Final Rights

Disclaimers

The opinions expressed in this book are those of the authors. None of the material has been approved by the boards of directors of the Funeral Consumers Alliance or the Funeral Ethics Organization. These organizations are listed only to identify the positions held by the authors.

Legal information and opinions in this book are carefully researched but cannot be guaranteed and cannot substitute for guidance from your lawyer.

Final Rights

Reclaiming the
American Way of Death

Joshua Slocum

and

Lisa Carlson

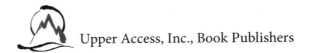

Upper Access, Inc., Book Publishers

Upper Access, Inc., Book Publishers
87 Upper Access Road, Hinesburg, Vermont 05461
(802)482-2988 - http://www.upperaccess.com

Cover and Interior Design by Kitty Werner, RSBPress, Waitsfield, Vermont
Woodblock Illustration by Mary Azarian, Plainfield, Vermont
Index by Carlson Indexing, Portland, Oregon
Photo on front cover © iStockphoto.com/spxChrome

ISBN 978-0-942679-34-2

Library of Congress Cataloging-in-Publication Data

Slocum, Joshua.
  Final rights : reclaiming the American way of death / Joshua Slocum and Lisa
Carlson.
      p. cm.
  Includes index.
  ISBN 978-0-942679-34-2 (trade pbk. : alk. paper)
  1. Burial laws--United States--Popular works. 2. Undertakers and undertaking-
-Law and legislation--United States--Popular works. 3. Funeral rites and
ceremonies--Economic aspects--United States. 4. Consumer protection--United
States. I. Carlson, Lisa, 1938- II. Title.
  KF3781.S59 2011
  344.7304'5--dc22
                            2011000565

Printed in the United States of America

11 / 10 9 8 7 6 5 4 3 2 1

Contents

Lisa Carlson

Preface

IN A SENSE, THIS BOOK is a successor to two earlier ones, updating the research on funeral law for consumers originally published in 1987 and in 1998. Those who keep *Caring for the Dead* on their shelf for ready reference should replace it with this book, to accommodate all the changes in laws, regulations, services, and the like. (In the future, updates to that information will be made available for Internet download at the Funeral Consumers Alliance website, <www.funerals.org>.)

That said, *Final Rights* is a new book, not just an update to an older one. Josh Slocum, now the nation's foremost advocate for funeral consumer rights, has joined as coauthor, bringing with him his considerable experience and insights. Between us, we've taken a new look at the death-care business as it exists in 2011, exposing corruption where it exists (in far too many places) while giving credit where due.

Our goal is to help consumers navigate around the barriers erected by the funeral industry (and government agencies that are supposed to be regulating it), to reclaim the traditional rights of families to care for their own dead, to say goodbye in the best ways they can without paying extortionate fees for goods and services they neither need nor want.

My own involvement in these issues began in 1981, well after Jessica Mitford's *The American Way of Death* had exposed widespread deception and misdeeds in the funeral industry but with disappointingly little to show in the way of cleaning things up. In that year, Sally Cavanaugh, a fellow member of my writers' group, brought us an article "How to Bury Your Own Dead in Vermont," a historical look-back at how our great-grandparents handled death in ways that were still legal.

Six months later, when my husband committed suicide at the age of 31, I needed that information. John had been a first-grade teacher; our daughter was eligible for free lunch at school; I didn't even know if I could cash John's next paycheck. In a few generations, we Americans had lost the common lore of what to do at the time of death.

I'd known when I married this super-sensitive person that suicide was always an out for John when he felt the world wasn't fair. He had tried twice before. So we lived each day as a gift. Our two children, ages three and five, were asleep when I found John's body in his red pick-up truck with the note, "I can't stand the pain any more."

It had been a wonderful marriage and I needed to stay close, even in death. So I told the funeral director who was taking the body for the autopsy to call us when he got back and we would pick up John's body and do the rest ourselves. I asked the janitor from school if he would help me drive John's body to the crematory. "I'd be honored," Rip said, "John was my friend."

Rip and I drove John's body to the crematory ourselves. I buried the cremains near John's flower garden and marked the spot with a hand-chiseled stone. At this difficult time, the direct involvement was therapeutic, especially for me. One mistake I made, however, was to take the body to the crematory too quickly, before the children had a chance for their own goodbyes.

I married Steve Carlson almost two years later. In 1986, his mother, Mary Jane, died of AIDS. It was a death we handled as a family, just as we had cared for her during her illness. I got the paperwork while two of the sons built a plain pine box. The four adult sons lifted her into the box and drove to family country property where they dug her grave by hand.

Mary Jane had encouraged my writing before she died, and Steve, also a writer, knew it was important to me to see a book on this subject in print. At a time when the small-press movement was exploding, it was exciting to start our own publishing company. It was, after all, the small presses that first wrote about alternative medicine, alternative education, and alternative lifestyles. *Caring for Your Own Dead* was published in 1987. Steve has stayed active in the independent press business ever since, publishing nonfiction from a wide variety of authors.

As I got involved with the funeral consumer movement, I was interested in the rights of all funeral consumers, not just the do-it-yourselfers. After twice as much legal research, we published *Caring for the Dead: Your Final Act of Love* in 1998 while I was executive director of Funeral Consumers Alliance (FCA).

Joshua Slocum took over as executive director at FCA when I "retired" in 2003. His passionate commitment, his great sense of humor, and his intellectual smarts have continued to raise the visibility and influence of FCA. From that vantage point, he had the best up-to-date stories to tell that make Part 1 of this book such a compelling new read, while I was able to concentrate on researching and updating the legal and practical information.

After leaving FCA, I started the Funeral Ethics Organization (FEO) to work with the industry to raise the bar for ethical practices. For information about FEO, visit <www.funeralethics.org>. The good guys and gals in the funeral business are deeply hurt by the mischief-makers. I extend a special "thank you" to funeral director Randy Garner for his trust and friendship. There are many others in the funeral industry I'm proud to call my friends, too. I am also grateful to the FEO board for letting me off the hook for a newsletter while working on the state-chapter research. And FEO board member David Zinner has an eagle eye for editing. Despite all the industry's ills, which are necessarily the focus of this book, there are some funeral directors who dedicate themselves daily to the cause of helping people at a time of grief, with compassion and professionalism.

Additional valuable help came from Jeri Helen, a skilled professional editor who volunteered her time to work out style issues and awkward wordings at the time of typesetting. Beyond that, the list of people who provided ideas and information to make this a better book is too long to attempt here. You know who you are, and you have my deep gratitude.

—*Lisa Carlson*

Joshua Slocum

Preface

ALMOST EVERYONE I MEET WHO knows about my career at Funeral Consumers Alliance asks, "How did you get into this line of work?" It's a fair question; no colleges offer majors in "Funeral Consumer Advocacy," and as a child, I didn't daydream about becoming a professional burr under the funeral industry's saddle. But the signs were there. For my eighth-grade English class, I had to interview a local business person in town and submit a report for class-wide publication titled "We Are Cortland!" My classmates wrote about the museum curator, the city councilman, the dentist, the Episcopal priest. I went to the undertaker.

Looking back at the answers he gave to my softball questions, I chuckle at how vague and pat they were. The most satisfying part of his job, he said, was "Having people express their gratitude when it's all over. I like to hear, 'Thanks, you helped a lot'." Oh, sure, he talked about how he had to "plan the services" and make sure the bodies were "properly embalmed." But there was no peek behind the velvet curtain. When I quietly let myself in the front door and tip-toed into one of the viewing rooms to see whose nose was sticking up above the open casket rim, the funeral director's hand came down on my shoulder. He guided me away from the reality of death and into what I now know was the "arrangements room," where frank conversation dies and euphemisms are born.

I closed my report by writing, "Well, I don't know if I would have the stomach for a job like this, but I must say it is interesting work."

Is it ever. So interesting that the industry doesn't want to share the fun. It was the industry's resistance to transparency—and the government's collusion—that propelled me into this work. As a young reporter at a daily paper in Virginia, I was looking for a subject for a weekend feature story. Someone put a copy of Jessica Mitford's famous book, *The American Way of Death*, on my desk, and I stayed up all night reading it. I knew I'd found my muse.

When I learned the largest funeral chain in the world, Service Corporation International (SCI) had bought what everyone in town still thought were "family" funeral homes I smelled a story. What had happened to the prices and sales practices over the years since these establishments had been taken over by Wall Street? I spent months trying to pry paperwork out of the Virginia Board of Embalmers and Funeral Directors. They stymied me at every turn, denying me copies of such simple documents as the price lists that the Federal Trade Commission requires funeral homes to hand out to consumers. I only learned much later the extent to which the industry controls or heavily influences these supposed "regulatory" boards.

My editor at the paper was no help either. Having struck up a phone and e-mail friendship with Lisa Carlson, who gave me an unbelievable amount of working knowledge about the funeral business, I'd compiled a three-inch-thick binder on the business, complete with research on the underhanded sales practices common to corporate funeral homes. Bob, my editor, called me into his office. When I closed the door and sat down, he said, "Josh, have you been screwed by an undertaker or something?" The idea that something might be wrong with the way funerals were sold to Americans was so beyond the pale that my interest could only be chalked up to a personal beef. He never let me continue the story.

I realized that if a skeptical reporter who knew his way around open-records laws couldn't even get a simple price list out of a government body that purported to protect the grieving public, the bereaved didn't stand a chance. No one was looking out for the funeral consumer—except for the nonprofit FCA. To my delight, Lisa Carlson offered me a job in the fall of 2002. When she retired in 2003 as executive director, the FCA governing board appointed me to the position.

When you read this book, I hope you will have many of the same reactions I did when I started digging beneath the surface of the American way of death. I want you to be surprised at the options you didn't know you had and emerge knowledgeable enough to have a frank conversation with your family about the things you, and they, do and don't want in a funeral.

I also hope you will be indignant enough to join your local nonprofit FCA, or to start one if none exists in your area. What compelled me to join Funeral Consumers Alliance was my enthusiastic agreement with its social and economic justice mission. Contrary to the industry caricature of the "memorial society folks" who just got together to collectively bargain for "cheap" funerals, FCA cares about protecting every individual's right to choose the last hurrah that fits her taste and her budget. You may want a week-long affair, or you may want a simple cremation with no fuss, or something in between. But whether you spend $1 or $10,000, you won't love or miss or honor the dead any more or less.

Many in the funeral and burial business will accuse Carlson and me of "painting with a broad brush" and of "hating funeral directors." They'll say that abuses in the business are unfortunate but few and that we shouldn't let a few bad apples spoil the barrel. I've learned it's hard for many to believe that the misdeeds we catalogue are as common as they are. "I've been in funeral service for 30 years, and I've never seen this kind of behavior" is a common retort. But many funeral directors have limited exposure to the industry as a whole. They run quiet businesses in their hometown without coming into contact with thousands of funeral consumers every year the way consumer advocates do.

But no amount of disclaiming or qualifying will quell those broad-brush accusations, because we are not merely calling out those who actually violate laws and regulations. In the foreword to The American Way of Death, Jessica Mitford wrote:

> This would normally be the place to say (as critics of the American funeral trade invariably do), 'I am not, of course, speaking of the vast majority of ethical undertakers.' But the vast majority of ethical undertakers is precisely the subject of this book. To be 'ethical' merely means to adhere to a prevailing code of morality, in this case one devised over the years by the undertakers themselves for their own purposes. The outlook of the average undertaker, who does adhere to the code of his calling, is to me more significant than that of his shadier colleagues, who are merely small-time crooks such as may be found operating in any sphere of business.

So it is with us. We are questioning the validity of the most basic assumptions that underpin the contemporary funeral business: the notion that money spent equals love shown, the idea that funeral directors are so indispensable that no family can cope with death without their expertise, the idea that funeral homes and cemeteries have a natural right to the patronage of every family experiencing a death. These ideas are deeply rooted in the American death trade. We cannot make progress in protecting grieving people from manipulation without confronting them candidly.

This book is not a publication of Funeral Consumers Alliance, but I couldn't have co-written it without the knowledge I've gained as executive director. The small staff have been privileged to talk with thousands of Americans who've written or called to ask for help or advice, to lodge a complaint or just to tell their stories. Because the FCA national office represents the more than 90 local, volunteer-run, nonprofit funeral information groups that make up our federation, we've met countless kind-hearted and spirited volunteers who give their own time to speak out for the rights and interests of the grieving public. No one else lobbies for the rights of the bereaved. Please support them with your time, your talent, and your dollars. Find them at <www.funerals.org>.

Acknowledgements:

Members of the governing board of FCA, both past and present, have been incredibly supportive of this project, and have allowed me to take the time I needed to research and write this book—thank you. FCA's administrator, Sherry Swett, has been amazingly helpful and patient with my odd schedule as I juggled the book and my ordinary duties at FCA. Without her, the national office just wouldn't run. FCA's administrative assistant, Leda Nutting, provides indispensable support, maintaining our database and helping thousands of consumers and FCA volunteers by phone and e-mail each year. The many friends and correspondents who read and critiqued draft chapters were a great help and sounding board.

I've been lucky to know many upstanding people in funeral service over the years whose counsel has been valuable. Even when we disagree, their friendly challenges have pushed me to think more subtly and (believe it or not) to change my mind more than a few times. Ron Hast, longtime funeral director and publisher of Mortuary Management, has been a consistent correspondent over the years and was the first funeral director to talk plainly and honestly to me when I began researching the business. Tom Parmalee, editor of Funeral Service Insider and American Funeral Director, has given me a surprising number of opportunities to speak for funeral consumers in the pages of his publications, despite my unpopularity with the subscriber base. Vermont funeral director Randy Garner, who started as a "critic of the critics" when he first encountered FCA, has become a trusted friend. He is the best example I know of a funeral director who runs his business with a conscience.

Though not directly involved in this project, my mother, Bonnie Cook, is behind it nonetheless. She sent me out into the world with a passion for just causes and with the loud mouth necessary to bring attention to them. I love you, Mom.

—*Josh Slocum*

Part 1
Bodies, Business, and Traditions
for Saying Goodbye

Circling the Hearses 1

THREE-YEAR-OLD LORENZO FARMER'S TINY BODY lay locked up in a Salt Lake City hospital morgue for days in 2006. It wasn't that he had no family; his grief-stricken parents had been by his side. It wasn't that the family didn't know what to do for his funeral; they were unusually clear-minded and resolute. Lorenzo was going back to the Fort Hall Indian Reservation in Idaho for a traditional Native American funeral. But the hospital wouldn't release Lorenzo to his own mother and father thanks to a new state law that made the dead in Utah hostages of the funeral industry.

"It was like a wall. Everybody was telling us 'No, no, no. We can't release the body to a family member. A funeral home has to be involved,'" Lorenzo's grandmother, Wendy Rodriguez, told the *Herald Extra*.

Until 2006, Utah law followed those of most other states; if no funeral director was involved, the family member *acting as the funeral director* could sign the spot on the death certificate describing the final disposition of the body. After May 1 of that year, however, only a funeral director could. Lorenzo finally made it back to his parents' arms, but not until Fort Hall consumer advocates David Robles and Marcia Racehorse-Robles found a sympathetic funeral director—as shocked at this law as we were—who signed the certificate and refused to take a fee. And not before Lorenzo's parents, Adrian and Crystal, had to endure the outrage of being denied the custody of their own son and the prospect that a mortuary might forcibly embalm his tiny body.

"You just go with whatever they tell you to," said Rodriguez. "We were just going to have to do it because we thought that was the only way we were going to get him back home."

The Utah Funeral Director's Association (UFDA) and the legislators who danced to their tune were responsible for this family's misery. In a brazen act of self-dealing, the UFDA told state lawmakers the slight change in wording in the death certificate law was part of a housekeeping bill to clean up technicalities. The bill slipped onto the "consent calendar," where non-controversial acts get a rubber stamp.

17

"The primary goal was to protect the consumer more than anything," UFDA President Tod Bonzo told the *Herald Extra* when the story broke. "It is a protection for human health . . . ."

It defies believability that UFDA was trying to protect the public by requiring that every citizen pay for the services of their dues-paying funeral homes. Utah was the latest to join the few other states with laws that restrict or prohibit full family control over their funeral rituals.

Fortunately, consumer activists stepped up. Joyce Mitchell, President of FCA of Utah, gathered families, consumer advocates, and Native American tribal representatives to testify against the restrictive law. Dave Robles and his wife, Marcia Racehorse-Robles, drove from Idaho and stalked the halls of the Utah legislature with Mitchell, pushing hard to restore this important family right. Their collective efforts sparked newspaper coverage and support from influential talk-radio hosts. Thanks to Mitchell's Representative, Brad Daw (R-Orem), HB 265 passed the House overwhelmingly, and Senator Luz Robles (D–Salt Lake, no relation to Dave Robles) became an enthusiastic Senate sponsor. The governor signed the corrective bill into law in 2009.

State Laws Denying Rights of Grieving Families

Eight other states continue to restrict families' rights to funeral privacy. Every one of these nonsensical prohibitions offends fairness and decency and reeks of an industry meddling to prevent consumer choice and protect its members' income:

- Connecticut requires a funeral director's signature on the death certificate and bars anyone but a funeral director or embalmer from removing a body or transporting it.

- The Illinois administrative code (which appears to have been changed after the publication of Carlson's 1998 book) defines "funeral director or person acting as such" to include only funeral directors or their employees or "associates." This means a mother couldn't obtain a disposition permit for her own deceased child, but any anonymous "associate" of a licensed funeral director could.

- Indiana law says burial permits can be given only to funeral directors, even though other statutes clearly refer broadly to the "person in charge" of the disposition, the next-of-kin.

- Louisiana law mandates funeral-director involvement in obtaining all necessary permits and funeral director presence at the final disposition of the body. Who knows what nefarious activities families and preachers might get up to if left alone at the grave with a casket! New York has similar requirements.

- Michigan health department officials have always been uncooperative with home-funeral families, and statutory changes in 2003 and 2006 now give them a legal excuse for their resistance. All death certificates must now be "certified" by a funeral director—though the statute doesn't even define what that means. Even more strangely, the wills and probate section of the law requires all body dispositions to be conducted by a licensed funeral director.

- Nebraska law requires a funeral director to supervise all dispositions and gives funeral directors the right and authority to issue "transit permits" to move the body out of state.

- New Jersey statutes changed after the publication of Carlson's 1998 book, revising sections of law that had allowed families to care for their own dead before that. References to the "person acting as" her own funeral director disappeared from the law.

While family-directed funerals are still permissible in Minnesota, the state tightened the screws in 2007. The law change barred families from using pickup trucks for transporting their dead (a hearse would be just fine, though). When Carlson and Slocum complained about this in response to a press interview, David Benke, director of the Health Department's mortuary science section said, "If that's what you want, go to one of those countries where they have no rules or regulations. You can dig a hole and bury a body in your back yard." (Mr. Benke was apparently unaware that Minnesota law did allow for family cemeteries on private land.)

Also, the state decided to keep its one-of-a-kind law requiring embalming for public viewing—religious or personal objections be damned. Once again, consumer activists mobilized, and they found the sympathetic ear of Representative Carolyn Laine. Laine successfully shepherded a bill into law in 2010 that rolled back these nonsensical restrictions and finally ended Minnesota's dubious claim to fame as the only state that required embalming for public viewing.

Funeral Directors Write Their Own Laws

The great majority of laws covering funeral licensing and practice were historically instigated by the National Funeral Directors Association and its handmaidens at the state level. Nearly all funeral licensing boards in the various states are dominated by funeral directors. They routinely ignore legitimate consumer complaints and sweep abuses under the rug.

Take Alabama as an example. The Alabama Examiner of Public Accounts (the state's inspector general) published a scathing audit of the Alabama Board of Funeral Service in 2007. Some of the findings showed that the board lacked transparency or even any kind of reasonable record keeping. The Examiner found the Board didn't have a website (it does now), Board members didn't respond to e-mails, the majority of office records were hand-written on paper (in 2006!), and the Board couldn't even provide a list of all licensed funeral homes in the state, as required by law. More worrisome, the report also indicates (though in careful language) that the Board falsified its own inspection records, claiming to have inspected far more funeral homes than any human could have in the time allotted. What's more, three funeral homes told the Examiner that the Board's associate executive secretary "requested money (other than normal fees) for board services."

Too often, state regulatory boards and the trade associations they align with lobby for laws that keep out competition—and write regulations to thwart entrepreneurs who want to lower funeral costs. As they see it, they're following a grand American tradition. As the 10th Circuit Court of Appeals put it in a bizarre decision upholding Oklahoma's right to outlaw direct-to-consumer casket sales, "Dishing out special economic benefits to certain in-state industries remains the favored pastime of state and local governments."

Most people who have a bad experience with a commercial funeral home quickly learn the difference between consumer protection and *industry protectionism*. Missouri widow Marilyn Oehlschlaeger called Funeral Consumers Alliance in 2006 after her husband's funeral. She claimed the funeral home never gave her a price list, and when she got the bill (more than $9,000) there were hundreds of dollars in charges for items she never asked for and didn't want. Oehlschlaeger and her two daughters told Slocum they repeatedly asked the funeral director for specific services and told him to strike off the extras they didn't want. "He kept saying, 'But we have these packages now,'" Oehlschlaeger said. "I told him we didn't want a package."

Slocum wrote a detailed letter to the state funeral board and the Attorney General pointing out the funeral home's legal misdeeds under the Federal Trade Commission's Funeral Rule and state law. During the complaint process, funeral home employees harassed Oehlschlaeger continually, calling her at home and pressuring her to meet with them and resolve the issue (a favorite ploy of corporate mortuary chains to make sure their *pattern* of misbehavior goes undetected). Slocum advised her not to meet with them—especially without a lawyer—and to let the complaint process play out. In the end, all she got from the state board (five funeral directors and one public member) was a one-paragraph letter saying the board hadn't found any legal violations. No explanation was given for how the board failed to see the statutory violations Slocum pointed out. The Attorney General's office did no better, claiming it had no jurisdiction over the funeral board.

How We Got Here

> The legal profession have their associations for mutual improvement. So do clergymen, chemists, Boards of Health, civil and mining engineers, physicians and surveyors . . . . It is well known that we can never have an educated profession of funeral directors unless we compel it by legal enactments as a sanitary measure . . . . I would have a law regulating the care and burial of the dead the same as there is for medicine.
>
> —Hudson Samson, President of the National Funeral Directors Association, addressing NFDA's fifth annual convention in 1886.

President Samson would be pleased with the progress trade groups have made over the past 124 years. All 50 states today have laws controlling the business of undertaking (though Colorado and Hawaii have no specific regulatory body enforcing them). Some are so detailed they prescribe in feet the length of the room in which the dead are embalmed or bar the use of profanities or "unprofessional" language in the presence of the deceased. So far as we know, none of the dainty dead have complained.

Today 48 states and the District of Columbia require some level of education, usually two years of college, before a person can get a funeral director's license. The majority require funeral businesses to have on-site embalming rooms. Many require funeral homes to have casket showrooms and chapels with minimum seating capacities. Massachusetts requires funeral homes to haul bodies in a vehicle used exclusively for transporting corpses—it's illegal to take the van out to McDonalds on one's lunch hour.

There is, of course, much justification for government regulation of the funeral industry. Very few people buy more than one or two funerals during their lifetime, and, when they do, it's almost always at a time of grief and vulnerability. The problem is that instead of protecting the public from deceptive sales practices and fraud, the laws and regulations too often protect the dismal traders from public accountability.

The funeral business is so effectively insulated from free-market competition that many families can't even imagine a funeral home free of faux-Victorian sitting rooms and a fleet of Cadillacs. Rules and regulations that make it hard for simple-burial businesses to thrive force consumers to pay for the upkeep and taxes that go along with a fancy facility.

Real consumer-protection laws are rare. It is no accident that the deck is stacked in favor of undertakers and their pocketbooks. When the National

Funeral Directors Association first organized, the motivation to establish an "educated profession" wasn't learning for learning's sake. The founding funeral directors knew that if they could convince lawmakers to require elaborate facilities and special schooling and certification, the burgeoning trade could keep out competition while raising prices to an "appropriately" high level.

NFDA's longtime apologist-in-chief, William Lamers, compiled 100 years of "The Words And Deeds of Funeral Service Practitioners" into *A Centurama of Conventions.* This thin 1981 paperback mixes gravitas and fawning. (One half expects to find "I ♥ my undertaker!" scribbled in the margins.) Sympathetic though he is to the undertakers' plight, Lamers states their aims more candidly than they do:

> One of these [concerns] was securing passage of laws setting high standards of training and education for admission to funeral service. Such laws would make certain that only qualified persons would be licensed by public authority.

The idea of undertakers as a Capital P Profession wasn't easy to put over. Before the last quarter of the 19th century, most Americans called on their undertaker (often a local cabinetmaker) to supply a coffin, bring chairs to the home, and to lend a general helping hand to the family members as they buried their dead. It would have seemed absurd that such prosaic work needed the eagle eye of a state bureaucracy to enforce complicated educational and legal requirements. Surely undertakers did not need the level of training required of doctors, lawyers, and other highly paid professionals.

Indeed, 19th-century undertakers complained bitterly about the difficulty of convincing the public and politicians to clear all obstacles on their road to Professionalism:

> The greatest assistance we want, and in my humble opinion the strongest protection we stand in need of, is the recognition before the law we justly deserve, and that the law shall require at our hands that degree of proficiency our calling is capable of, and that mead of protection we are competent to give and the public stand in need of and should demand . . . . Although in every state where we tried, our bill has fallen and failed of passage . . . ."
>
> — NFDA President Robert Bringhurst, 1890

If only President Bringhurst were around today; the campaign to lock up the funeral market has been a stunning success. While some states (California, Texas and Florida, for example) allow stripped-down, simple funeral businesses to exist in the form of "direct disposition" establishments, many others prevent innovation with arbitrary and picayune requirements. And while most states require funeral homes to have an embalming room, they don't require them to have their own refrigerator to serve those who object to embalming on personal or religious grounds.

Enforcing Petty Rules While Ignoring Consumer Protection

Massachusetts is typical. Funeral directors have long complained that instead of rooting out crooks, employees of the Board of Registration of Funeral Directors and Embalmers slap businesses with fines for all sorts of minor infractions that have nothing to do with consumer protection.

A 2006 press release from the Board brags that inspectors collected $2,200 in fines after finding "code violations" in the embalming rooms at six funeral homes. Small wonder, as state regulations give the overzealous inspector (tax collector) a smorgasbord of opportunities. Massachusetts funeral homes must:

- have a "chapel sufficiently large and sufficiently equipped for the conduct of an average funeral service" with a minimum of 300 square feet;

- not have any living space on the same floor as the funeral business unless the owner promises not to offer customers food or drinks;

- be physically connected, if the business consists of multiple buildings; and

- have an embalming room at least 12' by 14' with a tile or cement floor; any rubber mats used have to be at least 3/16" thick, and the room must have "one standard-type sanitary operating table; one flush-rim sink, one floor drain. . . one sanitary waste receptacle which is opened by a foot pedal; and a standard-type instrument sterilizer."

Anyone who wants to open a funeral home offering customers low-cost, no frills-burials can forget it. They'll have to sink money into a for-profit chapel even if the religious service is at a church, or even if there is no service. They will pay for an elaborate embalming room, with nice thick mats, even if, like an increasing number of Americans, their customers reject embalming. Consumers pay for this frippery through higher prices, even if they choose a simple burial or cremation—all those sunk costs have to be paid for somehow.

Not only that, but the Massachusetts board has been operating in secrecy, going into illegal executive (closed) sessions, according to a longtime volunteer for the Funeral Consumers Alliance of Eastern Massachusetts. Byron Blanchard says the board refused to e-mail him copies of the minutes of its public meetings in 2006 and now refuses to even give him a paper copy. See the Massachusetts chapter for more of the state's secretive, anti-consumer behavior.

(In fairness, we should add that Massachusetts has taken some pro-consumer actions. Regulators announced in 2009 they'd inspect 175 funeral homes and found 25 percent were violating the FTC Funeral Rule, with offenses such as failing to give price lists to undercover shoppers. In addition, the Division of Professional Licensure named the scofflaws—something the FTC refuses to do—and filed legal action against 46 businesses.)

Georgia has been going on prep-room raids, too. The state board (six undertakers, one consumer member) congratulated itself in a 2008 press release for catching red-handed two funeral homes for "failure to maintain in inventory the required 24 bottles of arterial fluid and 24 bottles of cavity fluid in the embalming room." The inspectors must have been too busy counting bottles of Firmatone and Cavity King (yes, they really are called that) to notice that the Federal Trade Commission found 13 of 15 Georgia funeral homes inspected in 2007 had Funeral Rule violations. Perhaps the vapors from all that formalin can also explain why the Board has ignored a complaint from an elderly man who claims a funeral home substituted a much cheaper casket for his wife's funeral than the one he paid for. Or, maybe it's because the funeral director cited in the complaint was a member of the state board.

The Wisconsin Funeral Directors' Examining Board suspended Cassandra Clarson's business license for a year after ruling she "aided and abetted unlicensed practice" by letting her partner, Roger Henke, "make funeral arrangements without a license." Henke's crimes? "Obtaining obituary information and preparing obituaries; meeting with families to discuss type of funeral services; contacting clergy to set the times and locations for funerals; discussing the costs of funeral services and the monies to be advanced."

The *Janesville Gazette* editorialized on August 23, 2007:

> The rules appear to protect business interests and hinder competition that would benefit consumers . . . . Why can't a business manager handle such duties? Are we to assume that spouses of licensed funeral directors don't engage in such "unauthorized activity" in small funeral homes around Wisconsin? . . . If funeral homes must be licensed so they don't take advantage of grieving loved ones, shouldn't companies selling headstones or burial vaults be licensed?

Consumers Fight Back

All this hearse-circling has some state boards so dizzy they've forgotten they're not a sovereign power. In 2005, the Missouri State Board of Embalmers and Funeral Directors went after Larry Gegner, an elderly man who sold caskets on the weekend at a flea market, when they found out he was telling people they had the right to bypass funeral homes and bury their own dead. The five morticians and one public member of the Board took Gegner to court on a laundry list of charges. These included "unlicensed activities" such as selling caskets to the public—*but state law specifically permits citizens to sell caskets to the public without a license.* The Board also charged Gegner with vague violations such as "arranging" funerals without a license.

Funeral Consumers Alliance and a nonprofit law firm, the Institute for Justice, pushed back. FCA sent several letters to the Board pointing out their legal errors, and IJ lawyer Valerie Bayham appeared at hearings to defend Gegner. Eventually Gegner and the Board reached a court settlement in which he promised not to engage in "funeral directing" (although he never had done so), and the Board acknowledged his right to sell caskets as well as his free-speech right to give advice on family-directed funerals. Before the settlement, the Board made a final attempt to dictate the behavior of private citizens by inserting into the funeral directing regulations, "Whether a fee is charged shall not be dispositive in determining whether one is engaged in the practice of funeral directing." Translation from Lawyerese to English: "We have the right to control anything anyone in Missouri does with a dead body, even private families or religious groups, whether or not money changes hands."

After pressure from FCA, they backed off this position and, at the time of this writing have drafted new regulations making it clear families have the right to conduct their own funerals. The Federal Trade Commission also sued the Board, resulting in a consent agreement barring the Board from enacting further regulations that restricted casket and vault sales.

An Irrational Basis

Why do so many cockeyed laws stay on the books? Few consumers or advocacy groups realize there's a problem in the first place. The rat's maze of industry regulation is designed to stymie people with bureaucratic bafflegab. Even fewer organizations know how to effectively challenge these laws, and those who do spend a lot of time pushing rocks up hills.

"There is a presumption that any law the government passes is a valid law, and that the burden is on the citizen to overcome this," according to Clark Neily, a lawyer for the Institute for Justice.

IJ does battle with the regulatory gatekeepers that keep small entrepreneurs out of fields from flower arranging to bug spraying. At any given time,
IJ is apt to be fighting the Arizona Structural Pest Control Commission for
bullying a teenager who made pocket money rat-proofing his neighbors'
roofs without a license, or the Louisiana Horticultural Commission, which
stands between helpless consumers and rogue florists who haven't passed
a state test proving they know how to stuff daisies in a pitcher "so that the
whole composition will be of good design."

The industry's arbitrary restrictions on who can sell what kind of boxes
has given IJ plenty of grist for its mill. When Tennessee threatened the Reverend Nathaniel Craigmiles with criminal prosecution for selling coffins
directly to the public, IJ sued the state in federal court and won. The 6th Circuit US Court of Appeals unanimously struck down the state's ban on retail
casket sales as unconstitutional under the 14th Amendment.

Tennessee scraped the bottom of the vault to justify the ban; casket retailers don't have the necessary "psychological training" and retail caskets don't
"protect the public health" the way mortuary caskets do. The Court didn't
buy it:

> . . .survivors must deal with a panoply of vendors in order to make fu-
> neral arrangements, from churches to food vendors for a wake, none
> of whom is required to have this psychological training. This justifica-
> tion is very weak indeed.
>
> Indeed, the only difference between the caskets is that those sold
> by licensed funeral directors are systematically more expensive.
>
> — Craigmiles et al v. Giles et al, 2002

IJ tried to rack up another victory against those Jessica Mitford called the
"bier barons" with a similar suit against Oklahoma. Kim Powers and Dennis Bridges started an on-line casket business, only to be smacked down by
the State Board of Embalmers and Funeral Directors. The Board thought
the best use of taxpayer dollars was to fight for the right to require casket
sellers to become full-fledged morticians with two years of college, a year
of apprenticeship, and 25 properly preserved Loved Ones under their belts.
The district court ruling described the uses to which undertakers put this
specialized training:

> Oklahoma funeral homes have attempted to increase the amount
> of money a consumer spends on a casket by showing higher-priced
> caskets more favorably in a showroom by strategic use of lighting,
> by placement of high-end caskets on rugs or beside sentimental
> sculpture, and by displaying less expensive caskets in unattractive
> colors alongside expensive caskets displayed in attractive colors. In at

*least one case, an Oklahoma funeral home priced a low-end casket at
$695, which had a probable wholesale cost of between $150 and $120.*

Yet the court *ruled for the state.* So did the 10th Circuit Court of Appeals,
even though the court acknowledged that "Consumer interests appear to be
harmed rather than protected by the limitation of choice and price encouraged by the licensing restrictions on intrastate casket sales." Even worse, the
court ruled against free trade, even while acknowledging that "dishing out
special economic benefits to certain in-state industries remains the favored
pastime of state and local governments." IJ appealed to the Supreme Court
in 2005 but the Supremes declined to hear the case.

How can judges support such bald-faced nonsense? Through the richly-
named "rational basis" test. Ever since a precedent-setting 1877 Supreme
Court case, US courts have bent over backwards to show deference to the
supposed wisdom of state legislatures when they enact laws, no matter how
transparently unfair. IJ's Clark Neily explains:

> *The original legal definition of insanity is the inability to tell right
> from wrong. So it is the first irony of the "rational" basis test that it is,
> according to that definition, insane . . . the rational basis test is noth-
> ing more than a Magic Eight Ball that randomly generates different
> answers to key constitutional questions depending on who happens to
> be shaking it and with what level of vigor. . . .*
>
> *[The rational basis test leads to] judges simultaneously recogniz-
> ing and refusing to protect fundamental constitutional rights; permit-
> ting government lawyers and witnesses to misrepresent—or at least
> disregard—material facts; preferring conjecture over evidence; sad-
> dling plaintiffs with a burden of proof that is technically impossible to
> discharge.*
>
> —*No Such Thing: Litigating Under the Rational Basis
> Test, NY Journal of Law and Liberty, v. 1, no. 2*

Courts that adhere strictly to this test (like the 10th Circuit in the Powers
casket case) abandon facts and fairness. As long as the government can offer
any justification whatsoever for the law, no matter how far-fetched or plainly
dishonest, the Court will uphold it. Said a Second Circuit Court decision:

> *. . .the Government is under no obligation to produce evidence or em-
> pirical data to sustain the rationality of a statutory classification and
> can base its statutes on rational speculation.*

Pretend an auto dealer's association gets sore over dealerships losing business to low-priced outfits like Jiffy Lube. So they send their lobbyist to get a

law passed outlawing grease-and-lube drive-ups and requiring all oil changes to be performed by a licensed dealership. Say a would-be Jiffy Lube owner takes the state to court, and shows the law was concocted to funnel business into full-service dealerships. But no, the state says, we created the law to protect consumers from fly-by-night grease jockeys who might wreck their engines. Under the rational basis test, the court would rule for the state, because the state *could have* meant to protect consumers, "rationally" speaking, even though everyone knows the truth.

That's exactly what the 10th Circuit Court did in the Oklahoma casket case. The ruling is pure through-the-looking-glass reasoning:

> *The licensing scheme at issue here leaves much to be desired. The record makes it clear that limitations on the free market of casket sales have outlived whatever usefulness they may have had. Consumer interests appear to be harmed rather than protected by the limitation of choice and price encouraged by the licensing restrictions on intrastate casket sales. Oklahoma's general consumer protection laws appear to be a more than adequate vehicle to allow consumer redress of abusive marketing practices. . . . But the majority is surely right that the battle over this issue must be fought in the Oklahoma legislature, the ultimate arbiter of state regulatory policy. I therefore conclude that the legislative scheme here meets the rational basis test and join in the judgment of the majority.*

"Consumer Protection" in Regulating Crematories

Many states have fallen for plainly dishonest "consumer protection" arguments when they finally got around to regulating crematories. Seven states require crematories to be owned by, run, or affiliated with full-service funeral homes. Twelve states bar crematories from selling to the public directly; crematories in these states are relegated to working as wholesale trade jobbers for full-service funeral homes that purport to be selling cremation to their clients, but who do nothing but haul the body and file the death certificate. Most consumers would be shocked to find out the average cost of the actual cremation at the crematory is just a few hundred dollars. You're unlikely to pay the undertaker less than a thousand.

Arizona funeral homes have just such a sweet deal. Now, you don't have to be a funeral director to own or operate a crematory. You just have to have an incorporated business, pass a criminal and professional background check, and "be of good moral character." But the law says you can't sell a cremation that isn't "arranged by a funeral establishment" unless "otherwise permitted by law." We'd argue that since families clearly have the right to care for their own dead in Arizona, that selling a cremation to a family that brings the body and the legal paperwork is permitted. Not so, claims the state. And what justification is there for forcing crematories to serve as second-class businesses at the beck and call of full-service mortuaries? We have to be able to regulate cremation, says the state. Then why not just regulate crematories *themselves*?

Such nonsense is par for the course when you start digging into the rationale for protectionist schemes. In 2002, Georgia regulators discovered 334 rotting bodies lying un-cremated on the back lawn and in broken-down hearses at the now infamous Tri-State crematory in Noble. Smelling an opportunity, the state's undertakers got behind a new law that they claimed closed a loophole that had allowed the Tri-State crematory to operate without regulation.

Under the old law, in effect at that time, a crematory that dealt directly with the public needed to be operated by a licensed funeral director. A crematory that dealt *only* with funeral directors was not regulated. The assumption, presumably, was that the funeral directors dealing with the crematory would check to be sure that the services they contracted for were being provided.

Because Tri-State dealt only with funeral directors, not with the general public, it did not need to be licensed or inspected. Think about this scenario: All the duly-licensed undertakers that sent bodies to Tri-State clearly didn't bother to do the most cursory checking; 334 corpses scattered about the property are hard to miss. In most instances, the funeral directors marked up the crematory charges by at least 100 percent, and usually more, when they passed them along to the consumer. Just *what* were all those undertakers doing to justify those prices?

The new law required all crematories to be inspected. That is obviously justifiable, given the horrible scene discovered at Tri-State. But none of the proponents of the new law could explain why requiring funeral director supervision of crematories was necessary to protect the public. Despite the evidence to the contrary, (especially in this specific case) we are supposed to believe funeral directors are inherently more ethical and conscientious than grubby old crematory operators.

Mortuary Schools Gloss Over Cremation Basics

The idea that crematory operators need the "special" training mortuary school provides falls apart when you look at what the 50-odd schools actually teach. There's little to nothing in many curricula on cremation, and the national board exam study guide for aspiring funeral directors—published by the International Conference of Funeral Service Examining Boards (ICFSEB)—glosses right over it. Carlson's Spring, 2005 *Newsletter for the Funeral Ethics Organization* found:

Only two questions out of 150 deal with cremation in the Funeral Arts section of ICFSEB's National Board Study Guide. The purpose of the exam, it states, is to determine "the MINIMUM QUALIFI- CATIONS to function as an entry level funeral director"—

2. Cremation first gained widespread acceptance and practice in:

A. ancient Rome
B. Hebrew lands
C. ancient Greece
D. Scandinavian countries

12. The proper terminology for the placing of cremated remains into a final container is

A. interment
B. inurnment
C. entombment
D. cremains interment

Cremation isn't rocket science, but requires basic skills such as retort op- eration, maintaining a documented chain of custody for the body, and un- derstanding the various state laws on who can legally authorize a cremation. These things aren't taught in many embalming schools. States would do far better for the public's protection and pocketbook to get rid of the funeral director monopoly and set up reasonable training and inspection require- ments for crematories that serve the public. In fact, prospective crematory owners get more relevant training from the short courses offered by the Cre- mation Association of North America than they would from two years at America's mortuary colleges.

Where We're Going

There's cause for hope—and for worry. Most state boards are still dominat- ed by the industry members they purport to regulate, and the consequences to consumers are dire. In 2006, the Kentucky legislature caved to industry fat-cat demands by outlawing lower-cost funeral homes from opening. Not outright, of course, but by requiring every funeral home to meet the most elaborate standards—an embalming room, visitation and ceremonial space, etc. They even tried to do away with citizens' rights to conduct private fu- nerals until FCA stepped in. The new law, backed by the state board of four funeral directors and one "public member" (whose wife worked at a funeral home) was aimed at an upstart undertaker who wanted to offer low-cost direct burials and cremations from a storefront office.

A lawmaker in Wisconsin tried similar shenanigans, and only a good old-fashioned public humiliation in the media—courtesy FCA—persuaded

Phil Montgomery to amend his 2005 bill that would have outlawed "strip mall" funeral homes. In truth, the bill was written *by* the Wisconsin Funeral Directors Association. Montgomery justified his bill to a TV station thus: "The fact that when you squeeze one in between a Dunkin' Donuts, you know, and a Hooters, I don't believe it serves the industry, or the consumers well." We must conclude it didn't occur to Mr. Montgomery that those who objected to the staff attire at beach-themed restaurants need only stay next door and keep their eyes at casket level. Or that nobody would be required to go to a low-cost establishment if they preferred one in a tonier neighborhood.

The worst abuse of power we've seen so far came in 2007, when the North Carolina Board of Funeral Service accused the volunteer President of the Funeral Consumers Alliance of the Central Carolinas of practicing funeral service without a license and threatened her with criminal prosecution. The charges? Publishing an obituary that would lead the public to think this consumer group sold funerals. The only problem—President Mary Brack didn't publish any obituaries. An FCA member family merely thanked the group for its help in one line in the obituary, "The Funeral Consumers Alliance of the Central Carolinas assisted the family." Of course, we are to believe this had nothing to do with the fact that the nine-member board has seven funeral directors, six of them picked by the state's two largest undertaker trade groups, *a right guaranteed to these lobbying groups by state law.*

Fortunately, at least a few lawmakers in a few states are wising up to rent-seeking rackets. Marilyn Oehlschlaeger—the Missouri widow whose case was discussed earlier in this chapter—became so disgusted with the regulators she went to state Representative Brian Baker's office for help. Baker promptly filed House Bill 1588 in 2007. The bill would have put five new consumer advocates on the board to break the undertakers' monopoly voting bloc. Sadly, it didn't pass.

In Maryland, Representative Joanne Benson became fed up with the eight-undertaker majority on the state board thwarting her efforts to break the monopolistic licensing system in Maryland. She solicited testimony from FCA and its state chapter about the need to reform the board. Benson's crusade successfully remade the board. Before 2008, the 12-member board consisted of eight funeral directors and four consumer members. The new board has 11 members; six are funeral directors, and five are consumer members. While the undertakers still have a majority, it's a big step in the right direction.

The Lynch Lawsuit

Lawmakers in Michigan have told us they're willing to work to restore families' rights to perform their own funerals, but it will be an uphill battle against well-heeled lobbyists who swarm out of the woodwork like drowning termites whenever such bills are filed. Advocates will likely have to contend with the silver-tongued Thomas Lynch, too. Lynch, an award-winning poet and author as well as the owner of several Michigan funeral homes, very much dislikes being questioned, and he appears to believe that dislike overrides the First Amendment rights of his critics.

In 2008 Lynch sued the Funeral Ethics Organization, Lisa Carlson personally, Funeral Consumers Alliance, and the Funeral Consumers Alliance of Idaho for libel in federal court. On what grounds? Carlson wrote an article in the FEO newsletter in which she noted that members of the Lynch family have publicly opposed families' rights to care for their own dead without using a funeral director (which they have). In a posting to an e-mail discussion list, Carlson also noted (correctly) that, in the PBS Frontline documentary *The Undertaking,* which profiled the Lynch funeral homes, funeral home staff were not shown giving consumers General Price Lists as required by the FTC. The tiny, volunteer-run, low-budget FCA of Idaho got dragged into the suit for reprinting this comment in their newsletter. And FCA's sin? A PowerPoint presentation titled "Deconstructing Thomas Lynch" that suggested profit was probably Lynch's motivation for writing a particular article praising lavish funerals. (The article is posted at <www.funerals.org>).

The court threw out the suit, of course, correctly observing that none of these statements was false or malicious. While it is tempting to comment further on Mr. Lynch's shenanigans, we don't think he deserves a stage for any more theatrics. For anyone interested, however, the lawsuit and various commentaries are on the FEO website: <www.funeralethics.org/newsletter>. The Funeral Consumers Alliance's website, <www.funerals.org>, also contains a number of articles on *l'affaire Lynch.*

Recommendations

It's time to bury the status quo in an unmarked grave. Industry-dominated regulation has done a whole lot to prop up outrageous funeral prices but almost nothing to stop consumer abuses. The near-universal requirement to go through two years of mortuary school before opening a funeral home only ensures the next generation of funeral directors will be indoctrinated by an outdated curriculum that's still harping on the "value of viewing and embalming" while teaching students little about cremation, green burial, alternative funeral options, religious diversity in funerals, or even how to set up a business website.

Sensible, fair, and effective regulation would:

- Restore families' constitutional rights to care for their own dead in the states where restrictions exist.

- Eliminate the need for expertise in embalming as a requirement to run a funeral home. Embalmers who serve the public should be required to have this training, of course, but there's no reason a simple disposition business owner should have to take classes in flooding the abdomen with formaldehyde.

- Eliminate requirements for funeral homes to have embalming rooms, "chapels," and other vestiges of old-school funeral parlors. Let the market decide what services are on offer. After all, no law requires McDonald's to sell poached salmon in dill sauce.

- Develop a test for prospective licensees that focuses on what's important for consumer protection. Test them on the FTC Funeral Rule, knowledge of state laws on funeral directing, prepaid funeral accounting requirements, and who has the legal right to make funeral decisions on behalf of a decedent.

- Require prospective licensees to do an apprenticeship of a reasonable length with a funeral business to gain practical experience. Vermont used to require that embalmers serve a one-year apprenticeship and funeral directors to assist with at least 30 funerals before becoming licensed. This worked perfectly well from time immemorial, but predictably, the Vermont Funeral Director's Association convinced lawmakers to require mortuary school attendance for licensure starting in 2009.

- Reform state licensing boards so industry does not have a majority voting bloc. A properly constituted board would ensure a spot for representatives of all trades regulated by the board—crematories, cemeteries, etc.—not just full-service funeral directors. Licensing boards should include as many or more disinterested consumer members as industry representatives.

- Consider abolishing the licensing boards altogether and place responsibility for licensing and oversight with a dedicated civil service staff, perhaps with an advisory board of funeral directors and public members to consult.

- Establish a clear, efficient complaint process for consumers with a grievance. Employ adequate staff sufficiently trained in funeral laws and regulations to fairly resolve complaints. Make complaints and resolutions public documents.

Are all of these reforms likely to take place in the foreseeable future? Of course not. Back in the 1980s, passage of the FTC Funeral Rule seemed to many to spell final victory for funeral consumers, and some predicted that CAFMS (the former name of FCA) would be out of business, with its goals accomplished. What a pleasant—but naïve—thought that was. But it is well worth the effort to work for reform and to help consumers to learn how the system works so they can protect themselves, especially when the regulators won't.

Tricks of the Funeral Trade 2

IN MOST BUSINESSES, THE FORCES of supply and demand keep goods and services within the affordability range of those who will use them. Not so with funeral and cemetery purchases. According to a 1995 study done by the Wirthlin Group at the behest of the funeral industry, almost 90 percent of consumers did not shop around for a funeral: 45 percent picked a funeral home that served someone else in the family; 33 percent called the nearest mortuary (perhaps the only one in town); and 11 percent picked a funeral home based on the perceived ethnic or religious affiliation.

While we have seen an increase in the amount of price and service comparison shopping since that time, most people still say they choose a funeral home based on past use, proximity, or affiliation. But how do you know if "your family's funeral home" that's been burying your relatives for generations is charging reasonable prices? How will you know if their business practices are good or bad if you've had no other experience? Most of us will arrange one, maybe two, funerals in our entire lives. That's not much to go on, and if you're looking for the best service at a reasonable price, reflexively calling only the last funeral home your family used is not a wise decision. Funeral directors are well aware of these tendencies. In the trade magazines, they refer to consumers like you as "my families."

Years ago, there was a funeral home in every other small town, and death care was acknowledged as a part-time job. When Carlson was growing up, the sign in Craftsbury Common, Vermont read "Upholstery—Hardware—Undertaking." Little by little, morticians found they could raise their prices, and the sideline jobs diminished. If the funeral business were indeed a full-time, five-days-a-week job, the number of funeral homes that would be needed for the death-rate in each state would be far fewer than the number that exist (see chart on the next page).

Many funeral homes can handle more than one funeral a day, reducing the "needed" number accordingly. This probably explains the figures for California, Hawaii, and Nevada. In rural areas with sparse population, a funeral director does not expect the dying business to be full-time, and more

Funeral Homes

	Have	Needed		Have	Needed
Alabama	460	188	Montana	74	35
Alaska	26	14	Nebraska	287	59
Arizona	161	180	Nevada	59	78
Arkansas	349	114	New Hampshire	105	41
California	960	919	New Jersey	724	270
Colorado	186	124	New Mexico	76	61
Connecticut	296	114	New York	1878	582
Delaware	70	31	North Carolina	751	308
DC	40	19	North Dakota	109	24
Florida	852	677	Ohio	1167	427
Georgia	703	267	Oklahoma	414	142
Hawaii	18	39	Oregon	193	125
Idaho	85	44	Pennsylvania	1664	495
Illinois	1232	395	Rhode Island	93	38
Indiana	649	222	South Carolina	557	151
Iowa	600	110	South Dakota	101	28
Kansas	383	94	Tennessee	548	231
Kentucky	497	162	Texas	1339	645
Louisiana	400	160	Utah	98	57
Maine	151	50	Vermont	70	20
Maryland	294	174	Virginia	488	234
Massachusetts	644	207	Washington	237	192
Michigan	729	343	West Virginia	309	84
Minnesota	559	152	Wisconsin	549	181
Mississippi	450	112	Wyoming	35	17
Missouri	681	218			

Source: Funeral home numbers were obtained from state regulatory boards for year 2010. Mortality rates used to calculate the number of "needed" funeral homes were taken from CDC death statistics from year 2009.

establishments will be needed to cover the geographic area than the number generated by a simple death-rate formula. In most states, however, the number of funeral homes far exceeds that which can be reasonably supported—full-time—by the death-rate. In Kansas, Pennsylvania, and Vermont, an average funeral home might get only two funerals per week; in Iowa and Nebraska, there may be only one funeral per week. When that is the situation, the funeral bill is likely to be severely inflated in order to support the under-utilized staff and facilities.

Remember, you have but one life to give to your undertaker. Restaurants and clothing stores can induce you to become a repeat customer, perhaps dozens of times, but even the most cleverly marketed mortuary cannot. The more funeral homes per capita, the more thinly customers are spread. When volume is low, the only way to pay the bills is to raise prices.

Are You Going to Be a Willing Victim?

Most mortuary students say they go into the business to be of service to the grieving public. It's after they're hit with the hard facts of making a living and the slow rate of business that steering consumers to more expensive options becomes a preoccupation.

There is only one chance to get the funeral right. Therefore, you—as the buyer—have a special burden to inform yourself about your choices and educate yourself about the pitfalls. Since most of us will never arrange for more than one or two funerals, you won't have much practice. Knowledge is your best self-defense.

How Much Can You Afford?

There are, of course, ethical funeral directors who would consider it a professional embarrassment to push a family into buying more than they can afford. The sales pitches we describe below won't happen at every funeral home. But they're not rare, either. What most people forget is that a funeral is not just an emotional ritual; it is a *business transaction*. The funeral home staff have mortgages and taxes to pay just like everyone else, and they have a right to earn a living. Too often, though, funeral homes *sell themselves* on the idea of their importance—their unique, can't-be-replaced position in society. Don't make the mistake of believing that the more services you choose, the more "respect" you're showing for the dead. No fancy casket or elaborate funeral will mean you love or grieve your dead any more or less.

Josephine Black Pesaresi, daughter of the late Supreme Court Justice Hugo L. Black, described how her family honored her father's request for "simple and cheap":

> Our family had heard my father's views about funerals for many years. Appalled by the high costs, he felt that funeral merchants often took advantage of grieving families when they were at their most vulnerable. Coming from a humble background, he had seen families spend themselves into debt. He was equally appalled by any person who wished an elaborate and expensive funeral, seeing this as evidence that the person was "puffed up about his own importance in the scheme of things."

. . . Huddling for a final conference, someone asked, "Shall we get the pink, the cheapest?" And we all gave a resounding 'YES.' We said we would buy the pink for $165 with the cloth stripped off. The salesman said that was impossible, it would look terrible. We, however, wanted to see for ourselves since this was our coffin of choice. First one of us pulled away a little cloth to take a peek, then another ripped more forcefully, and finally we all started ripping off the fabric with careless abandon. Off came the bows, the coffin skirt, and all but a few patches of stubbornly glued pink organza. There stood a perfectly fine plain pine box. The debris littered the elegant carpet, but we were practically euphoric. We had followed my father's directive almost to a tee, with the added bonus of deflating pretensions in this very pretentious room (though my father would have felt some compassion for the poor coffin salesman).

For the full, delightful essay, visit: <www.funerals.org/faq/51-qsimple-and-cheapq-my-father-said>.

When you arrive at some funeral homes, the car you drive or the way you're dressed might be sized up. If your family is already known in that area, funeral directors probably have a rough idea of your income and financial worth. That's part of the funeral director's job—to anticipate what you might want. After all, a car dealer won't try to sell you a Kia if it appears you can afford a BMW.

You will probably be on your best behavior once you enter the funeral home, which is probably more elegant than your own residence. While the formal aura of many funeral establishments is set to honor the dead, it can also be intimidating. How would you respond to the following?

- "Given your position in the community, I'm sure you'll want to . . ."

- "Your mother had excellent taste. When she made arrangements for Aunt Nellie, this is what she chose."

- "I'm sure you want the best for your mother."

- "Most of our families pick the *traditional* package."

Most of these sample quotes fall into the category of "controlling with guilt." But you don't have to fall for this. You're the only one who can determine the most loving and meaningful way to say goodbye. It may be helpful to bring along a friend who's not as emotionally invested in the death, someone you trust to help you make the most rational choices.

Keep the following response in mind, even if you don't speak it aloud: *"If I spent according to how much I care, I'd be penniless—I'd be paying you for the rest of my life!"*

Funeral directors will usually ask how you plan to pay for the funeral, to see if there is insurance to cover the costs. If a policy is made out to the funeral director, you should find out if any unused portion can be returned to the estate, particularly if money is also needed for other expenses. If a specific funeral home is *not* the beneficiary of an insurance policy, it's probably better not to divulge the amount of any insurance. The cost of an insurance-covered funeral has a strange way of ending up to be just about the same amount as the policy, once that amount is known. One widow told the funeral home her husband wanted "any old wood box." But, knowing that she had walked in with a $12,000 policy in her purse, the funeral director showed her a $6,000 casket and told her it was "the only suitable thing for a man" that they had. The total bill was . . . you guessed it.

If there is no insurance and family funds are limited, don't be embarrassed to state that early in the funeral arrangements—you're not alone. Be careful about obligating yourself for more than you can reasonably afford. The beautiful $10,000 funeral might not seem so wise six months down the road when you're facing increasing rent or college costs for children. Federal regulations require funeral homes to give you prices by phone. Shop around ahead of time—it could save you thousands of dollars. In addition, your local Funeral Consumers Alliance may have done some of the price-shopping for you.

Understanding the Paperwork

According to the Federal Trade Commission's Funeral Rule, you must be given a General Price List (GPL), a casket price list, and an outer burial container price list when you inquire about arrangements and prices. You may keep the GPL, though funeral homes don't have to let you keep the other lists. You must be given an itemized statement of your final choices when contracting for a funeral *before the funeral takes place.* Make sure the final statement has only those items you have selected. Don't leave the arrangements conference without this itemized receipt.

And while funeral homes may ask you to sign the contract, be sure to read the fine print carefully. Some contracts contain statements and conditions that we believe are illegal and unfair, such as "I was given all paperwork and disclosures required by the Federal Trade Commission." Most consumers won't know whether they've been given everything the law requires; they just want to sign the form and get it over with. This could harm your chances of bringing a complaint later, if that unfortunate necessity arises. Some state regulators have refused to hear consumer complaints about illegal sales practices because the family signed off on such contracts, even though they did so at a time of grief and confusion. We recommend you cross out any provision of the contract that you feel uncomfortable agreeing to before you sign it.

Professional Services Fees

The Federal Trade Commission allows a mortuary establishment to set a non-declinable fee for "Basic services of staff." You must pay this fee in addition to the cost of specific funeral goods and services you select. The consumer gets almost nothing for this fee; it is sort of a cover charge or bench fee. As defined by the FTC, this may include the following:

- The funeral director's time in helping you plan the funeral. (You're paying to listen to a sales pitch. Do you pay your travel agent extra to try to sell you more expensive trips?)

- The time it takes to make arrangements with a cemetery, crematory or other funeral home if the body will be shipped out of the area (but burial, cremation, and shipping are listed elsewhere on the price list).

- The time needed to obtain required permits. (In some states, funeral directors can sign their own. A car salesman tosses in this kind of service as part of the cost of doing business.)

- The time for the funeral director to transcribe the death certificate information (which you must supply) and file the certificate.

- Faxing or e-mailing the obituary (which you may have written, and for which you may pay an extra charge to the newspaper for the advertising of the funeral home).

In addition to these basic services, the FTC *also* allows this fee to cover "unallocated overhead"—or even "all overhead," according to an FTC staff publication. No other business is so protected; all others must recoup their costs for capital investment, taxes, insurance, answering services, and advertising by the price charged for each item offered. (See Chapter 8: "The Federal Trade Commission," for a more complete description of this problem.)

Over time, most funeral homes have loaded more and more of their profits into the non-declinable fee, while low-balling the *actual* goods and services you receive (the funeral ceremony, the casket, etc.). By 2006, the average non-declinable fee was $1,595 according to the National Funeral Directors Association, and it has risen since that time. It's not uncommon to see fees as high as $2,500, with some over $3,000. This fee is almost always higher than any of the actual services (such as a visitation) that you pick. This has perverted the intent of the Funeral Rule—to allow cost control through consumer choice. Families who make simpler arrangements pay just as much overhead as those who have a full-service, one-of-everything funeral.

To have the greatest control over what you spend for a funeral, determine the type of funeral you want ahead of time. A memorial service at your church would limit the amount of services required from a funeral home. In that case, finding one with a low charge for the "Basic services fee" may be particularly important to your pocketbook.

Embalming

Embalming is *not legally required* for most deaths. When burial or cremation will be delayed for several days, refrigeration can substitute for embalming in many states, though there are exceptions. Not all funeral homes have refrigerated storage, but most hospitals do. Most funeral homes—by policy—will not allow a public viewing of a body without embalming, but there is no state law that says the body must be embalmed and restored to a "life-like" condition for such an observance. In other countries, embalming is seldom done. A more complete description of embalming is given in Chapter 4.

The cost of embalming will be listed on the General Price List, but there may be additional related charges such as "other preparation of the body—dressing and casketing." For some families, dressing Grandma and fixing her hair, rather than leaving it to the funeral director, might be a loving way to say goodbye. Keep in mind that all fees are optional once you've paid the non-declinable fee.

Shelter of Remains

This might not appear on a price list at all, but, if it does, it should apply only after the four or five days that it might take to complete all funeral arrangements. The FTC does *not* permit a storage fee during usual funeral transactions. Unfortunately, the FTC issued an opinion in 2007 that allows funeral homes to charge for refrigerating unembalmed bodies. (FCA argued this should be considered ordinary custodial care). Be sure to ask if the funeral home's refrigeration charge is per-day or a flat fee.

Forwarding Remains

All general price lists will carry a charge for the handling of a body to be shipped out of the area. The price should include a description of what is covered. This usually includes paperwork, staff time, local transportation of the body, embalming, scheduling shipment, and a shipping container.

Several companies specialize in shipping bodies. Inman Nationwide is one that has contracted with local funeral homes to serve as agents in every state. It pays those agents about $900 (in 2010) for forwarding remains. Airfare is extra.

If you need to ship a body to another state and you're not going to conduct ceremonies in the state where death occurred, it's usually better to call a funeral home on the receiving end and let that business make arrangements. Why? Because most funeral homes charge far more for forwarding remains when arranged by *retail* customers (you) than the $900 wholesale business-to-business charge.

Beware of Misleading Package Fees

If you are price-shopping among several funeral homes for a "direct cremation," be sure to ask if the package price includes the cost of a minimum container and the cost for the cremation process and permits. Many funeral homes do not have their own crematories, and this will be an additional expense which may not be apparent on first inquiry. It's hard to imagine how you can have a "direct cremation" without cremation, but this bit of mischief is permitted by the FTC.

If you choose "immediate burial," one package price may be a lot higher than another because it includes a minimum casket and a grave-liner or vault. In addition, some funeral homes have jacked up their service prices on immediate burial but offer a "discount" if you purchase the casket at the funeral home. This means a handling charge has been built into the services fees, a practice outlawed by the FTC.

Cash Advances

You might need goods and services from outside vendors: an organist, the obituary, special flower arrangements, opening and closing the grave. Some funeral homes add a fee for arranging these, but it must be so stated on the price list, something like, "We charge you for purchasing these goods and services." When a funeral director says, "We'll take care of everything—we'll get the new lettering on the stone," you might be paying more than you need to. While it may be convenient to let the funeral home make these arrangements for you, you may wish to consider saving money by making the contacts on your own.

ID Viewing and Other Cremation Ploys

"Yes, [identification viewing] is self-serving," admitted the speaker during an industry presentation titled "Keys to Cremation Success." "Often after viewing Mom in a cardboard box, the family will ask if we have something a little nicer." His talk was titled "How to Add $1,400 to Your Cremation Calls," given at a symposium sponsored by the *Funeral Service Insider*. One Florida SCI funeral director pitched a grim mental picture and a guilt trip ahead of time. To a woman phoning for the price of an immediate cremation for her aunt, he said, "You'll probably want to upgrade to a cremation casket [$350 more, she later learned]. There will be an identification viewing, and most families don't want to see their loved one in a cardboard box."

With the growing cremation rate (36 percent nationally, and approaching 70 percent in some states), mortuaries are scrambling to recover the income they would otherwise be making from what Jessica Mitford called "the full-fig funeral." Over the years, some manipulative tactics have emerged, and "ID viewing" is one of the worst. It is one thing for a family to request a private visitation. It is quite another for the funeral home to require such a viewing.

One Vermont funeral director threatened "to wash my hands of this whole affair" when the family didn't want to view the grandmother's body. Terrified and feeling helpless (this was the only funeral home in town and the body was already there), they agreed. But they were traumatized by the experience: Grandma's body was on a cold metal table, her blouse undone and hanging open, and splotchy rouge on her cheeks. That was not how they'd wanted to remember her.

Many funeral directors insist ID viewing is necessary to make sure the right body is cremated. But the funeral home knows whose body it is when picking up the dead person from the hospital, nursing home, or family residence. ID viewing at the funeral home is unnecessary except under the very rare circumstances in which the identity of the deceased may be in doubt.

The statutes in Delaware and Maryland have specific language to require identification of the deceased by next-of-kin before a cremation can occur, but the identification, even in those states, can occur at the hospital, nursing home, private residence, or other place of death. A caretaker is almost always another "qualified person." Every state should require that a body be tagged before removal, a practice which would eliminate the industry's mischief with this ruse and avert mix-ups at chain-own businesses that use a central prep facility.

Some funeral homes have actually charged for ID viewing itself, rather than just using it as a sales tactic for more expensive merchandise. Others charge for "preparation for ID viewing." Except where required by state law any such fee may be declined unless the family requested such services; this was confirmed by the FTC on October 31, 1997. Families who were made to believe the viewing was obligatory and who would not have chosen it otherwise should request a refund of any related charges.

Finally, some funeral homes and crematories try to induce you to buy expensive urns by stamping TEMPORARY CONTAINER—NOT SUITABLE FOR LONG-TERM STORAGE on the plastic or cardboard container in which they return the ashes. The Texas Legislature danced to the funeral industry's tune and enacted a law in 2007 mandating that all crematories stamp such a warning on containers. Don't be manipulated. *You* get to decide what container is "permanent" or "suitable."

Carlson's father-in-law was a great believer in education. When his cremated remains were returned from the medical school in a box marked TEMPORARY, the family decided he would be a permanent example of this sleazy tactic. The box now often accompanies Slocum for his educational talks.

Funeral Conglomerates

Before you finish this book, you will have found many references to the problems at chain-owned mortuaries—especially Service Corporation International (SCI) and Stewart Enterprises. In the '80s and '90s, companies such as SCI, The Loewen Group (since bankrupt and bought by SCI), and Stewart went on a mortuary-buying spree, snatching up locally owned funeral homes at a rapid clip. If a funeral home was Palmer's Funeral Home yesterday (owned by John and Mary Palmer, third-generation funeral directors, born and raised in town), it will still be Palmer's Funeral Home tomorrow, even if the new owners are stockholders from around the world. But the prices and practices of the new owners may not resemble the business considerations of the Palmers at all.

It's common for these companies to keep on members of the original family in order to capitalize on their local reputation. You, the consumer, may have no idea that anything has changed—until you get sticker shock. SCI funeral homes, for example, are almost always among the highest-priced establishments in any market, sometimes three times more costly than other funeral homes. Some ex-owners who have stayed on in management positions have become disillusioned with the hard-sell tactics being promoted by the corporations and can hardly wait for their contracts to run out. In addition, many employees have told us privately over the years that management hounds them to sell, sell, sell, creating pressure on the workforce that leaves many feeling dirty about taking financial advantage of the grieving.

Pricey packages are the name of the game for SCI, which uses "Dignity" as its brand name. The "Smith" family's complaint (name changed to protect privacy) illustrates what Dignity looks like from the customer's point of view. When Mrs. Smith's father, "Mr. Collins," died in 2002, they went to the same funeral home they'd used when Mom died in 1996, having no idea it had since been bought by SCI. They wanted a funeral as close as possible to what they'd had for Mom, nothing more and nothing less. Mr. and Mrs. Smith and their son wrote separate letters to the Texas Funeral Service Commission describing a grueling hours-long arrangements conference (emphasis added below):

[The funeral director] Mr. Simpson left the room for a while and returned with a list of funeral service packages that were available. These packages contained a number of items such as the service, the casket, the outer burial container, flowers, and so on. The family asked Mr. Simpson whether or not the options provided in the funeral service package [were] similar in kind to that provided for Mrs. Collins' funeral. He replied that it was and that the funeral service package was the best option because it provided an additional discount . . . *thus there was no reason to look at a pricing list for individual items.*

[Simpson] again explained that we would not save money by doing the funeral *a la carte* because the "packages" were so heavily discounted that the basics, e.g., casket, liner, hearse, and graveside services, were actually less expensive in a package than they were if purchased individually, and besides, all the extras were thrown in the package. We asked [him] to provide us with an estimate of the service we had purchased for Mrs. Collins at today's prices in an *a la carte* manner, and he "dodged" the question and failed, in retrospect, to truly answer any of our questions in that area.

Mrs. Smith continued to press for an itemized price list and objected to paying for things the family didn't want:

Mr. Simpson countered that "now" they were offering packages and that we would want the least expensive packages, as that would provide us with the best savings. As he went through the individual parts of the package, I noted that we did not plan to use the chapel as we were having a graveside service as we did in my mother's service. He explained that we still had to pay for the chapel because it was part of the package "that was saving us money."

And the price of Dignity? $13,000 for the Smith family.

Comments by an SCI Employee

Jobvent.com lets you post anonymously about your employer. Of 10 SCI employees, only one had anything positive to say when we visited the site recently. Among the comments left:

We were told to sell Dignity plans, collect all monies immediately, give seamless service and ask for 10s on the J. D. Power surveys. It was quite difficult to sell the plans because they seemed overpriced to most consumers and the offerings in the plans did not seem valuable to the families served.

Another example comes from an on-line mortuary chat:

> I was employed by SCI for three years . . . . Once I was at a regional meeting. All were asked if they were funeral directors or sales people. The ones who raised their hands saying they were funeral directors were reprimanded and told they were not funeral directors but sales people . . . . . Families do not matter to officials at SCI. Only the almighty dollar, and their prices are high.

"Counselors" are asked to visit mourners just a few days after a burial to get sales leads from friends and relatives of the deceased. Even more humiliating is the insistence of management to go door-knocking in neighborhoods to sell prepaid funerals and burial property. This is a company that goes under the brand name of Dignity Memorial. What is the dignity of taking advantage of people on what may be the worst day of their lives?

It may seem that we're piling on SCI in particular, but the company has long been a disproportionately large source of consumers' complaints to the FCA office. The complaints from families using SCI-owned facilities in states around the country are suspiciously alike and indicate to us a company-wide pattern. Similar behavior appears in an SCI manual leaked to the FCA office.

Of course, not every experience with a corporate-owned funeral home will be a bad one. In fact, we've spoken to employees at some chain-owned funeral homes over the years (in the course of helping consumers with complicated arrangements) who proved to be competent, straightforward, and genuinely warm. But if price and ownership are important to you, it's wise to check out just who owns "your family's funeral home." If it turns out to be a large chain, you may be faced with high prices and uncomfortable pressure you're not expecting. In that case, don't be afraid to walk out or move the body to another funeral home.

Corporate Trend is Slowing

It's worth noting that corporate purchases of funeral homes have slowed in recent years, and some of the large corporations have sold off some of their properties after realizing they had overbought (and overpaid). While it is true that the publicly traded chains are the biggest funeral companies in the country and they have outsized market power in some ways, there's a common misconception that *most* funeral homes are now owned by these corporations. Not true. The big chains have owned between 10 and 15 percent of funeral homes in America over the years; the remainder are independent. Beware, though, that in some metropolitan areas (particularly in Florida with its concentration of elderly people) corporate chains have a near-monopoly.

Don't Put it Off

We teach our kids about religion, politics, money, and maybe even sex. But few of us teach our children about how to shop for a funeral. Said one funeral director, "Picking a funeral home without shopping around is like handing the funeral director a blank check." The most effective way to avoid excessive purchases at a time of emotional vulnerability is to talk about funeral options with your family ahead of time.

Talking about death won't make you die any more than talking about contraception will make you pregnant. While broaching the topic can seem uncomfortable or downright scary, countless families have told us over the years, "I feel so much better after having a frank talk about this; the fear is gone." Local Funeral Consumers Alliance groups have material on a variety of funeral topics, as well as local price information.

And if your family is especially hesitant, try some humor. Check out Carlson's book *I Died Laughing*.

Caskets, Other Boxes, Memorials, and Markers 3

YEARS AGO, THE MARK-UP ON CASKETS was often 200 to 500 percent to cover the other goods and services such as embalming, viewing, the funeral service itself, and transportation. If funds were limited, you were expected to pick a lesser casket, not skip the embalming or viewing. However, those choosing the least expensive caskets could expect a pretty short service.

After the Federal Trade Commission Funeral Rule went into effect in 1984, services had to be listed separately, but many funeral homes never reduced the casket prices to compensate for the other new charges. Consequently, it is not uncommon to see caskets—especially low-end ones—marked up to the point where the casket accounts for one-third of the total funeral bill.

Since 2000, and especially after Funeral Consumers Alliance filed a federal lawsuit against the major funeral chains and the biggest casket maker in 2005, many funeral homes are doing "price realignment." In order to discourage consumers from buying discount caskets from third parties—even Costco, WalMart, and Amazon.com now sell them—some funeral homes have been lowering their casket prices to match, or nearly match, the competition. The funeral director will happily show you that he's got a low-cost model, too, and it's a brand-name!

But it's a funereal shell game; once the casket price drops from $2,000 to $1,200, the basic service fee rises from $1,200 to $2,000. The bottom line for you is the same, but you lose the option to save money by purchasing a casket elsewhere. The trade magazines are pushing this concept to funeral directors, characterizing it as "putting your profits where they should be, in your services." The truth is more prosaic: since the basic services fee is the only one the consumer can't decline to pay, the undertaker can guarantee he gets as much profit from you as he believes he's due. Cost-conscious consumers will want to compare a funeral home's casket prices *and* service fees to find the best value.

Like any other business, the funeral industry has studied buying patterns. People tend to purchase one of the first three caskets they are shown—hurrying, perhaps, through a difficult choice. It isn't hard to figure out that among those first three will be ones with a good profit margin for the mortuary. When people are shown one casket marked $1,000, one marked $1,800, and one marked $2,500, which would you guess gets picked most often? We are, indeed, a society of middle-of-the-roaders. "I didn't want to pick the cheapest," said one woman about her mother's casket. Many other families have told us they picked a "moderately priced casket." When we asked how they chose it, they invariably contrast the price with one that was more expensive, and one that was cheaper. "Moderately priced" appears to mean any price at all, as long as it's in the middle. So if a funeral home wants to make a bigger profit next year, there's a good chance that the first three caskets shown might be listed at $1,800, $2,500, and $3,200—so now the $2,500-casket will become the popular model.

Showing caskets by catalog—with large glossy photos—is becoming more common. It reduces inventory cost and makes another room available for public use. Most funeral directors carry such catalogs when they visit nursing homes and private residences. In states that require a minimum display of, say, "five adult caskets," that may be all you'll find on hand, with others shown by catalog only. Industry reports claim that consumers seem more comfortable with the catalog or computer selections, and that casket revenues actually increase.

The FTC requires that a casket price range be included on the General Price List and that a full casket price list be supplied before showing any caskets. Carlson mentioned this to a *Chicago Sun Times* reporter who was getting ready to take an AARP volunteer "shopping" for a funeral. If the lowest-cost casket is not on display, she suggested, ask to see it anyway. (Some funeral homes hide the low-cost ones.) A couple of weeks later the writer called back: "You were right. When the nice gentleman I was with asked to see some less expensive caskets, they took us to a hallway on the way to the boiler room."

Similarly, a New Hampshire widow didn't think she could afford a $2,500 casket, the least expensive one on display. Her irate daughter reported that the mother was taken to a dark cold basement full of cobwebs. Half-way down the stairs her mother turned and fled. As a result, her dad's body ended up in the $2,500 casket.

"Protective" Caskets

The FTC's Funeral Rule makes it illegal for funeral homes to claim caskets will preserve the body indefinitely, but many flout the spirit of the law with deceptive language that refers to "protective" caskets. It is not uncommon to see something like this on price lists:

We offer many different styles and prices of caskets and an alternative container from which to select. Since many caskets that appear similar in appearance may differ greatly in quality and construction, we offer the following in order to assist you in making an informed decision.

- **PROTECTIVE**: These caskets are designed by the manufacturer to resist the entrance of air, water and other outside elements. They may be constructed of varying gauges of steel, copper or bronze.

- **NON-PROTECTIVE**: These caskets are not designed by the manufacturer to resist the entrance of air, water or other outside elements. They may be constructed of metal, hardwood, or wood products covered with fabric.

One is tempted to imagine a casket maker sitting down with the designers and saying, "Make sure these won't keep out air, water, or other elements."

The rubber gasket on a so-called protective casket adds just a few dollars to the manufacturing cost, but it may add hundreds to the retail price. A "sealer"—as many funeral directors call them—will not stop the decomposition of the body; it actually complicates the process. Instead of the natural dehydration that would otherwise occur, the body will putrefy in the oxygen-free environment. These gaskets are actually supposed to be one-way seals that let out the build-up of gases inside, but—as described in the company literature—they're subjected to a vacuum test before shipping to make sure no air can get in. You might call them "self-burping" caskets.

If, however, they are closed too tightly, the gasses can't get out and the caskets explode, as one Jacksonville, Florida woman found out three years after her father was entombed in his mausoleum crypt. A new funeral home was then contacted, a new casket was supplied by the manufacturer, and—after a change of clothing and a quick clean-up—a new entombment ceremony was held, sort of, amidst the stench. (See the Cemeteries chapter for a more complete description of the problem).

In addition to the seal, some of the more expensive Batesville steel caskets offer "cathodic protection"—a bar of magnesium serving as a "sacrificial cathode" to deter rusting. Similar mechanisms are used in water heaters, providing protection for three years or so. Batesville, however, used to stand behind its 16-gauge steel caskets for up to 50 years. Following several lawsuits, it has drastically lowered the number of years it will warranty a casket.

To its credit, California requires the following disclosure on all price lists:

THERE IS NO SCIENTIFIC OR OTHER EVIDENCE THAT ANY CASKET WITH A SEALING DEVICE WILL PRESERVE HUMAN REMAINS

It's wise to step back for a second and consider whether a "protective" or "warranteed" casket makes any sense at all. No casket will make the deceased any less dead, no casket will prevent decomposition, and how many of us are likely to exhume grandma decades later to make sure she's still dry?

Deception on this issue has occurred for a long time, despite consistent evidence that the gaskets serve no worthy purpose. Back in 1994, Clarence Miller wrote in *The Funeral Book*:

> Do not for one moment think that just because a casket has a rubber gasket designed to keep out air and water that it will. I have seen caskets disinterred after one month that were full of water though they were sold as "air and water tight. . . ." In more than 35 years as a mortician, I do not have any faith at all in so-called "sealer" caskets.

Even a Batesville representative said recently that he was uncomfortable with the word "sealer." "They're water and leak *resistant*," he said.

Responsible funeral homes have realized that making unrealistic promises is not only unethical; it can lead to lawsuits from aggrieved consumers. Some are describing their caskets in more factual, and less emotionally manipulative, terms, such as "gasketed" instead of "protective." A few have even said they won't sell "sealers" unless a customer insists, because they're a waste of money and a scam.

But not all. Slocum and a colleague, Sherry Swett, joined an undercover camera crew from Good Morning America in 2004 to go "funeral shopping." Posing as a family planning for Aunt Lillian's imminent demise, they stopped at several Connecticut funeral homes. In the casket room at one, the funeral director was eager to fulfill their every final wish. One member of the crew "innocently" asked about the price differences between the various models, and our host lit up. "This one's sealed," he said patting the top of a costly silver-colored model. "Won't let air or water in." "What does that mean?" Swett asked. The funeral director explained that it would keep Aunt Lillian in perfect shape. "Now, I've pulled up some caskets over the years, and these really work. We could open it up 30 years later and"—kissing the tips of his fingers as if to say *'magnifique!'*—"she'd look just like the day she died."

The second funeral home said we shouldn't buy "one of those caskets" from a discount retailer because they were "all seconds," and "tin cans."

In an article in the January 1998 issue of *Mortuary Management*, David Walkinshaw wrote: "From consumer surveys, it is clear that families select caskets mainly on eye appeal. . . . That is the reason that casket companies produce inexpensive caskets in rather unflattering finishes. If they looked too good, people would buy them."

Of course, there are well-made caskets that cost less than $800—or at least *should* cost less than that. But as Walkinshaw noted, to discourage customers from selecting low-end merchandise, these otherwise perfectly dignified caskets are often ordered in "ugly" colors—the most common being those covered with dull gray cloth (wholesale cost about $200). Some funeral homes refer to them as "welfare caskets." Yet when a priest or nun who has taken a vow of poverty dies, this same casket might be ordered in burgundy or navy blue. Suddenly, it is no longer a "welfare casket." If the price and basic design of a modest casket seem right for you, ask what other colors can be ordered. Usually a funeral home can get a more attractive replacement within a day or so.

Third-Party Casket Sellers

It is illegal for a funeral home to charge a handling fee if you use a family-built casket or purchase one elsewhere. We have seen some price lists that say that any such casket must meet state and cemetery or crematory requirements. Few such requirements exist. Occasionally, a funeral home will state that the casket must be "deemed suitable" by the funeral director. This is manipulative and illegal because the funeral director may not refuse your choice of a casket. Some establishments may make it inconvenient to use another firm's box, insisting that you be present when the casket is delivered, so they won't be "responsible," though this is also a violation of the Funeral Rule. On the other hand, you just might want to be there—to assure that no one "finds" a torn lining, a dent or scratch, or a smear of dirt and grease on the third-party casket after it is delivered. Retail casket sellers have long complained of such underhanded tactics.

Though it's been 27 years since the Funeral Rule became effective, there's a surprising amount of drama from the trade still swirling around the issue of third-party caskets. The trade magazines and blogs are filled with what can only be called whining from funeral directors looking for an excuse—any excuse—to find fault with any box they don't sell. The FTC has issued more than 10 years' worth of advisory opinions in an attempt to clarify what seems to be a very simple concept. The Commission states:

- Funeral homes can't require you to be present when the casket is delivered.

- Funeral homes can't require you to inspect the casket on delivery.

- Funeral homes can't refuse to allow third-party delivery staff to use the funeral home's equipment to bring the casket inside.

- Funeral homes can't refuse to accept a third-party casket during any time period in which the funeral home would ordinarily accept delivery from its own casket supplier.

Only three states still require that only a funeral director sell caskets—Louisiana, Oklahoma, and Virginia—clearly a ploy by the local undertakers to shut out competition and a violation of the intent of the Funeral Rule. Columnist George Will compared this to a hypothetical law requiring everyone who sold shoes to be a licensed podiatrist. Casket artisans and retailers in those states might call the boxes they're selling "hope chests"—there is no state that forbids a family from burying a body in a hope chest. Of course, consumers in those states may order a casket shipped in from another state, and a mortuary may **not** refuse the family's right to use it. Check on-line for retail casket sellers. Both Costco and WalMart now sell caskets on-line, too.

Caskets and Cremation

The Funeral Rule gives you the right to refuse a casket for cremation. All funeral homes must provide a minimum "alternative container." The least expensive would be a cardboard container for perhaps as low as $50, but some funeral homes are known to charge $395 or more for such a box. By law, you have a right to supply your own.

With the rapid growth of the cremation rate, some funeral homes have set up separate displays of cremation caskets, with separate listings on the Casket Price List. But funeral directors may not stop you from using a lower-cost cremation casket for viewing or burial, although some have tried. While certain containers may be suggested to families who are planning a viewing prior to cremation, any comment that one is "not suitable for viewing" is manipulative and illegal, yet still common.

Many funeral homes also offer rental caskets for viewing before cremation. These look just like ordinary caskets—they're usually wood—but the interior bedding is attached to a replaceable cardboard liner. When the viewing is over, the bottom end of the casket swings out like the hinge on a pick-up truck, and the cardboard insert slides out and goes to the crematory. The funeral home can then order another lined insert for about $100, and rent the same casket shell repeatedly.

You're likely to pay $700 to $900 per day for a rental casket to hold a dead body. By comparison, the most expensive room at the Waldorf-Astoria in New York City (priced on April 27, 2010) cost $559 per night and sleeps two living people, with some rooms as low as $259. Does your rental casket feature high-speed wireless Internet, mini-bar, maid service, and a marble bathroom?

Outer Burial Containers

Outer burial containers (vaults or grave-liners) can be as expensive as caskets, with some prices going as high as $7,000 or more. These, too, may have "sealer" mechanisms, which may offer the caskets some "protection" from ground water if the cemetery is built near a high-water zone. In that case, it may seem reasonable at first blush to choose a "sealer" vault. But unfortunately, a sealer is likely to pop to the surface during a flood and float away. That's what happened during the 1993 flood in the Midwest and the 1998 flood in the southeast, and cemetery personnel had a terrible time getting everyone buried again where they belonged. Even if high water is not a problem, what is one protecting with an expensive vault? Decomposition of the body will occur regardless.

A grave-liner (a simpler container that serves the same function) is usually less expensive than a vault. A basic concrete model (without the gold-spray paint or the bronze lining) will probably cost $400 to $900. A polypropylene "bell cover" should be another option and is easier to install. The vault or grave-liner keeps the ground from settling after burial so the cemetery people can enjoy easy mowing and maintenance. Because not all cemeteries require liners or vaults, be sure to check the policy yourself if you'd prefer to avoid this expense. No state has a law requiring an outer burial container and some national cemeteries (including Arlington) do not use them.

In an effort to sell an expensive vault, one Vermont funeral director told the ladies in his arrangements room, "I know a woman who told her husband to buy a cheap casket but an expensive vault because she was afraid of snakes." As it turned out, this made it easier for them to opt for cremation before the transaction was over, much to the funeral director's dismay.

Many vault companies have refused to sell directly to consumers, or to retailers that sell to consumers. Some that do sell to consumers have been boycotted by funeral directors. For Mary Lynn Broe, who handled funeral plans for her mother without a funeral director, getting the vault became a huge problem. When she tried to order a vault from an Illinois funeral home, the owners insisted she had to hire their unwanted services as well.

Some states, including New York and Vermont, allow consumers to refuse a vault on religious grounds. But good luck getting cemeteries to acknowledge this. New York's on-line consumer guide doesn't mention this option despite our reminders over the years, and staff at the Burlington city cemetery still tell the public (incorrectly) that "state law" *requires* a vault. (NY does allow cemeteries to charge a reasonable fee, however, for ground maintenance.)

Little Vaults for Urns

Stung by the rapid rise in cremation (and thus the decline in whole-body burial), many cemeteries are now requiring an "urn vault"—an outer container in which to put the box of cremated remains. While cemeteries that use heavy mowing equipment may have some legitimate concern about keeping the ground stable above caskets, urn vaults are truly a posthumous Russian nesting-doll racket. Some cemeterians will say, with a straight face, they require them in case someone wants to disinter the urn sometime in the future. The vault will guarantee that the urn or box remains intact or that you won't "put a fork through Mum," as one SCI salesman in Australia put it. An urn vault price of, say, $595 may be mentioned by the sales rep, who is not likely to volunteer that less expensive ones are also available (see the Cemeteries chapter for some suggestions). Although you may wish to shop around, any saving could be offset by an "inspection fee," "installation fee" or "opening and closing fee," all bogus charges to make up for lost profit.

Some states restrict who may sell a vault. Cemeteries that do sell such items may not forbid you from purchasing them—or memorials—elsewhere.

Memorials & Markers

While it is a violation of the Sherman Anti-Trust Act for cemeteries to refuse to accept monuments bought from outside dealers, few state regulators are on top of the problem. We've seen many consumer complaints that cemeteries refuse to accept a third-party monument, or have come up with trumped-up fees or bogus policies. The daughter of a veteran wrote to FCA telling of how one cemetery refused to place a temporary marker on her father's grave pending the arrival of his government headstone:

> My father was a veteran of the Air Force and Navy. He was career military. Unfortunately, we did as many people do and did not make burial plans until my father died.
>
> Upon arriving at Pine Ridge, the manager—Tom—took us into his office to help us make decisions. We asked about the veteran's marker. We were told that they take a very long time to arrive at the cemetery (7 months at the minimum) [the VA reports 90 days] and that we would have to pay extra to have it installed at the cemetery and that the cemetery would not maintain a veteran's marker. Tom told us that if we bought a marker from them that my father's grave would not go unmarked and that they would place a temporary marker on his grave until the one we selected arrived.
>
> We selected and ordered a Pine Ridge marker. The cost was over $4,000 for the interment and Marker. Several days after my father died, I visited the grave, and it was not yet marked.

Another family wrote:

> My grandfather died in 1983 and still has no headstone, the 3rd wife never paid for it. So I know he is a veteran (navy) and is eligible for a VA headstone/marker. This cemetery only does flat markers, that's fine. They will not accept the 24×12×4 stone marker but do accept the 24×12×3/4 bronze marker plate. The kicker is that the bronze marker plate requires a stone base . . . which would cost additional monies. Keep in mind the plate is the same size as the plain stone without a bronze plate. They insist upon the base being 28×18×4. My

guess is to boost sales of stone through their company. Sure they accept other bases from outside companies that are 28×18×4 but who would do that? They clearly came up with a way to charge outrageous amounts extra. Oh and they charge an 83 cents [per square inch] installation fee which is 3× most cemeteries. Then they charge a lower than normal amount for the stone, so it worked out the same in the end but functions to make it appear cheaper though them.

The state of Georgia has been very good to cemeteries. In 2006, the legislature passed a bill allowing cemeteries to charge customers $125 (up from $50) if they buy a monument from someone other than the cemetery. The law calls this "reimbursing" the cemetery for "reasonable costs in assisting in the siting of a monument," and "supervision and inspection of the installation," but this is really just a penalty for smart shoppers who find a cheaper tombstone elsewhere.

While it's a good idea to complain loudly (and perhaps threaten to go to the local TV or newspaper consumer reporter) if you find yourself strong-armed this way, it can be difficult to get state regulators to take action. Cemeteries are very poorly regulated, and most states don't have specific laws prohibiting this kind of behavior.

Consumers have run into trouble with independent monument dealers, too. Just as we don't recommend paying for your funeral or grave in advance, we advise against buying a marker ahead of time (unless, perhaps, you plan to have it installed at the cemetery immediately). Some people have lost their money when the monument store they paid years in advance has gone out of business.

When shopping for a marker:

- Get a copy of the cemetery's rules and regulations. You'll want to know what monuments are permitted ahead of time so you won't waste money on a stone the cemetery won't accept.

- Shop around. Independent monument companies may have better prices than the cemetery (if the cemetery sells monuments).

- Get a schematic or drawing of the marker and the lettering ahead of time for your approval before consenting to have the stone made. It's better to catch mistakes before they're carved in stone.

- Do business in writing. Too many families rely on a business's "word" over the phone, and if the marker doesn't get installed for a long period of time, or if the design is wrong, they have nothing on paper to prove the business made a mistake.

Embalming
A beautiful memory picture?

4

MOST PEOPLE DON'T KNOW THAT embalming is almost never required. In some circumstances, state laws may dictate embalming if there will be delayed disposition, but even then, in most cases, refrigeration can usually suffice. In 19 states, embalming is never required under any circumstance.

And contrary to the widespread misperception that embalming preserves a body indefinitely, cosmetic funeral-type embalming usually only holds a body for a few days. A stronger solution of chemicals (such as medical schools use to keep cadavers preserved for years) might turn the body to shoe-leather, inconsistent with the industry's description of a "beautiful memory picture."

The misconceptions can have unfortunate results. In one case that came to our attention, S.S., a 21-year-old only child, died on Friday from an accidental overdose of prescription drugs. He was embalmed on Saturday, and there were visitations for this devastated family all day Sunday, Monday, and half of Tuesday. The stench started on Monday, however, and by Wednesday—while arranging for burial in the next state—it was unbearable.

While the funeral industry has long promoted the myth that embalming "protects the public health," in reality it creates a danger for embalmers while offering no health benefit to the living. Embalmers open bodies that might otherwise be intact, thus potentially exposing themselves to fluid-borne pathogens. The formaldehyde they use is highly toxic and is a respiratory irritant. The Centers for Disease Control report embalmers have a 13 percent higher death rate (over any given time period) as compared to the population at large, and a 2009 study reports an increased risk of some forms of cancer from formaldehyde exposure in funeral service jobs. (See the November 24, 2009 issue of *Journal of the National Cancer Institute*.)

No "Pretty" Options

Randy Garner, a trusted funeral director friend of ours, read a draft version of this chapter and made a point worth highlighting: Nothing that happens to our bodies after death is "pretty." Embalming is not unique in that respect. Cremation, obviously, burns the body until there's nothing left but bone. Decay of the body, depending on many factors, can range from going back to the earth in a compost-like fashion to a situation in which the body putrefies and turns to a smelly liquid. One of the newest options, alkaline hydrolysis (see the Green Burial chapter) dissolves the body in lye, and few of us would want to open the canister and watch.

So why are we writing a chapter singling out embalming? Because of the widespread public ignorance about what the process is, why it's used, and when it's "required." There is no single aspect of the conventional American funeral process that is so widely misunderstood or that has been so forcefully marketed to the funeral-buying public. Many people are shocked to learn that the US and Canada are the only countries where embalming is so widespread as to be considered routine and ordinary. It is rarely done in most other countries (although the international US and Canadian funeral conglomerates are now pushing it hard elsewhere including Japan, England, and Australia).

Worse still, the majority of the public believes embalming is usually required by law when the opposite is true. In a 2007 article for *The Journal of Consumer Affairs*, researchers Steve Kopp and Elyria Kemp surveyed more than 200 adults to determine their knowledge (or lack thereof) of funeral rights and requirements. Sixty-six percent of those surveyed thought embalming was required by their state's laws if the body was not immediately buried. That is **never** the case in **any** state. This comports with our experience talking to thousands of Americans—most people default to the idea that embalming is usually or often required by law, and almost all of them report believing that the law requires embalming for a public viewing of the body.

No one needs to explain that cremation means burning or that cadaver donation to the medical school means dissection. But since embalming is so widely misunderstood, and since it is often used as the foundation from which to sell the most costly type of send-off, it deserves special attention.

History of Embalming

The Egyptians began embalming the bodies of wealthy and important people sometime before 4000 BC, and the practice spread to other ancient cultures. Generally, the bodies were soaked in a carbonate of soda, and the viscera and brains were removed. Herbs, salts, and aromatic substances were packed into the body cavities. Then the bodies were wrapped in cloth that had been soaked with preservatives. Variations of these procedures were employed as embalming spread to other cultures. For example, Alexander the Great was reportedly embalmed with wax and honey. Knowledge of embalming moved to parts of Europe about 500 AD but was not widespread, although the bodies of several well-known historical figures (including King Canute and William the Conqueror) were preserved.

In the 19th century, Italian and French scientists developed techniques to inject preservatives into veins and arteries. The practice reached the US during the Civil War, when it was used to delay decomposition of the bodies of war victims that needed to be transported long distances before burial. When President Lincoln was assassinated, his body was embalmed to allow public viewing in locations throughout the country. It was considered an unusual step to take, in an unusual period of national sorrow.

In his book *Inventing the American Way of Death, 1830–1920*, James Farrell comments: "Before 1880, people viewed embalming only as an historical phenomenon, an exotic custom of the ancient Egyptians." He notes that with organized encouragement from a rapidly emerging funeral industry, "... by 1920, almost all dead bodies were embalmed, not just those intended for transport."

As an example of how sophisticated the practice had become in those four decades, Farrell cites a 1920 advertisement by a Boston undertaker:

> For composing the features, $1.
>
> For giving the features a look of quiet resignation, $2
>
> For giving the features the appearance of Christian hope and contentment, $5.

The Reverend William L. Coleman, in his book *It's Your Funeral*, notes that "The science of embalming had largely been abandoned for 1,500 years" and its sudden re-emergence in the late 19th and early 20th centuries was controversial. "Both Christians and humanitarians often objected strenuously," Coleman writes. "They had visions of bodies being severely mutilated. Ministers denounced it as a desecration of the 'temple of God'." That view continues to be held by some religions, including Orthodox Judaism.

Yet despite such objections, embalming became an expected part of the majority of death arrangement packages offered by US funeral directors. Why? What are the benefits that have come into demand in North America but seem less important to the rest of the world?

"Sanitation" and Other Snake Oil

Embalming was promoted early on as a means of preventing premature burial, a horror that had been verified in several instances in the late 19th and early 20th centuries. Even today, we've heard older folks expressing this concern. Farrell quotes the Portland, Oregon, city attorney in an address to the 1910 convention of the National Funeral Directors Association (NFDA) as saying: "There is consolation in the thought that when a man's undertaker is finished with him, he can be reasonably sure he is not in a trance." That seems a harsher form of "consolation" than the practice of some religious groups which delay body disposition for three days to allow time for the exit of the spirit. Is it really more horrific to wake up underground or on a porcelain table with formaldehyde coursing through one's arteries?

Sanitation was another—and perhaps the most emphatic—argument made by the funeral industry in its early promotion of embalming. The idea was that embalming served to disinfect bodies, preventing the spread of diseases. The funeral industry, emerging between 1880 and 1920, successfully convinced the public (through the efforts of the newly formed National Funeral Directors Association) that professional services were necessary for proper care of the dead—with compatible laws and regulations quickly following.

Embalming was the centerpiece of that effort. Families could place a body on ice to slow its deterioration, but only an experienced "professional" could embalm. In fact, embalming remains the only specific skill undertakers possess that any business person of ordinary competence does not. The livery drivers, the carpenters, the furniture sellers, and others involved in body disposition, quickly found they could—with minimal training in a mysterious art—leap to a whole new social status in the community. Most of the time, all it took was the stomach for a little blood-letting.

As justification for elaborate funerals that include embalming, morticians often cite a quote attributed to Gladstone: "Show me the manner in which a nation or a community cares for its dead and I will measure with mathematical exactness the tender mercies of its people, their respect for the law, and their loyalty to high ideals." A recent past president of the National Funeral Directors Association wrote of how he'd embalmed his own mother, describing it as a "gentle cleansing process." That is a fine sentiment, but it would be a hard sell to anybody who has actually witnessed a modern embalming.

Modern Embalming Practices

The major differences between current funeral practices and those used by the Egyptians are the use of modern chemicals and equipment and an emphasis on temporary cosmetic restoration rather than mummification. The process consists of both arterial embalming (draining the blood and filling the veins and arteries with pink-colored chemicals) and cavity embalming (emptying fluids from the chest and abdomen, replacing them with sufficient preservatives to afford a temporary delay in decomposition).

The job is performed on an embalming table, which is surrounded by a conduit to catch body fluids and route them to a special container or—more often—the sewer system. First, the body is washed with a disinfectant solution. Then the limbs and joints are massaged to counter the effects of rigor mortis so the body can be positioned. The face is restored and features set, using prickly-topped plastic cups under the eyelids to keep them from sliding open and wire or suture to close the jaws. A little Vaseline or super-glue can keep the lips together.

Then arterial embalming begins. The embalmer chooses one of several (or in some cases many) locations in which a major artery and vein are in close proximity—the armpits, the neck, and/or the groin—and makes an incision. An injection needle is placed into the artery and drainage forceps into the vein to allow blood to flow into the table trough. An injection machine pumps a chemical solution (dyed for the proper effect on body color) into the artery while body parts are massaged to assist the flow. If the embalming is done too quickly, the features are likely to swell. So far, it's a relatively "surgical" procedure.

The next step, however, is cavity embalming. A trocar (a large-bore hollow needle) is connected to an electric aspirator (a pump that removes fluids from abdominal and chest cavities). The trocar is inserted near the naval and jabbed around inside the abdomen and chest to puncture various organs while the blood and waste are pumped out. The body is then filled with a formalin solution to kill microorganisms and retard decay. The anus and vagina are packed with cotton. Or—if the practitioner is up-to-date on the latest devices—the "A/V Closure" (a 4½" white plastic self-tapping screw) might be used to prevent leakage "while preserving the dignity of the deceased." Up to this point, the process has taken about 45 minutes to one hour.

In most cases the body is then cosmetically restored. The extent of this depends on the condition of the corpse and the wishes of the family. Sometimes a little rouge, face cream, and hair styling will do. But if the face appears somewhat emaciated, additional steps may include injection of tissue-builder with a hypodermic needle to flesh out the cheeks. If the body is severely mutilated or decayed the embalmer will do whatever it takes to restore the body to recognizable form with wax, plaster of Paris, and additional make-up. Dinair Airbrush Systems—a company that touts its equipment for stage and screen—has also been giving demonstrations of cosmetic magic to morticians, even recreating the little crow's feet and wrinkles if need be.

The Myth of Sanitation

The belief that embalming prevents the spread of disease is still widely held, but public health as a reason for embalming has long been refuted by medical authorities. Back in 1977, the Consumer Reports book on funerals (*Funerals: Consumers' Last Rights*, Copyright 1977, Consumers Union of United States, Inc., Mount Vernon, NY 10553) noted that disease does not run rampant in countries where bodies are seldom embalmed. Furthermore, studies show that embalming does not affect certain bacteria or viruses. Evidence of tuberculosis, smallpox, anthrax, tetanus, and AIDS have all been found in embalmed bodies shortly after death.

Even more revealing is an admonition from a sales rep for Dodge Chemical, which manufactures embalming fluids. In the case of death from Creutzfeld-Jakobs disease, the rep said don't even take the body into the funeral home. One form of embalming fluid actually keeps the disease alive.

There's nothing new about the knowledge that embalming does more to endanger public health than to preserve it. In 1977, a British Columbia deputy health minister was quoted as saying, "It is our view that the process of embalming serves no useful purpose in preventing the transmission of communicable disease. In those few cases where a person dies of a highly infectious disease, a far better procedure would be to wrap and securely seal the body in heavy plastic sheeting before removing it from the room where death occurred." Other Canadian health authorities have gone even further; in several provinces, embalming is forbidden for about 12 infectious diseases.

Astonishingly, however, as late as this writing in 2011, eight US states still *require* embalming for infectious or communicable diseases. Only six states recognize the potential health hazard *from* embalming. Delaware, Hawaii, Missouri, Montana, North Carolina, and Ohio specifically forbid it in the case of infectious disease, or require immediate disposition, which would preclude embalming.

Dr. Michael T. Osterholm, Director of the Center for Infectious Disease Research and Policy at the University of Minnesota, was surprised at the misinformation the Minnesota Funeral Directors Association was putting before lawmakers on this subject. He testified during a 2010 hearing on a bill that would improve families' rights to care for their own dead. In a supporting letter, he wrote:

> In the recent Senate hearing, I had the opportunity to hear the testimony of a representative of the Minnesota Funeral Directors Association. Frankly, I was extremely disappointed by the scare tactics they used in that testimony to suggest to the Committee that dead bodies in general pose a significant infectious disease risk.

Osterholm's letter is one of the most candid statements of the scientific consensus on this issue, and it's worth quoting at length:

> In this regard, I also render my best professional judgment that the mere presence of a dead body without regard to its embalmed status and one that is not leaking blood from an open wound or perforation, does not pose any increased risk of infectious disease transmission for the person who might handle that body or review it in a

private setting. Once a human dies, infectious agents that would be of any concern, including those on the individual's skin or internal organs is greatly diminished.

The lack of risk of infectious disease transmission in the handling of a dead human body without incisions or perforations is obvious when one realizes that today many dying individuals receive hospice care in their own home from family and loved ones without health-care training and without measurable infectious disease risk to these same persons. To now suggest that somehow the death of that individual makes that body a new and major infectious disease concern is simply without scientific merit. I believe the scientific facts supporting the course of actions provided under the provisions of your bill will allow loved ones to more intimately grieve the loss of their family member, colleague or close friend without increasing the risk of the transmission of infectious diseases to any of these individuals.

We have contacted the Centers for Disease Control many times over the years, and each time they've confirmed that CDC has *never* prescribed embalming as a public health measure. In short, there is *no* genuine controversy—it's a scientific fact that dead bodies do not pose a health risk to anyone except in very rare cases. As Ron Hast, a longtime funeral director and publisher of *Mortuary Management* magazine has noted, it's hard to square the fact that funeral directors cry out in alarm over the danger of unembalmed bodies when they pick them up all the time from hospitals and homes, and they're certainly not wearing HazMat suits when they do.

The sanitation argument is still widely believed, however. Until recently, the NFDA perpetuated that myth on its website and through its Consumer Education Series Brochures: "The foremost reason for embalming is the protection of public health. . . . Untreated remains pose serious public health concerns."

Those states with embalming requirements for any reason should eliminate them. After reading the chapter on embalming in Carlson's 1987 book, Mack Smith, executive director of the state funeral board in Kansas, had the good sense to seek amendments to that state's regulations, eliminating the embalming requirement for many diseases including AIDS. (The old embalming requirement had not allowed those who had cared for ailing AIDS friends prior to death to continue their care after death.) Immediate cremation or burial is now an alternative to embalming for the virulent diseases such as Ebola and rabies.

Embalming Costs

While embalming fees vary greatly, the national average at this writing is in the neighborhood of $500, though SCI funeral homes are charging up to $1,495. The price varies according to the amount of restoration that is needed or requested. There might be an additional $200 charge for autopsied bodies, for example. Medical examiners and coroners have a very mixed reputation on the condition in which they release a body, so sometimes an additional charge may be justified.

Actually, a $500 embalming fee strikes us as an extremely modest charge for a service that requires training, significant expertise, overhead expense, is not particularly pleasant, and which puts workers in jeopardy of blood-borne pathogens as well as exposure to highly toxic chemicals. On the other hand, embalming is usually performed as part of a larger package that includes other items with high-profit opportunity.

Why Embalm?

If you donate your body to a medical school, you can expect it to be embalmed, although the procedures are quite different from those used by undertakers. Schools generally keep bodies for six months to two years, and there is no other practical way to keep a body intact for that long.

Some state laws—until they are changed—may require embalming in certain circumstances. For example, Idaho requires that a body be embalmed or refrigerated if it will not reach its destination within 24 hours of death.

Even if there is no statutory requirement in your state, some form of preservation may be desired if there will be a delay of several days in gathering kin and scheduling services. However, refrigeration is just as effective (or more so) at preservation and involves no toxic chemicals or invasive procedures. Dry ice can also be used, as it is, for example, by medical couriers when carrying organs for transplant. Check on-line or in the Yellow Pages for a source. Frozen gel packs may also be used. In the past, people stored bodies on ice for long periods because it sometimes took relatives a week or more to arrive.

Another factor to consider is that the population has become more mobile, so most funerals can now be held within two or three days after death. For ordinary purposes, such as a private family-directed wake at home, temperature control is usually sufficient. In most cases (though there are exceptions), a body will keep for two to three days at 70 degrees or cooler without offensive decomposition or odor.

The most common argument for funeral-type embalming today is that friends and family have an emotional need to see the body one last time before final disposition. But having spoken with a great many people on the subject, we have heard that viewing a restored corpse did not always fulfill that need. In some cases, the body was made to appear so lifelike that it became even harder to say goodbye. In other cases, it looked like nothing more than a statue or mannequin, a caricature of the departed friend or relative.

Viewing

After the FTC's Funeral Rule was passed, funeral homes were required to print the following disclosure on the General Price List:

> Except in certain special cases, embalming is not required by law. Embalming may be necessary, however, if you select certain funeral arrangements, such as a funeral with viewing. If you do not want embalming, you usually have the right to choose an arrangement that does not require you to pay for it, such as direct cremation or immediate burial.

While the Rule now keeps funeral homes from insisting upon or charging for embalming when minimal services are selected, it fails to acknowledge a number of issues—including religious or moral objections to embalming—for funeral plans that did not call for "immediate" disposition.

Many funeral directors have remarked that the phrasing suggests it isn't possible to have a viewing without embalming. The original Rule was drafted in the late 1970s and early '80s, an era when it was unheard of in the US to have a viewing of any type without embalming. Today, many more funeral homes are offering private family viewing without embalming, and many West Coast funeral directors tell us that presenting a body without embalming has long been considered acceptable.

FCA, in its efforts to seek Rule amendments, will ask that "or other timely arrangements" be added to the above disclosure. With other options for keeping a body from decomposing, it should be the choice of the family whether or not the body is embalmed prior to viewing, not a funeral industry or state mandate.

The Difference between Viewing and Visitation

While there are regional differences in the use of these terms (sometimes also called "calling hours") the authors have chosen the following descriptions for clarity. A viewing is when the body is visible. A visitation may be with a closed casket or with the body not present at all.

In the case of an unexpected death—when a family is grappling with the reality of what has happened—there is often a strong need to see the body of the person who died and to hold or touch the person. In most of these situations, the body will have been taken to a hospital for rescue efforts or to determine the cause of death.

Some hospitals will be very cooperative in letting the family spend time with the body over many hours, especially with an infant or child death. Others may have limited space and will expect the body to be moved quickly. When you have out-of-town family that can not arrive for 24 hours and you choose to use a mortuary, you may want to ask for "private family viewing." Only occasionally is this listed on a General Price List, so there may not be a charge, but you should expect to pay a fee of around $150 to $200 if you request the body be cleaned up, dressed, etc. Sometimes the GPL will limit this to "no more than one hour"—a practice we find appalling if it shortens the family's grieving time. You may certainly demand the time you need but be willing to pay any additional fees for extended use of the facilities.

There is less formality with a private family viewing, and the body is often laid out on a covered table. A casket is distancing, making it more difficult to get close—to cradle one's arms around the dead person.

Whether you choose to have the body embalmed for this private time is a personal decision. There is no legal reason that would require embalming for such a viewing, and the funeral home may not impose embalming if it is not required by state law for the time period elapsed since death.

In the case of an expected death, most people have begun to say their good-byes, and there is less need to see the body to accept the reality of events. When the end comes, it may be seen as the end of a period of intense pain and therefore a blessing. Many undertakers insist, however, that a viewing is necessary for "closure." That you will probably pick a more expensive casket is surely part of the motivation in promoting a viewing rather than just a visitation.

In the past it was common to have two or three days of viewing or visitation. Today, industry reports indicate that consumers who want a viewing or visitation at all are asking for only one day or even just a few hours prior to the funeral.

A visitation also offers informal time for gathering and remembrances, but the casket is either closed or not there at all. A visitation without the casket present can be scheduled anywhere, anytime—without the cost or formality of funeral home involvement. Those who have opted for visitation—not viewing—have found the occasion to be intimate, personal, and in some instances more comfortable. Whether in quiet banter, surprised laughter, or tender tears, spontaneous sharing is comforting. There certainly is value for the family when friends and colleagues talk freely about the significance of their relationships with the deceased.

Cemeteries
For-profit and non-profit

5

WHILE MAJOR CEMETERY SCANDALS SEEM to occur every few years, 2009 was the year the federal government woke up to the need for regulation. In July, investigators discovered at least 300 graves dug up—the remains strewn about the property—in Chicago's Burr Oak Cemetery. Hundreds of family members poured through the gates, frantic to discover whether their relatives were among the desecrated.

The historic cemetery was vitally important to Chicago's black community. It was the final resting place for jazz legend Dinah Washington, many other prominent African American activists and entertainers, and thousands of everyday Chicago citizens. A newspaper photo showed the rusting casket of Emmet Till, tossed on a junk heap in an outbuilding, the torn satin lining visible through the glass viewing window. (This is the casket photographed in national magazines following Till's brutal murder in 1955, a graphic display that helped to galvanize the civil rights movement. Following the casket's reappearance in 2009, Till's family donated it to the Smithsonian Institution.)

On July 27, Representative Bobby Rush convened a hearing on cemetery regulation before the House Energy and Commerce Committee's Subcommittee on Consumer Protection.

Forty-two-year-old Roxie Williams, a Chicago mother with relatives buried at Burr Oak, was the unfortunate star witness. Flanked at an oak table by the Rev. Jesse Jackson, Jr., and Dinah Washington's great-grandson, the Rev. Don E. Grayson, she told the committee how her mother scrimped and saved to bury Roxie's father, who died when she was 11. Years later when she went to visit the grave, the cemetery had "lost" him.

"This was a time I first realized that something went terribly wrong at this place," she told the committee. "I went where I had always gone to see my father, and the headstone was gone and it was just grass there. I freaked out . . . . There was no headstone for my father, only my grandmother . . . . When I explained what happened, the lady told me not to worry about it—she would look into the incident and give me a call. I refused to leave until she gave me an answer of where my father's headstone was. She said it must be a mistake, because although they had a record for my grandmother, they did not have a record for my dad. My whole heart sank."

Slocum testified on behalf of FCA at the same hearing, delivering a grim verdict: With no federal oversight of cemeteries, the states had failed to protect grieving consumers from the most common frauds. While heart-wrenching stories about desecrated graves get national attention, he said, regulators have failed to address the everyday ongoing abuses of cemetery consumers that don't make the headlines. Because cemeteries don't even have to comply with the FTC Funeral Rule's requirements of printed price disclosures and freedom of choice in purchasing, grieving families are routinely subjected to deceptive sales practices that drain their wallets and stymie their choices.

Following the hearing, Rep. Rush introduced HR3655, the Bereaved Consumers Protection Act, which would force a recalcitrant Federal Trade Commission to expand the Funeral Rule to cover cemeteries, crematories, and third-party merchandise sellers. The bill had not passed into law by the close of the 2010 session. At that time, though, investigations were under way by both the Government Accountability Office and 60 Minutes, so there's room for hope that the issue won't be dropped. Until and unless such legislation re-emerges, it's "buyer beware" in most states. This chapter will show what to expect when you buy from a cemetery and how to avoid some of the most common misunderstandings and deceptive practices.

From Churchyards to "Memorial Parks"

No one knows how many cemeteries exist in the United States. If you count family burial grounds, historic or abandoned graveyards, and the thousands of currently operating cemeteries, there are likely hundreds of thousands, maybe more. The earliest cemeteries, like those found in rural parts of New England and the South, are simple affairs, often located on family property or next to churches. If you live in a sparsely populated area, you may still be able to find a grave at a quiet, unpretentious graveyard run by a nonprofit association (often governed by neighbors who do so as a community service). In the small towns of Vermont, it's not uncommon to pay a few hundred dollars for a grave and a few hundred more for the guy with the backhoe.

While driving across the Shoshone-Bannock reservation in Idaho for a conference on Native American funerals, Carlson and Slocum were shown how the locals have maintained the simplest burial traditions. The graves had a quiet, timeless simplicity, the earth mounded gently over the top to sink naturally with time, each grave bordered with white stones.

At the other end of the spectrum are the modern descendants of Southern California's Forest Lawn Cemetery. Long the king of kitsch in cemeteries

(Evelyn Waugh satirized it in his 1948 novel *The Loved One* for strewing the landscape with reproductions of high art such as Michelangelo's David while at the same time running a gift shop full of tchotchkes and souvenir ashtrays), Forest Lawn inaugurated the age of the "memorial park." Throughout the 20th century, the dominant aesthetic in cemeteries was to make them look and sound like *anything but* a cemetery. No gloomy, draped urns or Victoriana in our modern "gardens of memory," just regimented rows of identical markers flush to the impossibly well-groomed ground—Levittowns for the dead.

The prices and practices among American cemeteries vary as widely as their landscapes. While some cemeteries still follow the historical model that burial grounds should be operated as a public good, a cemetery's nonprofit or religious status by itself is no guarantee of reasonable prices or practices. Some states require that cemeteries be incorporated as nonprofits, but that doesn't necessarily assure that they are inexpensive or ethical.

When his mother died in 2003, David Lahey inquired about buying a two-grave parcel in the historic section of Cincinnati's Spring Grove Cemetery. He wanted to be sure the cemetery would let him erect a fairly substantial central monument, that the lot would always be visible from the road, and that Spring Grove wouldn't add any more burials or plantings that would obstruct that view. Finicky? Certainly, but Lahey—a well-known and wealthy retired businessman—was willing to pay for what he wanted.

According to court documents from Lahey's 2010 suit against Spring Grove, the saleswoman told him there weren't any two-grave sections available, but there was a four-grave parcel. Lahey claims the saleswoman assured them the cemetery wouldn't bury anyone or plant any trees that would obstruct the view, because Spring Grove's rules would prevent this. So, he bought the parcel for $29,130 and buried his mother. He then exhumed his father from a grave in Arkansas and had him reburied next to his mom.

Lahey's suit describes a series of meetings with cemetery staff members who contradicted what the saleswoman told him and offered ever-more-expensive remedies. If he wanted to guarantee the view on his parcel, Lahey would have to purchase up to $14,800 in additional square footage. Given that his parents were already buried there, Lahey shelled out the money. Spring Grove never gave him a copy of the rules and regulations, and the cemetery's director admitted in a deposition that it was "very much not typical" for sales staff to give customers a copy of the rules before they buy. Had Lahey seen them, he might have thought twice—Spring Grove's rules give the cemetery the right to buy back any graves, at any time, with no mention of obtaining the family's permission (or any word on what they'd do with the body in an already-occupied grave).

Religious Cemeteries

Religious cemeteries are sometimes no better. Unknown to most parishioners, the largest Catholic archdiocese in the country runs its burial operations in a partnership with the second-largest for-profit funeral and cemetery chain on Wall Street. In 1997, the Los Angeles Archdiocese announced it would allow Stewart Enterprises to build and operate for-profit mortuaries in its cemeteries. Operating under the name "Catholic Mortuary Services," Stewart Enterprises today runs six funeral homes on the grounds of the LA Archdiocese's nonprofit cemeteries, and the archbishop has a new cathedral.

The archdiocese isn't shy about applying spiritual pressure to parishioners. From its website:

> The final expression of our faith as Catholics is the blessed and sacred burial in a Catholic cemetery. It is our opportunity to rest among fellow believers, awaiting the resurrection to life everlasting in union with God. . . .
>
> Burial in a Catholic Cemetery is an act of reverence and respect for the body which has housed our soul during our life in fellowship with Christ. Heavenly glory is the destiny for which God intends us. Death is not the end, but a rite of passage to eternal life, to full union with God. It is the sacred right, privilege and loving **duty** of every Catholic to choose such a burial [emphasis added].

Many grieving Catholics will doubtless find it to be their loving duty to pay for the expensive services of the church-sanctioned commercial funeral homes located at the cemetery, too. While the Archdiocese and Stewart Enterprises have characterized this partnership as offering one-stop arrangements that minister to the spiritual needs of Catholics, promotional materials suggest more temporal motivations. A Glendale man sent FCA a letter he received urging him to prepay for funeral and burial through "Catholic Mortuary Services." The letterhead includes a stylized Christian cross, and lists the names of six Catholic cemeteries in the Los Angeles Archdiocese: All Souls, Calvary, Holy Cross, Queen of Heaven, Resurrection, and San Fernando Mission. The letter states, in part:

> In order to serve the needs of Catholic families better, the Archdiocese of Los Angeles has authorized the construction of mortuaries on land leased at six of its cemeteries . . . . Most importantly, families like yours can now preplan your funeral arrangements . . . . We will be happy to discuss with you in further detail the benefits of preplanning and how the new mortuaries will mean better service for Catholic families.

P.S. Mail the postcard in no later than November 26 to receive a preconstruction discount of $200 off preplanned funeral services.

The letter did *not* say that Catholic Mortuary Services is a trade name of the for-profit Stewart Enterprises. For all any parishioner would know, this letter came directly from the church. And just how did Stewart Enterprises get hold of the names and addresses of the archdiocese's congregants?

Another Los Angeles Catholic sent FCA a similar flier she received. Co-branded "Catholic Cemeteries" and "Catholic Mortuaries" with a stylized cross. Under the headline **Preplan Your Catholic Heritage**, the flier features discounts on plots, crypts, and other property, with the exhortation "Buy now for **BEST LOCATION**." The discounts are good "till November only!!!" One hardly sees the 6-point type that reads "A subsidiary of Stewart Enterprises."

Like some funeral homes, some cemeteries capitalize on consumers' allegiance to their faith by explicitly naming or identifying the operation as religious. For example, the biggest funeral home and cemetery chain in the country, Service Corporation International (SCI) operates cemeteries catering to Jewish people with names such as Menorah Gardens and King David. For their sales materials, they use the brand name Dignity Memorial.

There are many reasons to choose a cemetery, including location, burial with other family members, or religious preference. But don't assume that just because a cemetery has a religious name that it's necessarily operated by a religious organization or that it's run according to your idea of appropriate religious principles. Such cemeteries' sales literature may be deliberately appealing to your emotions. It's wise to consider whether you're willing to have your religious allegiances exploited for commercial gain.

Mausoleums: Not So Clean, Not So Dry

Are you afraid of bugs? Does the thought of burial in the dank, dark earth leave you cold? Well, maybe a mausoleum is for you. Or maybe not.

Crypt space above ground has long been marketed as a "clean and dry" alternative to earth burial. Mausoleum operators aren't above appealing to your squeamishness to sell you a slot. But from an engineering perspective, shelving whole human bodies behind a thin wall and inviting mourners to come "visit" was never a good idea. Dead people decompose, and unless the mausoleum is properly engineered, they do it in a messy way.

A well-engineered mausoleum promotes air flow to dehydrate the bodies, with crypt slots angled backward to drain fluids that can otherwise breach the casket and run out the front. But many of these posthumous high-rises are shoddily constructed, and using the wrong kind of casket can lead to disaster. So-called sealer (or "protective") caskets have a rubber gasket that seals the space between the lid and the bottom. That is exactly what you *don't* want. Trapping moisture and gases causes the body to putrefy into a festering soup. People from around the country have filed suit against funeral homes, casket companies, and mausoleums for duping them into believing these "protective" caskets and above-ground crypts would keep mom clean and dry. Horrified families have sent us photographs showing liquefied remains inside the casket and stains on the sidewalk from leaking fluids.

Many in the industry know the truth but conceal it in order to keep selling to the unwary public. At least four brands of Tyvek-type bags are peddled in the mortuary trade journals with coy claims to envelop the casket to "protect it." But they're not protecting the casket; they're protecting the mausoleum *from the casket*, as described in this ad in a funeral trade magazine:

Let Nature Take Its Course

We know what happens after the crypt is sealed. Your clients do not know, or do not want to know. Provide comforting visits over decades with Ensure-A-Seal's new and improved Casket Protector. Durable and strong, the cover is designed for both metal and wood caskets. The ONE-WAY check valve allows gases to escape. The NEW seamless, chemically hardened fiberboard tray contains liquids. Don't let natural processes destroy your facility's reputation.

Carlson's Funeral Ethics Organization newsletter unearthed a 1994 study on mausoleums by the Monument Builders of North America that examined how caskets held up over time in above-ground crypts:

MBNA found that the Catholic Cemetery Association was documenting an 86% failure rate for problems with wood and cloth-covered caskets, 62% for nonsealing metal, and 46% for "protective" or "sealer" caskets. Even with the somewhat better results, the report states in bold print, "It is highly unlikely that such protective sealer metal caskets employ sufficient mechanisms to contain body fluids or gases."

Betty Greiman learned the truth about mausoleums the hard way. "The crypt was open to put his casket in and when we looked in, we saw that my mother's casket was propped open with what looked like 2×4s. And I was hysterical," she said to a reporter for WKRC in Cincinnati.

Greiman filed suit against Forest Lawn Cemetery in Erlanger, Ohio, after discovering the owners were propping open all the caskets to ventilate them. Ventilation is, of course, exactly what a sensible mausoleum operator wants, but propping open the coffins without telling the families?

We've long wondered why mausoleums would even accept sealer caskets, let alone require them, as some do. And why would funeral directors—the supposed professionals—sell such a casket to a family choosing a mausoleum interment? Perhaps many of them are genuinely (if inexcusably) confused. Many mausoleums require embalming on the grounds that it will prevent odors, but that won't help for more than a few weeks or months. Apparently some undertakers actually believe this is an acceptable long-term solution.

So do some mausoleum managers. Slocum had a bizarre conversation with the manager of a Florida mausoleum in 2003. A woman from Michigan who wanted to bury her husband in a crypt they owned in Florida sent FCA a copy of a letter from a "Planning Specialist" at Forest Hills Memorial Park and Funeral Home in Palm City, owned by Stewart Enterprises. In the letter, saleswoman Deanna Mitchell told the customer her husband would "need to be embalmed and in at least an 18-gauge steel casket for placement into the mausoleum crypt." The woman didn't want to embalm her husband and saw no need to waste money on a heavy 18-gauge casket.

Slocum asked the saleswoman why the mausoleum required embalming. "For preservation," she said. He then asked Stewart's regional sales manager why Forest Hills required an 18-gauge casket. Bill Baggett tried to claim "bylaws from the state of Florida" required an 18-gauge; it took some pressing for him to admit these were merely the cemetery's own bylaws (rules) that had been *filed with* the state regulatory office. So, why the 18-gauge? "Well, our 18-gauge caskets seal," he said. Given the problems associated with sealer caskets in warm climates, Slocum asked why the cemetery would even *want* a sealer in its crypt.

"Over the years we've transferred many of our *patients* to different spaces and we've never had that problem," Baggett replied.

Mr. Baggett must not read his trade journals. The weekly *Funeral Service Insider* published an article on "exploding casket syndrome" in 2003. FSI offered its readers four approaches to consider: do nothing, cut chunks out of the rubber seal, leave off some of the casket hardware so air can get it, or just unseal the box completely. Cutting pieces from the casket seal (the rubber gasket you paid hundreds more for because it would "protect" your loved one) was an idea from Curt Rostad, a well-known funeral director and industry commentator.

If you feel you must have mausoleum burial, take these precautions:

- Tour the buildings, and note any odors and any stains on the front of crypts or the floor or sidewalk beneath them.

- Do not purchase a sealer casket. If the mausoleum claims these are required, cross the mausoleum off your list.

- It's probably worth a few hundred dollars to buy an enclosure bag to zip up around the casket

What to Expect and What to Watch Out For

Because cemeteries are poorly regulated, many of the protections you have when shopping at a funeral home don't apply at the graveyard. Cemetery practices and terminology are widely misunderstood, too. Keep the following in mind before you buy.

Get the cemetery's rules and regulations—Few states require cemeteries to hand these to you, so you'll have to ask. Don't do business with any cemetery that won't hand them out. You need to know in advance what type of monuments (size, material, base, etc.) and decorations the cemetery allows. It's legitimate for cemeteries to set rules on the size, appearance, and materials for markers. Most cemeteries restrict the decorations you can leave on a grave; glass jars, decorative fencing, pinwheels and the like are often barred for aesthetic and/or safety reasons.

Understand what you're buying—A grave is not "real property" like your house and land. You don't own a 6×9 parcel of land outright, you've bought *the right to be buried there.* In ordinary parlance, we speak of "buying a grave," but what you've really bought is a *right of interment* at a particular spot. This is why you can't put up an unlimited number of decorations on the grave or erect any monument you want. Think of it like an apartment complex or a condo governed by an association; you have the right to live there, but you have to follow common rules.

Don't believe anyone who tells you something's required or barred by law—You can be almost certain that any claim about what the law requires or prohibits is false. Insist the salesman give you the legal citation on paper. So-called "family service counselors" making their living on commission are usually poorly trained and will often make up non-existent "laws" to get you to spend more. Mrs. B, a 70-year-old widow from Virginia, was browsing graves at a cemetery near Washington, D.C. "I didn't want a lot of folderol," she said. "So I asked if I could be buried in the pine boxes they used next door at King David Memorial Gardens. They told me the federal government wouldn't let me be buried in a pine box—'that was only for the Jews'."

No state requires a casket, a vault, or an outer burial container of any kind as a condition of burial. Most cemeteries, however, require at least a concrete liner to surround the casket to prevent the grave from collapsing. In New York and Vermont you can refuse a vault on religious grounds.

Don't be swayed by promises of "protection"—Any cemetery (or funeral home) that tells you a certain sealed or lined vault will "protect your loved one" is preying on your sentiments and lying to you. Any honest gravedigger will confirm it's impossible to predict the condition of a casket and vault if it's later exhumed. Some remain dry and intact; others (including the expensive "protective" type) are cracked and filled with water. No box of any sort will keep the body from decomposing. None will keep water or dirt out for any certain length of time. If you would like an expensive casket for appearances at a funeral that's fine, but don't be fooled into thinking it will serve any function beyond what a minimal container can do.

Be aware of additional charges—Many people mistakenly believe once they buy the right of interment (the grave), that settles the matter. It doesn't. Even if you buy the grave ahead of time, you'll have to pay an opening/closing fee when the grave is actually dug and filled back in. Depending on the cemetery, this can range from $200 to $2,000 ($800 to $1,300 is typical, according to reports from consumers).

"Perpetual care" may not be—Many cemeteries will take a portion of the price you pay for the grave (5 to 15 percent) and put it in a perpetual care fund toward upkeep. In theory, the principal should stay intact, with the cemetery drawing the interest to pay for maintenance. In reality, that money often isn't enough, especially when the cemetery runs out of space and can't count on new sales revenue to bolster the meager earnings from the care fund. Consumer complaints of raggedy-looking or abandoned cemeteries have increased over the past 10 years.

Also, there are dozens of news stories every year about cemetery owners raiding the prepaid or perpetual care funds. An Oklahoma oil speculator was accused of draining $20 million in funds prepaid by 13,000 Tennessee families and another $70 million from 28 cemeteries he owned in Michigan. The Hawaii Attorney General is trying to recover over $22 million That the state says a company known as Rightstar failed to deposit. See Chapter 8 for more examples. Many cemeteries, of course, manage their money responsibly, but it can be hard to know what will happen down the line.

Think twice (or three times) before buying in advance—We estimate there are hundreds of thousands, maybe even millions, of already-bought graves nationwide that will never be used by the people they were intended for. Decades ago it was common for families to buy a grave for everyone in the household. They thought they were taking care of an unpleasant necessity ahead of time.

But it's not 1955 anymore. Few of us graduate high school, then attend the local college, marry a childhood sweetheart, get a job at the local company, then retire, then die and get buried in the hometown cemetery. Most people move several times during their careers, and even retirees frequently end up several states distant from where they thought they'd make their last home. More families are choosing cremation for this reason, and it's becoming less common for folks to make regular pilgrimages to burial spots.

Many elderly couples say they want to buy their own lots ahead of time "because my kids will want some place to come to remember me." But the truth is, many of them won't, and that doesn't mean they don't love their parents. It means people are finding different ways to remember the dead that aren't bound to where the remains are buried. Perhaps your letters, recipes, or photographs mean more to them than the location of your coffin. What seems like a favor to your survivors may actually be an unwanted burden after you're gone. If the children need to choose cremation for financial or geographical regions, they may be left with feelings of guilt because they couldn't afford to ship mom's casket across the country or they couldn't afford to fly "home" to visit the grave.

And what to do with these unused graves? There's a glut of pre-bought but unwanted graves on the secondary market, and it can be quite hard to unload one. With the rising cremation rate, the market for graves isn't likely to grow.

That said, if you're looking for a grave on the secondary market, prices are in your favor. It's worth checking to see if anyone in your area is selling one for less than the cemetery would sell it at retail price. To start your search, try <www.finalarrangementsnetwork.com> or <www.gravesolutions.com>.

Disposition of Cremated Remains

There are few restrictions on where ashes can be scattered or buried. You can to do so on your own land or on someone else's with their permission in all states. While parks and national forests frown on scattering and may have rules against it (for fear that families may create a shrine), officials will privately admit they turn a blind eye as it's impossible to enforce a ban anyway. If you do, be discreet, and spread the ashes over a reasonable area. The remains look like white aquarium gravel, and dumping a quantity equivalent to about a five-pound bag of sugar on one spot is conspicuous.

And what about scattering at sea? Section 229.1 of the Federal Environmental Protection Agency law says anyone in the US can bury remains at sea so long as they take the remains three miles out from shore and report the "burial" within a month to the closest EPA office. But an EPA staffer said the agency is totally uninterested in enforcing this, and only one family in his decades of experience even bothered to file a report. "I don't care about cremated remains," he said. "We're trying to deal with real polluters." Cremated remains are nothing but small bits of bone, composed mainly of calcium. They're sterile and pose no health risk to people or the environment.

What about families who stand on the beach and scatter? Burials or scatterings that take place within three miles of shore fall under the Clean Water Act, rather than the EPA rules. States, not the federal government, enforce the CWA. We've never heard of a single state trying to stop families from scattering at the beach. If anyone "warns" you about the prohibitions on scattering, it's probably safe to thank them for their concern and go on your way. However, if you live in California, Indiana, or South Dakota, check your state chapter for some minimal but easy-to-work-around requirements.

If you're flying with cremated remains, be sure to keep them in a container that can be scanned by the X-ray machines at the airport (no metal boxes, and avoid heavy ceramics). The Transportation Security Administration won't let you through if the machine can't see inside, and they refuse to open any container that contains cremated remains for a hand inspection (likely because they don't want to be accused of tampering with someone's mom). Though it's not required by law, it's a good idea to bring a copy of the death certificate and crematory receipt with you in case anybody asks.

Cemeteries are counting on the burial of ashes to make up for some of the revenue they're losing as whole-body burial declines. Most offer in-ground urn burial, and many have built columbaria or set aside a portion of their mausoleums for urn-sized niches. Just as with whole-body burial, cemeteries have techniques to part you from your cremation dollars. One of the most common is the "urn vault." While you can make an argument that grave liners sometimes serve a purpose by keeping the ground level as the casket deteriorates over time, the tiny vaults-for-urns are a pure scam.

Cemeteries that require urn vaults insist they're necessary so that people can find and retrieve the ashes if they decide to disinter them later, or that they "keep the ground from collapsing." How many people are likely to dig up grandpa's ashes later? How far can a hole really collapse when the only thing to disintegrate is a jar the size of a flour tin?

Lucy Smith learned the name of the game when she tried to get out from under this expensive "Russian nesting box" racket. When Cadillac Memorial Gardens tried to sell her a polystyrene urn vault for $275 (remember, this is a piece of plastic the size of a bread box), she went on the Internet and found the *exact same model*, direct from the manufacturer, for $50 at the Triple-H site, <www.triplehcompany.com>. (Triple-H willingly sells directly to consumers, and we've found the staff to be helpful and polite over the phone.)

However, cemetery manager Jim Goodman refused to use it, first saying he was "liable," then claiming he had to make sure it could withstand 3,000 pounds of pressure per square inch. Slocum called him and asked why he wouldn't take the vault. Goodman hemmed and hawed and finally admitted the vault Lucy Smith had bought was "a Triple-H vault, the same one I use. It's fine." Then why did you tell Smith you wouldn't accept it? "I never told her that," Goodman said.

But he'd already given himself away the minute he picked up the phone: "Here's the problem—she's just tryin' to save a little money."

Just as with whole-body burial, **no** state requires an "urn vault" to surround the urn when burying ashes, and **no** state requires an urn as a condition of burying ashes.

Home Burial

Home burial is a fine old American tradition. A drive through the countryside will turn up many family cemeteries on private land. They add charm and genealogical interest, and many families are proud to have them. For those with land in rural or semi-rural areas, home burials are usually possible. Check your state chapter in this book and also your local zoning ordinances.

Whole-body burial sites should be at least 150 feet from any water supply. The slope of the land and the soil conditions should also be taken into account, especially where the earth is shallow, over ledge, or clay. Power lines should be avoided, because overhead power may be replaced with buried cable in the future.

There is strong historical precedent in the establishment of a family burial plot, but you should consider the long-range implications on land value in doing so because a graveyard becomes a permanent easement on the property in many states. In a 1959 Oklahoma case, Heiligman *vs.* Chambers, a grandson sued to keep the new landowner from moving family bodies to a town cemetery. The court upheld the right to permanency created by any such family burial ground, at least in that state. Other states have provisions for moving the graves from "abandoned" burial sites.

A family must realize that someone else in future years may not maintain a family cemetery after ownership changes. And while visitation rights may be protected by the Oklahoma precedent and common law, how would you feel returning to land that is no longer in the family?

For many, these deterrents are minimal compared to the satisfaction and personal identity that a home burial offers. No one else sets visitation hours, you don't have to buy an expensive vault, and the plantings or markers can be appropriate to the family or individual. When she buried the ashes of her husband, John, Carlson found a rough piece of slate, one too large to be moved easily, but one she could manage. She carved his name and death date on the one flat surface, using a Boy-Scout jackknife and a screwdriver. Acid rain will probably fade the writing in 50 years, but perhaps it won't matter by then. Because John was cremated, she was free to pick the garden site she wanted for his spot, without a permit. But because this is not registered in the town clerk's office as an official home burial site, there will be no guarantee of permanency in preserving recognition there. The slate marker may stay, but then again it may get moved.

Veterans' Burial Benefits

All honorably discharged veterans, their spouses, and dependents, are eligible for free burial in a national cemetery run by the Veterans Administration.

Remember, "free burial" *does not include funeral-home costs.* The family is responsible for all services from a funeral home, including transportation, embalming, any ceremonies at the funeral home, the casket, etc. If you choose to be buried somewhere other than a national cemetery, the government will provide a standard military marker, but you will have to pay for the grave, the opening and closing, the vault, and any other cemetery charges. Many states have set up cemeteries for veterans, especially if there is no VA cemetery in the state. You can expect to pay something at such a cemetery but probably at a significant saving compared to other options.

There are some special circumstances and benefits:

- **Death during active duty**—All funeral expenses will be paid by the military, including body preparation, casket, transportation to the place of disposition, interment (if in a national cemetery), and marker. In addition, as of July, 2005, next-of-kin are entitled to a "death gratuity" of $100,000, retroactive to October 7, 2001.

- **Death due to a service-related injury**—There is a $2,000 "burial allowance" which may be used to cover some of the funeral director's expenses, the casket, and transportation to the cemetery. **If** death occurred in a VA facility, transport of the body to the cemetery will be paid, provided it is no farther than the last place of residence. If burial is not in a national cemetery, there is a $300 "interment allowance," but it is unlikely that will cover opening and closing or vault charges, let alone the cost of the lot.

- **Non-service-related death in a VA facility or while collecting a VA pension or disability compensation**—There is a $300 allowance which may be used to defray some of the usual funeral expenses. Although burial in a national cemetery is free to these veterans, all other mortuary expenses are the responsibility of the family. Transportation to a national cemetery (not farther than the residence of the deceased) will be provided *only* if the death occurs in a VA facility. There is an additional $300 interment allowance that applies **only** when burial is in **other** than a national cemetery.

- **Death of a veteran outside a VA facility, not receiving military pension or compensation**—There will be no funeral or burial allowances, nor will survivors be reimbursed for transportation to the cemetery. The lot in a national cemetery, any required vault, interment, a marker, and flag are the only burial benefits.

Preneed Sales
It's NOT "all taken care of"

6

WHEN SLOCUM FIRST USED THE word *preneed* in conversation with his friend Paul (who knew nothing about the funeral business), Paul burst out laughing. With a deadly serious tone, he riffed off the old Caress soap commercials: "Before you need . . . you *pre*-need." The idea of paying for a funeral before you're dead—and the notion of selling it without using the words "funeral" or "dead"—seemed astonishing. But it seems like a very good idea indeed to many older Americans. According to industry reports, between a quarter and a third of all funerals performed annually have been prepaid.

Who are these Americans rushing off to the mortuary while they're still alive, eager to slap down $7,000 or more for a party they won't attend until years from now? They're people like you, people like your parents, folks you go to church with. Why do they buy? Because the preneed sales industry knows very well how to take advantage of the anxieties and uncertainty most of us feel when we contemplate our own demise. Will my funeral be dignified? Will my children be able to afford it? Won't my death be hard enough without my survivors having to make stressful decisions while they're grieving?

Step into my parlor, said the "preneed counselor" to the prospect. Sign here on the dotted line, and don't forget to sign the check. No matter how much funeral costs rise in the future, you'll never have to pay another dime. And think of the kindness you're doing your children; all they have to do is call us at the time of need . . . and everything will be taken care of.

Who wouldn't find that impressive? No one likes buying funerals, and, boy, if you can beat inflation with a price-guarantee, it doesn't get much better than that. But wait a second—if a car dealer told you that if you prepaid for a model year 2020 Honda at today's retail cost and you'd never have to pay another dime, would you believe him? Wouldn't you wonder if the model you prepaid for would even be built in 2020? Would the dealership still be in business? Would you still want the same car when the time comes? Wouldn't you suspect there must be a catch, since the dealer has to make his profit somehow? Most of us would be highly skeptical of such too-good-to-be-true promises. Unfortunately, too many otherwise savvy families walk into a funeral home doe-eyed, eager to believe the most unrealistic promises. Hearing soothing white lies is easier than having to face the cold emotional and financial facts about our own deaths. But this can cost you, or your next-of-kin, dearly.

Pat and Bud Cairns retired to Myrtle Beach in the mid '90s. They put most of their modest savings into a new mobile home and got by on Social Security. They also prepaid for their funerals, preferring to get what they thought *had to be* a huge expense out of the way. But, by Pat's own admission, they weren't thinking clearly when that decision was made. When the financial drain of monthly payments on graves and coffins they weren't yet occupying got to be too great, they had second thoughts. Trouble was, they prepaid a funeral home in Ohio, but they were living in South Carolina. The Cairnses had bought graves in Ohio, where they used to live, and while they were visiting Ohio, they thought it would be best to "take care of everything," but they hadn't thought the process through. Pat wrote to FCA in 2003:

> My [insurance policy that will fund my funeral] will not be paid up for another two years, and should I die before that time, my husband or children would have to come up with the additional costs of my funeral . . . . [M]y question is, can I transfer my husband's contract to a funeral home in Myrtle Beach but choose a less-expensive funeral? Direct cremation, etc.? I'm sure the funeral home in Ohio would retain a generous portion of my husband's money, but if we could get what we need and can afford at the local establishment, matching it as closely as possible to the transferred total amount, it would be a blessing. I have been having nightmares thinking about what will happen if I, or any other relative on his side, had to pay the entire funeral bill.

Slocum wrote back to Pat, asking for all the contracts and financial records pertaining to her funeral. What he discovered was a shocking examples of a funeral home (and an insurance company) taking financial advantage of an elderly. While there were similar problems with Bud's prepaid funeral, we'll use Pat's as an example.

Pat bought a full-service funeral—embalming, viewing, funeral ceremony, casket, grave-vault, hearse—the works. But the itemized bill from the Ohio funeral home was written up as if Pat were likely to die in Ohio. The funeral home knew full-well the Cairnses lived in South Carolina (they paid for the funeral while visiting family in Ohio). How would this help her if, as was almost certain, she died at her home in the South? While Pat admits she should have been more alert, the mortuary certainly didn't ask any questions.

The funeral home talked Pat into making the agreement *irrevocable*. Irrevocable is a term that means the buyer can't cash out the money she's paid in ahead of time; it has to stay in a trust, or in an insurance policy. This protects the money from seizure by Medicaid if she ever needs Medicaid to pay for nursing care. Pat wasn't even close to going on Medicaid, but she was told this would "protect her money if ever she did." She'd unwittingly signed away the right to a refund based on the *chance* she'd go on Medicaid, not because she needed to immediately. In addition, Pat said, when she tried to transfer the money to a funeral home in South Carolina, the Ohio funeral home told her *irrevocable* meant she had no right to transfer her money to another funeral home—even though she couldn't use an Ohio mortuary when she died in South Carolina.

The financing was the most jaw-dropping part. Like many mortuaries, the Ohio funeral home sold insurance policies to customers, the proceeds of which would pay for the eventual funeral. And like many such policies, the customer can pay the premium in one lump-sum up front or by monthly payments over time. Pat chose the "affordable" monthly payments of $82, for ten years. But if she completed 10 years of payments, she would have spent $9,879 for a life insurance policy that would pay a maximum of $5,745. You read that right. It's as if she'd walked into a bank and deposited $10,000, only to have the teller say "Your deposit is worth only $6,000, should you ever want to withdraw it." The insurance company, of course, would defend itself by saying that Pat was entitled to the full death benefit even if she died after making only one payment of $82, but they know that's not likely to happen. By the time Pat contacted FCA, she'd already paid $2,428 more than the policy would ever pay out for her funeral.

After pressure from FCA, the funeral home released Pat and Bud from their contracts, and the insurance company issued a full refund. In 2008, Pat wrote:

> Dear Joshua,
>
> Bud passed away on Wednesday. I chose [a funeral home] just a few miles away from our home and the funeral director was fair and honest, answering all of my questions and meeting my needs, without attempting to sell me anything I did not need. Bud was cremated February 7 and I have his ashes here at home in an inexpensive urn we purchased years ago at a thrift shop. It is an ice bucket, but so attractive we decided that at least one of us would be using it eventually.

And the total cost? Less than $2,000. But this kind of resolution is unusual. Many families get locked into expensive prepaid contracts they can't get out of and have to chalk it up as a bitter lesson learned. Pat kindly agreed to let us tell her story as a warning to other families. She readily admits she and her husband didn't read the fine print and were basically sleepwalking through the purchase of a full-service funeral that they really didn't want anyway. It was just easier, she said, to go along with what the funeral home called "traditional" than it was to think carefully about what they felt was really important and within their budget.

The Pitch

All successful companies must market their products. Sex sells, we know, and so does emotion. Since even the cleverest marketer would have difficulty using bikini beauties to sell coffins, preneed salesmen must resort to a subtler appeal. Maybe "that nice young man" from the local funeral home has stopped by your grandmother's house. If so, chances are he's been well-trained to find just the right buttons to push to get in the front door and back out again with a check.

National Prearranged Services developed this into an art. The Missouri-based company was the brain-child of James Douglas Cassity, whom the *Kansas City Star* described as a disbarred Springfield, Missouri, attorney who served a six-month stretch in federal prison for fraud in an unrelated tax-shelter scheme. Cassity's funereal empire included a chain of funeral homes in Missouri and more than a dozen other entities including life insurance companies. NPS worked around the country, signing up funeral homes as customers. NPS agents would sell prepaid funerals to citizens (funded by an NPS life insurance policy) on behalf of the funeral home, pocketing a hefty commission.

A Leaked Sales Manual

A sales manual leaked to FCA by a former NPS "Family Service Counselor" describes several techniques to use:

Getting in the Front Door

Good Samaritan:

"Hi, I'm Joe Counselor from ABC Funeral Home. I was visiting with Blanch Jones and she included you in some of her private plans. I need to visit with you for just a moment or so, then I'll be on my way."

Public Relations:

"Hello _____, I'm _____ with ABC Funeral Home. Mr. Funeral Director asked me to stop by. I need to visit with you just a moment or so, then I'll be on my way."

If Joe Counselor isn't successful as a Good Samaritan or PR man, the guide suggests that he can employ a "survey":

> "Hi, Mrs. Jones, my name is _____ and I'm a counselor with _____Funeral Home, and we could use your help. We are conducting a survey to help us better serve the community. I need to ask you a few questions. May I come in?"

If that doesn't work, the guide assures us, simply repeat the script. Verbatim. Once comfortably inside, Joe Counselor is to spend 30 minutes to "develop a relationship that is warm and sincere." This is accomplished by asking about Mrs. Jones' children, her job, and her hobbies. With Mrs. Jones suitably warmed, Joe Counselor should then "pick up kit, stand up and start moving toward the kitchen" while saying:

> "Mr./Mrs. _____made some private arrangements for their family, and they included you as someone they thought this could also help. May we use your kitchen table?"

Now the real softening begins. After sizing up his mark, Joe Counselor picks from one of three sentimental stories meant to illustrate the consequences of failing to pay for your funeral before you need it. The "Wrong Way" vignette tells the story of "Verna," an elderly lady who got into a fight with her sister when arranging their mother's funeral. Which wouldn't have happened if mom had paid for it ahead of time. For a "single woman with children," Joe Counselor uses the "Widow Story":

> "Mrs. Bell, it gives you peace of mind today knowing that you are right there helping your kids like you always have. You know, Mrs. Bell, I have thought would my own mom be interested in something like this for financial reasons? No, probably not. But then I thought, what does my mom really care about? That would be her two boys . . . . That's why a lot of folks simply deposit this amount into their Memorial Account to have it over and done with. Would this be comfortable for you today?"

There are plenty of other ways for companies to induce you to prepay for your funeral or buy insurance for it. Even if they're less smarmy than NPS's theatrics, they all follow a pattern: Create a "problem" in the customer's mind, then offer a pricey solution. Late-night television ads for life insurance blare, "Did you know the average cost of today's funeral can be $10,000 or more?!" People around the country get come-ons in the mail that feature bar graphs showing the rising cost of funerals over time. Better call us today to "lock-in prices," they say. But does your funeral *have to* cost $10,000? Of course not. However, if you're like most Americans, you've never compared prices at several funeral homes, and you probably don't know you have the right to pick and choose from the mortuary's price list to make a funeral that fits your budget. And even if you do choose a full-service funeral, Funeral Consumers Alliance chapters around the country routinely find the prices can vary by thousands of dollars, all within the same city.

Don't Bank on it

A series of high-dollar, high-profile financial meltdowns in the preneed industry kicked off in 2006, exposing the lax patchwork of inadequate regulation around the country. Clayton Smart, an oil speculator, shocked 13,500 families in Tennessee when he announced that the funeral homes and cemeteries he bought in 2004 wouldn't make good on the guaranteed preneed contracts the families purchased since the 1960s. Barry Yeoman, writing for AARP Magazine, described it this way:

> The Brewers had no reason to question the honesty of Forest Hill. Its three locations had been in business since 1888, serving the rich and the poor alike, including such luminaries as Elvis Presley and his mother, Gladys. Like the Brewers, thousands of customers from Tennessee, Mississippi, and Arkansas had also trusted the company's reputation enough to buy pre-need policies. Then in July 2006, one of Forest Hill's new owners, Oklahoma oilman Clayton Smart, called a press conference to announce he was invalidating 13,500 pre-paid funeral contracts, including the Brewers'. While police stood by to prevent a customer riot, Smart explained that any contract holder who wanted to use his or her pre-need policy would have to pay an additional $4,000, more or less, at the time of death, even if the plan was already paid in full. "Obviously, things were a lot cheaper in 1965," Smart explained. "I wouldn't have bought the business if I thought I'd have to honor those contracts."

Dozens of Forest Hill customers wrote to FCA in a panic. "We have recently spoken with a 'Family Service Counselor' at Forest Hill East, who informed us that the most we can expect to receive is $899 per funeral," wrote one man who paid $1,798 in 1980 for two full-service funerals for himself and his wife. "He said they are currently offering a service 'at cost' for $4,000."

To its credit, Tennessee acted aggressively (although the horse was already out of the barn). The Department of Commerce and Insurance sued Smart's company, and the courts put a state receiver in charge of Forest Hill. The charges against Smart included violating the Federal Trade Commission's Funeral Rule, failing to submit accurate records of prepaid funeral accounts to the state, and failing to deposit 100 percent of customers' prepaid money in a trust account as required by Tennessee law. The insurance department said Forest Hill failed to report more than $21 million in trust account money to the state in 2006, and simply never deposited $705,014.70 it collected from new customers that year.

Meanwhile in Michigan, the state claimed Smart—who owned 28 cemeteries there—made off with more than $70 million from the trust funds. All that money came from families who bought graves ahead of time in good faith. Authorities in Tennessee recovered enough of the missing money to keep Forest Hill operating and making good on prepaid funerals, but proper regulation could have prevented the entire affair. (Note: At this writing, Smart's case is set to go to trial in March, 2011.)

The mother of all preneed meltdowns came in 2008, courtesy our friends at National Prearranged Services. Though most of its preneed sales were in Missouri, NPS sold a great number of preneed insurance policies in Texas and 42 other states. After placing the company under "confidential supervision" in early 2008, the Texas Department of Insurance ordered it to stop doing business and put it, and its satellite companies, into receivership by the fall.

Regulators in several other states had suspended NPS's business licenses too. Texas found the company was $987 million in the red. In plain terms, it owed 200,000 customers payment for their eventual funerals, but was almost a billion dollars in the hole.

What happened? Investigators charged that NPS was cashing in the whole-life insurance policies it sold to customers to pay for their funerals, then replacing them with less valuable—and more expensive, premium-wise—term life policies. In a classic Ponzi scheme, the company desperately drummed up more innocent customers to pay the bills coming due as current customers died.

Fortunately for preneed customers, the life insurance industry has a fund to pay out when companies go bust. Unfortunately for funeral home owners, they'll only get paid face value on the contracts (no growth or interest). This means funeral homes that offered customers price guarantees on funerals will have to eat the difference, and we suspect some of them will try to squeeze survivors who may not know what they're entitled to. Indeed, one Texas insurance official told Slocum she was already getting calls from funeral directors asking "How am I supposed to service these contracts if there's no growth on the policies?" She told them, "That's your problem; you signed a contract with the customer."

The NPS debacle pulled the curtain back on the sorry state of preneed regulation. For a time, it looked like states would get tough. Slocum testified to Missouri lawmakers as part of a working committee on preneed reform and pushed for 100 percent deposit of preneed money and tougher oversight.

Incredibly, legislators caved to whining from Big Preneed. At a hearing, one local funeral magnate said, "If you force me to deposit all this money up front, I won't be able to pay my preneed counselors to go out into the community and perform this valuable planning service for our citizens."

Missouri law allowed preneed sellers to skim 20 percent of a customer's prepaid money off the top along with interest. If Mrs. Jones changed her mind or moved, that 20 percent and all the interest was gone. Even worse, this encouraged a financial house of cards by allowing funeral homes to take tomorrow's profits today, creating a scheme dependent on new preneed customers to pay for the cost of those dying today. In the end, lawmakers gave in. While they tightened up oversight of preneed accounts and barred interest skimming, they barely nudged the deposit requirement—from 80 percent to 85 percent.

Constructive Delivery and Creative Accounting

You've probably never heard of the legal fiction "constructive delivery." It works like this. Say you buy a full-service funeral ahead of time. Embalming, viewing, graveside service, casket—the works. In states that permit constructive delivery, the funeral home can hand you a certificate stating you're the proud owner of Acme Casket 45-A, valued at $2,000, and that it's in their warehouse. Under the law, that casket has been "delivered" to you. The same would apply to a vault purchased preneed with a grave. You're no longer entitled to a refund if you change your mind before you lie down in it. In some cases, the funeral home hasn't even ordered the casket or depleted its inventory. By law, you've taken delivery of the casket, and the funeral home or cemetery is now the owner of your money. Few states actually audit the warehousing.

Some states either permit constructive delivery or don't explicitly bar it, while others outlaw the practice, recognizing it as a sham. Be sure to check the state chapters for the laws in your state. Florida laws are among the worst. Cemeteries are allowed to consider monuments and vaults "delivered" to you, the customer, if they're stored on cemetery grounds in a "protected environment." And while the law cagily tries to pretend constructive delivery of caskets is prohibited, the devil is in the details:

> [Consumer refunds on prepaid merchandise] shall be provided **only if at the time that the preneed licensee is required to fulfill its obligations** under the preneed contract the preneed licensee **does not or cannot comply** with the terms of the contract **by actually delivering the merchandise, within a reasonable time**, depending upon the nature of the merchandise purchased, after having been requested to do so.

So if you buy a casket ahead of time in Florida, then move to New York, the funeral home doesn't have to refund your money unless it "can't" or "won't" deliver the casket *at the time of your death*. What good does this do Mr. Jones who no longer wants the casket because he's decided on cremation? What about Mrs. Smith who's moved back north — should she tell her kids to just hope the Florida funeral home will ship the casket to the new funeral home by overnight express? One Florida woman paid for her funeral there but died during a trip to New Jersey. The service funds were transferred, but the New Jersey funeral director was told that the casket was in a warehouse in Florida and he would have to make arrangements to pick it up. In order to be sure they had a casket in time for the viewing, the family ended up buying a new one in New Jersey. There was no refund on the casket they didn't use.

Florida's Consumer FAQ page "helpfully" notes, "A licensee that is willing and capable of delivering the purchased merchandise is not required to make a refund. A purchaser does reserve the right to sell the merchandise if he or she so desires." Should the kids put the casket up for sale on eBay?

Worse still, Florida laws (and it's not the only state where this is true) let preneed sellers pocket a huge portion of your money up front. Sure, the law entitles the customer to a 100 percent refund of money paid on *services* but will you get it? It's hard to see how. The funeral home or cemetery has to deposit only 70 percent of what you prepay for services, and just 30 percent (or 110 percent of the *wholesale cost*) of the goods you buy in advance. Where's the money going to come from for that 100 percent refund you're entitled to?

Neptune Society Contracts

At least one company has expertly exploited such loopholes. The Neptune Society, a direct cremation company licensed in 49 states, aggressively markets its prepaid and overpriced cremations through direct mail and telephone calls. Consumers have complained to Funeral Consumers Alliance for years about the company's high-pressure tactics and deceptive contracts. When Carlson was executive director of FCA, she filed a complaint against Neptune with the Securities and Exchange Commission. Naturally, she didn't hear a word back.

Fast forward to 2008 when Colorado regulators were taking Neptune to court for the very things FCA has been warning about for more than a decade. The charges? In a rare example of readable, consumer-friendly language, the Colorado Division of Insurance put out a press release titled *Neptune Society Used "Bait and Switch" to Lure Consumers to Purchase Pre-Need Funeral Contracts:*

> Allegedly, Neptune Society skirted the law by inducing consumers to purchase a "package deal" and sign two contracts: one for future

funeral and/or cremation services, and a separate contract for the immediate purchase of merchandise, such as a funeral urn, at grossly inflated prices. Most of the funds from the funeral services contract were held in trust, as required, but the funds from the "merchandise" contract were not trusted.

As an example,

- One contract purchaser paid a total package price of nearly $1,333.

- Of that amount, 55 percent of the package price (about $700) was charged for "up front merchandise" on a separate contract.

- Rather than place three-fourths of the entire $1333 into trust as required by law, Neptune chose to place *only 75 percent* of the remaining $610 into trust.

- This means a customer who had paid nearly $1400 for a preneed funeral contract had *less than $560 trusted.*

- In addition, the "merchandise" costs were inflated with a charge of $349 for a funeral urn *valued at approximately $13.*

The state also alleged Neptune—which relies on contracts with crematories around the country to do the actual cremation for them—lied about a non-existent agreement between the company and a crematory operator. The crematory owners said they had no contract to provide cremations for Neptune and that Neptune forged the owner's signature on legal paperwork.

Bottom line: Except in a handful of states, you can't trust the law or your representatives to look out for your financial well-being if you prepay for a funeral. Only 11 states get close to what we'd consider adequate protection for preneed consumers. In all other states you don't have the right to a 100-percent refund or transfer of your prepaid funeral money if you move or change your mind. Until that changes, you're far better off keeping your money in a pay-on-death account at your bank or credit union.

Trust or Insurance?

There are two primary ways to prepay for a funeral. A *trust fund* is like a bank account. Depending on your state laws, when you buy a trust-funded funeral some or all of your money is deposited at a financial institution. The second option is funeral insurance—you buy a whole-life policy designated to pay the funeral home at your death.

If you use insurance, you can usually pay a single premium up front or pay monthly premiums over time. Don and Gail Zeman went to Christy Smith Funeral Home in Sioux City, Iowa, to make funeral arrangements ahead of time. They each chose a $7,000-plus funeral. Not having the $14,000 they thought it would cost, the funeral director sold them Homesteaders funeral insurance policies. They would later regret that purchase.

The Zemans' paperwork shows that the total funeral benefit for one funeral is $7,262.37, and with the ten-year plans the monthly payments would be $115—or $230 total for the two of them. It was their understanding that they had up to ten years to cover the full cost. After paying nearly $11,000 over the course of four years, the Zemans wanted to see what the exact balance was. They were shocked to learn that they were locked into those payments for the full ten years, with total payments of nearly $28,000.

The Iowa Insurance Department has not protected consumers from this practice. Nothing on any of the paperwork showed that the payments would total nearly double the benefit at death. If the Zemans had been told that, they would have walked out the door. Now that they've stopped payments, the $11,000 they've spent is worth only about $6,000. They'll be using a different funeral home when the time comes.

Typical insurance policies pay limited death benefits during the first few years of premium payments. It's like Vegas—the house always wins. The insurance companies know how likely you are to die before you've paid up, and they've adjusted their rates accordingly. Most policies are held for at least five years before a death occurs. You can see what the odds are and why there is great profit in the funeral insurance business.

Beware of converting your trust-funded funeral to insurance! If a funeral home tries to get you to convert your trust to insurance, it's almost always a bad move. If you ever decide to cash out a trust fund (provided your state entitles you to a sizeable refund), you'll get most or all of your money. With insurance, the cash-out value is far less, often only half of what you paid in premiums. Funeral homes that want you to convert your trust to insurance are making a commission from the insurance company. They're not likely to tell you the downside, and neither are the insurance companies.

FCA received a leaked copy of a letter sent by a Connecticut funeral director to his colleagues just days before a law took effect requiring funeral homes to get the customer's permission before an insurance conversion (grammatical mistakes as in the original):

> That whole line about "making lemonade from lemons" is *apres poi* as I write this message to my Connecticut friends. Laws were created so that come October 1 funeral homes doing trust conversions to insurance would have to inform their families. I quickly offered folks an incentive to "take action now"—and so they did! And for that, I am grateful. What a response! In addition, a thorough review of the law by our attorneys tells us that a CT funeral home has right

up until Friday, September 29, 2006, to avoid the notification letters. So my offer continues to stand: **9% versus 7%** for any portfolio transfer from a trust to ACA Assurance. A $500,000 transfer would yield you a check in the amount of $45,000 . . . So when comparing preneed Trusts to preneed Insurance, it's only fitting that I quote the Burger King and say, "Have it your way."

ACA was put in "rehabilitation" again in 2008 by the New Hampshire Insurance Department for poor financial management. Policies lost 25 percent of face value, gained no interest, and a moratorium was put on cash-outs. Because it was a nonprofit fraternal corporation, the typical guarantee fund for the insurance industry could not be used.

Guaranteed Confusion

Beating inflation by locking in today's prices on a funeral is the major selling point for prepaid arrangements. But there's never a free lunch, and most people don't understand the downside of these contracts. Some states require funeral homes to refund to your estate any excess money in your trust account or insurance policy left over after the prepaid funeral has been performed. But many don't. In those cases, consumers sign away the right to any growth on their account in exchange for a price guarantee.

Unfortunately, in today's financial world, the investments—trust or insurance—won't keep up with funeral inflation. Funeral directors are cautioned by advisors and accountants not to guarantee prepaid funerals, as they can get more from walk-in arrangements at the time of death. In practice, funeral homes that have been stuck with less money than expected in prepaid funds have often pulled less-than-ethical maneuvers to make up the difference. Examples include switching a lower-cost casket for the "model that is no longer available" or billing survivors for the difference.

In addition, most people don't understand that cash advance items—things the funeral home buys for you from other retailers—can't be price-guaranteed. Flowers, grave-digging, fees for musicians or clergy—are out of the funeral homes' control and your survivors will have to pick up the tab for any rise in prices. This is a nasty surprise for adult children, who often call FCA complaining bitterly.

In our experience, people who prepay for their funerals usually leave their children *less prepared* to deal with death than those who don't prepay—especially compared to families that make funeral planning an open discussion where survivors are *empowered* to navigate the funeral transaction. Most people who buy prepaid funerals don't understand the contracts themselves, so they can't explain them to their children. The father of one of Slocum's close friends refused to discuss his prepaid contract with his son. He sealed it in an envelope labeled "to be opened only upon my death." This is worse than doing nothing; it's ensuring your survivors will go through the confusion and heartache you thought you were preventing.

It Always Pays to Plan Ahead; It Rarely Pays to Pay Ahead

The goal of this book is to empower you to plan funerals wisely. That means giving some thought to what you want and what your family wants—and maybe what they don't want. It's important to know your rights and to feel confident to pick a funeral that fits your taste and budget. Most of all, we want to help you help your survivors. You can't "take care of everything" for them. But you can give them the know-how and self-confidence they need to carry out your wishes and theirs in an affordable and meaningful way.

It's not as hard as you might think. We've spoken to thousands of people over the phone who were terrified to even use the word "funeral." "I'm calling you to find out what to do *if ever I should* pass away" is surprisingly common. We've always tried to be kind, but we don't soft-peddle tough questions. It's very satisfying for us when a caller says, "I was so scared to even think about this, but after talking to you, that's lifted. You're the first person I've spoken to about my funeral plans that didn't run away or change the subject. Thanks for talking to me like an adult who can handle it." Don't underestimate your survivors. They can handle it too, and they'll be grateful you insisted. They'll also appreciate it if you do it before things become dire or "immediate" and can be discussed casually—perhaps even with occasional humor, which has proven healing capabilities.

There is *one situation* in which it may be a good idea to prepay. If you're applying for Medicaid, all states allow you to prepay for a funeral in order to shelter some money from consideration for Medicaid eligibility. This is known as a "spend-down." You have to exhaust your own money (to a certain degree) before Medicaid will kick in to pay for various medical expenses. But the amounts you can shelter in a prepaid funeral vary by state, so be sure to ask Medicaid what the limits are.

To shelter your funeral or burial money in order to qualify for Medicaid, you have to put it in an *irrevocable* account or plan. That means you can't cash out the insurance policy or trust fund and use it for something other than your funeral. But beware—unscrupulous funeral homes may tell you that *irrevocable* means "You can never change your mind about funeral homes and you're locked in to using my mortuary." That's not true, except in Pennsylvania. Medicaid doesn't care which funeral home you use, and it doesn't care if you change to a different funeral home. It cares only that the money you set aside be used only for your funeral or burial expenses.

Don't be tempted by a funeral home or cemetery into prepaying into an irrevocable plan "just in case you should ever go on Medicaid." Once you've deposited money into an irrevocable account or insurance policy, it can be much harder to get a refund if you ever change your mind and decide on a less-expensive funeral.

Only purchase an irrevocable plan when you absolutely need to qualify for Medicaid in the here and now. Unethical funeral homes have used this ploy to convince consumers they're making a wise choice for the future, knowing full well that many consumers will falsely believe they're locked in forever to using that funeral home, even if circumstances change.

The best option if you're not applying for Medicaid is to deposit your funeral money in a Pay on Death (POD) account at your bank or credit union. You name a beneficiary—your child, a trusted friend, anyone—and the money is released to that person on your death without having to go through probate. The money stays in your name, the interest is yours, and the account is portable. If your roof springs a leak and you need a dry house more than you need an eventual cremation, you can cash it out and replenish it later. For the pros and cons of each kind of funeral funding for your state, check the brochures at <www.funeralethics.org/preneed> or your state chapter.

Body Parts
Big business, little regulation

7

WHEN SUE SEDGWICK EXPRESSED CONCERN about her mother's poor hospital care (which may have contributed to Florence's death), the funeral director suggested a private autopsy, which he could arrange. He took Sue's payment of $2,000. Two days later, Sue received the expected cremated remains in the urn she had picked out but no autopsy report.

Weeks later and after many phone calls, Sue received a report: for a woman with gray hair instead of red, a woman 50 pounds heavier than her mother and five inches shorter. This was not her mother's autopsy.

A visit to John C. Lincoln Hospital in Phoenix, where the body had been taken, turned up the unhappy discovery of Florence Sedgwick's name in a log book of organ and tissue donors. At that point, Sue didn't know what or who was in the urn she had. Not only had Sue not given permission for any organ or tissue donation, there is a strong possibility that Florence died of septicemia, making her tissues totally unsuitable even for most research studies, given the risk to handlers.

This is hardly the first scandal involving body parts. For a chilling read, try the story of David Sconce and Lamb Funeral Home in *Chop Shop* by Kathy Braidhill (1993). Or check out the misdeeds at UCLA med school, Tulane University, National Anatomical Services, and Biomedical Tissue Services among others, in *Body Brokers* by Annie Cheney (2006). A 2005 scandal involving stolen bones and tissue received worldwide publicity because one of the bodies was that of *Masterpiece Theatre* host Alistair Cooke. Cooke's daughter, Reverend Susan Kittredge, says her father never would have agreed to body donation given the kind of person he was and, of course, Kittredge was concerned that the body parts were fraudulently obtained from a funeral home. But she also points out that if enough people were to donate, there would be no need to steal body parts.

Little or No Regulation

Organ and tissue donation *for transplant* is regulated by the FDA and the Uniform Anatomical Gift Act (UAGA) which has been adopted in every state, but the UAGA's authors did not anticipate the other needs for cadaver tissue and bones. The rapid growth of the bio-tech industry in the past 20 years has brought many advances in medical treatments. Bone paste from cadavers has been used for spine repair. Doctors need real knees to practice the latest orthoscopic surgery. But the lack of regulation, especially of non-transplant tissue, has permitted a black market to thrive and has spawned dozens of for-profit entrepreneurs like ScienceCare in Arizona and Colorado and BioGift in Oregon.

The most logical way to address these problems would have been to amend the UAGA. Carlson, on behalf of the Funeral Ethics Organization, and Slocum, on behalf of Funeral Consumers Alliance, each sent thick binders of documentation to the Vermont lawyer on the UAGA update committee in 2003. But the window of opportunity for meaningful reform was squandered. When the revised UAGA came out a couple of years later, none of the changes addressed the needs for regulating the body parts business.

Troubling Questions

Has the donor family given informed consent? Troubles arise when body parts are stolen or the family does not clearly understand the actual intended use. Is it okay to blow up a body to test protective gear against the damage done by land mines if all the family was told was that such a donation is "advancing science"? Does a family understand that when a body is "segmented," it will be cut up in various parts for various different uses and sent, perhaps, all over the country, all over the world? As Brent Bardsley of the nonprofit Anatomy Gift Registry points out, the nonacademic companies generally do a better job of stating clearly what will happen to the body. Most people donating a body to a medical school think they'll be the center of attention in an anatomy lab prior to cremation. But most academic institutions also support research, and some share cadavers with other institutions. What if a few brains are needed for Alzheimer studies? Or a few hands for carpel tunnel studies? Would the donor have minded if they ended up there instead? Doesn't a family have a right to know?

Has the donated tissue been tested for disease? Some companies use tissue and bone for research as well as transplant purposes. Such crossover use is not uncommon within the same company. The criteria for transplant should clearly protect a recipient from harmful infections, yet by 2003 the Centers for Disease Control (CDC) had documented 62 such cases of infected patients. There may be hazards to researchers working with donated tissues, too. Tracking the tissue during all travels is imperative to the public safety but is not always being done, even though the technology exists. Read the excellent article by Scott Brubaker on the website of the

American Association of Tissue Banks: "Tissue Tracking Failures and Lessons Learned: Hope for the Future." (www.aatb.org)

Is the use and final disposition of each body part respectful and accounted for? One company's report lists the sale of "vagina with clitoris—$375." Who is buying this and for what purpose? (There may be legitimate uses, but the casual trade in such body parts with no accountability seems disrespectful.) Seven knees were shipped to the Miami Sheraton for a doctors' conference, with no record of what happened to them afterward. In Arizona, LifeLegacy sent bodies and body parts to a cemetery's crematory, and later, a cemetery visitor called police after spotting bones and skulls heaped in a pit. These were recognizable bone fragments that had not been pulverized per the industry standard for all crematories.

Does the state limit profiteering by monitoring fees? What is a "reasonable" fee to cover the costs associated with harvesting tissue? Some "nonprofit" companies like the Musculoskeletal Transplant Foundation (MTF) are paying six-figure salaries to high-level executives, with the CEO's salary over $600,000 in 2008. Carlson discovered that MTF is the tissue bank for most hospitals in Vermont and is called any time there is a death of a potential tissue donor. Other tissue banks are openly for-profit. And profit motive has surely fueled unsafe and less-than-ethical practices.

Is there a system for setting priority use, especially for the living? When there is greater revenue generated by the "sale" of skin to plastic surgeons, then skin for burn victims may be diverted. Will the competition for body donors short-change the needs of medical schools? Should there be a priority allocation of donor resources? The demand still exceeds the supply, according to some in the business.

A Patchwork Quilt of State Regulation

While federal regulators have neglected their oversight duties, a few states have picked up the ball. The District of Columbia, Ohio, Oklahoma, and Virginia require a tissue bank to be licensed by the state and accredited by the American Association of Tissue Banks (AATB). New Jersey law has elements similar to the new AATB standards for testing, tracking, and disposition but also requires that all tissue banks be nonprofit. Oregon requires tissue banks to be registered with the state, but there are no statutory standards.

New York would appear to have excellent rules, but unfortunately their enforcement is lacking. Companies must document that informed consent is obtained. A company must disclose to the state on request its income and expenses. It must disclose the body parts it harvests, the prices charged for each, and to whom it's selling. Prices must be "reasonable." Body parts must be tracked and the form of disposition noted. Unfortunately, staffers in Albany told Carlson they had no model for informed consent and no criteria by which to assess a company's consent procedure. "It's a process, not a piece of paper," she was told. Lawyers hired by donor families might not agree. New York is not asking companies for financial information or the charge for body parts, even though 17 of the 73 licensed entities appear to be for-profit companies.

Statutes and regulations will be of little use if the regulatory agencies do not have adequate funding and staff to do the job. In 2009, Carlson wrote to the Health Commissioner in Vermont to get her support for regulating tissue bank activity in that state. She got no response, probably because the Health Department already feels overworked. The Food and Drug Administration adopted the AATB standards for transplant. Perhaps every state should require nontransplant tissue banks to be accredited by AATB, as well. That might be easier legislation to pass, with no fiscal or staff implications for an overworked state health department.

Given the strong new standards at AATB, why would anyone start another accrediting agency? In September 2009, Arizona funeral home owner Garland Shreves incorporated the for-profit Research for Life, a company that accepts whole body donations. Seven months later, he incorporated American Medical Education and Research Association (AMERA) to accredit nontransplant companies such as his. The organization, which touts itself as "nationally recognized," held its first meeting in October 2010. Functionaries with AMERA include Bryan Avery and his wife Lucy Lessard who own the nonprofit Gifts for Life in Hawaii. According the AMERA website <www.ameraus.org>, two of the four pending accreditations are Gifts for Life and Research for Life. The AMERA standards are not on their website and won't be, Carlson was told.

Michael Meyer, a medical ethicist and professor at Santa Clara University in California, says, "National standards are the first step toward transparency. There can't be a patchwork quilt." Perhaps Arizona and Hawaii will be among the next states to require AATB accreditation for all tissue banks, and suspect outfits like AMERA will quietly go away.

We support the idea of donating one's body for medical science. We would all like to know that our surgeon practiced on a cadaver before performing surgery on us. And for-profit companies have a role to play in developing innovative medical technologies. But the body parts business today is little better than the Wild West, and it will stay that way until regulators take the issue seriously. Already, we've heard from people who have cancelled their bequests to an anatomical gift program out of disgust with the scandals and theft. Legitimate medical schools are almost always short of cadavers, and the "see no evil" attitude of regulators, sadly, will contribute to making the problem worse.

Federal Trade Commission
A fickle consumer ally

8

STAFF AT THE FEDERAL TRADE Commission are fond of saying that FTC stands for "For The Consumer." A few critics have suggested a more colorful phrase.

The fact is, the FTC is given the job of helping consumers, and it has some dedicated staffers who do their best to fulfill that role. But over the years, with some exceptions, the Commission has done little to enforce the Funeral Rule—the first and only federal regulation giving grieving consumers specific rights.

Funeral Consumers Alliance has been reporting funeral home violations of the Rule since 1996, and the agency has done nothing to address these problems aside from sporadic undercover "sweeps" that ding funeral homes for failing to give out itemized price lists to shoppers at the appropriate time. That's all well and good, but does it matter *when* the customer gets a price list if it's full of misrepresentations and illegal charges?

The Funeral Rule

The Funeral Rule regulates how funeral homes present their goods and services to their customers, and, in the process, gives significant rights to consumers. The Rule was proposed by the Federal Trade Commission in 1974, and given "final" FTC approval in 1982. Because of strong opposition from the funeral industry, congressional review stretched the process out for another two years. FCA and its member societies, along with other consumer groups, actively supported and promoted the Rule at every step and celebrated final implementation in 1986. The Rule:

- Gives you the right to **pick and choose** only what you want—funeral homes can't force you to buy a complete package and they may not condition the sale of one item on the purchase of another.

- Gives you the right to a **printed, itemized price list** at the very beginning of any discussion about arrangements.

- Gives you the right to obtain **price quotes over the phone.**

98

- Gives you the right to see a **casket price list** before being taken into the showroom or shown any caskets by catalog or computer.

- Bars funeral homes from **lying about nonexistent laws** in order to sell you embalming, caskets, vaults, or anything else you may not want or need.

- Bars funeral homes from **refusing to serve you if you build the casket or buy one** from an outside source.

- Bars funeral homes from charging you a **handling fee** if you bring in your own casket. (Prior to the Rule, many charged a casket "corking fee" to discourage outside coffins)

Before the Rule was adopted, funeral homes routinely forced consumers to buy a full package. The price of the casket included embalming, viewing, a funeral ceremony, etc., whether you wanted all that or not. Consumer advocates hailed the Rule as a grieving consumer's bill of rights. We assumed (naively, in retrospect) that the days of mortuaries lying to consumers to jack up the funeral bill would come to a close.

When Carlson began as FCA Executive Director in 1996, she started grading thousands of General Price Lists (GPLs) from funeral homes coast to coast. At least 50 percent had major Funeral Rule violations—missing consumer disclosures, no simple cremation or burials available without all the trimmings, illegal "handling fees" for families who brought their own caskets. When Slocum took over at FCA in 2003, he continued the practice, forwarding his findings to the FTC, which never offered any comment on them.

PR Trumps Enforcement

When the FTC announced its first-ever Funeral Rule compliance conference in Dallas in April 2006 (22 years after the Rule went into effect), it seemed like a good time to show the feds what was really going on. Slocum tabulated the violations he found in 272 GPLs from six states. **Eighty-six percent** had at least one Rule violation, and most had many more. Meanwhile, the FTC was pumping out press releases crowing about how well Texas funeral directors were doing:

> The Federal Trade Commission announced today that it found a high level of compliance in East Texas with the FTC's Funeral Rule, which protects consumers from abusive practices in the funeral industry. In a recent sweep of funeral homes in the Tyler, Texas area, nine of the 10 funeral homes shopped were found to be in compliance with the rule. —November, 2005

Intriguing, since Slocum found the exact opposite: nine out of the ten Tyler funeral homes had violations on their GPLs when he examined them. Thinking the FTC might want to know this before Slocum made it public at the Dallas meeting, he left messages and e-mails for Commission staff. What was the response? A concerted effort by the FTC to exclude any messengers of unpleasant information.

One lawyer from the Southwest Regional Office tipped his hand by accidentally copying to Slocum the following e-mail he wrote to an FTC colleague:

> I will defer to you regarding contact with Josh Slocum. However, we don't have caller ID here, so I could possibly answer his call without knowing . . . given the apparent sensitivity of his issues, I'd rather he be dealt with "officially." I sincerely hope we don't have a "scene" on Thursday when he arrives or during the meeting. We have worked so hard down here to plan a wonderful conference, and I am disappointed with the controversy he has stirred up. What do you think we should do?

The only scene that took place in Dallas was the FTC's attempt to eject a national FCA board member when he and Slocum arrived for the meeting. At 8:30 that morning, FTC attorney Janette Gosha told Jim Bates that he didn't register early enough and would have to leave. Bates reminded her that this was a public meeting paid for with taxpayer dollars. Well, there aren't enough chairs, Gosha said. So Bates offered to stand in the corner. There wasn't enough food, Gosha countered. She relented only after Bates produced a receipt for the $20 he had paid for the day's lunch buffet.

From the start, it was obvious the FTC was more interested in silencing consumers than in regulating the funeral industry. Thomas Carter, Senior Staff Attorney for the Southwest Regional Office, opened the morning with, "The good news is Texas funeral homes are doing a great job following the Funeral Rule, based on our investigations." Carter then described the "partnership" between the FTC and National Funeral Directors Association.

"The old 'gotcha' system wasn't working," he said. "So we put on our thinking caps and came up with the Funeral Rule Offenders Program. FROP is one of the most successful public/private partnerships in history."

FROP: Foxes Guarding the Henhouse

Back in 1996, the National Funeral Directors Association struck a deal with the FTC to create FROP. Under the deal, Funeral Rule violators can enroll in the program, which is administered by NFDA. In exchange for fees paid to NFDA and a "voluntary" payment to the US Treasury—instead of the $11,000 fine the FTC was empowered by law to levy at that time (since raised to $16,000)—errant funeral homes undergo three years of remedial training and testing by NFDA.

Keep in mind that the NFDA is a trade association, whose main job is to promote the funeral industry, boosting its image and its profits. As a special bonus, the FTC agreed to keep the names of Funeral Rule violators out of its press releases. So the job of guarding the henhouse goes to the fox, who operates in total secrecy, with guarantees that any mischief will be hidden from the public.

When Slocum wrote up the Dallas incident in the Spring 2006 FCA Newsletter, a casket retail store owner sent this e-mail:

> I am a casket retailer located in Tyler and have been in business since 1996. During this period I have witnessed or been told of many violations of the Funeral Rule. I firmly believe the Funeral Rule is not worth the paper it is printed on. My wife and I opened our casket store after a personal experience with a funeral home. The long and short is that my family decided that we were not going to put up with the FH's tactics and we buried my uncle ourselves—built the box, dug the grave . . .Only after this experience did I find out about the Funeral Rule.
>
> . . . Some FH's in Tyler flat out tell families that they don't accept caskets from an outside source, use various methods to discourage and hamper those who do attempt to buy a casket from an outside source, and have artificially inflated prices so that there will be an illusion of a discount on package funerals.

Contrary to the sunny pronouncements in Dallas, Rule enforcement has been so weak that mortuaries feel free to get away with violating its core requirements. A suspiciously high number of complaints come from families who patronize funeral homes owned by Service Corporation International (SCI), what one lawyer calls the "largest funeral home chain in the galaxy." SCI prefers, of course, to be referred to by its consumer brand name, Dignity Memorial. One consumer, Brooke Horne, wrote to FCA about her dignified experience:

> My mother passed away this week. She specifically wanted a 'no frills' direct cremation. We asked for nothing more than the cardboard box for cremation, the cardboard box for the remains. We were charged a package price with lots of things included which we did not want. They told us it was one price: $2,950. This can't be correct. What can I do?

Horne said Houston's Calvary Hill Funeral home told her that a Dignity Memorial package was the cheapest option. The package included many items—an "aftercare planner" and flowers, for example—that she didn't want. FCA advised her how many rules Calvary Hill broke and called the funeral home to let them know we expected them to lower the bill and start following federal regulations. Armed with knowledge of her rights, Horne returned to find them singing a very different tune. She wrote back to us:

> I cannot tell you how pleased my mother would be knowing that we had busted their "chops" a little. I can't thank you enough. By the time I got back to the funeral home the director was falling all over himself to be agreeable. We settled on $850, taxes included. I said I wanted to pay the fair price and I was very happy with that. He said he would like to send flowers to her memorial and I asked that he send a donation to the Sierra Club. He said he would send $100 out of his own pocket. What did you say to these folks? They are giving us all the stuff that comes with the "package" and I said fine, we would donate it all to the senior center including the flower arrangement.

SCI has a huge financial incentive to break the rules. The company's 2003 annual report noted, "On a burial funeral, Dignity packaged sales generate on average approximately $2,800 more than non-Dignity sales. On a cremation service, Dignity packaged sales generate approximately $1,700 more than non-Dignity sales."

Speaking to Slocum under the promise of anonymity, a California SCI employee offered another explanation:

> We are specifically directed by SCI to tell our customers that they are not allowed to make changes to the prepackaged plans because of an FTC rule of some kind. They browbeat the people that work for them into believing this is some kind of FTC regulation. Nobody bothers to look it up. You have to sell these packages and if anybody wants to make a substitution, then you have to tell them, "The FTC does not allow us to make a change to the package."

Despite a 2006 letter from FCA pleading with the FTC to investigate SCI's everyday sales practices, the Commission continues "sweeping" funeral homes with a toothbrush. Meanwhile, complaints pour into the FCA office from consumers reporting the kind of trickery the Rule was meant to end. Here is another example:

> I called Eden Memorial Park Cemetery in Los Angeles today to discuss the cost of burial plots for my mother, who is still alive. Among the many charges [the salesman] listed was for a burial container. I asked if that was the 3-sided container (top and sides)

or a complete vault. He sounded appalled at the question, and said that, of course, it was the complete, sealed enclosure, "which is required by law." I said, "Um, actually, the FTC website states 'Outer burial containers are not required by state law anywhere in the US, but many cemeteries require them'." He feigned surprise and said he'd always been under the impression they were required by law. I offered to give him the URL of the FTC web page stating this, but he said, "Oh, no—I'll take your word for it." Right! As if he wouldn't be fully aware of the laws regarding this! The sleazebag!

The salesman called her back a minute later to say he'd forgotten they were having a sale on graves—wouldn't she like to save $1,000 by purchasing today?

Unlike this woman, most consumers don't even know the Funeral Rule exists, leaving one to wonder how many uninformed families are duped by these expensive lies. People write and call FCA from around the country reporting they never received a price list, that the funeral director simply filled out the family's itemized receipt during the arrangements conference with "everything you'll need" (usually a one-of-everything funeral), and misrepresented legal requirements.

When Slocum joined FCA in 2002, the Funeral Rule had been law for 18 years. He assumed that was long enough for morticians to understand what it required and what it prohibited. Yet after years on the job, he found many undertakers are still ignorant about the Rule. Linda McLemore, a fiery FCA volunteer from Georgia, forwarded an e-mail exchange with a funeral director at Williams Funeral Home in Columbus. She wrote Spencer Williams a polite letter asking him to amend the false claims on the consumer FAQ page on his website because the statements were untrue and in violation of the Rule. The worst was Williams' claim that embalming was required *by the FTC* for an open-casket viewing. His response (with unusual capitalization and sentence structure preserved from the original) is sadly typical:

Mrs. McLemore,

I am completely unaware of anything on my Q&A page that is not accurate for my Georgia customers. These are not State Laws that were quoted on this page. I actually quoted those laws as part of the Federal Trade Commission's FTC Funeral Rule.

(1.) Actually, as far as the open casket and embalming, ...
. . . Aside from this being part of the Federal Trade Commission's FTC Funeral Rule, when we take our oath as Funeral Directors and Embalmers, we take on a responsibility as "Guardians of the Public Health." Whereas most people are under the false assumption that

the only purpose for embalming is for preservation, the truth is that embalming is multi-purpose. Some of the main purposes for Embalming include: **Sanitation** (the embalming fluid is actually a strong disinfectant), restoration & preservation.

(**2.**) Again, this is not a State Law, it is Federal Law. That Law is known as the Federal Trade Commission's FTC Funeral Rule.

(**3.**) Once more, this is part of the FTC Funeral Rule that states, "Embalming is required if burial will not take place within 72 hours, unless refrigeration is available." and unfortunately, refrigeration is not available within our area.

I do appreciate your inquiry, however, I am striving to keep our webpage accurate. I do not wish to misinform anyone or misrepresent to any family that comes to us for information. My concern is that you are under the belief that my page is wrong. My page is true, complete, and accurate.

Of course, the Funeral Rule has no such requirements, nor does Georgia law. Since misrepresenting the law is banned by the Funeral Rule, it seems particularly alarming when funeral directors cite the Rule itself as the source of this misinformation.

These examples are a tiny sample from a file box in Slocum's office labeled, in red marker, FTC FUNERAL RULE EVIDENCE, set aside for the next hearings on reforming the Rule. That day may be far off—the FTC astonished consumer advocates by voting to close the Rule review in 2008 with no amendments.

FTC Guts Its Own Rule

Nothing has kept the cost of funerals artificially high as much as the so-called "Basic Services Fee." Originally conceived as a modest charge funeral homes would assess for the administration common to any funeral—the initial conference with the family, writing up the contract—the "basic" fee has ballooned to the single most expensive item at most mortuaries. Much of the time it beats out caskets, which were historically the most hyper-inflated item on the menu. And it's the one "service" you *can't* decline to pay for.

From 1982 to 1988, the average Basic Services Fee increased by 73 percent, according to FTC studies. And yet, the FTC's commentary in its 1988 report wondered why the cost of funerals was rising faster than inflation in the years immediately after the Rule went into effect. When a single item (the one item for which there was no accountability at all) had risen from 11 percent to almost 20 percent of the total funeral cost, one has a hard time imagining how the FTC staff missed it.

Consumer groups testified against the basic services fee during a Rule review in the late 1980s, showing how any cost-savings that itemization might have brought were being gobbled up by the anything-goes "basic" fee. Perversely, the FTC's amended definition of the fee in 1994 loosened it even further, making a joke of the Rule's promise to help consumers control costs by declining optional services. The following is from the FTC publication *Complying With the Funeral Rule:*

> The basic services fee also may include overhead from various aspects of your business operation, such as the parking lot, reception and arrangements rooms, and other common areas. It also may include insurance, staff salaries, taxes, and fees that you must pay. Alternatively, instead of including all overhead in your basic services fee, you can spread the overhead charges across the various individual goods and services you offer. . . .

Mortuaries typically charge $1,500 to $3,000 just to get in the door, then low-ball the prices of the *actual goods and services you choose.* Someone arranging a direct cremation over the telephone or planning all services at a church is not filling the parking lot or using the reception rooms and should not be forced to pay for such. What other industry is given government permission to charge a non-declinable fee that is unrelated to the goods and services selected?

By keeping funeral prices artificially high, the Basic Services Fee has helped to prop up thousands of mortuaries that would likely have gone out of business due to normal market forces. Unlike in almost every other sphere of commerce, the higher the number of businesses selling funerals, the higher prices tend to be. Since a funeral home can sell only one funeral per person, if there are "too many" funeral homes for the population, the demand is spread thin. The only way to make up for this is to charge ever-higher prices to each customer. The bloated basic fee helps keep three funeral homes going in a town that can really support only one. What other business is so completely insulated from the forces of supply and demand?

The abuse of this fee continues, and once a mortuary has been purchased by a corporate funeral chain, it tends to rise with alarming regularity. Lamar Hankins, past President of Funeral Consumers Alliance, wrote in the Spring, 2007 newsletter of the Austin Memorial and Burial Information Society (AMBIS):

> The results from the last two AMBIS funeral price surveys reveal the clear marketing strategy of Service Corporation International (SCI) for getting families to pay more for funerals. It is a five-prong strategy, involving decreases in prices for caskets and increases in prices for embalming, the non-declinable fee (the cost that is added

to all arrangements for the services of staff and overhead costs supposedly common to all arrangements), and refrigeration, along with high-pressure sales tactics.

In 2005, SCI was hit with a massive lawsuit filed by Funeral Consumers Alliance (FCA) and some individual consumers alleging price-fixing in the sale of caskets. Shortly thereafter, SCI lowered its charges for caskets. Simultaneously, it raised the price of embalming to the astronomical price of $1,395 locally, a price nearly 2½ times more than the local non-SCI average. Likewise, it raised its non-declinable fee in its four Austin funeral homes to more than $1,100 above the average for all 40 Austin-area funeral homes included in our survey. At $2,995, the four Cook-Walden funeral homes in Austin and Pflugerville are the highest in the survey. Only eight other funeral homes in the survey have non-declinable fees above $2,000, and two of them are also owned by SCI.

The National Funeral Directors Association cited the average charge for the non-declinable fee in 2006 at $1,595. In 2010, they cited the *median* price of the non-declinable fee at $1,817. The median is the price right in the middle, where half the survey respondents charged less than $1,817, and half the respondents charged more. Since NFDA has always used the *average* price in their past surveys, switching to the use of the *median* price in 2010 is likely to confuse and mislead. For example, the 2006 NFDA survey showed the *average* price of a full-service funeral at $7,323. Yet in 2010, they used the *median* price of $6,560—an attempt to suggest funeral prices have gone down in four years?

When it comes to the non-declinable fee, consumer groups often find it's much higher than the averages or medians reported by trade groups:

- The Funeral Consumers Alliance in Raleigh, North Carolina, found fees as high as $3,000 in 2003.

- The FCA of South Carolina found a range from $500 to $3,000 in the city of Columbia in 2007.

- In a 2010 survey in Connecticut, a least half the funeral homes had a Basic Fee of over $2,000.

- Slocum found one funeral home charging $5,000 for the basic services fee, then only $125 each for the actual visitation, funeral ceremony, and graveside service.

Also, in areas where there are retail casket sellers, funeral homes follow the advice of trade journals and lower their casket prices to compete, then raise their service prices. In other words, competition and market forces sometimes lower the price of the casket itself, but this does no good to the consumer who must make up the difference in the non-declinable fee. This is an excellent reason for consumers to shop around for reasonable prices on service fees as well as caskets.

Failed Efforts to Reform the Rule

In 1999, the FTC generated a list of questions to be answered during its mandatory five-year review of the Funeral Rule. FCA testified, backing that testimony with five cartons of documentation. These included price surveys and general price lists from over 2,000 funeral establishments that had been collected by volunteer members of local affiliates around the country, articles from trade journals that Carlson had been monitoring over the years, and a compilation of funeral and cemetery complaints received in the FCA office. When the actual hearings were scheduled, FCA was seated front and center. Our organization's goals:

- Abolish any non-declinable fee. (Replace current charges with an optional per-hour fee).

- Add an option for private viewing without embalming, with a per-hour charge permitted.

- List the cost for body donation to a medical school.

- List the cost of the cremation process. (The current listing implies that one may pick an immediate cremation only.)

- Include the cost of cremation in package pricing for all cremation options. (How can one have a direct cremation without cremation, as is now permitted by the FTC in the price listings? A consumer shopping for prices would have no way of knowing how much will be added for the cremation itself.)

- Standardize the description of the immediate burial option, so that consumers can compare prices charged by different funeral establishments.

- Require disclosure of any service charge or mark-up on cash-advance items purchased by the funeral director. This would apply to things like placement of the obituary, ordering flowers, or any other third-party item that the consumer could purchase independently.

- Expand the Rule to also cover cemeteries, casket vendors, and monument dealers. They, too, should be required to disclose the prices they are charging consumers and should be forbidden from committing deceptive practices or restraint of trade.

- Require disclosure of all conditions and cancellation risks on preneed contracts: trusting, "constructive delivery," interest income, fees and commissions, penalties, and substitution of merchandise.

On the whole, casket sellers and monument dealers were eager to see the Rule expanded and were unafraid of regulation. The National Funeral Directors Association has expressed support for expanding the Rule to cemeteries. However, the International Cemetery and Funeral Association (now the International Cemetery, Cremation, and Funeral Association—they have mission-creep) sent a letter to the FTC objecting to FCA's claims, stating that there was no evidence of cemetery consumer abuse. Hardly a credible source when one considers that almost all the officers of the organization at that time came from corporate-owned funeral and cemetery chains.

And what happened after the 1999 hearings? Absolutely nothing. Why? It's not hard to guess. George W. Bush was elected president in 2000. Robert Waltrip, founder of SCI, was a close friend of the Bush family and a donor to the George H. W. Bush Library as well as various political campaigns. When he was governor of Texas, Bush had fired the executive director of the Texas Funeral Service Commission when she fined SCI for using unlicensed embalmers there in Texas. SCI—and most of the rest of the industry players—certainly didn't want to see the non-declinable fee eliminated or its for-profit cemeteries regulated.

This was, of course, a period in which many industries were, essentially, deregulated. In some instances there may have been benefits, but this trend was at least partially responsible for America's economic meltdown and the massive oil spill in the Gulf of Mexico, among other large-scale problems. Consistent with this trend, the FTC became much friendlier to business interests and less concerned with its mandate to foster competition in the interest of consumers.

There was a glimmer of hope for Funeral Rule reform in 2002, when Senator Christopher Dodd introduced a bill that would have made the FTC's Funeral Rule into a more enforceable federal law and would have expanded it to cover cemeteries and other death-care businesses. Public interest in funeral regulation was running high that year with the Tri-State Crematory disaster (more than 300 rotting bodies on the property) fresh in everyone's minds. At the time, Carlson was head of Funeral Consumers Alliance and worked closely with congressional staff to improve the bill. After the bill went nowhere, Dodd reintroduced it in 2005. Again, it went nowhere.

The Kibosh

Considering the boxes of evidence detailing Funeral Rule abuses provided by FCA over the years, nothing could have been more shocking than the Commission's March 10, 2008 press release. The Commission voted to keep the Rule in its current form. No expansion to cover all players in the death business, no modification of the much-abused basic services fee, no changes to address the financial disaster prepaid funerals have become for families across the country. The Commission's 57-page report contained one jaw-dropper after another. From page 1:

> Because of insufficient support in the record, the Commission declines to propose amendments that some commenters have advocated, namely to: (1) expand the scope of the Rule; (2) to eliminate the basic services fee of the funeral director; (3) allow funeral providers to charge casket handling fees; (4) prohibit discount funeral packages; (5) require additional price information disclosures on the various disclosure documents; and (6) adopt additional regulations focused on contracts for funeral arrangements made on a pre-need basis.

"Insufficient evidence" is the mantra throughout the report. The FTC spends page after tortuous page claiming the record doesn't support reforming the Rule without ever explaining *why* the evidence isn't enough. As Carlson wrote to the Commission, "If the FTC was depending on consumer groups [to provide evidence], it would seem that staff failed to look at the five cartons of documentation and price surveys Funeral Consumers Alliance submitted for review. But that information can readily be updated. How many thousands of new price lists (GPLs) would you like to see, from how many funeral homes, in how many states?" From page 16 of the report:

> [S]everal commenters proposed changing the Rule to cover entities selling funeral goods or funeral services. However, the record evidence did not establish that these sellers, particularly cemeteries and crematories, engaged in the types of abuses addressed by the Rule (e.g., lack of price disclosure, forced bundling of goods and services, and misrepresentations of funeral goods and services).

It takes chutzpah to claim that, since there's "no evidence" cemeteries are withholding price information, the Rule shouldn't require them to disclose what they charge! While the report later acknowledges some cemeteries operate in a way that makes them subject to the Funeral Rule (so far, so good), failing to explicitly address them gives the bad apples enough leeway to argue their way out of complying. So they can get away with all manner of bad behavior the FTC has long recognized as abusive if done by funeral home staff.

The report's treatment of the non-declinable fee is especially galling. It's a mystery how educated people in the nation's fair trade office could accept and endorse self-serving industry defenses. From page 29:

> One commenter surmised that if the basic services fee were eliminated, funeral providers would have to spread their costs over other items, which, he believed would lead to higher prices. Commenter Charles Graham, a licensed funeral director and embalmer, also contended that prohibiting the non-declineable [sic] fee would require costs to once again be spread over other services and merchandise.

Yes, that's precisely the point. Consumers should pay their fair share of overhead for the goods and services they buy, but *only* their fair share. The non-declinable fee perverts the Rule's intent by allowing undertakers to charge exorbitant fees for "basic services," even for customers who choose limited arrangements. Cost-conscious families are forced to subsidize the mortuary's full overhead, even though they're not using it. Yet the FTC pretends it cannot understand why this is a problem.

The award for Best Doublespeak goes to the Commission's approach to casket-handling fees. The report acknowledges that charging a fee to consumers who buy a casket outside the funeral home is harmful, but then it states that "discount packages" are totally different and "confer benefits" on consumers. To evade the Rule's ban on handling fees, many funeral homes have constructed "discount packages" available only if the consumer buys a coffin from the funeral home. Those who buy a coffin elsewhere have to pay *higher itemized prices*, exactly the same financial penalty as the handling fees banned by the Rule. But that's not the same, according to the Commission. From page 35 of the report:

> While this practice could raise concerns if the discount effectively swallows any cost savings associated with purchasing a less expensive casket from a competitor, there is insufficient evidence [despite the report's own acknowledgement that 14 percent of NFDA members tie "discounts" to the purchase of a casket] to show a prevalent practice of funeral providers offering discount packages in a manner that unfairly interferes with consumers' ability to provide their own caskets.

If the reader is wondering why it's OK for some businesses to engage in abusive practices as long as not too many of them do so, we're wondering too. If the Commission recognizes that certain practices are harmful to consumers, why does it have to wait for a majority of funeral homes to use them in order to declare the practice illegal?

In 2009, consumer advocates got another chance to reform the Rule. Once again, a scandal provoked a bill. After investigators discovered that workers at Chicago's famous historically black Burr Oak cemetery were digging up old graves and reselling them, US Representative Bobby Rush convened a hearing before the House Subcommittee on Consumer Protection. Rush asked Slocum to testify about the problems families experience at cemeteries, particularly the abuses that don't make the headlines.

Following the hearing, Rush introduced HR3655, the Bereaved Consumers Bill of Rights Act of 2009. (See the Cemeteries chapter for a full description.) At the time of this writing, the bill has passed the full House Energy and Commerce Committee, though it was amended to exempt most "religious" cemeteries. However, it did not make its way through the legislative process by the end of the 2010 session. Will our lawmakers ever have the stomach to do the right thing by grieving consumers?

Funeral Rule Advisory Opinions

Interested parties can request FTC staff to make a ruling on whether certain practices are allowed or barred by the Funeral Rule in its current form, and FCA has submitted several. While not all requests have been answered, some of these give consumers ammunition to fight back against predatory practices:

> Opinion 08-1—Freestanding crematories that serve the public are subject to the Funeral Rule.

> Opinion 07-1—Funeral homes can't charge an additional fee for "service vehicles" used to file and retrieve permits; that has to be included in the Basic Services Fee. (Unfortunately, this opinion also states funeral homes are allowed to charge families extra for refrigerating unembalmed bodies, despite FCA's contention that this is just a double charge for "sheltering of remains" which is already billed in the Basic Services Fee.)

> Opinion 07-3—Funeral homes can't require families to be present at the funeral home to "inspect and accept" third-party caskets, a tactic used by some mortuaries to make buying a third-party casket onerous.

> Opinion 07-4—Funeral homes may not charge families for storing a third-party casket immediately prior to the funeral, and they can't charge families for throwing away the packaging in which outside caskets arrive.

Opinion 07-10—Funeral homes **must** offer direct cremation, the simplest kind of disposition, if they offer cremation at all. (Amazingly a funeral home owner wrote the FTC to ask if he could offer only more elaborate cremation packages.)

Opinion 04-1—Funeral homes can't require consumers to sign for the delivery of third-party caskets.

Opinion 97-4—Funeral homes can't require families to pay for "identification viewing" and any associated preparation of the body, unless required by state law (which is almost never the case).

Working with the FTC

In criticizing the Commission so bluntly, we know we run the risk of alienating an agency we need to work with. And we don't want to give the impression that no one at the FTC cares. The Commission has taken action recently against a state funeral board that tried to outlaw direct-to-consumer casket sales and has supported lawsuits that would open up competition in funeral sales. We've also gotten to know several staffers over the years who do yeoman's work trying to keep up with an extraordinary workload. Some of them have confided their disappointment at watching the Commission degenerate from a bold watchdog organization into a politically motivated bureaucracy whose lumbering pace lets industry off easy at the public's expense.

We appreciate these dedicated public servants, but the fact remains that the FTC as a whole has failed the funeral-buying public. Consumers and taxpayers have a right to expect the government to work for them not as an enabler to an industry well-known for its willingness to abuse the bereaved.

Filing an Effective Complaint 9
And what NOT to do

WHAT SHOULD YOU DO IF you are treated in a dishonest, unethical, and/or illegal way in your dealings with the funeral industry?

First, write down everything from the minute you feel you might have a complaint, to make sure you record details while they're fresh in your mind. If another person is with you and shares your concerns, ask that person to write down what happened, too. Sometimes that person will remember additional helpful information. Be sure to date all of your notes. Write down the names of everyone you deal with, even if it is just a first name or a description of what the person looked like. Keep a log of all phone conversations.

Try to settle your concerns with those involved first. That's how you would want to be treated if it were your business. Write a letter to the funeral home or cemetery outlining your concerns. Explain what went wrong and what remedy you would find acceptable. Send it by certified mail, return receipt requested. A telephone call may be helpful, as well, if you feel there is a good chance of working things out. But with a serious dispute, telephone calls are not sufficient, as there's no paper record. E-mail is not sufficient either, as there's no easy way to prove the business received it.

If you can't get satisfaction from the business, you may want to file a complaint with the state regulatory authorities. All states except Hawaii have an agency or a regulatory board that oversees funeral homes although oversight in Colorado is limited. Cemeteries are not as well-regulated, however, and you may have difficulty finding out which entity oversees them. Call the FCA national office if you have trouble finding the agency to which you should send your complaint. This will also help FCA's efforts to record and track complaints. The staff can also help you research your state laws, which may affect how your complaint is treated.

If your complaint involves a violation of the Funeral Rule, you should also send a copy to the FTC's Consumer Protection Bureau at 600 Pennsylvania Ave. NW, Washington, DC, 20580. The FTC *does not* investigate individual consumer complaints, but building a file helps the Commission and consumer advocates identify patterns of abuse that should be investigated.

Categories of Complaints

Funeral home and cemetery complaints generally fall into the following general categories or a combination of them.

- **Unreasonable or unexpected cost**—e.g., the price list shows that the least expensive casket available is $595, but the funeral director claims there is nothing available less than the $2,000 casket on display.

- **Unethical or unprofessional conduct**—e.g., you were told that embalming was required even for private family viewing or that the handles will fall off the casket you purchased from a retailer.

- **Negligence**—e.g., the funeral home failed to send the obituary to the newspaper and, as a result, no one showed up for the funeral.

- **Breach of contract**—e.g., the cemetery or monument dealer failed to deliver the marker you ordered, even after six months.

- **Funeral Rule violations**—e.g., you weren't given a price list to examine at the beginning of the arrangements conference.

Guidelines for Writing

When writing your complaint, follow these guidelines:

1. Identify yourself, the names of the businesses and staff involved, and the nature of the complaint at the top. Regulatory offices are chronically understaffed. Save them time by getting to the specifics right away. Remember that you're writing to someone who doesn't know you and probably doesn't know any of the parties involved.

2. Give enough detail so that the reader can understand the problem without being overwhelmed by irrelevancies. Begin at the beginning, and end at the end. Don't include a running travelogue of the times each relative arrived for the funeral-gone-wrong and on what airline. This doesn't matter, and it encourages the reader to put your complaint at the bottom of the pile.

Your choice of words is important. "It was a terrible funeral" or "It cost too much" are not valid complaints. You will be more effective in getting results when you can be specific or identify a law or regulation that was broken.

3. Try to keep emotional content to a minimum. Everyone's mom is the best mom who ever lived. Every parent who loses a child has lost the most important person in their world. But belaboring the emotional aspect of the death, and playing up the noble qualities of the deceased runs the risk of making you appear melodramatic even though your pain is genuine.

4. Consider the remedy that would satisfy you and ask for it but not for more than that. Most of us have internalized the idea that the only right and proper remedies to seek when a business lets us down are a full refund of our money or a lawsuit seeking damages. Make no mistake, we've seen plenty of instances where funeral or cemetery businesses engage in willful patterns of consumer abuse that cry out for a public trial and hefty damages.

But we also know funeral directors and cemetery staff make mistakes they regret. Sometimes funeral home or cemetery workers are desensitized to things that seem normal to them but bizarre or offensive to ordinary consumers. Before you decide to file a lawsuit or call for the state to shut down a funeral business, consider whether a more creative remedy would give you more satisfaction and contribute to better service for other families in the future. For example, if the wrong information is called in for the obituary, the best practical solution may be a corrected obituary, a partial refund, and a promise to institute safeguards against the same error happening with other families, rather than a lawsuit to try to shut down the business.

What to Expect

In some states, members of the funeral board themselves investigate. Many have a consumer representative on their boards, ideally one who would be a member of the investigating team. Some boards have investigators on their staffs. In other states, the complaint will be turned over to an enforcement department responsible for a number of agencies. Or sometimes the Attorney General's office is responsible for investigating consumer complaints.

Usually, a funeral board or the state agency has a number of options. Most (though this varies) can order a refund or reduction in the funeral bill, impose a fine, order an apology, or require additional education. The board might issue a warning, place the offender on probation, or even revoke a license. Taking a funeral director's license is generally done only for the most outrageous misconduct, such as embezzling preneed funeral money. If the only remedy available to the funeral board is revoking a license, you may be disappointed with the results of your complaint, as this is rarely done.

Unfortunately, most state funeral boards are dominated by members of the funeral industry. This conflict of interest results in many legitimate complaints being swept under the rug. You may find the process frustrating, and you may have to communicate in writing several times with the board or staff to get an adequate explanation of why your complaint was handled as it was. Sometimes, you just won't get an answer. But don't let this discourage you from filing. Some consumer complaints are handled fairly, and, when they're not, some consumers have been able to convince their elected representatives to tighten the laws or put pressure on the boards to do a more thorough job. If you're having a hard time being taken seriously, call or write the FCA office.

Remember, your complaint **may prevent a similar thing from happening to someone else.** Improvements for consumers occur most often when regulatory bodies know about problems. Filing a complaint may not only help you, but it may help *all* consumers.

Unreasonable Complaints

We're a nation of consumers, and we complain when we've been cheated or mistreated. But some people undercut their claim to the moral high ground by making demands for recompense out of proportion to the crime.

The majority of disgruntled consumers really do have a point: the funeral home charged them for things they didn't need or want or swapped out a cheaper casket than what they had paid for, or the cemetery slapped on a fee when the family wanted to buy a less expensive marker from an outside dealer. But some complaints are sparked by misunderstanding on the consumer's part. A simple lack of knowledge can spark a consumer's anger, which is sometimes misdirected toward a funeral or cemetery businesses that hasn't done anything wrong.

You might have an unreasonable complaint if . . .

- **You think funeral directors are probate court judges.** Too often, families fight over dead bodies. A common dispute involves who has the legal right to arrange and carry out the funeral. Who prevails if the kids are at war over whether dad wanted a viewing or whether he wanted burial or cremation? Families who can't come to agreement often expect the funeral director to adjudicate. Each person thinks the undertaker should side with him, of course. In reality, each state has laws setting out the order of legal priority. If the decedent left no written instructions, the common-law devolution of next-of-kin prevails: spouse, then adult children, then parents, then siblings, etc. Some state laws require a majority of any particular "class" (like a majority of kids) to sign off on the funeral. Other state laws allow just one member of that class to sign off, and still others, unhelpfully, leave it vague.

In many situations it's not clear who should have the final word. What if Bob has five kids who can't agree on burial versus cremation, and state law says all the children must agree? Should one child out of five be able to override the other four? What if the one hold-out is demanding a funeral that he can't OR won't pay for?

A New England funeral director tells of an unfortunate episode following the death of a young girl in a car crash:

> Her parents were divorced and remarried, and the girl had been raised by the grandparents. There were about a dozen folks making arrangements, split into two camps around each parent. When we got to deciding where she was to be buried, an argument ensued. Everyone looked at me to sort it out, and I told

them they needed to work it out among themselves. Then the name-calling began. One side accused the parent on the other side of having nothing to do with the kid, which of course got a similar response from the other side. Then a teenager on one side of the room pointed at a boy on the other and yelled, "Oh yeah, well you abused your sister," which caused the accused kid to run out of the room crying. I then stood up and told everyone we were through for the day. It was a Sunday afternoon, and I'd make an appointment for them with the probate judge Monday morning to decide where she would be buried and told them they needed to go home. As they were leaving, a young man looked at me with a scowl and said "Thanks a lot!"

If your family can't reach agreement, you'll need to petition the probate court (you don't need a lawyer in probate court, however you may if jurisdiction is in a district or circuit court) to resolve the situation.

We urge you to do everything possible to avoid this—it's painful and often ugly. Though it might not seem so at the moment, it's usually better to grit your teeth and hash it out with the family members you just can't stand than it is to drag the affair into court. But do not blame the funeral director, who has no control over the situation.

- **You think funeral directors are psychic.** A typical example is the woman who called FCA furious that a funeral home carried out a burial for her father without notifying her or asking permission. It turns out that dad had a girlfriend who'd lived with him for many years. When he died, the girlfriend arranged the funeral and didn't tell the funeral home that there were living children. The daughter called FCA on a mission to sue the funeral home. "Didn't the funeral director have to check to make sure she really had the legal right? Shouldn't the funeral home have contacted me?"

There isn't any comprehensive next-of-kin database to consult. A funeral director has no way to know that the person who shows up in the arrangements office is or isn't the decedent's wife. There's no way for the undertaker to know whether there are six children scattered around the country. "Well, shouldn't she have had to produce a marriage certificate?" the woman asked. Well, no, funeral directors aren't obligated to "card" their customers, and it's easy to see how offensive this would be to many families. Carlson isn't even sure where hers is.

Most states require funeral directors to make a good-faith effort to find out who has the legal right to make funeral arrangements. So long as they do so, these laws usually indemnify the funeral director from lawsuits. If someone who didn't have the legal authority to do so arranged a funeral for one of your family members, remember that your complaint is against that person, *not* the funeral director. Put yourself in the funeral director's shoes: Can you imagine any way that *you* would have been able to figure out if some person you met for the first time had a living sister six states away?

- **You think of the funeral home as a credit agency.** Many families mistakenly believe funeral homes are obliged to serve up an expensive, top-of-the-line funeral with no money down and then take payments of $100 a month for five years. In years past, many funeral homes offered payment plans, but few do so today, having learned a hard lesson from the number of customers who have skipped out on the bill. Funeral homes have to pay their staff salaries, their mortgages, taxes, and utility bills. If your boss suggested paying you over five years for the work you are doing now, you'd say no. Don't expect the funeral home to take a deal that wouldn't work for you.

  If you can't pay today for the funeral you want, then you can't afford it. Hundreds of consumers have called us over the years, upset that the funeral home won't set up a payment plan or that no charitable organization will pay for the final send-off "my mother deserved."A fancy funeral isn't an entitlement, and funeral homes have no obligation to take installment payments.

  If you can't afford the funeral you want, you can be creative. Choose a simple burial or cremation and put together a loving, personal memorial service. Have a potluck dinner at the family home, where everyone brings a dish and a story about the deceased. Call your clergy person to arrange a religious remembrance at your house of worship. Ask your intimate friends and family to work with you to put together a gathering for everyone. In all but eight states, a family can handle the entire affair, including preparing the body, without a funeral home.

  Note—Some funeral homes will refer you to loan agencies that do a quick turn-around, but these are almost always a bad deal. Such financing companies may charge ridiculous interest rates, draining your wallet for years after the burial.

- **You think funeral directors are security guards.** "Why can't we instruct the funeral home not to let Cousin George into the viewing? He never visited grandpa, he's awful to the rest of the family. . . ." It's surprising how many of these people have placed an obituary in the newspaper, *announcing calling hours.* A viewing or visitation announced in the paper is, by definition, a *public* event. If you don't want certain people showing up, don't tell the world about the event.

If you suspect that a troublemaking family member may show up anyway, be sure to alert the funeral home staff. There have been cases where the police had to be called because of an out-of-control attendee. If you suspect that will occur, talk to the staff and remember that it's the job of the police, not the funeral home, to handle the problem.

Another solution is to allow feuding sides of the family to have goodbye time with the deceased separately. A Vermont funeral director explains his method:

> It has been our policy not to accept responsibility for sorting out guests, as most of the time we wouldn't recognize the unwelcome person anyway. In situations like this, we ask that a family member (the bigger the better) be assigned to take care of watching for and warding off the unwelcome. That has worked really well. These families are often overflowing with contentious personalities, and finding someone for this duty is not usually very hard. It takes us completely out of it. We let them know that we can call the police for assistance if needed, but we stay out of it. My college bouncer days are well behind me.
>
> The separate visitation times has also worked well with feuding families. The unwelcome folks in question usually value some time alone with the deceased, more than being at the funeral with relatives they don't like, and it works out well for all.
>
> When making arrangements, we tell folks who want a private funeral that no matter who calls us for service info, they will be told the service is private, and no service time will be given out—even if they say they are family, because we have no idea who will consider themselves to be family. We refer them to the person in charge from the family for service details. In this way, the family is completely responsible for anyone who shows up.

- **You think Aunt Jane will look like Sleeping Beauty.** As Jessica Mitford wrote in *The American Way of Death*, "Few people die in the full bloom of health, unravaged by illness and unmarked by some disfigurement." Yet many families have complained about the appearance of the deceased. Some of these complaints are well-founded: failing to put in the dentures, obvious sutures leaking embalming fluid, eyes not fully closed. Even, in some extreme cases, maggots.

  That said, many factors affect how well an embalmer can present a body. Was the person emaciated or morbidly obese? What medications did he have in his system? Was the death physically traumatic? A sensitive funeral director will explain candidly what the family can expect and make recommendations.

We've seen some complaints, though, that are unrealistic. One woman wrote to FCA that the presentation of her "mother's body was less than perfect, which is unacceptable" and therefore "a sacrilege." Another family sent us color photos of their father's body, complaining that he looked awful. Of course, we didn't know what the gentleman looked like in life, but—as far as embalmed dead people go—he looked well-dressed and well-groomed. If the hairstyle is wrong, it can be fixed. But there's not much that can be done to avoid the distinctly funereal look of lying permanently on one's back.

- **You demand a pound of flesh for an ounce of sin.** Death is emotional, and funerals are deeply symbolic and important rituals for many people. But when funeral homes make mistakes—or even when they do wrong intentionally—customers should be sure the punishment they ask for fits the crime. One woman wrote to FCA with a complaint that contained what seemed to be some legitimate grievances. It looked as though the funeral home may have illegally substituted a cheaper casket and vault than the models the deceased had prepaid for. If true, that's plain old fraud, and the funeral home should be investigated by the state and fined sufficiently to deter that behavior.

  But the complainant went too far. The woman sought a full refund, criminal and civil charges against the funeral home, reimbursement to her and her four sisters for the time they spent compiling paperwork, the state stripping *every employee* of their licenses, and permanent closure of the funeral home. We think the funeral home (if guilty) should pay a hefty fine for the casket swap-out and should be placed on tight probation under the supervision of state regulators. But to call for every employee of the business to be de-licensed, and to have the whole enterprise closed by the state is unreasonable.

Most of the advice in this chapter is simple common sense, but worth emphasizing because funeral misdeeds can be so frustrating to deal with. A person you love has died, you are in a stressful situation dealing with friends and relatives, and you feel cheated by a professional to whom you are paying a lot of money. Then if you complain, government agencies may try to whitewash the misdeeds instead of helping you as a consumer. It's human nature to either give up (and perhaps stew about it for the rest of your life) or else go into a rage that can become less than completely rational.

At a time like that, try to stand back, take a deep breath, and act in a cool, methodical manner. That will give you the best chance of righting the wrong and of protecting other consumers from similar problems in the future.

Mortuary Education
A dead end

10

So you want to be a funeral director? Most states require that you pass the "National Board Exam" (NBE) first. To see what you will have to know, let's take a look at the study guide. It's put out by the International Conference of Funeral Service Examining Boards (ICFSEB). These are folks from around the country who sit on state funeral boards and are practicing funeral directors.

Study Guide for the Exam

We should mention first that some of the excerpts quoted in this chapter were earlier quoted in an article by Carlson in the FEO newsletter, and at that time a lawyer for ICFSEB wrote to complain that the quotations violated the Conference's copyright on the material. Carlson responded by noting that only very small portions of the material were quoted and that this was consistent with "Fair Use" because the context is criticism, which would be impossible without being able to quote the original source. If you are interested in that controversy, the exchange is posted at <http://www.funeralethics.org/newsletter>.

The purpose of the exam, according to the study guide, is to determine who meets the "MINIMUM qualifications to function as an entry level funeral director and/or embalmer." Here is a sampling from the Sociology section. The "correct" answers are in bold.

1. A funeral rite that in essence is devoid of religious connotation is known as:

   A. adaptive
   B. traditional
   C. humanistic
   D. memorial service

10. In a nuclear family, when the spouse dies, the surviving spouse:

   A. never marries

B. raises the children alone

C. depends on relatives to raise the children

D. returns to his or her family to let them raise the children.

11. A joint family would most likely be found in which of the following settings?

    A. metropolitan

    B. urban

    C. suburban

    D. rural

15. Which of the family types traditionally practices patriarchal governance?

    A. joint

    B. nuclear

    C. blended

    D. egalitarian

The first four questions in the history section are:

1. The first secular funeral director in the western world was:

    A. Praecio

    B. Libitina

    C. Kher-heb

    D. Litibinarius [*sic*] (apparent misspelling of Libitinarius)

2. Cremation first gained widespread acceptance and practice in:

    A. ancient Rome

    B. Hebrew lands

    C. ancient Greece

    D. Scandinavian countries

3. The Roman funeral was typically carried out by:

    A. the family

    B. the church

    C. Military legions

    D. public officials and paid secular functionaries

4. To keep down the cost of funerals in the Middle Ages, people often formed:

    A. Burial Clubs

    B. Church groups

    C. Memorial Societies

    D. Insurance Associations.

Now peek at the "Psychology and Counseling" section:

2. A person who expresses anxiety and discomfort while attending a visitation at a funeral home is most likely experiencing a/an:

A. inborn response
B. reaction displacement
C. conditioned response
D. delayed response

3. Which of the following is a determinant of grief?

A. feelings
B. concurrent stresses
C. behaviors
D. hostile reactions

6. According to Bowlby, attachments come from a need for:

A. sex
B. love
C. food and protection
D. safety and security

11. Psychology is defined as the study of:

A. emotion
B. human behavior
C. social groups
D. the mind

19. Which of the following acts of mourning is to experience the pain of loss?

A. First
B. Second
C. Third
D. Fourth

Would you feel reassured that a person is competent to handle a funeral of a loved family member based on ability to answer these questions? We'll stop quoting here, but the list goes on and on with questions that are equally useless, vague, badly worded, and/or irrelevant.

What's missing is coverage of the issues that really do matter. Only two superficial questions in the Funeral Law section mention the Federal Trade Commission's Funeral Rule, yet a violation of the Rule could result in a $16,000 fine. Knowledge of religious and cultural diversity? That might be handy, but it's not covered if your family is, say, Native American or from the continents of Asia or Africa. No ethics questions at all. No questions on who, other than next-of-kin, might have the legal authority to arrange a funeral, even though 40 states now have a designated-agent law. No questions on prepaid funerals. No contemporary cremation questions at a time when the cremation rate in some states is 50 percent or more.

Origins Veiled in Secrecy

How was the exam developed? On one page, the study guide refers to an organization with which it has had a somewhat rocky history: "All the questions . . . are linked . . . to the curriculum outline of the American Board of Funeral Service Education . . . ." ABFSE is a group that is made up of mortuary school educators who nudged the Conference out of the business of accrediting schools in the middle of the last century. ABFSE seems willing to let the Conference continue the testing, however.

On a subsequent page of the Study Guide, ICFSEB has lurched out in a totally different direction. "In order to determine what tasks the entry level funeral director and/or embalmer should be able to perform, a geographically diverse group of funeral directors and embalmers drew up an initial list of tasks which funeral directors and embalmers performed in the field.[1985]" The list was up-dated in 1991, 1998 and 2004, we are told. But who was in the group doing the drawing up and updating? When Michael LuBrant, director of the four-year mortuary program at the University of Minnesota asked ICFSEB to see the data in the process of his Ph.D. work on criteria for mortuary education, they declined to share their information. What legitimate educational organization would operate in such secrecy or be so fearful of academic scrutiny?

The other group, ABFSE, hides behind the same curtains. When Carlson was working on a cremation article for the FEO newsletter, "Lighting a Fire Under Mortuary Education" (see <http://www.funeralethics.org/spring05.pdf>), she asked to get a copy of the mortuary school curriculum. She was refused. Fortunately, in the process of surveying all the mortuary schools to see what they were teaching—or not—about cremation, one brave soul agreed to leak an extra copy. Out of over four hundred pages, only two cover cremation and cremation merchandise. Several schools gladly shared that they went way beyond what was required in the curriculum guide, and one provided an excellent outline of the course work covering cremation. Other schools simply acknowledged that they "teach to the exam."

Bad Reviews from Funeral Directors

What does go on in mortuary schools? When Carlson asked on a funeral directors' Internet discussion group, "How relevant was your mortuary education," she was not surprised to get answers like these : "Not relevant at all" . . . "Little to none. All they were good for was to pass the boards.". . .

"The focus was to get us prepared for the board exams. Since the school was owned by a chemical company the underlying focus was to feature their chemicals in classroom settings."... "The word 'cremation' rarely came up in classes."

A woman who later became a nurse described her mortuary education this way:

> Besides doing my own personal research into the development of the funeral industry in the United States, I attended courses in the Mortuary Science Department at San Antonio College in San Antonio, Texas. It was there that I got a behind-the-scenes look of the industry and what individuals wishing to become funeral directors were taught. It was during one of the first class meetings that the instructor stated, and I quote, "This is about making money off the dead, and if that is not what you are here for, you are in the wrong program." I was struck by his honesty but also tremendously shocked, disheartened and dismayed by the coldness of this statement. This was something that I had suspected but hoped against hope that I was wrong. As in the case of all industries in this country, the almighty dollar is the driving force of this one. In all of the courses I took, this remained quite apparent.

Another offered this commentary:

> The problem for me was that, for all of the time devoted to sales and marketing, not to mention discussions of ancient peoples' burial practices, the intricacies of tort law, and the utter dissection of Mitch Album's *Tuesdays With Morrie,* there also was almost no mention of any non-traditional family relationships. The typical "client" always seemed to be middle to upper-middle class, loved by all family members, straight, religious and "traditional" in that they wanted a conventional funeral service. Never mind the rest of us.
>
> The embalming instructor often stepped up on her soap box to proclaim that we were doing the most sacred work known to man and that respect for the deceased was the utmost responsibility of the embalmer. I wonder how she missed the idea that some people's idea of sacred and respectful did not include plunging a trocar into their heart and lungs? By not teaching, or even allowing the idea of natural death care into the classroom, and even worse, by coyly implying that unembalmed bodies were potentially menaces to society, she sends class after class of mortuary practitioners out into the field with no foundation or inclination to provide assistance in caring for an unembalmed body. This perpetuates the idea that it is illegal, because no funeral director wants to experiment or learn on

the job how this type of work should be done, so they say that it can not be done.

The one part of my mortuary education that bothers me the most is the fact that I had to go to those outside of the industry, to those who often oppose the practices of the industry, to learn how to care for families who come to me for help. There is no reason that the entire mortuary program, while it does a nice little dance around Judaism, Islam and Hinduism (all religions that specifically forbid embalming) in the religion course, could not include instruction on how to care for a body without embalming. The fact that the use of dry ice was a totally new concept to me when I saw it in the video "A Family Undertaking," as I was about to graduate from mortuary school, is deeply disconcerting to me.

Slocum has received similar reports at the FCA office. Several mortuary school students, apparently sensing something wasn't right, have contacted FCA to verify that what their instructors were telling them was true. One Texas student wrote asking for all the materials pertaining to the Federal Trade Commission's Funeral Rule. He said he was learning precious little about it in his mortuary law class and felt a duty to understand it before he went into business. Would that his instructors felt the same. Another student claimed the mortuary law teacher (are you detecting a pattern?) stated that *failing to embalm* a body was considered "abuse of a corpse" and grounds for a lawsuit against the funeral home. Baffled, the student asked, "Shouldn't it be the other way around, with the family's permission required before embalming?" Well, yes.

Mortuary education today seems a little like incest with unwilling partners, partners who have no idea how to talk to each other, and both of whom seem stuck in practices and ideas that are 40 years out of date. Mortuary schools have little choice but to teach the prescribed material, no matter how irrelevant it may be. In order to be accredited by ABFSE, 60 percent of a mortuary school's students must pass the ICFSEB exam on the first try. It's no wonder schools are teaching to the exam, and—in some cases—ignoring any other curriculum requirements that might improve their graduates' ability to perform well in the field.

In addition to the National Board Exam, the ICFSEB website states, "The Conference provides administrative support for some state examinations." Vermont is among the 16 states listed, and Carlson was eager to see what kind of state exam the Conference was giving to Vermonters. So she asked the Funeral Board administrator to request a copy of the exam. The Conference refused. One suspects it is the same exam that is given under the NBE title, as that is the only study guide suggested to students.

In other words, Vermont's Board of Funeral Service requires new funeral director applicants to pass a test it has never seen in order to be licensed in the state of Vermont. What sense does that make? (Other states for which ICFSEB says it has state exams are Alabama, Alaska, Arizona, Hawaii, Idaho, Louisiana, Mississippi, North Carolina, Nevada, Ohio, Oregon, South Carolina, Tennessee, Texas, and Washington.)

Recommendations

Ideas on how to improve mortuary education, at least in any detail, would be beyond the scope of this book. But it clearly serves no public purpose to just require a little jargon and sales techniques to convince families in grief to part with more of their money. States should be encouraged to eliminate mortuary school, at least in its present form, and the NBE as licensing requirements. A good liberal arts education, a one-year internship, and a real state-generated exam make far more sense. At the very least, any trade school purporting to prepare students for the contemporary, real-world funeral business should focus much more attention on the Funeral Rule, cremation procedures, the legal rights of consumers and their designated agents, preparation and presentation of bodies without chemical embalming, and the growing interest in natural burials.

Home Funerals
A returning tradition

11

ALTHOUGH FIRM STATISTICS ARE HARD to come by, home funerals, once the standard practice in America, are making a comeback.

This is a recent phenomenon. When Carlson's first book, *Caring For Your Own Dead*, was published in 1987, her mission to alert the public that they had a right to take funerals back into the family was met with near-universal shock and derision. She recalls appearing on the Phil Donahue show (the most-watched talk show at that time) just after the book was published:

> Donahue had not read the book, and his staffers had equated my ideas with the funeral kooks. I mean, I was on his show with the mummification people [Summum, a "religious" nonprofit in Utah that will mummify you for $67,000]. The poor funeral director from the National Funeral Directors Association, sent to represent the industry, sat there ramrod straight and wide-eyed, not sure what to say. The audience took Donahue's lead—he clearly thought he had a bunch of weirdos on his hands, including me, because he sneered about "schlepping dead bodies around in pickup trucks."

Carlson managed to soften Donahue a little after he learned that she knew one of his heroes, Jessica Mitford, and after she discussed the historical traditions of caring for the dead. In fact, Donahue later invited Carlson back for a second appearance to discuss how families can save money by taking on some of the aspects of funeral care themselves. But the initial reaction was telling.

"Back in those days, we couldn't give the book away to hospice. We thought that was a perfectly logical extension of the hospice ideal and a logical audience for the book," Carlson recalled. "But the national hospice organization wanted nothing to do with it. A minister, chairman of my local hospice's education committee, refused to accept a gift copy of the book, claiming 'nobody would be interested in that'."

John Blake, executive director of the Continental Association of Funeral and Memorial Societies (CAFMS, the organization that later became

Funeral Consumers Alliance) approved of the idea of giving consumers an inexpensive way to bypass dealings with the commercial funeral industry, but many local funeral consumer organizations around the country were wary of or indifferent to the idea of families caring for their own dead.

"John liked it, but I quickly found I was considered a freak," Carlson said. "I simply soft-pedaled it in my relationship with the funeral societies. But many of them came to appreciate the legal information on a wide variety of funeral issues. Once I got involved in funeral consumer advocacy, I became interested in the rights of *all* consumers, not just the do-it-yourselfers. And because of that, the legal research for the 1998 version of the book was much broader. I figured that even some home funerals will involve working with the industry to a degree, and you damned well better know what your rights are when you do."

Progress in helping people to understand the home death-care movement has been substantial. The "green funeral" movement, discussed later in this book, has worked its way into American culture, aided by such events as a moving natural-burial scene in the television series "Six Feet Under."

Yet as recently as December of 2005, a major television pundit, Keith Olbermann, decided that Carlson was that day's "Worst Person in the World." Olbermann's verdict was based on an inaccurate four-paragraph news story describing her goal of establishing a memorial park that would include opportunities for green burial by families caring for their own dead. Olbermann's off-the-wall description went like this:

> That's right: families could go dig their own graves, for their own loved ones. No fuss, no muss, no caskets, no embalming. Just bring your own shovels, and fill 'er up.

There was some obvious intent of humor in Olbermann's comments on a slow news day when he couldn't think of anything more horrible than letting families care for their dead in an environmentally sound manner, and, of course, Carlson took it in that spirit. But clearly we had, and still have, a long way to go in getting the message across that there is nothing the least bit bizarre about families wanting to say goodbye to loved ones in a more personal way than just writing a big check to a funeral director.

The authors of this book strongly advocate the right of families to care for their own dead and we are pleased to see the resurgence of interest and acceptance of this tradition. But because our modern society has lost the common knowledge of how to care for the dead, it may be particularly difficult for many people to go through that learning curve at a time of immense grief. It is, therefore, encouraging to see the emergence of a new group of helping professionals and volunteers serving as home funeral guides.

The practical details of caring for the dead—filing death certificates, moving the body, etc.—are discussed in Part 2 of this book, beginning with the necessary general information followed by the specifics for each state.

Home Funeral Guides

Most funeral directors say they entered the field to help people manage one of the most difficult times of their lives, and we think most of them mean that sincerely. Home funeral guides say much the same thing, but they have a very different idea of how to help the grieving. These women (almost all of the ones we know about are women) universally express a desire to *empower* families to make their own decisions. They don't want to *direct* the funeral; they want to ensure that the family has the practical knowledge they need to direct it themselves. In contrast to the conventional funeral industry, much of which is still reluctant to give consumers truthful information, home funeral guides are among the best sources of accurate information on funeral options and families' legal rights.

We refer to these women as home funeral guides, although not all of them go by that title. Some call themselves death midwives, some consultants, and some have not adopted a title of any kind, but "home funeral guides" seems like the best generic description.

Jerrigrace Lyons of northern California is the *grande dame* of the home funeral guides. One of the first people in the country to put herself in the public eye as a death midwife and home funeral educator in the 1990s, Lyons has conducted workshops around the country training people on everything from the practicalities to the (in her view) spiritual aspects of home funerals. She founded *Final Passages* in 1995 after her friend Carolyn Whiting died. While Carolyn's death was unexpected, she'd thought about her funeral in advance and left detailed instructions to her friends requesting a mortuary-free funeral at home. Since then, Final Passages has helped more than 150 families bury their dead privately, and the group offers seminars for health-care workers, complete with state-required continuing education credits.

Beth Knox of Maryland founded *Crossings* after her daughter was killed by an airbag in a low-speed car wreck. She describes it as follows:

> She left suddenly twelve years ago at the age of seven. When the life support at the hospital was about to be removed, I was told that the hospital could only release her to a funeral home. I had given birth to her. She had lived with me every day of her life. I had carefully chosen what she was exposed to, what she ate, where she went to school. I was required by law to care well for her. But now that her heart had stopped beating, I was being told that her care was no longer my concern.

As it turns out, the hospital was wrong. I had the legal right to care for my daughter, but I didn't find that out until later. In the meantime, I found a funeral home that was willing to "pick her up" but then bring her directly to our home. (I later found out that I had the right to transport her in the van in which I had driven her to school each day. I was not required by law to call a funeral home at all.) I cared for her at home for three days, bathing her, watching her, taking in slowly the painful reality that she has passed from this life, and sharing my grief with her classmates and brothers and grandparents and our wonderful community of friends, before finally letting go of her body.

Now an educator and advocate, Knox teaches the things she didn't know until it was too late. According to her website, at <www.crossings.net>:

We are a home funeral and green burial resource center—particularly educating the family to act as funeral director—which is legal in almost all 50 States. We do this through:

Education—letting families know that they are THE decision-makers in after-death care and can exercise choices that will bring about greater healing.

Information—making information available on the exact choices available to you in creating a better experience in after-death care whether working with or without a funeral director.

Support from Enlightened Funeral Directors

Until the early 2000s, Lyons and Knox were the only prominent names in this new field. As of 2011, <homefuneraldirectory.com> lists more than 60 individual consultants, support groups, and organizations nationwide that give advice on home funerals. To our great pleasure, a few brave funeral directors are among them. It's not easy for an undertaker to rebel against the industry climate of fear and territorialism, but if home funerals are to become anything more than a secretive "fringe" option, forward-thinking funeral directors need to take up the banner.

Char Barrett is one such pioneer. A relentlessly upbeat businesswoman in Seattle, Barrett runs a funeral business specializing in home funerals. She came to the field in a roundabout way. Interested in hospice work after her father's death, Barrett was surprised by a friend's suggestion that she become a funeral director.

"I resisted at first, then I researched it. I didn't want to leave Seattle to get a degree, but I did get my associate's degree in mortuary science," said Barrett. The worst part, she said, was the requirement to practice embalming:

I had to, which was absolutely traumatic to me. I had to do so to meet degree requirements. Literally in a 2-year degree, I spent a whole year learning about embalming. And the rest of the classes—understanding grief and loss—anything about the role of a funeral director was a *quarter* of the classes. It's ridiculous how weighted the curriculum is to embalming. But I have to say, having gone through that, I can stand toe to toe with the rest of these guys. I can say "Hey, I've been through this, I know what embalming's about."

While Barrett will do a conventional funeral for anyone who requests it, most of her clients don't want a "one-of-everything" affair. Whether a family hires her for consultation and paperwork only, or whether they ask her to help put back together a disfigured victim of a car accident, Barrett says her place is to do just what—and no more than—a family wants and needs.

Some Funeral Directors Find It Good for Business

Some more conventional funeral directors, too, are sensitive to the needs of home-funeral families and will work with them to provide as much, or as little, service as they want. Indeed, it's good for business. Peter Stefan of Worcester, Massachusetts, relates that he got several full-service, quite profitable funerals from one extended family after helping one of them perform a home funeral for a minimal cost.

Randy Garner placed the following on his funeral home's website:

We realize that in Vermont, there is no requirement that you use a funeral director or funeral home provided merchandise or that you conform to a set of pre-determined packages or options. We recognize the value of family involvement in any portion of the death care and funeral process and will do our best to make sure that our charges are an accurate reflection of the duties you specifically ask us to perform.

Interest in home funerals has hit critical mass: The first national conference for home-funeral guides took place in Boulder, Colorado in October, 2009. Organized by Karen van Vuuren of Natural Transitions, a 501(c)(3) educational nonprofit, the meeting attracted 40 participants from around the country. She described the meeting as a first step toward building a national alliance of home funeral advocates.

There was consensus on one thing: Well-meaning people have to stand up more assertively for the right to choose a home funeral if advocates are to prevent the commercial industry from using state legislatures to shut the movement down.

"It's not just about protecting a family's rights, but protecting their rights to *choose the resources that support that choice*," said van Vuuren.

Van Vuuren and funeral director Char Barrett (with help from many others) launched the National Home Funeral Alliance in 2010, the first nonprofit group specifically devoted to protecting the rights of families to keep the funeral in their hands. One of NHFA's first projects will be a position paper, co-written with Funeral Consumers Alliance, laying out model state laws and guidelines. NHFA debuted at the 2010 home funeral conference in Boulder, which saw double the attendance over the year before. A code of ethics is on their website at <http://homefuneralalliance.org>.

Unlike conventional funeral homes, home funeral guides have no over-priced coffins to sell. They don't embalm, and they repudiate mortuary mythology. Home funeral guides charge various prices, but they're substantially lower than the average "get in the door" basic services fee at most funeral homes ($1,500 or more is typical at the mortuary). Beth Knox's Crossings is a nonprofit that works on donations and promises to help anyone in need. Home funeral guide Mary Kateada offers a free consultation, then asks for $25 to $35 an hour depending on how involved the family wants her to be. Holly Stevens, cofounder of the Funeral Consumers Alliance in Greensboro, NC, put together an amazingly comprehensive website and a free downloadable book at <www.undertakenwithlove.org>.

The Industry Fights Back

How much of a threat to consumers is a middle-aged woman giving a public talk at the library, telling people how to file a death certificate, how to wash and diaper the dead for a home wake, and the best way to put the body in a homemade coffin without straining your back? To Oregon State Senator Vicki Walker, such a woman is a menace indeed. In 2009, Walker drafted a bill that contained a provision requiring "death care consultants" to get a state license:

> Regardless of any title used by the individual, an individual practices as a death care consultant if the individual offers, for payment, consultations or workshops to individuals or groups regarding funeral or final disposition services.

In plain English, anyone who takes even a dollar in exchange for explaining how to arrange a memorial service, how to navigate a funeral home's price list, or the cremation process, would need a state license. One can immediately see how clergy, secular celebrants, or officiants-for-hire, even consumer advocacy groups, could run afoul of the law. One estate-planning lawyer called Slocum in shock at the idea that his law degree and specialization in end-of-life planning would be considered insufficient.

Given the widespread lack of knowledge about the funeral industry and its effect on the public—not to mention the knee-jerk response provoked whenever anyone utters the dreaded words "dead body" or "funeral"—lawmakers easily passed it and the governor signed it.

The bill included no guidance on how death care consultants (DCCs) should be licensed or even what criteria the state should use. It simply gave the Oregon Mortuary and Cemetery Board—the agency that regulates the conventional high-cost death industry—the power to set its own standards without even giving those to be regulated any representation on the board.

Sen. Walker never responded to a detailed letter of concern Slocum sent on behalf of Funeral Consumers Alliance. FCA pointed out the obvious constitutional issues that arise when a state requires a license in order for a citizen to engage in free speech. Slocum also noted how strange it was to want to crack down on private citizens whose entire mission was to empower and educate grieving consumers and to demystify the funeral process so families might protect themselves from commercial abuse.

The state board's executive director put together an advisory committee that included two home funeral guides. But the rules drafted by the committee were ignored, and the executive director submitted her own to the board. No education was required for these new licensees, there was no description of the exam they would have to pass, no professional standards spelled out. But authors and those who gave workshops were excluded. Several home funeral guides quickly decided to offer their services for free, payment being the primary trigger for licensing. (Read the Oregon chapter for the adventures Carlson had flying to Oregon to take the DCC exam.)

A Close Call in Colorado

Things almost went very badly in Colorado, too. Karen van Vuuren, a soft-spoken English expatriate, feared she'd be barred by law from helping families when state representative Nancy Todd, a former schoolteacher, introduced House Bill 1202. Todd claimed she was alarmed that Colorado was the only state that didn't regulate the funeral industry, a legitimate concern. But she consulted exclusively with the Colorado Funeral Directors Association and ignored letters from Funeral Consumers Alliance urging her to amend the bill's overly broad language. The original version appeared to bar anyone from offering advice on arranging a funeral unless that person had thousands of hours of experience in the conventional funeral industry—an inappropriate requirement for people like van Vuuren, whose mission is to help families *avoid* formaldehyde.

"We are being brought under the auspices of controlling bodies who don't really understand who we are and are trying to regulate us like we're mortuaries," van Vuuren said.

Representative Todd fell for scare tactics too. She told a television news reporter she was alarmed that home funerals were legal, because, she mused, what was to stop someone from killing grandma and burying her quietly in the backyard? (A total non-sequitur, as funeral directors have no role to play in deterring murder coverups. That's why we have death certificates, burial transit permits, and autopsy requirements for suspicious deaths.)

Fortunately, the final version of the bill that passed exempted nonprofit organizations from the requirements imposed on commercial mortuaries, but it still appears to prevent people like van Vuuren from so much as touching a body to help a private family lift it into a casket. Though the amended bill was better than the original, she said it was far from perfect.

"I think it remains to be seen [how the new law will affect groups like ours]," said van Vuuren. "The amendment that went in, I didn't want it to just refer to nonprofits [but] it was a total last minute thing."

In Pennsylvania, Reverend Lynn Acquafondata, who serves as an "end-of-life guide" offering grief support, was paid a visit by the investigator for the State Funeral Board. Afterward she wrote:

> I was able to get a *pro bono* lawyer who is doing an excellent job. She met with me when I talked to the state investigator. Some of his questions were friendly, some hostile. He does not make the decision, only presents the facts to the board of funeral directors. At the end he mentioned that he is a funeral director himself.

Acquafondata's focus is on the spiritual aspects at a time of death. Although she does have information about biodegradable caskets and shrouds on her website, the website states clearly that she does not do the things that funeral directors do such as washing and transporting bodies. She notes that families can do those things for themselves.

When Phyllis Ingold and her sister had a home funeral for their mom, a policeman arrived at their door, "because I hear there's a dead person here." Two weeks later, Phyllis received a letter from the lawyer for the Pennsylvania Funeral Board, accusing her of behavior for which she had to be licensed as a funeral director, citing occupational code. He stated that, while the investigation was closed without action, any "future complaints of this nature" would result in a $10,000 fine. Phyllis, of course, had no intention of going into the funeral business. Neither did Rabbi Wasserman in the Pittsburgh area, when he helped members of his congregation with funerals as part of Jewish tradition. He, too, has been paid a visit by the Board's inspector.

It seems most likely that these complaints have come from those in the industry. When Carlson sent an e-mail to John Eirkson, president of PFDA, offering to set up a continuing ed course on home funerals and what PA law permitted, she got no response. It certainly paints the Pennsylvania undertakers as mean-spirited and lacking the traits typically cultivated—compassion and understanding.

Cracks in the Dam

We worry that the events in Oregon and Colorado—and maybe Pennsylvania—are the cracks in the dam that will unleash a flood of misguided state laws that could stifle the growing home-funeral movement.

We've certainly seen no evidence of harm to consumers from home funeral guides. And it's unclear what harm such laws would seek to prevent anyway. The philosophy underlying the Federal Trade Commission's Funeral Rule is the recognition that the real harm to consumers comes in the form of emotional manipulation that costs grieving people a great deal of money. Over and over again, we've seen instances of funeral directors who make up non-existent laws about the necessity for embalming or sealing caskets, who pressure the grieving into believing that the more money they spend, the more effective "grief-therapy" they will receive. State regulation, however, is still mired in the outmoded propaganda that undertakers are a vital part of "protecting the public health" and that only those with a degree in mortuary "science" could be trusted to handle the dead.

Pros and Cons of Regulation

The question of regulation—whether home funeral guides should be licensed or whether there should be required training—remains more divisive. We e-mailed or called several home funeral guides to ask their opinions. The women who responded made valid points for and against the idea of regulation. Here's a sampling (we've condensed some responses):

> I myself am torn on the issue of regulation. There is no problem, of course, as long as money is not involved in the relationship between guide and client. *Undertaken With Love* is squeaky clean in this regard as nobody is earning anything from our project; any small donations we get go right back in to our education efforts. . . . I'm not saying home funeral guides ought not to charge for their services, but once money enters the picture, two areas of concern arise. Home funeral educators become vulnerable to funeral industry assertions that they are practicing funeral service without a license because of the vague and broad definitions of funeral service in most states' statutes. Also, the practice of home funeral guiding itself, if it ever is seen to be lucrative, will lure those who are motivated primarily by greed rather than by service. . . .
>
> — *Holly Stevens, FCA of the Piedmont (North Carolina), author of Undertaken With Love*

I know that in Oregon, the idea of licensing was not well received by all of the women. I believe only three women were supportive and that was because they thought they could be a part of creating the licensing test or regulations. I highly doubt that they would be allowed much input on this.

—*Jerrigrace Lyons, Final Passages*

Do we need regulating? I haven't explored this fully, but my gut says yes we do. I feel it would bring recognition, credibility, legitimacy, but I would only want it if it would not curtail family rights. I just have to compare it to, for example, the home birth movement. In Colorado, they were underground, but they were serving a need. Then they bit the bullet and became registered with the state. [Regulation or licensure] is protectionist to a degree, but it is protectionist toward the consumer. . . . It's definitely a hard thing, regulation. It's not as if it's clear it's absolutely the right thing to do. . . .

— *Karen van Vuuren, Natural Transitions*

The authors are undecided on the question of regulating home funeral guides. The traditional legal trigger for licensure has been whether someone takes money in exchange for hands-on services such as moving or washing the body. Recognizing the vulnerability and lack of knowledge most families have when it comes to buying funeral services, there's an argument to be made for seeing that as a reasonable "bright line" test.

By comparison, most states require licensing of electricians and plumbers. You can wire your own outlets and snake your own drain—the licensing requirement kicks in if you charge money to do these things for others. After all, as a botched wiring job could set a house on fire and an incompetent plumber could leave a basement swimming in sewage. An "incompetent" home funeral guide can't make Grandpa any more dead than he already is. And nearly every state requires unnecessary training in embalming, casket-merchandising, and the trappings of the costly "traditional funeral," in order to be licensed. Neither consumers nor home funeral guides would be well-served by these sales-oriented "educational" rules.

Funeral directors, of course, have complained about death midwives, asking "Why don't they have to get a license before they haul bodies and perform wakes, just like I do?" Well, death midwives don't belong to an industry that has taken massive economic advantage of the bereaved, they don't lie about the legal or health necessity of embalming, and they don't manipulate the legislative system to shut down consumer choice.

It's also true that building professional organizations of home funeral guides, and perhaps creating a separate licensing or registration system, could increase public awareness of and confidence in home funeral care as a legitimate option. But the analogy with actual midwifery goes only so far; there are real potential medical dangers to mothers and infants during birth. There is no such danger when the client is already dead. Moreover, nearly every trade that organizes and strives for legal recognition as a profession ends up using its clout to raise prices and shut out competition through bogus legal restrictions. No one doubts the good intentions of the pioneering women in this project, but neither is anyone immune to the seductions of exclusivity and prestige.

Entrepreneurs in the home-funeral field who haven't done their homework could also spark a regulatory backlash that could endanger the rights of ordinary citizens to care for their own dead. One woman from Georgia wrote to Carlson to say she "quickly" needed to know the laws in her state, as she was setting up a home funeral business—not exactly confidence-inspiring. A Vermont man set up a website selling "green" funeral services with no apparent knowledge that he needed a funeral director's license to sell his services in transporting bodies and filing legal paperwork for customers. While the "educational" requirements for an undertaker's license are questionable, it's no good to flout the law and provoke a crackdown.

Given the momentum behind the home funeral movement, it seems inevitable these issues will be debated by regulators and legislatures around the country. We have every reason to worry that funeral trade groups will do everything in their power to marginalize or shut down those who offer home funeral services. It will be crucial for home funeral guides, consumer advocates, and interested citizens to be on guard against such attacks.

Home Funerals without Guides

We've focused much of this chapter on home funeral guides because they play an increasingly important role and because of the controversies about state regulation. In closing, it's appropriate to remind readers that in the past, most families handled most deaths themselves without funeral directors or guides.

Although managing death is no longer part of the common knowledge of our culture, families still have the right to do so in most states, and most are more than capable of handling all requirements themselves. But for some, at a time of intense grief, an experienced guide can help with the process, and we find that movement to be constructive and encouraging.

Green Burial
What they used to just call "burial"

12

IT'S AMUSING HOW OFTEN JOURNALISTS call the Funeral Consumers Alliance wanting hear about "that new kind of burial." What's become known as "green burial" is what people throughout history have called, simply, burial. It involves laying the body in the earth without chemical embalming, a metal casket, or a vault. Our ancestors from the late 19th century and further back would recognize it; devout Jews and Muslims still practice it.

But the full-service formaldehyde funeral has been the new "normal" for more than a century, so getting society to think outside the box isn't easy. Consumers and reporters often ask "Is green burial allowed in my state?" This question presumes that one needs the law's permission to skip embalming, steel caskets, and burial vaults. In fact, no state laws require embalming or the use of a coffin or outer burial container as a condition of burial (though many cemeteries have policies that require vaults).

Interest in green burial is growing, and so is the number of cemeteries that allow it. Anyone considering green burial, however, will have to contend with the growing pains of this "new" idea that's beginning to make headway into the staid burial business. While the funeral industry as a whole seems more welcoming to green burial than it was to cremation 30 years ago, undertakers and cemeteries in many areas know little about it—or write it off as an affectation confined to "liberal tree-huggers" on the coasts.

And while green burial would seem intuitively to be cheaper than a conventional funeral, some green cemeteries charge premium prices, as their primary goal is to conserve virgin land, and that takes money. The American entrepreneurial impulse is having its effect too, with manufacturers and vendors hawking all manner of "sustainably sourced" wood coffins and the like at *boutique* prices. If you're not careful, your low-carbon-footprint, back-to-nature burial might cost as much as a conventional funeral.

Everything Old is New Again

As it was with cremation, the United Kingdom is ahead of the US when it comes to green burial. As of this writing, there are more than 200 "woodland burial grounds" in the UK. No agency keeps track of all so-called green cemeteries in the US; we found about 30 in our research. That number may be out of date by the time you read this. A good place to look for information is the Green Burial Council's website, <www.greenburialcouncil.org>.

Green burial grounds can be quite different from each other. Some are parcels of virgin land operated so as to ensure indigenous plants and wildlife are not disturbed; think of them as nature preserves. Others are a bit less strict, and still others are conventional cemeteries that have set aside parcels where coffin-less burial is permitted. What they have in common is that they don't permit embalming, a vault, or a non-degradable coffin.

Billy Campbell a small-town doctor in Westminster, South Carolina, and his wife, Kimberly, a British expatriate, are pioneers in the green burial movement. Billy first wrote about the idea in a local environmentalist magazine in 1988. That germ of an idea grew into the opening of Ramsey Creek Preserve in 1998, the first natural burial ground in the US. See <www.memorialecosystems.com>. By all accounts, the rural land with a creek running through it is breathtakingly beautiful and peaceful.

Billy first started thinking about the connection between death and environmentalism in college. By the early 1990s, he said, "If you got more than three drinks in me at a party I'd go on and on about it . . . . Kimberly told me I should stop talking about it and do it." While intensely interested in conserving open land, Billy is quick to point out that that doesn't mean keeping *people* out—quite the opposite.

"I think we have this idea that land is just something we use, that it's just a backdrop for recreation," he said. "I think there was something really missing when we urbanized in the last century. There [were, historically,] families who really loved their land and felt connected to it. I think we lost that."

Marrying burial with protection of the natural landscape seemed like a sensible way to restore some of that connection. Interestingly, this is a contemporary extension of what was known as the rural cemetery movement in the 19th century, a time when cemeteries were moved to the suburbs and designed to include rolling hills, trees, and *charm*. Proponents hoped families would enjoy the landscape and see the burial grounds as a place to stroll and to picnic, not merely as an overcrowded repository for the dead.

Obstacles to Green Burial

Those ideas had lost currency by the 1990s, and there was a great deal of suspicion when the Campbells first opened Ramsey Creek. "Some people went so far as to say we were actually throwing bodies in Ramsey Creek or feeding them to the buzzards," Billy said, laughing as he recalled it. "But it's no longer cool to make fun of Ramsey Creek around here, since you might know someone who's buried here!"

The idea has met with even more suspicion elsewhere. In what we hope will remain a unique example of hysteria, Bibb County Georgia became the first municipality in the country to ban simple, cost-effective, environmentally friendly burials. The supreme irony of Bibb County's 2008 ordinance was that it was enacted, supporters claimed, to *protect the environment*. Misinformation and fear ran amok when residents Beth Collins and Jim Wood announced plans to open a green cemetery on a 58-acre parcel they owned. Despite having already given Collins and Wood a permit for this use, county commissioners back-pedaled and enacted an ordinance that:

- Requires all bodies to be inside "leak-proof" caskets and vaults, though no such products exist. In fact, it's a violation of the Funeral Rule for undertakers to make such claims about their products.

- Requires all burials to be 1,000 feet from water, which is also impossible, as one will almost certainly hit water if drilling straight down that far.

- Requires all new cemeteries to be walled off to keep out "wild animals." How a wall will stop birds and groundhogs from getting in—or why anyone would want to—is unclear.

- Requires families to buy an "appropriate" and "permanent" grave marker, a bizarre reaction to the practice of using indigenous stones (or no marker at all) at green burial sites.

- Bans private burial on family land, and requires a funeral director to oversee all deaths from "communicable disease." (The flu is communicable, yet we don't require families to hire a registered nurse whenever little Johnny comes down with it).

What was Bibb County so afraid of? We can't be sure, since county officials never responded to a seven-page letter from Funeral Consumers Alliance outlining the logical and legal problems with the new green burial ban. But it's a safe bet that misplaced fears and myths about the "contagion" from dead bodies overtook common sense.

A surprising number of people treat dead bodies as if they were one-person Superfund sites, ready to leak dreaded contaminants into the ground water. Until 2010, the Vermont Veterans' Memorial Cemetery actually required all bodies to be embalmed, out of concern for groundwater quality. That's right—the state supposed that burying carcinogenic formaldehyde close to the town wells was a safer idea than letting people decay naturally.

This becomes even more puzzling when you take a drive out to the (quite beautiful) cemetery itself; dairy cows are pastured directly across the street, but no one seems worried about water "contaminated" with cow flops.

But the unembalmed and uncoffined dead pose no danger to the living. Disease-causing organisms die with the person. As a writer for the Pan-American Health Organization noted, "The microorganisms that are involved in decomposition are not the kind that cause disease."

Cost, Conscience, and Greenwashing

In our capitalist nation, vendors like nothing better than coming up with something "new and improved"—with a suitably upgraded price. This is a particular concern when it comes to green burial and the stodgy conventional funeral industry.

To give credit where it's due, funeral directors as a whole have been much more welcoming of green burial than they were of cremation when it started gaining popularity. For 30 years undertakers fought cremation with every weapon at their disposal (some going so far as to show families gruesome pictures of actual bodies on fire). By comparison, today, the funeral trade magazines talk about green burial regularly and invite experts to their trade conferences, despite continued skepticism in many areas.

But consumers need to be wary. Funeral homes realize that green burial could threaten their cash flow if they don't handle it carefully. After all, green burial is about what you *don't buy*. Cross off the metal casket and go for a shroud, skip the embalming and use dry ice instead, and forget that bronze-lined burial vault. A boon for your wallet, but not for the mortician's wallet. Expect that some funeral homes will start marketing green burial as a premium service with a premium price, perhaps by appealing to your sense of doing right by the environment. It makes sense to ask, "Why am I paying you more money for fewer products and services?"

There's a hint of fear, perhaps bordering on desperation, lurking behind some of the more fanciful ads in the funeral trade magazines—green burial isn't a welcome development for companies that make their living selling boxes for burning and burial. Matthews International, maker of crematory equipment and monuments, took out a full-color ad featuring a wooded glade and the improbable assertion that "Taking Care of the Environment Is In Our Nature." The ad copy goes on, "Our latest advancement in technology, the M-pyre system, lowers fuel consumption, reduces emissions and increases performance of cremation equipment." Which is all well and good but not likely to win over those who object on principle to the energy and emissions associated with cremation.

Wilbert, one of the largest vault-makers, is straining even harder with an ad that reads, "Concrete Burial Vaults—a Natural Choice?"

> You may not think of a traditional ground burial as being green. But there are steps you can take—beginning with the use of a lined

concrete burial vault—to make ground burial more environmentally friendly. . . .A lined concrete vault also protects the environment by preventing chemicals from escaping the vault's interior and seeping into the earth.

The *piece de resistance* comes at the end:

At the same time, it helps protect a family's loved one nestled inside by helping resist the entry of outside elements. Isn't it nice to know families can protect their loved one *and* the environment? **Now that's something to think about.**

Indeed it is.

You can't consume your way to conservation, and you shouldn't have to spend more in order to waste less. When author Mark Harris called Slocum during the research phase for his book *Grave Matters*, he wanted advice for his chapter on caskets. "What's the greenest casket you can buy?" he asked. Slocum replied, "The greenest casket you can buy is the one you *don't* buy."

There are all manner of "green" coffins coming on the market—made of recycled paper, sustainably harvested woven willow, etc.—but some of them are imported from overseas. How "green" is it to have something flown in for your funeral on a jet? And the cost? The "Ecopod"—which looks like a cross between a willow seed and a science fiction hibernation chamber—retails for several thousand dollars. A homemade box from local scrap lumber might be more appealing to both environmentalists and the budget-minded.

If the funeral home you're considering offers green burial, a quick way to gauge whether the price is reasonable is to compare it to the charge for immediate burial (which is, after all, basically a green burial). We see no reason why a green burial package ought to cost any more than an immediate burial unless you request extra services or merchandise.

Joe Sehee, Executive Director of the Green Burial Council, says he is concerned about "greenwashing"—tarting up products and services as environmentally sound when they aren't. He formed the GBC in 2005 to set standards for green cemeteries, and quickly found a need to make inroads with funeral homes, too. "The original idea was to set standards just for burial grounds, but we realized this wasn't going to get any traction if the funeral service industry wasn't on board," he said. "If you didn't have people willing to handle un-embalmed bodies, how were you going to do green burial?"

The GBC began recruiting funeral homes to build a network of "approved providers," but many mortuaries turned out to be green in name only. Carlson investigated some of them for her FEO newsletter in the fall of 2008, and found funeral homes requiring embalming after 24 hours, listing steel caskets as "protective" (implicitly discouraging green burial), and charging far more for green burial than for comparable simple options.

Sehee argued that the GBC didn't want to "set the bar too high" at first, considering how skittish funeral homes are about anything unconventional. Better to get a foot in the door and raise the standards in increments, he said. He was, however, alarmed at what Carlson found.

"That was a real opportunity for a teachable moment, and I appreciate Lisa for that, even though I wish it was a little less public and painful," he chuckled to Slocum afterward. "That actually had a huge impact on how we're evaluating funeral homes now."

But Carlson still found vetting problems in January 2011, two years later. A quick check of three states found that in Virginia, two of the three "approved" funeral homes have nothing "green" on their websites. No prices are listed on the one "green" funeral home site, but prices are sky high at the others. One has a "Basic Burial Package" starting at $7,060.

Twelve were "approved" in Pennsylvania. Two had green information but no prices. Another had green packages—for burial at $4,725 and for cremation (hardly green) for $4,520. Eight had no green information at all, but five of those posted the GBC logo, and one had a bad web link

New Jersey had eleven "approved" funeral homes. Fertig and Prout Funeral Homes did a fairly nice job of describing green options but disclosed no prices. Another offered a natural burial package at $5,685, with embalming, although that may be with one of the new formaldehyde-free chemicals. The web links were broken for two funeral homes, and another had no web presence. The other five mention nothing about green burials.

In short, consumers need to do their own green rating. FEO has a checklist for this at <http://www.funeralethics.org/green.htm>.

Once you find green options, how much do they cost? All cemeteries—green or not—charge different prices. Whole-body burial at Ramsey Creek will cost $2,500, comparable to the charge at many commercial cemeteries but higher than some. Billy Campbell points out, however, that families are free to act as their own funeral directors and dig the graves themselves, avoiding a bill from the funeral home that could otherwise add thousands to the bill. Burial at Greensprings Natural Cemetery in upstate New York will run you $1,450 for a whole-body burial. If shopping around, don't forget to check your local rural or municipal cemeteries. Some of them, especially in small communities, will gladly let you bury without a coffin or vault, and may charge less than $1,000 for a grave. In addition, we're seeing more municipal cemeteries setting aside sections for natural burial, and we expect this mainstreaming of green burial will continue.

Green Alternatives to Cremation

Two new methods of body disposition, described as gentler on the environment than cremation, are making headlines: *Promession* and *alkaline hydrolysis.* It's unclear whether either one will catch on, though Slocum thinks alkaline hydrolysis has a better chance. Carlson disagrees and thinks people will find Promession less offensive than dissolving a body in a lye bath.

Promession, patented by a Swedish company, is the posthumous version of the popular high school science class demonstration of dipping a rose or a rubber ball in super-cold liquid nitrogen then shattering it like glass. The body is chilled to brittle fragility, then mechanically shaken until it's reduced to a fine powder. Emissions-free, certainly, but the process does seem like a Rube Goldberg approach to burial—why go to such much trouble when nature will do the same job underground (if more slowly)? Carlson has been in contact with a British company that is starting up to do this, but the process is not yet available anywhere in the US as of this writing.

Alkaline hydrolysis is a fancy term for dissolving the body in lye. It's sometimes called *resomation*, a word coined by the Scottish company that makes the equipment for the process. The corpse is immersed in a solution of water and potassium hydroxide, then heated under pressure for a few hours. What's left is an inert liquid and bone fragments, which are then pulverized much like cremated remains. While this may conjure up gruesome images of Mafiosos taking care of customers who didn't pay for protection, is it really any "worse" than putting the body in a flaming oven? After all, people fussed and fumed over cremation when it was first introduced to the US in the 1870s, calling it a violent desecration of the body.

Matthews International, a crematory manufacturer which distributes the Scottish-made machines in the US, calls the process "Bio Cremation," which strikes us as misleading (and a little precious—what makes it any more "bio" than burial or cremation?). It's not cremation at all, of course. On the other hand, the company may be trying to avoid legal tangles in states where the law specifically permits only earth burial, cremation, or anatomical donation as methods of body disposition.

Unless researchers or lawmakers have evidence that the liquid remaining after the process is in any way harmful to the sewer system or environment (and we know of no such evidence), it would be unreasonable to restrict the process. Feelings of "ickiness" about certain methods of disposition are understandable, but they're not a basis on which to form public policy. Unfortunately, one New York State lawmaker feels otherwise, and helped defeat a 2008 bill that would have made the process legal. He called it the "Hannibal Lecter bill," an offensive reference to the infamous fictional serial killer from *The Silence of the Lambs.*

Meanwhile, the Mayo Clinic has been using alkaline hydrolysis since 2002 to dispose of the remains of donor bodies, and many veterinary clinics also use the process. Funeral homes in Florida and Maine have committed to offering this service, but it remains to be seen how popular it will become.

The NFDA's Position

The National Funeral Directors Associations' response to green burial has been . . . interesting. In the August, 2008 edition of its magazine, General Counsel Scott Gilligan printed a green burial indemnification form for funeral directors to get customers to sign. The primary purpose seemed to be scaring them out of their wits with misinformation:

> The FUNERAL HOME can provide no assurances regarding the appearance or the condition of DECEDENT's remains. . . that there can be substantial risks of physical injury to pallbearers from holding, carrying, and transporting a body in a container that may not be designed to hold the weight or to be safely lifted and carried. . . it may be difficult or impossible to locate the grave due to the lack of a permanent marker or monument. . . .

Slocum wrote Gilligan an open letter taking the form apart point by point, and received a lawyerly, evasive response by mail. Interesting, the form seems to have disappeared from NFDA's website. Perhaps it's because they've changed their tune? As of this writing, the website says member funeral homes who want to be certified as green must, among other things:

> [O]ffer one or more temporary preservation options such as refrigeration, dry ice, conventional ice or other non-formaldehyde chemical products for open casket viewing, as allowed by state law.

The Future of Green Burial

It is probably apparent that we expect green burial will become much more commonplace very quickly, for excellent reasons. In its simplest form, green burial is by far the most environmentally sound method of disposition. It is also conducive to family participation, which can have great therapeutic value. If your family owns appropriate land in a rural location, green burial is also a logical way to care for your own dead. For some, the idea of planting a tree over the grave site, perpetuating the cycle of life, is especially attractive.

Changes in death-care customs tend to occur gradually, as it is natural for people to think in terms of the traditions they grew up with, and for many, the traditions are intertwined with religious or cultural beliefs. But public acceptance of the dignity of natural burial is spreading quickly. If somebody picks up a copy of this book 20 years after publication, he or she may be surprised by our use of the word "new" to describe a process that was, after all, predominant for the millennia leading up to the last century, and for very good reasons due for a comeback.

Part 2
Funeral Law and Related Information for Consumers

Caring for the Dead
Necessary Information for Family Involvement

THIS CHAPTER SUMMARIZES THE MAIN issues to consider in caring for the dead, but be sure to also read the subsequent chapter for the specific state where the death occurred.

Many people over the years have asked for a checklist for performing a family-directed funeral. Would that it were so easy! While the process is not excessively complicated, there are many things families need to contemplate and many differences in state laws, so it is impossible to distill the process into a sound-byte-style checklist.

There are, however, some basic components common to every family-directed disposition:

1. A doctor, medical examiner, or nurse practitioner must certify the death by completing the medical information on the death certificate.

2. The death certificate must be completed and filed before the body is buried or cremated.

3. Most states require you to get a permit for transportation or disposition before moving the body and before final disposition.

4. You will need to do a walk-through ahead of time with all parties involved, from the local registrar of vital statistics to the cemetery, crematory, or medical school where the body will end up. Some of these parties may need to be shown in advance that what you're doing is legal if they haven't experienced a family-directed funeral before.

Avoiding Careless Errors

Those who choose to handle death privately must take great care to follow all state and local regulations. The requirements are not complex, but failure to meet them can lead to unpleasant situations and create a climate in which professionals become less willing to work with families.

One crematory, for example, was sued for rejecting a body sent by a family. The case was thrown out of court, and rightly so, because the family had merely hired someone to deliver the body without a death certificate, transit permit, or authorization from next-of-kin for cremation. Another crematory will no longer accept bodies directly from families because in one case, the family had assumed that medical personnel would fill out the forms properly. While that seems like a reasonable assumption, in this case the cause of death as stated by the medical examiner on the permit to cremate was not written exactly as it had been on the death certificate, and the state later made an issue of it. In short, the procedures are quite simple and straightforward, but it is necessary to pay close attention to the details and to be vigilant about errors that may be made by others.

Death Certificate

Great care must be taken in completing the death certificate. Whiteout or other corrections are not usually permitted. If an error is made, you may have to start over again with a new certificate. Most states have implemented an Electronic Death Registration (EDR) system, which doctors and funeral directors can log into rather than writing on a piece of paper. Private individuals will not be allowed to use the on-line system, but vital statistics departments should have a paper alternative for families who perform their own funerals. Check your state chapter and your local vital statistics office ahead of time for the proper procedure.

For all deaths, a death certificate signed by a doctor stating the cause of death must be filed—usually in the county or district where death occurs, or where a body is found, or where a body is removed from a public conveyance or vehicle.

If complicated laboratory work is needed to accurately determine the exact cause of death, the physician or medical examiner may write "pending" or a similar phrase for the cause of death and release the body for disposition. In those few cases, a delayed or corrected death certificate will be sent to the state registrar by the physician when the cause of death is known.

In addition to the medical portion, facts such as "mother's maiden name" must be provided by the family. Unless the signature of a licensed funeral director is required by state statute, the family or church member who is handling the arrangements must sign the death certificate (or paper alternative in states with EDR) in the space marked "funeral director," followed by his or her relationship to the deceased, immediately after the signature.

States vary in the time required for filing the death certificate with the local registrar, but this must usually be accomplished before other permits are granted and before final disposition.

Fetal Deaths and Miscarriages

A special death certificate or fetal death report is required in all but two states for fetal deaths. Eleven states seem to require registration of all fetal deaths. In a majority of states, a fetal death must be registered if it occurs after 20 weeks of pregnancy. In Hawaii, the requirement goes into effect after 24 weeks.

Some states gauge pregnancy duration by fetal weight, e.g., 350 grams (12½ oz.), and because any unattended death—including fetal death—could require a coroner's investigation, a physician should be called.

Even if there is uncertainty as to whether reporting requirements are applicable, reporting a fetal death may be helpful in obtaining insurance benefits in some situations.

Autopsies: Dealing with a Coroner/Medical Examiner's Office

Autopsies are generally required when cause of death is violent, unexpected, uncertain, or "unusual," including suicide. For this reason, the police should be called when death occurs outside a hospital or nursing home, is "unattended," and falls into one of the categories above. But it is not necessary to call 911 for an ambulance or police if the death is not unusual. For example, it wouldn't make sense to call 911 if Grandma died in her sleep at 85, and doing so would bring on unnecessary commotion.

Death from a contagious or infectious disease may also necessitate involvement with a coroner or local health officer.

When donating the body to a medical school, a family should request that no autopsy be performed. The decision will depend on circumstances surrounding the death, and the state may order an autopsy in suspicious cases.

The practices in coroners' offices vary widely. In California, it is legal for medical examiners to amputate fingers for identification and remove tissue and organs for study. One woman discovered that her father had been buried without his heart when she arrived at a workers' compensation hearing and saw the heart presented as evidence.

The condition in which a medical examiner or coroner returns an autopsied body varies considerably. We've had reports from families and home funeral guides stating the body was barely tacked back together, and work had to be done to better sew up the incisions. Some families planning a home funeral might wish to engage a funeral director for this. On the other hand, we've heard from several families who did this work themselves.

The term *medical examiner* is usually reserved for those with medical training, and the person in such a position is often appointed by the department of health. In a few states, the word *coroner* is used interchangeably with medical examiner. Generally, however, the term coroner implies an elected position. In California, a medical degree is required for a candidate to run for coroner. In many other states, however, anyone may run for the office, with or without medical training.

A coroner may be a practicing funeral director or have a direct relationship with a funeral home. In Pennsylvania, more than half the coroners' offices have a funeral director on the staff. To avoid any appearance of impropriety, a coroner or medical examiner may rotate pick-up calls among all funeral homes within the jurisdiction, but this is not always the case. Funeral directors from various states have complained that a local coroner-funeral director ends up getting more business when he's on duty as the coroner. This is unethical, and consumers have no obligation to use the funeral home whose director is acting for the state as a coroner.

Home Death, Home Visitation

With hospice support, many people are able to die at home in familiar surroundings, near familiar faces. In some states, an "expected" death can be certified by an attending nurse.

A home death can allow the family time to obtain permits and make necessary arrangements. Turning off the heat in a room or turning on an air-conditioner can make it reasonable to contain a body without further action for 24 to 72 hours or more. People often ask, "Doesn't the body smell?" No, not usually for the first two or three days, at 70 degrees or less, but each situation must be considered individually. Often in waning days a failing person stops eating and drinking, so the body will become somewhat dehydrated before death. Noxious odors are therefore unlikely during the next few days. The robust body of someone who finished a meal of corned beef and cabbage just prior to death, however, might produce telltale odors.

For some, there is therapeutic value in keeping the body at home for at least a brief period, allowing the family a chance to congregate and deal with the death, as often occurred in the front parlor two or three generations ago.

Nursing Home Death

When death is anticipated in a nursing home, it will be important to work out your plans with the nursing home staff ahead of time. If the deceased has had only a semi-private room, for example, the nursing home may have no other location to hold the body while paperwork and other errands are done. Staff members are accustomed to calling a funeral director, regardless of the hour, for quick removal. Out of consideration for other residents, it may not be feasible for the nursing home personnel to allow a long delay while permits, a container, and vehicle are obtained.

When Carlson's Uncle Henry died at a care facility, she didn't have a dignified way to move the body out. She called a friendly funeral director to pick up and bring the body to her home where it was placed in a cremation box. She and her husband drove it from there to the crematory.

Hospital Death

Disposition of a fetal or infant death can be handled entirely by the hospital as a courtesy if a family so chooses. When other deaths occur in a hospital, the relative on hand should ask the nursing staff to remove any life-support articles such as catheters, IV needles, and feeding or breathing tubes. A catheter is held in place by a "balloon" and is not as simple to remove as an IV needle. Some of the nasal tubes appear especially disfiguring after death and may be of concern to other family members who are expected later to help with the death arrangements.

Some hospitals may be reluctant to release a body directly to a family without the use of a funeral director. If the death is expected, you should alert the hospital staff of your intentions ahead of time. If hospital personnel are confused or believe incorrectly that they can refuse to release the body to the family, a telephone call from your lawyer (or Funeral Consumers Alliance) may be in order.

It is also important for families to recognize the legitimate needs of hospitals. Some hospitals may have no storage facilities for dead bodies while permits are obtained and may insist on calling a funeral director for immediate removal after death if there is to be any significant delay.

Body and Organ Donation

Donation of eyes and other organs must be done under sterile conditions and usually within a short time after death. Because organ-donor cards may not be immediately available to hospital personnel, next-of-kin should make the decision to donate known to attending staff at the earliest time possible.

Hospital employees are often reluctant to approach a grieving, distressed family. Anyone who can find emotional healing in a gift of life or sight is encouraged to take the initiative in making such an offer even if the time of death is uncertain. The corneas of elderly persons can usually be used, and eyes (and sometimes skin) may be donated even if total body donation to a medical school is subsequently planned.

With the increasing success of organ transplants, consideration should be given to whether organ donation takes priority over body donation. There may develop a competition between those needing body parts and those who need whole bodies. Loss of a major organ involving a thoracic incision usually makes a body unacceptable for a teaching donation because of the difficulty in embalming a system interrupted by recent surgery. Carlson and her husband, Steve, have written in on the body donation cards they carry that organ donation is to be considered first. If organ donation is not needed, only then should their bodies be considered for body donation to a medical school. If their bodies are not accepted, they want a plain pine box send-off.

Body donation to a medical school may be an option even if the deceased has not enrolled in such a program. For up-to-date information about the needs and requirements of medical schools, as well as for-profit and non-profit companies that accept body donations, check our website:

<www.finalrights.org>

Embalming

No state requires routine embalming of all bodies. Special circumstances—such as an extended time between death and disposition—may make it necessary under state law. Interstate transportation by a common carrier may also necessitate embalming, although most airlines will waive that requirement if there are religious objections. Refrigeration or dry ice can take the place of embalming in many instances. Check the Yellow Pages (or the on-line equivalent) for a source of dry ice. Frozen gel packs such as those used for picnic coolers can also work, though you will need enough to swap out when one set gets warm. In some states, embalming may be required by law if the person has died of a communicable disease, although this is a seriously flawed requirement. (See Chapter 4 and your state chapter.)

Moving A Body

Never move a body without a permit (or without medical permission if your state allows that in lieu of a permit)! Always call ahead before moving a body even if you have a permit. A medical school, cemetery, or crematory staff member who is unprepared, or a town clerk who just isn't sure about family burial plots may need some time and help in doing his or her job. By calling first to make arrangements at the destination, you will be expected and prepared. Remember that even if your state permits families to perform their own funerals, crematories, cemeteries, and medical schools are not legally required to work directly with consumers. You will want to know in advance whether the staff will accept the body directly from you (and you may be able to persuade them to do so by explaining your plans in advance).

The use of a simple covered box allows some dignity for all involved in the handling and moving of a body, regardless of final disposition.

If a family chooses to build the container for delivery of a body for cremation, they should consider the size. A standard cremation chamber opening is 38 inches wide and 30 inches high. A container two feet wide and 14 to 18 inches deep is usually sufficient for most bodies, however. One crematory mentioned that most home-made boxes tend to be too large. Simple cardboard containers (or caskets) can be purchased from funeral homes (though some will refuse to sell the box only). Or check the internet; the FCA site at <www.funerals.org> has a listing of casket sellers in many parts of the country, and many will ship a simple cardboard or wood casket in knockdown form, ready to assemble. Some boxes are more expensive than others because of construction. Some are paraffin-coated, others plastic-lined, and some have plywood bottoms. You should also consider the length of the box when you choose the vehicle for transportation.

Most states require a permit for transportation or disposition. The death certificate must usually be completed first, and often a special permit-to-cremate is needed prior to cremation. In many states, funeral directors serve as deputy registrars. If death occurs when local municipal offices are closed, a funeral director may be needed to furnish or sign the disposition or transit permit, especially in states using electronic death registration (EDR) widely. As a deputy of the state in this function, the funeral director should not charge for this service unless such a charge is set by the state.

Body Fluids

After death, the blood in a body settles to the lowest points, leaving the upper portions pale and waxy, with purple mottling below. Some parts of the body may swell a little. Fluids may be discharged from body orifices. It will be helpful to use absorbent material—such as towels or newspapers—underneath. A sheet can help with wrapping and moving the body. If the person has died from a communicable disease, it will be important to take all health precautions. Use a pair of latex rubber gloves. Your state may require the use of a funeral director in such a case. Consult your family doctor for instructions if the information for your state is not specific or if you are concerned.

When an autopsy has been performed or death occurs from trauma, the body may be wrapped in a vinyl body bag—available from a funeral director—to prevent additional leakage or seepage. A plastic, zippered mattress cover might work as well. However, if you plan on cremation, avoid any such materials whenever possible.

Out-of-State Disposition

All states honor properly acquired permits of other states when a body is to be moved interstate. There may be local regulations for disposition, however. Check by telephone before setting out for the destination.

Burial

In some states, when burial will be outside the county or town where death occurred, you will need an additional permit to inter (whether on private land or in a cemetery) from the local registrar in that area. The statutes and regulations of some states include depth requirements for burial; these are listed in the state chapters in this book. Standard practice in many states is to place the top of the coffin at least three feet below the natural surface of the earth. A burial location should be 150 feet or more from a water supply and outside the easement for any utility or power lines.

Cremation

When cremation is chosen, an additional permit is often required from the local coroner or medical examiner. There is a fee for this which varies by state; the highest we know of is Oklahoma's $150 charge. If the deceased did not sign a cremation authorization prior to death, authorization from next-of-kin or a designated agent is required by most crematories. Usually this can be obtained by fax, Western Union, or overnight mail if family members live out of state.

Next-of-kin is determined in this order (although it varies slightly from state to state):

(1) surviving spouse
(2) adult sons and daughters
(3) parents
(4) adult siblings
(5) guardian or "person in charge"

That is, if there is a surviving spouse, his or her permission is all that is required. If there is no surviving spouse but several children, all adult sons and daughters may be required to grant permission for disposition by cremation (though some states require only one adult child to consent). Adult siblings must assume responsibility if no spouse, offspring, or parents survive.

Be sure to check the chapter for your state to see if the law allows you to designate an agent to carry out your wishes for final disposition. "Designated agent" laws allow a person to choose anyone (it need not be a family member) to have the sole legal authority to direct the cremation or other form of disposition. It is extremely helpful to name an agent ahead of time so that family disputes will not hold up the arrangements or wind up in probate court. Gay, lesbian, and transgender people should take special care to designate an agent if their state has a designated-agent law. We have seen some terrible problems with blood families swooping in to take the body away from the decedent's same-sex partner. (This problem can also be averted, of course, in the increasing numbers of states with same-sex marriage.)

A pacemaker must be removed before cremation. The services of an attending physician, the medical examiner, or a funeral director can be requested for this. On the other hand, one funeral director told Carlson, "Anyone can do it." A pacemaker is about the size of a silver dollar, embedded just under the skin, usually near the neck or lower on the rib cage. A shallow incision with an X-Acto knife would make it readily accessible, and the wires to which it is attached should be snipped. If a pacemaker is not removed and explodes during the cremation process, repairing damage to the cremation chamber may be the liability of the person delivering the body.

Selecting a Crematory

There is no consistency among the states when it comes to the operation of crematories. Some states allow only cemeteries to run crematories, barring funeral homes from owning them. A few other states allow only funeral homes to operate crematories, and bar freestanding crematories from doing business directly with the public. Still other states permit crematories to operate independently and do business with consumers directly. Check your state chapter for details.

Generally, crematories run by funeral homes are less likely to work directly with a family, as they want consumers to pay them to do everything. At Cook-Walden funeral home in Austin, Texas (owned by SCI), the staff told an FCA board member that they would accept the body and the death certificate directly from the family, but the direct cremation price was the same ($2,400!) even though the family would be doing almost all the work.

As with all entities involved in a family-directed funeral, you may need to contact several crematories ahead of time to find one that will work with you. Carlson took Uncle Henry to a crematory an hour and a half away where the cost was $225. The nearby crematory would not take a body from a family, and lists prices close to those in Austin.

Obituary (Death Notice)

Traditionally, an *obituary* is a news article published when a well-known person dies. A *death notice* is called in by the family or funeral director and published, usually at a price, to inform others that death has occurred. However, in current usage, the terms are generally interchangeable.

When a death occurs, it is almost impossible to personally notify everyone who knew or cared about the deceased. Close friends and relatives, of course, should be informed by phone before they read about the death in the newspaper. But a death notice may help assure that the news reaches a wider circle of acquaintances in a timely manner. It should mention any services planned, even if a memorial gathering is scheduled for a later date.

More people are learning about the deaths of friends and acquaintances on-line than ever before. As newspaper readership declines, putting a notice of death on your—or the decedent's—Facebook page (or other social media) may spread the news more quickly than relying on a newspaper obituary alone. While e-mail is considered by some to be the most impersonal form of communication, many people are grateful to be notified quickly by e-mail, especially if they spend a lot of time on-line.

If you do choose an obituary, call the paper to learn its policies and any costs. Your local paper may have a standard format for obituaries or expect certain information to be included. An obituary can generally be phoned in or e-mailed. If there is no funeral director involved, the person at the paper may ask for a copy of the death certificate just to be sure that the obit is not a practical joke (as has happened from time to time).

The cost varies a lot but can be quite high; it's not uncommon to see obituary charges of $500 or more. Of course, most people want the obituary to tell the story of the person who died, and the longer it is, the higher the price.

When Slocum's close friend died in 2010, the obituary Slocum wrote would have cost $700 to put in the *Syracuse Post-Standard* (and it wasn't that long). The funeral director suggested putting only the necessary details about the time and place for Michael's memorial service in the paper, and publishing the longer obituary on the funeral home's website, which they offered free. Thank you, Newcomer Funeral Home.

Lisa's Uncle Henry was a colorful character—a friendly, witty street person who got to know almost everybody he met. A long obit with several of his life stories was the only practical way to get the word out to everybody. It was expensive, but was the one costly item that seemed important.

Miscellaneous but Still Important

- It is not uncommon for family members to forget to remove jewelry at the time of death.

- A family using the time of a mortician for advice should find it reasonable to pay a consultant's fee.

- If a person who works in a funeral home or crematory offers to file a death certificate, you should expect to pay for the service.

When private death arrangements are made in an area of the country where the practice is still uncommon, you can expect some hesitancy on the part of involved persons such as registrars and town clerks. Some hospitals may even be reluctant to release the body to a family. We have tried to include in each state chapter relevant legal citations enabling family disposition. People in authority, accustomed to delegating their duties to funeral directors, may have to be informed of their responsibilities. That can be frustrating, particularly when you are enduring a time of loss and grief. The majority of these people will probably be concerned with performing their duties appropriately. Few will intentionally want to hinder your choice if you have followed all required procedures and if you seem well-informed.

Caring for the Dead
In Alabama

Please refer also to the general introduction to state chapters—"Caring for the Dead: Necessary Information."

Persons in Alabama may care for their own dead. The legal authority to do so is found in:

> *Title 22-9A-14(b): . . . The funeral director or person acting as the funeral director who first assumes custody of the dead body shall file the certificate of death . . .*

There are no other statutes that might require you to use a funeral director when no embalming is desired. A 1986 letter from John Wible, General Counsel, Alabama Department of Health, verified this interpretation for an earlier book, and nothing has changed in the laws since.

Death Certificate

If death occurs in a hospital or nursing home, the facility will initiate the death certificate and have the attending physician sign the medical portion of the form. The remaining personal or family information must be added, typewritten or in permanent ink. For death at home, a blank form and information on current procedures is available from the state Office of Vital Records, Health Statistics, in the Department of Health in Montgomery. The death certificate must be filed with the local registrar or county health department within five days and prior to cremation or removal from the state.

Alabama expects funeral directors and doctors to be using electronic death registration before long, but families caring for their own dead may still use a paper death certificate, obtainable from the state office.

Fetal Death

A fetal death report is required if death occurs after 20 weeks of gestation. All other procedures apply.

Transporting and Disposition Permit

A burial transit permit is no longer used in Alabama. A body may be moved with medical permission. A completed death certificate constitutes authorization for final disposition. If disposition is planned in another state and that state expects a burial transit permit, the funeral director doing the embalming required to cross state lines can obtain such a form.

Burial

There are no state statutes that specifically permit or prohibit home burial. It is also unlikely that there are local zoning regulations regarding home burial, but you should review them before planning a family cemetery. If your land is in a rural area, draw a map of the property showing where the burial ground will be and have it filed with the deed. That may be all you have to do to establish your family cemetery. There are no state burial statutes or regulations with regard to burial locations or depth. A sensible guideline is 150 feet from a water supply, 25 feet from a power line, with two or three feet of earth on top. Plan your family cemetery away from boundaries with neighbors, too.

Landowners have a legal obligation to permit descendants and interested others to visit graves on private property. Cemeteries may be declared "abandoned" and the bodies moved to a new location after public announcement and notification of descendants when known.

Cremation

A permit for cremation must be signed by a local medical examiner or coroner. If no medical examiner is available, the county sheriff will secure a licensed physician for this purpose. There is a 24-hour wait prior to cremation. Most crematories insist that a pacemaker be removed. Next-of-kin can override the wishes of the decedent regarding cremation, even if the decedent had prepaid and pre-authorized his or her own cremation. In the case of surviving adult children, all children must agree, not just a majority. If the crematory will not permit the authorizing person(s) to witness the cremation, this must be disclosed prior to the cremation arrangements.

All crematories are affiliated with mortuaries. Some may resent your desire to bypass their other funeral operations. You may wish to get the assistance of your family physician in negotiating arrangements ahead of time if the crematory fails to acknowledge your rights.

There are no laws regarding the disposition of cremated remains. You may do as you wish.

Other Requirements

Embalming or cremation is required by statute before removing a body from the state unless the body will be used for medical research purposes. Off-the-record conversations with those in the industry reveal that funeral directors from neighboring states often pick up a body without embalming first, and some here have shipped a body with dry ice when there are religious objections to embalming.

There are no other circumstances that require embalming. Alabama has no requirements controlling the time schedule for the disposition of unembalmed bodies. Weather and reasonable planning should be considered.

If the person died of a contagious or communicable disease, the doctor in attendance should be consulted.

Medical Schools for Body Donation

Body donation to a medical school is another option for disposition. Find the information for Alabama at <www.finalrights.org>.

State Governance

The Alabama Board of Funeral Service has seven members; no more than four may be of the same race. There are no consumer representatives. Website: <www.fsb.alabama.gov/>.

A legislatively mandated audit of the Funeral Service Board in 2007 is, frankly, quite shocking:

<www.examiners.state.al.us/PDFs/Audit28S-0013.pdf>

Three people reported to the auditor that a staff person had solicited money other than normal fees. The report of establishment inspections seemed bogus, as it would be physically impossible to travel the miles between the facilities listed in a single day. The office was run with paper and pencil, without the benefit of any computerized efficiency; the office could not easily produce a list of licensees for the audit. Indeed, it seemed unaware (and unconcerned) that there were a number of unlicensed funeral establishments in the state. The board was failing a number of state-mandated tasks such as supplying a list of laws and regulations to licensees in a timely way.

Apparently, the audit shook things up, as the office now has a website and e-mail at least.

Crematories must be affiliated with a funeral establishment and are regulated by the Board of Funeral Service.

There is no state agency governing the day-to-day operation of cemeteries. According to state statute, cemeteries are required to post a complete list of prices for all burial services and merchandise offered.

The Department of Insurance regulates funeral and cemetery preneed sales.

Prepaid Cemetery and Funeral Funds

Unless the funeral home is using an insurance policy to fund the preneed, 75% of the funds for *funeral services and merchandise* must be placed in **trust**, 60% of the outer burial container cost, and 100% of cash advance items. A full refund can be requested during the first 30 days. No trust deposit is required until the account is paid in full, which might take quite a few years for some families. These preneed laws, passed in 2002, are probably worse than no laws at all, as they give funeral homes the right to keep 20% of what a consumer paid if the consumer moves and needs to change funeral plans. So the funeral home will have to ante up 5% of what it pocketed earlier in order to refund 80%, as required by the Insurance Department's standard contract. The seller may keep the interest. If funded by insurance, the cash value is all a consumer can reclaim if the policy is cancelled, considerably less than what was paid. The full value of the policy can be transferred, however.

Prepaid *cemetery merchandise* (markers) must be in **trust** at the rate of 110% of the wholesale cost. Sixty percent of *vaults and services* must be in trust. Constructive delivery (warehousing) can avoid all trusting requirements. There is no provision for a consumer to cancel cemetery purchases. This would be desirable if one were to change plans from body burial to cremation and no longer needed a vault. In fact, the Alabama law is particularly bad for the poor because it permits a cemetery to cancel a contract entirely and keep all funds paid if the purchaser comes upon hard times and is more than 90 days late with payments.

The model preneed contracts on the Insurance Department's web site is written in six-point type and nearly impossible for even a young pair of eyes to read. We found no requirement that a contract be written in a more legible type size.

Consumer Concerns

- The death rate in Alabama can support approximately 188 full-time mortuaries; there are, however, 460. Funeral prices tend to be higher in areas where there are "too many" funeral homes.
- There is no state board governing cemeteries.

- There is no consumer representation on the Funeral Board. Ideally, it should have majority consumer representation, and should also be expanded into a funeral-cemetery board.

- Trusting requirements for prepaid funeral and cemetery purchases are inadequate and should be increased to 100%, with a full refund, including interest, if the purchaser needs to transfer or cancel the contract.

- There is no requirement to provide consumers with an annual report of all prepaid funeral funds.

- There is no state protection in the case of default on prepaid funeral monies.

- Until the Alabama laws are changed, it is probably a terrible idea to prepay for a funeral or any cemetery merchandise and services, given the lack of adequate protection for consumers. Your own pay-on-death account in the bank will be safer.

- Identification and tagging of a body is now required by state law, but the Board of Funeral Service has failed to promulgate a regulation to make this happen.

- The standards for ethical, professional conduct are inadequate and should be strengthened. That would make it easier for a consumer to prevail when filing a complaint. (See Appendix.)

- Complaint procedures are unclear and inadequate.

- The executive director of the funeral board told Carlson ten years ago that he had no intention of enforcing the FTC Funeral Rule. If the feds are going to pass laws, let them enforce them, he said. When calling to update information for this chapter, Carlson asked if the Funeral Rule had been adopted yet in Alabama. The secretary said, "What's the Funeral Rule?"

- Current Alabama regulations require "a card or brochure in each casket stating the price of the funeral service using said casket and listing the services and other merchandise included in the price." It does permit the funeral home to attach separate prices to each item on the list in the casket, but the total-funeral-per-casket package pricing is not in compliance with the FTC Rule; only the basic service charge may be included in the casket price in some instances. Alabama consumers, then, may not be getting a separate itemized list of funeral options from which to choose at every funeral establishment. If you decided not to have embalming, for example, how much would that save? If you chose to use your own vehicles instead of a limo to the church, how much would that save? The FTC permits a family to choose funeral goods and services separately, selecting only those options they want.

- The FTC Funeral Rule should be adopted by reference.

- The regulations require that at least eight adult caskets be on display, but there is no requirement that low-cost caskets be included in that display. With computer presentation, the consumer is likely to have a much wider choice, and the casket showroom could be eliminated altogether.

- There is no provision either forbidding a mark-up on cash advance items or requiring the disclosure of how much the mark-up would be if permitted.

- The law requiring embalming or cremation when crossing state lines is routinely ignored but, when enforced, it is an offense to some religious groups and is entirely unnecessary.

- There is no law that allows you to state your funeral preferences or to name a designated agent to make your final arrangements. In situations where you are estranged from next-of-kin, this could be important.

- Coroners are elected. Some are medical people but, according to one report, nearly 75% are funeral directors or have an affiliation with a funeral home. When that is the case, there is a serious conflict-of-interest. Consumers should feel free to have a body moved to the funeral home of their choice if a coroner has sent the body to a funeral home that otherwise would not have been selected.

- Alabama is one of the few states where crematories must be run by a funeral director. There is nothing on the study guide for the national funeral directors exam about running a crematory. There is nothing in the curriculum of most mortuary schools on running a crematory. To make sure that some price competition remains in the deathcare industry, crematories should be independently licensed.

- [The chairman of the Department of Surgery at the University of Alabama-Birmingham is authorized by law to regulate the acquisition of bones and tissue for study and transplant. This responsibility has been turned over to the Alabama Organ Center, which is doing tissue retrieval for certain biotech companies. Other body parts brokers are operating independently, however, arranging to have bodies shipped out of state, without any oversight or regulation.

Miscellaneous Information

- Educational requirements for becoming a funeral director: 18 years of age, two years of apprenticeship, and passing an exam. For an embalmer: mortuary college (2 years), two years of apprenticeship, and a passing exam grade of 70%.

- Casket manufacturers and casket dealers must pay a license tax.

- Funeral directors may not hold a body for payment.

- It is unprofessional conduct to use "profane, indecent, or obscene language" in the presence of the family or a dead human body "not yet interred." (After that, watch out?)

- The Board of Funeral Service is authorized to make sure that all licensees know how to properly enucleate eyes (safely remove for transplant). In practice, most simply call the Eye Bank.

- A notice of disinterment must be filed with the local Health Department or the state Health Department indicating the new location for burial.

This chapter was reviewed (and corrected) by the State Registrar of Vital Statistics in the Alabama Department of Health and the Alabama Insurance Department. It was also sent for review to the Anatomy Department at the University of Alabama, the University of Southern Alabama, the Alabama Board of Funeral Service, and the Alabama Funeral Directors Association. Review does not necessarily imply approval or agreement with all of the statements.

Caring for the Dead
In Alaska

Please refer also to the general introduction to state chapters—"Caring for the Dead: Necessary Information."

No Alaska statute requires the use of a funeral director for body disposition. Indeed, AS-08.42.020(c) states that unlicensed persons may be granted a permit to dispose of the dead if no embalming is required.

Death Certificate

The family doctor or a local medical examiner will supply and sign the death certificate within 24 hours, stating the cause of death. The remaining information must be supplied, typewritten or in black ink. The death certificate must be filed with the local registrar or subregistrar within three days and prior to disposition. The registrar may grant a time extension in situations of hardship but this provision should not be abused.

Alaska expects funeral directors and doctors to be using electronic death registration at some time in the future. Procedures may change somewhat then, but it should not interfere with caring for your own dead.

Fetal Death

A fetal death certificate is required if death occurs after 20 weeks of gestation and must be filed with the registrar within three days and before final disposition. A physician must sign the fetal death certificate except in special problem cases handled by the Department of Health and Social Services.

Transporting and Disposition Permit

The local registrar or subregistrar will issue a burial-transit permit. The death certificate must be obtained first. The person in charge must keep a copy of all records.

Burial

There are no state statutes that specifically permit or prohibit home burial. It is also unlikely that there are local zoning regulations regarding home burial, but you may want to review them before planning a family cemetery. If your land is in a rural area, draw a map of the property showing where the burial ground will be and have it filed with the deed. That may be all you have to do to establish your family cemetery. There are no state burial statutes or regulations with regard to burial locations or depth. A sensible guideline is 150 feet from a water supply, 25 feet from a power line, with two or three feet of earth on top. Plan your family cemetery away from boundaries with neighbors, too.

If the death occurred outside the district where burial will take place, the burial-transit permit must be filed with a magistrate of the court in that district.

Property used exclusively for cemetery purposes is not taxed.

Cremation

Approval for cremation must be granted by a local medical examiner or magistrate. Most crematories insist that a pacemaker be removed, and authorization by next-of-kin usually is required. There are no laws regarding the disposition of cremated remains. You may do as you wish.

Other Requirements

The laws requiring embalming were repealed in 2006. Alaska has no requirements controlling the time schedule for the disposition of unembalmed bodies. Weather and reasonable planning should be considered.

When death occurs from smallpox, plague, anthrax, diphtheria, meningococcal meningitis, cholera, epidemic typhus, or any unusual and highly communicable disease, a physician shall advise appropriate precautionary measures.

The rate of autopsied deaths is high in Alaska. According to the Health Department regulations now being considered, a medical examiner is not required "to make the head, face, and hands of the deceased presentable . . ." after autopsy. Indeed, according to a funeral director Carlson spoke with, the body may not even be closed after autopsy. Any family choosing to handle a death personally under such circumstances may wish to ask for the assistance of a funeral director to at least place the body in a covered container.

Medical Schools for Body Donation

There are no medical schools in Alaska. Check the nearest states at <www. finalrights.org> and consider the time required for transportation.

State Governance

Alaska has no state funeral board. The Department of Commerce, Community and Economic Development, Division of Corporations, Business and Professional Licensing issues the license to a funeral director. Information is at <www.commerce.state.ak.us/occ/>

Crematories must be run under licensed funeral establishments

There is no state board governing cemeteries.

Prepaid Cemetery and Funeral Funds

Prepaid *cemetery* money and perpetual care funds are entrusted to the care and integrity of the cemetery's trade association without any state trusting requirements. Nonprofit cemeteries are tax-exempt.

All prepaid *funeral* money must be placed in a trust in an insured financial institution within five days. The trust must be in the name of the person on whose behalf the purchase is made, with interest and any excess accruing to the estate of that person if not used for funeral purposes. There appear to be no reporting requirements.

The seller of a prearranged funeral may charge a fee for arrangement services provided that fee is disclosed to the buyer. "Mrs. Brown. Let me sell you a funeral, but you'll have to pay a little extra for the privilege of giving it to me ahead of time, say, $50."

Consumer Concerns

- The death-rate in Alaska can support approximately 14 full-time mortuaries; there are, however, 26 commercial establishments—a modest number of facilities considering the vast geography of this state. Funeral prices do tend to be higher in areas where there are "too many" funeral homes or funeral homes that are under-utilized.

- There is no provision for a detailed description of merchandise selected preneed and no provision for substitution if not available at the time of death. Survivors should have the right to approve any substitutions, of like quality and construction, not "value." It is not uncommon for families to be told, "We don't have anything like that any more—" with subsequent pressure to purchase something more expensive because the prices have gone up.

- There is no requirement to send the consumer an annual report of prepaid funds, paperwork that may be useful to survivors. Such reporting would also help to enforce the trusting requirement and deter any temptation for embezzlement.

- There is no state protection for consumers in case of default on pre-paid funeral funds.

- Until the Alaska laws are changed, it is probably a terrible idea to prepay for a funeral or any cemetery merchandise and services, given the lack of adequate protection for consumers. Your own trust account in the bank will be safer.

- There is no law that allows you to state your funeral preferences or for naming a designated agent to make your final arrangements. In situations where you are estranged or distant from next-of-kin, this could be important.

- There is no requirement to identify and tag the body at the place of death before removal, a measure that would avoid mix-ups which have happened at large facilities.

- There is no requirement that low-cost caskets be included in any display.

- There is no provision either forbidding a mark-up on cash advance items or requiring the disclosure of how much the mark-up would be.

- Although there are other mentions of FTC regulations in the statutes, there is no specific reference to the Funeral Rule. Adoption of this would make it more enforceable in Alaska.

- Because crematories must be run only through licensed funeral establishments, this option is likely to be more expensive than it needs to be. There is nothing in the study guide for the national funeral directors' exam with regard to crematory operation nor does the subject appear in many mortuary curricula.

- Alaska has no regulation of the body parts business.

Miscellaneous Information

- Educational requirements for becoming a funeral director: one year of college (30 hours) and one year of apprenticeship. For an embalmer: mortuary college (2 years) and one year of apprenticeship. They must also pass a state and national exam.

- Alaska has a comprehensive Trade and Commerce statute to protect consumers which clearly identifies "Unlawful acts and practices." Some provisions are specific to funeral dealings, but facets of all others may apply as well.

- Medical examiners are appointed and must be licensed physicians.

- Fraternal benefit societies may not own funeral homes.

- Five or more persons of the same district may form a cemetery association. Land, not exceeding 80 acres, may be set aside for cemetery purposes and will not be subject to taxation.

- A disinterment permit must be obtained from a local registrar at the local health department.

- Coal mining is not permitted within 100 feet of a cemetery.

This chapter was reviewed by the Alaska Division of Professional Licensing and the Department of Health and Social Services, Vital Statistics. Review does not necessarily imply approval or agreement with all of the statements.

Caring for the Dead
In Arizona

Please refer also to the general introduction to state chapters—"Caring for the Dead: Necessary Information."

Persons in Arizona may care for their own dead. The legal authority to do so is found in:

> *Title 36-831-A: . . . The duty of burying the body of or providing other funeral and disposition arrangements for a dead person devolves in the following order:*
>
> *1. If the dead person was married, upon the surviving spouse . . . [goes on to designated agent and other next-of-kin]*
>
> *Title 36-326 Disposition transit permits: H. A local registrar, a deputy local registrar or the state registrar shall provide a disposition-transit permit to a funeral establishment or other responsible person if the information provided pursuant to subsection B complies with this chapter and rules adopted pursuant to this chapter.*

There are no other statutes that would require you to use a funeral director when no embalming is desired.

Death Certificate

The family doctor or a local medical examiner will supply and sign the death certificate within 72 hours, stating the cause of death. The remaining information must be supplied, typewritten or in black ink. The death certificate must be filed with the local registrar within three days and prior to cremation or removal.

If death has occurred without medical attendance on an Indian reservation and if no medical examiner is available, tribal law enforcement authority may certify the cause of death.

If death is in a hospital or nursing home and the certificate has not yet been completed, the institution will supply a Human Remains Release Form.

Arizona will soon move to electronic death registration. When that is up and running, a family will have to go to the county health department to register the death. (Someone is on-call for evenings, weekends, and holidays.) The family member will fill out a worksheet with the family information. Once that is entered into the system, it will be faxed to the doctor for a cause of death, unless the doctor will accompany you to the health department. Typically, this all needs to be done before a burial-transit permit can be issued.

Fetal Death

A fetal death certificate is required if death occurs after 20 weeks of gestation or if the weight is 350 grams or more (about 12 ounces). If no family physician is involved, the local medical examiner must sign the certificate.

Transporting and Disposition Permit

The local Health Department registrar will issue a burial-transit permit. If the death has occurred after usual business hours, a funeral director may be asked to supply the permit. The death certificate must be obtained first. If cremation is planned, the medical examiner's permit must also be obtained first.

The "state copy" must be mailed immediately to the state registrar as a notification of death. After disposition, the original page of the burial-transit permit must be signed and returned to the clerk of the county where it was issued or to the state registrar within ten days of disposition.

Burial

There are no state statutes that specifically permit or prohibit home burial. It is also unlikely that there are local zoning regulations regarding home burial, but you may want to review zoning before planning a family cemetery. If your land is in a rural area, draw a map of the property showing where the burial ground will be and have it filed with the deed *before* burial is planned.

Title 36-326 Disposition transit permits states: *I. A local registrar, a deputy local registrar or the state registrar shall provide a disposition-transit permit for interment of human remains in a cemetery only if the location of the cemetery has been recorded in the office of the county recorder in the county where the cemetery is located or the cemetery is located on federal or tribal land.*

There are no state burial statutes or regulations with regard to depth. A sensible guideline is 150 feet from a water supply, 25 feet from a power line, with two or three feet of earth on top. Plan your family cemetery away from boundaries with neighbors, too.

Only cemetery personnel may open and close a grave in an established cemetery. How too bad, given the religious traditions that can be very therapeutic to some. Arizona has a high cremation rate, and families should certainly be allowed to help with interment of cremated remains. Unnecessary restrictions may make the idea of home burial more appealing.

Cremation

When cremation is chosen, the signature of the local medical examiner must be obtained before the burial-transit permit can be issued. If no medical examiner is available, the county sheriff shall secure a licensed physician for this purpose. A fee may be charged. Most crematories insist that a pacemaker be removed, and authorization by next-of-kin is required if the deceased did not authorize cremation prior to death.

Crematories may not contract directly with the public, according to a statute that appears to conflict with the right of families to care for their own dead. This statute is clearly to protect full-service funeral homes from competition by low-cost providers. Carlson was told that many of the crematories are on the wrong side of the tracks, so to speak, and that the law is needed to protect consumers. But it that's so, wouldn't the neighborhoods be just as dangerous to funeral directors? Why doesn't the Funeral Board have the backbone to do its job—to regulate crematories and make sure the people who run them are knowledgeable and responsible? The Funeral Board should make sure that all crematories can accommodate family needs, either for witnessing or by assisting those families choosing home funerals with simple disposition.

There are no laws regarding the disposition of cremated remains. You may do as you wish.

Other Requirements

If the person died of a contagious or communicable disease, the doctor in attendance should be consulted.

If disposition does not occur within 24 hours, the body must be embalmed or refrigerated. According to a 1983 legislative audit of the Funeral Board:

> **Public Health Risks Are Minimal** — . . . Embalming is not essential to protect public health. An official of the US Public Health Service, Centers for Disease Control (CDC) told us that his experience provided no evidence that embalming serves a public health function. . . . He described embalming as a cosmetic procedure.

Medical Schools for Body Donation

Body donation to a medical school or bio tech company is another option for disposition. Find the information for Arizona at <www.finalrights.org>.

State Governance

The Arizona State Board of Funeral Directors and Embalmers has seven members. Three are consumer representatives. It has a website with a downloadable consumer rights brochure: <www.azfuneralboard.us/>.

Cemeteries are supposed to be regulated by the Real Estate Commission. A two-inch-thick report that documents the failure of the Real Estate Commission to deal with cemetery regulation and cemetery complaints was issued July 1, 1998 by the then executive director of the Funeral Board. Almost nothing has been done in the intervening 13 years. Cemetery information isn't evident anywhere on the Department of Real Estate's website, nor does the chart of organization assign "cemeteries" to any staffer. When Carlson asked the auditors in that division how often they audited cemetery perpetual care funds, she was told, "Our audits are primarily random and not predictable. We usually try to audit every four years, but there are many factors involved." That staffer refused to give out a list of cemeteries regulated by the Commission. Do they even know which they are?

A curious cemetery reference on the DRE website is for an "Application for Temporary Cemetery Salesperson License Or Membership Camping Certificate of Convenience." Does this department think a trip to the cemetery is convenient, a little like camping, and only temporary?

Crematory authority is no longer issued by the Real Estate Commission; a crematory must be licensed by the Funeral Board. One does not need to be a funeral director to run a crematory.

The Department of Banking shares regulation of preneed trusts with the Funeral Board. The Insurance Department regulates funeral insurance.

Prepaid Cemetery and Funeral Funds

The Real Estate Recovery Fund is supposed to cover claims stemming from the sale of cemetery lots, but it's not at all clear what that might be unless perhaps someone was selling lots that didn't exist. It doesn't cover mischief done by a corporation, only individual licensees. Even if one could prove that it was an individual who raided the perpetual care funds, for example (as has happened in Indiana, Michigan, and Tennessee, to name some recent cemetery disasters), restitution is limited to $90,000 per licensee. If the cemetery is now unkempt and in disrepair, it is unlikely that a consumer will see much if any relief from this fund, as each lot owner—dead or alive—would have to mow the lawn and then submit a receipt for the "actual and direct out-of-pocket loss" . . . every month, every year.

Cemeteries are required to prove financial responsibility for continued main-tenance, but there is no annual or biennial audit of cemetery trust funds. There are no trusting requirements for prepaid cemetery goods and services and apparently no procedures for dealing with cemetery complaints.

Responsibility for monitoring prepaid funeral funds is shared between the funeral board and the state Banking Department. Safe investment in a federally insured trust, inspections, and clear disclosures on the funeral agreement are well-defined. The preneed contract names the institution and account number into which monies will be deposited. The Department of Insurance is responsible for regulation of funeral insurance.

A funeral establishment may pocket 15% as an initial service fee, although that would be refunded if the consumer cancelled the arrangement within three days. The balance must go into trust. If you are making installment payments, the seller may keep up to half of each payment until the 15% com-mission has been claimed. The mortuary may also withdraw up to 10% of the interest each year for administering the funds. Consumers may ask to withdraw funds to reimburse themselves for taxes on the interest, once the taxes have been paid. Someone cancelling a prepaid account will lose the 15% service fee and at least some of the interest.

If a prepaid plan is a "fixed price" plan, all interest goes to the seller, with the agreement stipulating that the purchaser has agreed to this. If it is not a fixed-price plan, the excess is distributed to the estate. Let's hope survivors know enough to check the account balance listed on the prepay agreement before making the actual arrangements.

The seller of prepaid funeral plans must report on such funds annually to the state.

The seller must provide for a substitution of "substantially equivalent" fu-neral merchandise if the item selected—such as a casket—is no longer avail-able. A description of the construction material and lining must be included in the preneed contract.

The difference between cemetery sales and funeral sales is easily demon-strated by the practices at Sunland Memorial Park and Mortuary. One Ari-zona man and his wife arranged for immediate cremations preneed. Each received a "Preneed Funeral Arrangement Agreement" indicating a total cost of $806—$1,612 for the two of them; that covered the funeral director, refrigeration, body pick-up, body container, and miscellaneous items such as memorial cards and a guest book. 85% of that money was, presumably, placed in trust. On another sheet marked "Cemetery Arrangement Agree-ment," the total was $1,280.28; this covered the cost of two urns ($846), two cremation chamber fees ($300), with the balance for engraving and tax. None of this money was required to be placed in trust. Four years later—after receiving a hand-made wooden urn from a friend—the husband asked to cancel the urn purchase and get his money back. The Sunland manager—with calculating indifference but "most sincerely"—replied that the purchase of the urn was a cemetery contract and was binding. No refund, not even 85%, even though the items were sold by a salesman making the funeral arrangements. In fact, this slick cemetery-mortuary combo operation had pocketed more than half of what the couple paid by writing up a portion of the purchase as a cemetery agreement.

Consumer Concerns

- The death rate in Arizona can support approximately 180 full-time mortuaries; there are, in fact, only 161. This is one of the very few states where there is not a significant glut of funeral homes. Prices are competitive based on consumer surveys.

- Trusting requirements for preneed payments for cemetery goods and services are inadequate and should be increased to 100%.

- There is no apparent cemetery regulation and oversight or a procedure for dealing with cemetery complaints.

- There are statutory provisions for vacating a cemetery. While they are thoughtful provisions, it seems a little disconcerting that a cemetery isn't necessarily a permanent easement on the land.

- There is no statutory provision for transferring an irrevocable preneed contract.

- There is no annual reporting requirement to the purchaser of prepaid funeral goods and services, paperwork that might be useful to the family of a deceased to indicate prepayment and that would help to "enforce" trusting requirements.

- While there is a cemetery recovery fund for lot purchases, there is no state protection in case of defaulting funeral providers.

- Until the Arizona laws are changed to require 100% trusting of all money and interest for prepaid funeral and cemetery goods and services and better provisions for transfer, it is probably a terrible idea to prepay for these arrangements. Your own trust account in a bank will be safer.

- The standards for professional conduct are inadequate and could be strengthened. That would make it easier for a consumer to prevail when filing a complaint. (See Ethical Standards in Appendix.)

- Identification and tagging of the body at the place of death before removal is not required, which may contribute to body mix-ups at large facilities.

- There is no requirement to include low-cost caskets in any display.

- Although a mortuary must mail a price list on request (a postage and handling fee not to exceed two dollars may be charged), it is not required to supply a price list when making arrangements with someone who is out-of-state. With e-mail and fax machines in wide use, this exemption should be eliminated.

- To restrict crematories from dealing with the public appears to be a blatant restraint of trade, resulting in higher prices for consumers. Indeed, families may be more trustworthy in caring for their own dead than at least a few of the funeral directors. Crematories and cremationists should be sufficiently licensed and regulated that they can do business directly with the public if they choose. They should be checking the paperwork even for bodies delivered by funeral directors. The scandal in Noble, Georgia happened under the "watch" of funeral directors who didn't. That should be the state's job. There is nothing on the study guide for the national funeral directors' exam regarding cremation and little if any in mortuary school curricula on cremation.

- Although there is a statutory obligation to comply with the written wishes of the decedent as well as for naming an agent for body disposition, a spouse is named in another statute with the primary right of disposition unless legally separated at the time of death. Estrangement is not taken into account. Until this conflict in the laws is corrected, there is a possibility that a cranky soon-to-be-ex-spouse may muck up your funeral plans.

- This state has no laws regulating the body parts business.

Miscellaneous Information

- Educational requirements for becoming a funeral director and embalmer: mortuary college (2 years), pass a state equivalent or national exam, and one year of apprenticeship. Alas, the national exam is a total embarrassment, deemed "irrelevant" and "useless" by consumer advocates and industry practitioners alike.

- Cash advance items may not be marked up with a commission for the mortuary. They must be billed to the consumer in the same amount the funeral home is billed.

- A statement that a casket is not required must appear on the funeral purchase agreement.

- Reference is made to the FTC Funeral Rule which allows those provisions to be enforced by the state.

- Prices must be disclosed in a standardized format that makes it easy for consumers to shop and compare.

- Medical examiners are appointed and must be licensed physicians.

- Casket retailers may not sell caskets preneed. The casket must be delivered at the time of sale. (Some casket stores have gone out of business in other states, having spent the prepaid casket money, with no provision for future delivery.)

- A next-of-kin or legal representative may request a disinterment permit from the state registrar. No permit is required for reinterment in the same cemetery.

- In compliance with the statutes, Arizona funeral directors must give out a pamphlet describing a funeral consumer's rights, and it is quite good. It is on the Internet or may be obtained by writing or calling the office:

Arizona State Board of Funeral Directors and Embalmers
1400 Washington, Room 230
Phoenix, AZ 85007
602-542-3095

This chapter was sent for fact-checking and review to the Arizona Board of Funeral Directors and Embalmers, the Department of Health Services—Vital Records, and the Department of Real Estate. No response was received from the Department of Real Estate. The Executive Director for the Funeral Board felt some of the editorial comments were a little harsh, especially with regard to crematories.

Caring for the Dead

In Arkansas

Please refer also to the general introduction to state chapters—"Caring for the Dead: Necessary Information."

Persons in Arkansas may care for their own dead. Wording for such is found in the following statutes:

Title 20-18-601(b): The funeral director or person acting as the funeral director who first assumes custody of the dead body shall: 1. file the death certificate . . .

Title 20-17-303. Disposition of the body. After the [coroner's] examination has been completed, the dead body shall be delivered to the relatives or friends of the deceased person for burial.

However, Rule II promulgated by the Board of Embalmers and Funeral Directors states:

1. Every funeral conducted within the State of Arkansas must be under the personal supervision and direction and charge of a Funeral Director who holds a valid license from this Board. To conduct a funeral shall require the direct personal supervision of a Licensed Funeral Director until final disposition is completed.

Statutory mandate gives the board authority only over those in commercial funeral service. This rule—which would limit the actions of church groups and private citizens if applied to them—is outside the authority of the board. Therefore, persons in Arkansas may care for their own dead, provided that all permits and other health regulations are in compliance.

Death Certificate

The family doctor, a local medical examiner or coroner, or a hospice nurse will sign the death certificate within 24 hours stating the cause of death. The remaining information must be supplied, typewritten or in black, unfading ink. The death certificate must be filed with the local Vital Records registrar within ten days and before final disposition.

Arkansas will adopt electronic death registration within a few years. When that is in place procedures may change somewhat but families should still be able to file a paper death certificate, available from the local registrar at the Health Department. The Vital Statistics Office in Little Rock is very helpful.

Please note: At this writing, when a person dies at home under hospice care, the hospice nurse "may" sign the death certificate [20-18-601(c)(3)]. But in that case, the coroner must be called. That is not required under hospice care in an institution. A call from a frustrated son alerted Carlson to this problem. When the community care home where his mother was living out her last days told Scott they would not release her body to him for home funeral arrangements, Scott and his wife made plans to move his mother to their home and care for her with hospice help. However, in walking through the process ahead of time, he had a shocking experience with the local coroner who also happens to be a funeral director. "I've been in business for 37 years and I know what I'm doing," he said. "If you call me, I'm going to pick up the body." Replied Scott, "I'll sue your pants off if you do."

In re-reading the law, we both agreed that the statute says the hospice nurse "may"—not "shall"—sign the death certificate. His mother's doctor agreed to sign the death certificate instead, foiling the hopes of one greedy funeral director–coroner.

Fetal Death

A fetal death report is required when there is no sign of life at delivery after 20 weeks or more of gestation from last normal menses to delivery, or when the weight is 350 grams or more (about 12 ounces). The physician, coroner (in case of home delivery), medical examiner, or other qualified attendant must prepare the certificate. The certificate must be filed within five days.

Transporting and Disposition Permit

A body may be moved with the consent of a physician, medical examiner or county coroner. A burial-transit permit, obtained from the local registrar, is required when a body is transported into or out of the state or for cremation. No burial-transit permit is required for burial within the state.

Burial

All burials must be in an established cemetery. Family graveyards are exempt from taxation and must be registered with the county clerk before burial. There are no state burial statutes or regulations with regard to depth.

A sensible guideline is 150 feet from a water supply and three feet of earth on top. To establish a burial plot on private land, contact the Health Department at (501)661-2654. Check any local zoning laws too.

Cremation

All cremations must be in a licensed crematory. If the death was investigated by a coroner or medical examiner, a cremation authorization must be obtained from that agent. Otherwise, a cremation authorization must be submitted by the person who has the right to control disposition, the next-of-kin, or the deceased prior to death.

Under the Arkansas Final Disposition Rights Act (20-17-102), an individual may indicate final wishes prior to death including cremation, and others are bound to follow such direction in this statute. Funeral Board regulations, however, have not been amended to recognize that and still permit next-of-kin to change cremation plans, "unless such change is in conflict with current Arkansas law." Sadly, experience tells us that many funeral directors won't honor the law permitting the deceased's wishes to prevail if a more expensive option can be sold to the family, relying on this poorly worded rule to do so.

Crematories (and direct disposition services) may not contract directly with the public, according to Funeral Board regulations. This is undoubtedly to protect full-service funeral homes from competition by low-cost providers, and may ultimately be grounds for a restraint of trade lawsuit.

Most crematories insist that a pacemaker be removed.

If cremated remains are scattered on private land, the written permission of the landowner is required. There are no other limitations on the disposition of cremated remains.

Other Requirements

When disposition has not occurred within 24 hours, the body must be embalmed or refrigerated at 45 degrees or lower, unless cremation is planned. Embalming or refrigeration is not required for 48 hours if cremation is the method of disposition.

A body to be shipped by common carrier or out of state must be embalmed. Per Health Department regs—8.0 (c), "A body which cannot be embalmed, or is in a state of decomposition, shall be transported only after enclosure in an air-tight container." This exception should be available to those who have a religious or other serious objection to embalming.

If the person died of a contagious or communicable disease, the doctor in attendance should be consulted.

Medical Schools for Body Donation

Body donation to a medical school is another option for disposition. Find the information for Arkansas at <www.finalrights.org>.

State Governance

The Arkansas Board of Embalmers and Funeral Directors has seven members. There are two consumer representatives, including one senior citizen. <www.state.ar.us/fdemb/index.html>

The Board of Embalmers and Funeral Directors licenses and inspects crematories and direct disposition services. One does not have to be a funeral director, however, to run a crematory.

The Arkansas Cemetery Board has seven members: the Securities Commissioner or designee; four cemeterians; and two public members, at least one of whom must be over the age of 60.

The Department of Insurance regulates all preneed transactions. <http://insurance.arkansas.gov/>

Prepaid Cemetery and Funeral Funds

Before a cemetery may be established, the Department of Health must determine if there is a potential threat of groundwater pollution.

Cemeteries must make an annual report of their perpetual care funds to the Cemetery Board. Ten percent of each lot, niche, or mausoleum sale must be set aside in the permanent maintenance fund.

A lot owner wishing to sell cemetery space must first offer it to the cemetery at the going rate for similar space (20-17-1019).

The Arkansas Insurance Commissioner oversees prepaid *funeral* contracts. The contracts must specify the specific goods and services being purchased at a contract or guaranteed price. With funeral inflation exceeding general inflation, this may be asking for mischief. Although the funeral home must provide goods and services of "a like kind and quality" to those chosen—regardless of the price at a later date, it would not be difficult for a mortician to coerce family members into picking something else, probably at an additional cost because of all the new casket styles appearing each year. A clear description of the quality and construction for any merchandise selected should be included in all prepaid plans, and the survivors should have the right to approve any substitutions.

If insurance is not used as the funding vehicle, the seller must establish "a trust account" into which all prepaid funds are deposited, but the law does not specify a separate trust in the name of each buyer. Statutes provide that "net investment income or surplus" may be withdrawn by the seller at any time.

Annual reporting to the Insurance Department is required, including the total invested and the people it covers. People may contact that department to inquire about the value of their contract. If you have not checked on this, the mortician may be the only one who knows exactly how much your account is worth, and your survivors could be in the dark about what excess funds will be due for refund.

Contracts made after July 1995 may be cancelled or transferred at any time. However, the following note will appear on your contract: "If this contract is irrevocable and you choose to transfer this contract to a substitute provider, the entire amount of the contract will not be transferred and you may have to pay more to obtain 100% of the services provided for in the contract." That actually applies to a revocable one, as well, because all you will get back is the principal amount paid, not the interest.

Arkansas has established a fund to protect consumers from fraud and embezzlement of prepaid funeral monies. $5 of each prepaid account is remitted to the state for this fund.

Consumer Concerns

- The death rate in Arkansas can support approximately 114 full-time mortuaries; there are, however, 349. Funeral prices tend to be higher in areas where there are "too many" funeral homes.

- It appears that "constructive delivery" (warehousing) is permitted for prepaid cemetery merchandise such as vaults and markers. This should be eliminated, with 100% of all such prepaid monies put into trust against the possibility of cancellation.

- There is no annual reporting requirement to the purchaser of prepaid funeral goods and services. Such paperwork might be helpful to the family of a deceased to indicate prepayment and would help to "enforce" trusting requirements.

- Until the Arkansas laws are changed to require survivor approval for substitution of funeral merchandise, all interest earned to stay with the account, and full trusting of cemetery purchases, it is probably a terrible idea to prepay for these goods and services. Your own trust account in a bank will be safer.

- The standards for ethical, professional conduct are inadequate and should be strengthened to make it easier for a consumer to prevail when filing a complaint. (See Ethical Standards in Appendix.)

- Complaint procedures are unclear and inadequate.

- There is no requirement to identify and tag a body at the place of death before removal. Such a requirement would avoid body mix-up as sometimes happens at large facilities.

- The regulations require that at least five caskets be on display, but there is no requirement that low-cost caskets be included. With computer presentations for a wide variety of models now available, the casket display requirement is obsolete.

- Although the FTC Funeral Rule is listed on the Funeral Board's website and may be included in material sent to licensees, nothing in the statutes or regulations requires funeral directors to abide by it, making the Rule difficult to enforce in this state.

- Furthermore, current Arkansas regulations seem to permit funeral pricing and practices that are in conflict with the FTC Funeral Rule. The FTC requires an itemized list of prices for all options to be given to consumers at the beginning of any funeral arrangement and a casket price list prior to the showing of any caskets. Under "Disclosure," Arkansas regs require that all caskets have a visible price card showing what merchandise and/or services are included, the old bundling practice from days of yore. Only much later in the regs, buried some paragraphs and two headings later, does it state that a licensee must make "a full disclosure of all its available services and merchandise . . . prior to selection of the casket and services." One finds it easy to suspect that bundling may still be a widespread practice in Arkansas.

- The State Funeral Board's restriction to prevent crematories and body transporters from dealing directly with the public will keep consumer choices limited and costs high and is an unfair trade practice. The scandal in Noble, Georgia happened under the "watch" of funeral directors. That should be the state's job. Families may be more trustworthy in caring for the dead than some funeral directors. Furthermore, there is nothing in the study guide for the national funeral directors' exam regarding cremation and little if anything on cremation in mortuary school curricula.

- Coroners are elected. Some are medical people but many are funeral directors or have an affiliation with a funeral home. When that is the case, there is a serious conflict of interest. Consumers should feel free to have a body moved to the funeral home of their choice if a coroner has sent the body to a funeral home that otherwise would not have been selected. There is no code of ethics on the coroner's association website.

- This state has no laws regulating the body parts business.

Miscellaneous Information

- Educational requirements for a funeral director are a high school degree and two years of apprenticeship. One year of mortuary school may replace one year of apprenticeship. For an embalmer, high school and mortuary college (2 years) plus one year of apprenticeship are required. Both must pass a national and state exam. Alas, the national exam is an embarrassment, deemed "irrelevant" and "useless" by consumer advocates and some industry practitioners alike.

- Cash advance items must be billed in the amount of the actual cost paid by the funeral home, without a mark-up.

- You may name an agent for handling funeral arrangements in your declaration for disposition.

- A lot owner wishing to sell his/her cemetery plot must offer it to the cemetery first at the going rate.

- A permit for disinterment must be obtained from the State Registrar with the consent of the next-of-kin or their authorized agent, unless the disinterment is by court order. The disinterment must be under the direct supervision of a licensed funeral director. The casket may not be opened except by court order.

This chapter was sent for fact-checking and review to the Cemetery Board, the Insurance Department, the Arkansas Funeral Board, and the Department of Health's Vital Statistics Division. Although some information was verified by telephone, no written responses were received.

Caring for the Dead

In California

Please refer also to the general introduction to state chapters—"Caring for the Dead: Necessary Information."

Persons in California may care for their own dead. The legal authority to do so is in the California statutes, Chapter 3, section 7100:

> *(a) The right to control the disposition of the remains of a deceased person, the location and conditions of interment, and arrangements for funeral goods and services to be provided, unless other directions have been given by the decedent pursuant to Section 7100.1, vests in, and the duty of disposition and the liability for the reasonable cost of disposition of the remains [emphasis added] devolves upon, the following in the order named:*
>
> *(1) An agent under a power of attorney for health care who has the right and duty of disposition under Division 4.7 (commencing with Section 4600) of the Probate Code, except that the agent is liable for the costs of disposition only in either of the following cases:*
>
> > *(A) Where the agent makes a specific agreement to pay the costs of disposition.*
> >
> > *(B) Where, in the absence of a specific agreement, the agent makes decisions concerning disposition that incur costs, in which case the agent is liable only for the reasonable costs incurred as a result of the agent's decisions, to the extent that the decedent's estate or other appropriate fund is insufficient.*
>
> *(2) The competent surviving spouse.*
>
> *(3) The sole surviving competent adult child of the decedent, or if there is more than one competent adult child of the decedent, the majority of the surviving competent adult children. However, less than the majority of the surviving competent adult children shall be vested with*

the rights and duties of this section if they have used reasonable efforts to notify all other surviving competent adult children of their instructions and are not aware of any opposition to those instructions by the majority of all surviving competent adult children.

(4) The surviving competent parent or parents of the decedent. If one of the surviving competent parents is absent, the remaining competent parent shall be vested with the rights and duties of this section after reasonable efforts have been unsuccessful in locating the absent surviving competent parent.

(5) The sole surviving competent adult sibling of the decedent, or if there is more than one surviving competent adult sibling of the decedent, the majority of the surviving competent adult siblings. . .

(6) The surviving competent adult person or persons respectively in the next degrees of kinship . . . .

The duty to pay for a funeral is enforced only if you live in the state. There are no statutes that require you to use a funeral director.

Death Certificate

The family doctor will sign the death certificate within 15 hours, stating the cause of death. A coroner will supply a death certificate within three days.

California is now using electronic death registration in most counties. Paper death certificates are still being used in a few counties. A family can get a blank death certificate from the local health department.

Fetal Death

A fetal death certificate is required when death occurs after 20 weeks of gestation. If there is no family physician involved, the local medical examiner must sign the fetal death certificate.

Transporting and Disposition Permit

Upon presentation of a completed death certificate, the local registrar in the county health department will issue the permit for disposition. This must specify the cemetery, at sea, or crematory with final resting place for cremains. (It's fine to say you'll be taking them home.) One copy must be filed with the registrar of the county where disposition takes place and one must be returned to the issuing registrar within ten days. The charge for this permit is $7. After-hours service may not be available in all counties. Therefore, a family trying to make arrangements when death occurs during a weekend may find the process difficult. (Funeral directors have the advantage of electronic filing.)

Burial

Body burial must have 18 inches of earth on top; with a double-depth burial (one vault on top of another), at least 12 inches of cover is required. Burial must be in an established cemetery, so you will need to check with the county registrar for local zoning laws to see about establishing a cemetery for home burial. According to a 1939 statute, six or more bodies buried in one place—not the cremated remains of six—constitutes a "cemetery." One must wonder if they all have to die at once to start a new cemetery.

Local municipalities are given jurisdiction over cemetery matters, and it will be up to local officials to okay home burial in rural areas. Statute 8115 reads:

> *The governing body of any city or county, in the exercise of its police power, may by ordinance prescribe such standards governing burial, inurnment, and entombment and such standards of maintenance for cemeteries, including mausoleums and columbariums, as it shall determine to be reasonably necessary to protect the public health or safety, assure decent and respectful treatment of human remains, or prevent offensive deterioration of cemetery grounds, structures, and places of interment. Such standards may be made applicable to every public and private cemetery within the city or county.*

One has to wonder why local officials were unwilling to permit Michael Jackson's burial on family property.

In any event, if you are in a rural area and want to establish a family cemetery, draw a map of the property showing where the burial ground will be. A good practice is 150 feet from a water supply and 25 feet from a power line or neighbor's boundary. Then take it to the local zoning board or other municipal authority. That may be all you have to do to establish your family cemetery before having it recorded with the deed.

You might also show the municipal folks this 9700 statute: "*The owner of property may dedicate the property to pet cemetery purposes by a notarized dedication recorded with the county recorder of the county in which the property is situated . . . .*" If that's all it takes for a pet cemetery, a family cemetery shouldn't be considered a big deal either.

Cremation

No additional state-mandated permit for cremation is required. Most crematories insist that a pacemaker be removed.

If a crematory does not permit a family to witness the cremation, that must be disclosed prior to any contract.

A person may authorize his or her own cremation prior to death. Otherwise that must be done by the person(s) with the right to control disposition.

In addition, a new form has been added, Declaration for Disposition of Cremated Remains, in which to detail the disposition of cremated remains.

Having been removed from any container, cremated remains may be scattered at sea, at least 500 feet from shore and not from any bridge or pier. A verified statement must be filed with the local registrar nearest the point where scattering occurred. These provisions are unenforceable, and California families regularly, if discreetly, scatter cremains at beaches.

If not in a cemetery, cremated remains may be interred or scattered with the permission of the landowner; or they may be kept in the dwelling of the person having the right to control disposition. But the DCA website says, "You may not remove the cremated remains from the container and you must arrange for their disposition upon your death." We're not sure what self-important bureaucrat dreamed that one up. One woman put them in a whiskey bottle and made a lamp out of it, "because he lit up my life." What's going to be the penalty if you do something like that?

According to the DCA funeral and cemetery web page, "Cremated remains may not be transported without a permit from the county health department, and they may not be disposed of in refuse." Examining the statutes, however, it is hard to see that interpretation applied to every time you might move, perhaps to a new house in another town. Yes, the initial disposition permit must state the intended destination for the cremated remains, but there are no "cremains police" checking to see if they're still on your mantel, for example, 25 years from the date of death.

Legislation introduced in 2010 would add a provision for a disposition permit for every keepsake urn into which cremated remains were divided, with the home address and name of each person having one . . . for an extra fee for each such permit. This was not written up at the request of the DCA, so someone in the industry is busy making cremation more complicated for California folks. Maybe you should just take the cremated remains home and divvy up Mom there.

Except for South Dakota, there is no other state with such unenforceable and unnecessary requirements.

California licenses cremated remains disposers.

Other Requirements

Regulations, not statutes, require a body to be embalmed or refrigerated after 24 hours. That would apply to bodies in the possession of a funeral home licensee, not home funeral families.

Before a mortician may embalm a body, the person arranging for the body disposition must sign an authorization that discloses that embalming provides no permanent preservation.

If the person died of a contagious or communicable disease, the doctor in attendance or local health officer should be consulted.

If the body is to be shipped by common carrier, it must be embalmed or shipped in an airtight container. However, that section of the health and safety code also says "A dead body, which cannot be embalmed or is in a state of decomposition, shall be received for transportation by a common carrier if the body is placed in an airtight metal casket enclosed in a strong transportation case or in a sound casket enclosed in an airtight metal or metal-lined transportation case."

Those with objections to embalming should be able to take advantage of that exception. Longtime California funeral directors tell us they routinely ship Jewish bodies this way, and that no one is enforcing this unnecessary requirement.

Medical Schools for Body Donation

Body donation to a medical school is another option for disposition. Find the information for California at <www.finalrights.org>.

State Governance

The California legislature voted in 1995 not to fund the State Funeral and Cemetery Boards, giving oversight to the Consumer Affairs Division of the Attorney General's Office. It is overworked and understaffed, and one has to wonder whether the public is well-served by this change. It has an excellent website, however: <http://www.cfb.ca.gov/>.

For now, it's closed most Fridays.

Prepaid Cemetery and Funeral Funds

100% of cemetery goods and services must be placed in trust."Constructive delivery" can bypass the trusting requirement. "Delivery" usually is accomplished by issuing a certificate of ownership and warehousing the vault and/ or marker, although the state is not checking to see if the goods are actually there. Once "delivered," it is almost impossible to get a refund even if the items and services have never been used.

If the price for cemetery goods or services sold preneed is not guaranteed, a disclosure must appear on the contract indicating that additional charges may be due at the time of death.

A city or county cemetery may not sell markers or monuments.

Cemeteries must make an annual report to the state accounting for all pre-need and endowment funds. California has had some serious problems with cemeteries going out of business, due to lack of adequate maintenance or endowment funds. One has to wonder what the state has been doing with the reports or whether the reporting is even enforced.

California requires that 100% of all prepaid funeral funds be deposited in **trust** in a federally insured institution. Constructive delivery is not permitted for funeral merchandise. A 10% revocation fee may be charged by the seller if the plan is cancelled or transferred, payable from the interest only. The law permits the seller to withdraw 4% of the original amount from the earnings each year, which leaves little to accumulate for covering inflation. There won't be much to pay the seller a 10% revocation fee either.

Commingled preneed trust funds "shall be subject to an annual, independent certified financial audit" which is then to be filed with the state. There is no way for the state to know, however, if some funds were never put in trust. There is also nothing to prevent the loss of value if the trust funds were paid into the stock market as apparently happened with the California Funeral Directors Association's "Master Trust." In July 2010, the state released an audit showing the Master Trust misused $70 million in consumers' prepaid money on things like *lobbying* on behalf of funeral directors, and attendance at trade conventions (marketing extravaganzas).

Funeral and cemetery providers must disclose any prepaid contracts to those making the final arrangements or risk a fine of three times the amount if failing to do so.

Consumer Concerns

- The death rate in California can support approximately 904 full-time mortuaries; there are, in fact, 757. This is one of the very few states where there is not a significant glut of funeral homes, and prices are competitive in some areas. Consumers will have to shop around, however, as there is a huge difference from one funeral home to the next.

- There are statutory provisions for vacating a cemetery. While they are thoughtful provisions, it seems a little disconcerting that a cemetery in California isn't necessarily a permanent easement on the land.

- There is no requirement for annual reporting to the purchaser of prepaid funeral and cemetery goods and services. Such paperwork might be helpful to the family of a deceased to indicate prepayment and help to "enforce" the required trusting, as well.

- The buyer is at risk of losing all interest if a preneed contract is cancelled or transferred.

- There is no standard preneed contract that would require a detailed description of all merchandise selected. There is no requirement for a substitution of like quality and construction, approved by survivors, if the agreed-upon merchandise is not available.

- There is no guarantee fund to protect prepaid funeral money in case of default.

- Until the preneed loopholes are closed, it is probably a terrible idea to prepay for a funeral in California.

- There is no requirement to identify and tag the body at the place of death before removal.

- There is no requirement to include low-cost caskets in any display.

- Consumer price surveys show that at least some funeral homes are not using the standardized price format required by the state (to make it easy for consumers to shop and compare). Apparently the state inspectors are not checking on this.

- Information on funeral industry violators is no longer available to the public since the Department of Consumer Affairs took over. This takes away the consumer's right-to-know, the normal self-defense against unscrupulous businesses.

- The state has not adopted the Federal Trade Commission Funeral Rule by statute or regulation. Similar price disclosure is required, but the misrepresentation and anti-tying provisions of the Funeral Rule were omitted. (A link to the FTC's Rule is on their website.)

- High ethical standards in competence, honesty, and business practice are not clearly defined. If so, it would be easier for a consumer to prevail when filing a legitimate complaint. (See Appendix.)

- This state has no laws regulating the body parts business.

Miscellaneous Information

- Educational requirements for becoming an embalmer: One year of mortuary college, two years of apprenticeship, and an exam. For a funeral director: Associates Degree (2 years) and an exam. To be licensed as a funeral director one must be employed by or the owner of a funeral establishment. Other than a $400 licensing fee, there are no requirements for a funeral establishment other than a fixed place of business—no embalming room, no casket display, etc. This should make possible low-cost competition.

- Cash advance items may not be marked up with a commission for the mortuary. They must be billed to the consumer in the same amount the funeral home is billed.

- A statement that a casket is not required must appear on the funeral purchase agreement. There is also a regulation that requires the following statement to appear on each casket that has a sealing device: There is no scientific or other evidence that any casket with a sealing device will preserve human remains.

- There is a statutory duty to comply with the written wishes of the decedent if the deceased left sufficient funds. You may name an agent for body disposition in your Advance Directive document if you would prefer someone other than your legal next-of-kin to handle your affairs.

- In compliance with the statutes, California funeral directors and cemeterians must give out a pamphlet describing a funeral consumer's rights. It is available on-line <www.cfb.ca.gov/consumer/funeral.shtml> or may be obtained by writing or calling:

California Department of Consumer Affairs
Cemetery & Funeral Programs
800-952-5210
400 -R- St.,
Sacramento, CA 95814

The DCA website also has information for filing a complaint including an on-line form.

- Anyone responsible for the disposition of a body who fails to do so "within a reasonable time" is liable for three times the cost of another person's actually doing so in his or her stead, if a state resident.

- Undertakers are subject to disciplinary action for "using profane, indecent or obscene language in the course of the preparation for burial, removal or other disposition of or during the funeral service for a dead human body or within the immediate hearing of the family or relatives of a deceased, whose body has not yet been interred or otherwise disposed of." (After burial, watch out?)

- Coroners are elected. A medical examiner—a physician—may be appointed.

- A body may not be held for debt.

- A permit from the Health Department is required for disinterment and removal from a cemetery.

This chapter was sent for review to the California Department of Consumer Affairs and the Department of Public Health but they declined to comment.

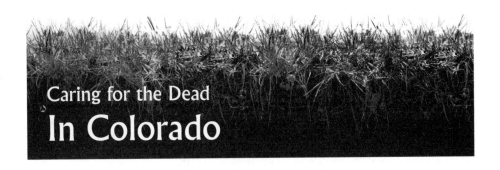

Caring for the Dead
In Colorado

Please refer also to the general introduction to state chapters—"Caring for the Dead: Necessary Information."

Persons in Colorado may care for their own dead. The legal authority to do so is found in:

Title 25-2-110 (3) The funeral director or person acting as such who first assumes custody of a dead body or dead fetus shall be responsible for the filing of the death certificate.

Title 12-54-119 [re statutes regulating the funeral profession] (2) This part shall not apply to, nor in any way interfere with, any custom or rite of any religious sect in the burial of its dead, and the members and followers of such religious sect may continue to care for, prepare, and bury the bodies of deceased members. . .

Death Certificate

The family doctor or coroner will sign the death certificate within 48 hours, stating the cause of death. The remaining information must be supplied, typewritten or in black ink. The death certificate must be filed with the local registrar in the county where death occurred within five days and prior to disposition.

Money problems have kept Colorado from implementing electronic death registration, but that will surely be coming, and when it does, the procedures will change somewhat. If Colorado follows the route other states have taken, a paper alternative will be available for the home funeral folks, and the local registrar or health department will type into the system the necessary demographic information. How to handle weekend and holiday deaths may be of concern.

Fetal Death

Fetal death must be reported if gestation is 20 weeks or greater. A physician's or coroner's signature is required.

Transporting and Disposition Permit

The county registrar or coroner will issue a disposition permit. The death certificate must be obtained first. The permit must be endorsed by the sexton or crematory and returned within five days to the issuing registrar.

Burial

In 2010 coroners rammed a bill through the legislature requiring that all burials on private property be recorded with the county within 30 days. The Coroners Association and legislative sponsors failed to return Carlson's phone and e-mail messages suggesting inclusion of guidelines such as 150 feet from a water supply, 25 feet from a power line or boundary, with two or three feet of earth on top. The Private Burial Affidavit form can be obtained from the local registrar or coroner.

Cremation

The disposition permit serves as the permit to cremate. No additional permit is required. Most crematories insist that a pacemaker be removed, and authorization by next-of-kin or the designated agent is required. There are no laws regarding the disposition of cremated remains. You may do as you wish.

Other Requirements

If disposition does not occur within 24 hours, the body must be embalmed or refrigerated.

If the person died of a contagious or communicable disease, the person acting as the funeral director must consult with the local or state health officer concerning disposition.

A body to be transported by common carrier must be prepared by a mortuary science practitioner and embalmed or shipped in a hermetically sealed casket.

Medical Schools for Body Donation

Body donation to a medical school is another option for disposition. Find the information for Colorado at <www.finalrights.org>.

State Governance

The Colorado funeral board was eliminated by sunset laws in 1983, and funeral directors are no longer licensed in this state. The Colorado Funeral Directors and Embalmers Association, a trade organization, has established the Mortuary Science Commission. The Commission "certifies" those applying for recognition who have successfully completed training and apprenticeship. The Commission has five members. Three are funeral directors, one represents the clergy, and one is a consumer representative.

In 2009, the Colorado legislature moved in a new direction which now requires the "registration" of all funeral homes and crematories with the Department of Regulatory Agencies (DORA). This seems little more than a ploy to gather funds for the state with new registration fees while clogging up files with useless paperwork. In addition, the legislation defined who may be called a "mortuary science practitioner" or "funeral director."

We suspect that, despite its denials, the Colorado Funeral Directors Association (which pushed the legislation) sees this as the first step back to full licensure to more efficiently restrict low-cost competition. COFDA described the bill as aiming for nothing more than "Title Protection." A "mortuary science practitioner" must graduate from an approved mortuary school, pass a national exam put out by the International Conference of Funeral Service Examining Boards (a test now being declared irrelevant and 40 years out of date by both industry and consumer critics), and serve 2,000 hours of apprenticeship. A "funeral director" needs only the 2,000 hours of apprenticeship that includes at least 50 services.

Odd Math

The legislation doesn't even require a test to see if a prospective funeral director understands state law or the FTC Funeral Rule. An "embalmer," however, has the burden of 4,000 hours (two years) of apprenticeship involving 50 dead human bodies. With the average embalming taking about two hours, that would use up 100 or so of the required hours. Just what did the legislators think these embalmers would be doing for the other 3,900 hours? A cremationist must apprentice for 500 hours with at least 50 bodies involved. More odd math here, as a typical cremation is only about 2½ hours—125 hours total. EMTs—the ones who work to keep you alive—need less than half the training embalmers do, and embalmers only have to make you look good after you're dead. (This gem was noted in a Funeral Consumer Society of Colorado newsletter).

Misconduct by Buildings?

Mind you, funeral directors or whatever you want to call them are still not licensed or registered in Colorado. Only the physical funeral or crematory establishment is registered and at risk of losing its registration at the beck and call of DORA. Apparently the legislators forgot that when they wrote, **"12-54-405. Letters of admonition—funeral homes and crematories. (1)**

When a complaint or investigation discloses an instance of misconduct . . ."
And just how can a building be guilty of misconduct? Now they really screw
things up: **"12-54-406. Cease-and-desist orders—procedure.** (1)(a) If it appears to the director, based upon credible evidence as presented in a written
complaint, that a person is acting in a manner that creates an imminent
threat to the health and safety of the public, or a person is acting or has acted
without the required registration, the director may issue an order to cease
and desist such activity. . . ." *But remember, persons are not required to be
registered.* Because no industry practitioners are licensed or even registered,
does DORA really have any authority to discipline them?

Foxes Guarding the Henhouse

If the legislature wanted to regulate the activities of funeral industry practitioners, they certainly made a muddle of it this time. There is no standard
of unprofessional conduct, unlike states such as New York that have detailed
such lists in their statutes. Indeed, in Colorado the director or administrative law judge "may consult with . . . an appropriate professional organization or association of businesses . . . weighing the appropriate standard of
care . . ." when adjudicating a complaint. In other words, if someone has filed
a complaint against a discount cremation service, the director can contact
the Colorado Funeral Directors Association to see what those folks think
the proper care should be. Many of the COFDA members run full-service
establishments that may be suffering from low-cost competition. And the
same business organizations may be consulted in the drafting of any rules,
too. Impartial opinions? Why didn't the statute require the director to also
consult with the Funeral Consumer Society of Colorado?

Crematories must be registered with DORA. One does not need to be a funeral director to run a crematory.

Prepaid Cemetery and Funeral Funds

The Insurance Division regulates preneed sales for both cemetery and funeral purchases, and licenses preneed sellers who may or may not be funeral
directors or cemeterians. With insurance usually a poor choice for funding
a funeral (due to high cost and/or poor growth), one has to wonder why that
was given to the insurance guys and gals instead of the Division of Financial
Services, the Division of Banking, or the Division of Securities.

Fifteen percent of the sales price of any grave and at least ten percent of the
sales price of any crypt or niche must be put into an endowment fund in a
state-authorized institution.

Although 85% of *cemetery goods* must be placed in trust, "constructive delivery" can bypass the trusting requirement. "Delivery" usually is accomplished by issuing a certificate of ownership and warehousing the vault and/or marker, but the state is not checking to see if the goods are actually there. Once "delivered," it is almost impossible to get a refund even if the items have never been used.

Only 75% of prepaid *funeral* money is required to be put in trust, which—in effect—permits the seller of preneed funeral goods and services to pocket an up-front "commission" of 25%. "Constructive delivery" can bypass the trusting requirements for funeral merchandise, too. If you have a $6,000 funeral contract of which $1,000 is for a vault and $2,000 for a casket, the seller may give you a slip of paper saying those are in a warehouse. Then the seller deposits 75% of the remaining $3,000—or a mere $2,250 of your original $6,000. With that kind of immediate financial gain and warehousing mischief, Colorado must be a paradise for preneed funeral merchants.

The law is vague about what happens if you change your mind. A consumer may cancel a preneed contract and get a full refund within seven days. You may cancel (or, presumably, transfer) a preneed policy after seven days, "for return of consideration." How much "consideration" you'll get seems iffy but surely will be missing the interest and likely the 25% the seller pocketed to begin with. And write off the casket and vault if they're in the warehouse.

If you default on payments, the funeral home is permitted to keep 15% of the contract price (not 15% of what you actually paid) as liquidated damages. The math doesn't work very well here, as the seller may have already pocketed 25%. Perhaps that means the seller must fork over the other 10% whether it's in the trust or not.

A tip sheet from DORA says that heirs may cancel a preneed contract after death and get 100% refunded, but this right seems murky given the contradictory legal provisions.

Not all those selling preneed funeral arrangements are morticians. Agents are required to make an annual report to the trustee holding prepaid funeral monies (such as a bank) so that the trustee or state can compare all accounts outstanding against funds being held. However, there seems to be no way for the state to check if all preneed sales are actually deposited and included in the report. In the case of one pair of agents, at least some money had been deposited, and—once the state had audited the account—they emptied the account, with over $100,000 in prepaid funeral money now missing. The funeral homes named as the suppliers for these arrangements have been gracious enough to honor them. Not a nice situation, however, for anyone.

To its credit, Colorado's Department of Insurance has tackled the Neptune Society's preneed racket which Carlson had reported to the SEC almost ten years earlier. The state's actions regarding this scam, which still exists in many other states, is described in the Chapter 6.

Consumer Concerns

- The death rate in Colorado can support approximately 118 full-time mortuaries; there are, however, 170. Funeral prices tend to be higher in areas where there are "too many" funeral homes.

- Constructive delivery is permitted, and trusting requirements for both cemetery and funeral purchases are inadequate. Twenty-nine other states require 100% trusting for funeral preneed contracts. Preneed is alive and well in those states. Why doesn't the legislature want the same protection for Colorado residents?

- The requirement that preneed contracts must be printed in at least eight-point type is inadequate for anyone with failing eyesight; this should be increased to ten or twelve.

- There is no requirement that the family or designated agent approve any substitution of merchandise, although substitutions must be of equal quality.

- There is no requirement for an annual report to the consumer specifying the institution of deposit and value of prepaid funeral funds. Such documents could be important to survivors who might not know about prepaid accounts and would help to enforce trusting requirements.

- There is no statutory provision to protect consumers against default of prepaid agreements if funds were never put in trust.

- Until the laws are amended, it is a terrible idea to prepay for a funeral in Colorado.

- There is no requirement to identify and tag the body at the place of death before removal.

- The requirement for embalming or refrigeration within 24 hours is unnecessarily restrictive and should be increased to 72 hours or eliminated to permit families to more readily care for their own dead and to honor individual preferences and religious tenets.

- Colorado has no way to put unethical practitioners out of business without licensing. (See Appendix for Ethical Standards.)

- The FTC Funeral Rule has not been adopted in the statutes which would make it more enforceable in this state.

- This state has no laws regulating the body parts business.

Miscellaneous Information

- Cash advance items may not be marked up with a commission for the mortuary. They must be billed to the consumer in the same amount the funeral home is billed. Anecdotally, however, there is evidence that this statute is being ignored.

- Coroners who have an interest in a funeral home may not, as a rule, direct business to their own establishments in the course of performing as a coroner unless there is an emergency. There is no code of ethics on the coroners' association website, however, to guard against such a conflict of interest.

- You may name a designated agent to carry out your funeral wishes which may be important if you are estranged from your next-of-kin.

- A permit for disinterment and removal from a cemetery must be obtained from the state registrar in the Health Department.

This chapter was sent for review and fact-checking to the State Registrar, DORA, the Division of Insurance, and the Colorado Funeral Directors Association. Helpful corrections were given by the state registrar's office. DORA's response was, "I think that the Funeral Directors Association is going to take the lead on this." What other state would imply that a trade organization is more competent than the state agency mandated with the regulation of that same trade? Colorado tax dollars are doing what for consumers?

Caring for the Dead

In Connecticut

Please refer also to the general introduction to state chapters—"Caring for the Dead: Necessary Information."

In Connecticut a dead body becomes a hostage of the funeral industry, one of only eight states that require the use of a funeral director. (Connecticut, Illinois, Indiana, Louisiana, Michigan, Nebraska, New Jersey, and New York.) In no other situation is a private citizen forced to use a for-profit business to fulfill the interests of the state. The statutes also conflict with each other:

> *Sec. 45a-318.* **Document directing or designating individual to have custody and control of disposition of deceased person's body. . . .(a)** *Any person eighteen years of age or older, and of sound mind, may execute in advance of such person's death a written document, subscribed by such person and attested by two witnesses, either: (1) Directing the disposition of such person's body upon the death of such person, which document may also designate an individual to have custody and control of such person's body and to act as agent to carry out such directions; or (2) if there are no directions for disposition, designating an individual to have custody and control of the disposition of such person's body upon the death of such person . . . .*

The statute goes on to list next-of-kin in the absence of an agent. But the rights granted in Section 45a-318 are completely voided by the following:

> *Sec. 7-62b.* **Death certificates. . .** *(a) A death certificate for each death which occurs in this state shall be completed in its entirety and filed with the registrar of vital statistics in the town in which the death occurred no later than five days after death if filing a paper certificate and no later than three days after death if filing through an electronic death registry system, in order to obtain a burial permit prior to final disposition. . . .*

(b) The funeral director or embalmer licensed by the department, or the funeral director or embalmer licensed in another state and complying with the terms of a reciprocal agreement on file with the department, in charge of the burial of the deceased person shall complete the death certificate on a form provided by the department. Said certificate shall be filed by a licensed embalmer or such embalmer's designee or a funeral director or such director's designee, in accordance with the provisions of this section, except when inquiry is required by the Chief Medical Examiner's Office. . . .Only a licensed embalmer may assume charge of the burial of a deceased person who had a communicable disease. . . .

Parents may file a birth certificate if no doctor is involved. What's the big deal about a death certificate?

*Sec. 7-69. **Removal of body of deceased person.** No person except a licensed embalmer or funeral director licensed by the department, or licensed in a state having a reciprocal agreement on file with the department and complying with the terms of such agreement, shall remove the body of a deceased person . . . .*

Title 7-62b—re Death certificates—refers to the licensed funeral director "in charge of the burial." What if the family doesn't want a funeral director in charge? Title 45a-318 specifically gives custody of the deceased to a designated agent or the family. Other states use the statutory wording "funeral director or person acting as such." This would be more to the point for the purpose of ensuring accurate vital statistics in the least restrictive manner possible. None of the information on the death certificate comes from the funeral director. The physician fills out the medical portion and the family has to supply the "mother's maiden name"-type details.

Title 7-69—requiring a funeral director to move a body—is again in conflict with 45a-318 that specifically gives custody to family. Furthermore, all one needs to drive a motor vehicle is the appropriate driver's license. We know of no special skills required for riding in the front seat when there is a body in the back. Title 7-69 is unnecessarily restrictive and of benefit to a special interest group only—funeral directors.

If the laws cannot be repealed, they will likely generate a court case contesting their Constitutionality. In a 1909 federal case, Wyeth v. Cambridge Board of Health, the court ruled:

. . . the refusal to permit one to bury the dead body of his relative or friend, except under an unreasonable limitation, is also an interference

with a private right that is not allowable under the Constitution of the Commonwealth or the Constitution of the United States.

Death Certificate

The death certificate must be signed by a physician within 24 hours and filed, prior to disposition, in the town where death occurred. Electronic death registration (EDR) began in late '09 in some towns and should be complete by early 2011. All town clerks as well as funeral directors will have the software.

Fetal Death

A fetal death report, signed by a medical examiner or physician, is required when death occurs after 20 weeks of gestation.

Transporting and Disposition Permit

With a paper system, the local registrar will issue a burial permit or a removal permit to a funeral director only. If cremation is planned, one must obtain the cremation certificate from the medical examiner before applying to the registrar for a cremation permit. A funeral director may serve as a sub-registrar for use on holidays and weekends but may not issue a cremation permit.

With EDR, the removal permit will be generated automatically when the death certificate has been filed electronically.

Burial

A burial permit must be obtained from the registrar of the town in which burial will occur. Burial must be 350 feet from a dwelling place, one-half mile from a reservoir, 600 feet from an ice pond, and the top of the casket must be 2½ feet from the surface of the earth. The sexton will return the burial permit to the registrar in a monthly report.

Cremation

There is no fee for a cremation certificate if the death is under the jurisdiction of a medical examiner. In all other cases, a cremation certificate from the medical examiner must be obtained. The fee for this is at least $40 but more typically set by the medical examiner at $75. Once the cremation certificate has been obtained, a registrar will issue a cremation permit. The charge for this is $3. Sub-registrars may not issue cremation permits.

The cremation permit must indicate the intended destination of the cremated remains. There are no cremains police to see if they are still on the shelf in the den in ten years, so you can effectively do as you wish.

There is a 48-hour wait before cremation unless death was from a communicable disease. A crematory may charge for storage or refrigeration if the body is delivered much before that time. Most crematories insist that pacemakers be removed, and authorization by next-of-kin usually is required.

Other Requirements

There are no embalming requirements in Connecticut, but if the person died of a communicable disease, disposition must be handled by a licensed embalmer. Disposition must occur within a "reasonable time."

Medical Schools for Body Donation

Body donation to a medical school is another option for disposition. Find the information for Connecticut at <www.finalrights.org>.

State Governance

The Department of Public Health is the agency that is given the responsibility to license and inspect funeral homes—not the Board of Examiners of Embalmers and Funeral Directors. Of what importance does the state of Connecticut see in having a Board of Examiners of Embalmers and Funeral Directors? From a statutory point of view, attendance at board meetings is of concern:

> *Title 20-208. Examining board. (b) Said board shall meet at least once during each calendar quarter . . . Any member who fails to attend three consecutive meetings or who fails to attend fifty per cent of all meetings held during any calendar year shall be deemed to have resigned from office.*

Is there any mandate to set ethical standards and protect funeral consumers? Not that we could find. The board is empowered to adjudicate complaints and impose sanctions, but that would be after the fact.

The Examining Board has five members. Three are embalmers and two are public members. When Carlson tried to get the names of the board members including the consumer representatives, she played number tag at the Department of Public Health before getting kicked off the line. There is no website for the Funeral Board and only one page on the Public Health website that even mentions them.

Crematories may be established on cemetery grounds or on other lots with the approval of selectmen.

Prepaid Cemetery and Funeral Funds

There is no state cemetery board. Perpetual care funds for cemeteries are usually entrusted to the town or state, as most cemeteries are municipal ones. Religious cemeteries are expected to put perpetual care funds into trust also. There is no other regulation of prepaid cemetery funds.

Prepaid *funeral* funds must be placed into federally insured accounts and both the consumer and seller must receive an annual report. Commingling of accounts is permitted.

The seller of a funeral contract is allowed to collect a 5% administrative fee if the purchaser defaults or moves the contract to another firm or simply wants to cancel the arrangement.

The funeral establishment is obligated to substitute merchandise "similar in style and at least equal in quality" for any items selected preneed, but there is no indication that an adequate description of merchandise will be included in any such contract.

Consumer Concerns

- The death rate in Connecticut can support approximately 114 full-time mortuaries; there are, however, 296. Funeral prices tend to be higher in areas where there are "too many" funeral homes.

- The laws in Connecticut restrict families from caring for their own dead and should be amended to protect the rights of individuals.

- A 5% penalty is permitted when cancelling a preneed funeral contract.

- There is no default fund to protect prepaid funeral accounts. With annual reporting, it is likely that few defaults will occur—but only if consumers know that they must get the annual report.

- There is no requirement for a detailed description of merchandise selected preneed. Survivors should approve any substitution.

- Although the preneed laws in Connecticut are better than in some states, it may be unwise to prepay for a funeral until the penalty for transferring an account is eliminated and survivors are given the right to approve substitution of merchandise.

- No statute or regulation requires display of low-cost caskets.

- The law does not distinguish between those dying of a "contagious" disease and a "communicable" disease. Immediate disposition without embalming would be a responsible requirement for contagious or infectious diseases. That provision, however, would be unnecessary for a communicable disease such as AIDS, and the family should be permitted to make all arrangements.

- The 48-hour wait before cremation serves no useful purpose for consumers. If all next-of-kin are in agreement, or the deceased signed a cremation authorization prior to death, and there are no suspicions surrounding the circumstances of death, then the 48-hour wait can and will be used to announce, "It is the policy of this funeral home that a body must be embalmed or refrigerated if it is held beyond 8 hours," as found on some SCI general price lists. Consumers will be stuck with an unnecessary charge for a procedure many consider an indignity if no refrigeration is available.

- The medical examiner's permit for cremation in the case of an anticipated death from natural causes is totally unnecessary and creates an additional burden and charge for families.

- There is no requirement to identify and tag the body at the place of death before removal.

- The FTC Funeral Rule has not been adopted in the statutes, a step that would make it more enforceable in this state.

- The standards for ethical conduct are not well-defined and should be strengthened. That would make it easier for a consumer to prevail when filing a complaint. (See Ethical Standards in Appendix.)

- There is inadequate public information on how to file a funeral complaint.

- This state has no laws regulating the body parts business.

Miscellaneous Information

- The educational requirement for becoming a funeral director/ embalmer is an associate degree (usually two years) and one year of apprenticeship. The applicant must also pass the national board exam. The exam is an embarrassment, deemed "irrelevant" and "useless" by consumer advocates and some industry practitioners.

- Cash advance items may not be marked up with a commission for the mortuary. They must be billed to the consumer in the same amount the funeral home is billed. (This restriction is not always honored by corporate chains, or a "processing fee" may be assessed, we are told.)

- Funeral homes may not operate on cemetery grounds.
- Medical examiners are appointed; they must be physicians.
- One may name a designated agent for body disposition.
- A permit for disinterment must be obtained from a registrar at the local Health Department.

This chapter was sent for review to the Connecticut Board of Examiners of Embalmers and Funeral Directors, the Department of Public Health, the state Registrar of Vital Records, the Attorney General's Office of Consumer Protection, and the Connecticut Funeral Directors Association. Only the lawyer for CFDA was kind enough to reply, with a small correction.

Caring for the Dead
In Delaware

Please refer also to the general introduction to state chapters—"Caring for the Dead: Necessary Information."

Church groups and residents in Delaware who might wish to care for their own dead may be faced with growing difficulty if they are not vigilant. After a family chose to handle a death privately, Delaware statutes were amended in 1993 to delete "the person in charge" and the phrase "funeral director or persons acting as such" from the registration of death statutes. That section now reads:

> *Title 16§ 3123 Registration of Deaths. . . (a) A certificate of death for each death which occurs in this State shall be filed with the Office of Vital Statistics . . . (b) The funeral director who assumes custody of the dead body shall file the certificate of death.*

Although this would imply that a paid "funeral director" must be involved, there are no statutes actually forbidding families or church groups from caring for their own dead. Indeed, it is usually the clergy who help the family in directing the funeral and whose congregations would lose out if a narrow interpretation of the law were to prevail. According to one Dover official, the Amish take over once the totally unnecessary embalming has been done. One has to wonder if someone has convinced them that embalming is required by law. The public health regulations still refer to "funeral director or person acting as such." Family members may file a birth certificate when there is no physician or hospital involved, so why shouldn't they be able to file a death certificate?

Although it was suggested by Health Department staff that morticians were the instigating force to alter the statutes, Delaware's professional and occupational statutes began the section on funeral directing with distinctively laudable aims when the predecessor to this book was written in 1998:

> *Recognizing that the practice of funeral services is a privilege and not a natural right of individuals, it is hereby deemed necessary . . . to*

provide rules and regulations . . . that the public shall be properly pro-
tected against price fixing and unprofessional, improper . . . unethical
conduct . . . . Accomplishment of that purpose shall be the primary
objective of the Board of Funeral Services.

In reading the Delaware funeral laws ten years later, one finds the same section of the statutes to read (Title 24, Chapter 31 § 3100):

The primary objective of the Board of Funeral Services, to which all
other objectives and purposes are secondary, is to protect the general
public, specifically those persons who are the direct recipients of ser-
vices regulated by this chapter, from unsafe practices and from occu-
pational practices which tend to reduce competition or fix the price of
services rendered.

The secondary objectives of the Board are to maintain minimum
standards of practitioner competency, and to maintain certain stan-
dards in the delivery of services to the public. In meeting its objectives,
the Board shall develop standards assuring professional competence;
shall monitor complaints brought against practitioners regulated by
the Board; shall adjudicate at formal hearings; shall promulgate rules
and regulations; and shall impose sanctions where necessary against
practitioners, licensed and formerly licensed.

While consumer protection is a proper goal, it's a shame the legislature
stripped out the fine sentiments of the earlier statutes. Current law seems to
assume that all citizens will use a funeral home, and we know that much of
the industry believes it does, indeed, have "a natural right" to your body and
your business.

Death Certificate

With electronic death registration (EDR) just starting in Delaware, not all
physicians are on-line although many funeral directors are. A paper death
certificate must be obtained if a family is caring for their own dead. If the
physician doesn't have a blank death certificate, one can be obtained from
a hospital or medical examiner. The remaining information must be supplied, typewritten or with ball point pen in black ink. (There are four carbons which must be clear.) The death certificate—copies one and two—must
be filed in any one of the three Vital Statistics offices (Dover, Georgetown, or
Wilmington) within three days and before final disposition. Copy four may
be retained by the hospital or physician.

Although an attending nurse may "declare" a death, the cause of death must be certified by a physician.

Fetal Death

A fetal death report is required when death occurs and the weight is 350 grams or more (about 12 ounces). If there is no family physician involved, the local medical examiner must sign the fetal death certificate.

Transporting and Disposition Permit

A body may be moved with medical permission. Copy three of the death certificate must be retained as a burial-transit permit.

Burial

Home burial is permissible outside town limits in Kent and Sussex counties. Check with the local registrar or health officer. The top of the casket must be 18 inches below the natural surface of the earth. Although not mentioned in the laws, a burial site should be 150 feet or so from a water supply.

Cremation

A permit for cremation may be obtained from the Office of Vital Statistics or from a funeral director. This permit must then be signed by the medical examiner (or deputy medical examiner). There is no fee for this authorization. These signatures could be difficult to obtain over a weekend. However, both parties involved—as officers of the state—can be expected to serve at any time. The telephone numbers to contact may be obtainable through a funeral director or a local law enforcement person. One copy of the cremation permit is to be retained by the crematory. The other copy filed with the death certificate.

Delaware requires identification by next-of-kin, a person authorized to make funeral arrangements, or a medical examiner prior to cremation. "ID viewing" has been used by the industry to tack on additional charges or for manipulative sales tactics to sell more expensive cremation containers. Until this law is modified, persons with relatives choosing cremation should insist on identifying the body before it goes to a Delaware funeral home. A more appropriate statutory provision would be to require—as does the state of Washington—that all bodies be identified at the place of death and tagged before removal. This would be a responsible procedure if, for example, Mom died in a nursing home while her children were all out-of-state and where it would be reasonable for a caretaker to identify the body. Cremation could then be readily arranged without delay, prior to any memorial plans. Body tagging is probably a more reliable method to keep from mistaking identities, which has happened after ID viewing in at least a few instances.

A cremation authorization must be signed by the next-of-kin or legal representative of the deceased. Most crematories insist that a pacemaker be removed. Delaware statutes permit a family to view cremation. All cremations must be performed in a licensed crematory. There are no laws regarding the disposition of cremated remains. You may do as you wish.

Other Requirements

Body disposition must be accomplished within five days. If disposition does not occur within 24 hours, the body must be embalmed or refrigerated.

Since the last edition of the book was written, the embalming requirement for infectious diseases has not only been abolished but such embalming is forbidden, with immediate cremation the preferred disposition. Exceptions can be made for religious reasons, but the casket must be sealed and the burial depth increased to two meters.

Medical Schools for Body Donation

There is no medical school in Delaware. Those considering body donation should check the nearest neighboring state.

State Governance

The Delaware Board of Funeral Service Practitioners has seven members, three of whom are public members, not connected with funeral service. "Such public members shall be accessible to complaints, inquiries and comments from the general public." Its website is:

< http://dpr.delaware.gov/boards/funeralservices/index.shtml>

Prepaid funeral transactions are regulated by the state Bank Commissioner. Preneed sellers are licensed by the Bank Commissioner and are not necessarily morticians.

<http://banking.delaware.gov/default.shtml>

Funeral and burial insurance is regulated by the Insurance Department.

There is no state board overseeing cemetery operation. The Attorney General may inspect cemetery records. Cemeteries may be run by nonprofit organizations only.

Crematories are regulated by the Delaware Department of Health.

Prepaid Cemetery and Funeral Funds

10% of the cemetery lot price must be placed in the perpetual care fund. Delaware has no other regulation of prepaid cemetery funds.

100% of prepaid *funeral* funds are to be placed in trust—in "an insured depository institution, or insured credit union, authorized to do business in Delaware"—along with accumulated interest. The seller must maintain records of all such agreements and make the records available for inspection.

If the preneed funds are placed in a revocable account, the purchaser has the right to a full refund, with interest, upon giving 15 days notice. Irrevocable accounts may not exceed $15,000.

There is no guarantee fund to protect consumers against the loss of prepaid funeral funds. However, sellers of preneed funeral services licensed by the Banking Department must supply a bond of between $50,000 and $200,000, to be determined by the Department. If an average funeral is about $5,000, this would cover only 10 to 40 funerals and would be quite insufficient if the seller embezzles the money from, say, 100 funerals sold.

There are no laws or regulations giving you specific protections or rights when buying cemetery services and merchandise preneed

Consumer Concerns

- The death rate in Delaware can support approximately 28 full-time mortuaries; there are, however, 66. Funeral prices tend to be higher in areas where there are "too many" funeral homes.

- There is no requirement that a consumer get an annual report of preneed funds. Although Delaware requires 100% of prepaid funeral money to be put in trust, such documents could be important to survivors who might not know about prepaid accounts otherwise. Embezzlement of funds that never made it into trust accounts has already happened in a number of states. This reporting would be an additional deterrent.

- There is insufficient statutory provision to protect consumers against default of prepaid funeral agreements if funds were never put in trust. A guarantee fund should be established.

- There is no statutory provision to allow the transfer of an irrevocable account should a person move or want to change which funeral home to use.

- When a prepaid funeral policy specifies particular merchandise, there is no protection for consumers if that item is no longer available.

An adequate description should be required, and consumers should be guaranteed a substitution of equal quality, with the approval of survivors.

- Until the preneed loopholes are closed, it is probably an unwise idea to prepay for a funeral in this state.

- There is no requirement that low-cost caskets be included in a casket display.

- The embalming or refrigeration requirement after 24 hours is burdensome and should be changed to 72 hours or eliminated altogether—to permit a family more choice. At 24 hours, funeral homes are likely to make an additional and unnecessary charge, even for the most minimal of arrangements. There has been no public health problem in the states without an embalming requirement.

- There is no requirement to identify and tag a body at the place of death prior to removal.

- Ethical standards are inadequate and should be clearly defined in order for valid consumer complaints to prevail. See Appendix.

- This state has no laws regulating the body parts business.

It is interesting to note that in the 10 years since the predecessor to this book was published, the Delaware legislature has addressed several of the "consumer concerns" listed:

- Embalming is no longer required for dangerous infectious diseases, surely an important protection for funeral personnel.

- The FTC Funeral Rule has been adopted, a regulation that requires funeral homes to provide consumers with price and option information and forbids funeral homes from misrepresenting the laws.

- One may now name a designated agent for body disposition or express one's preferences for final disposition in an advance directive.

We hope that this edition will motivate some Delaware legislators to clarify the rights of families and church groups to care for their own dead as well as addressing the other issues of consumer concerns that we have listed.

Miscellaneous Information

- Educational requirements for becoming a funeral director in Delaware are: two years of college plus one year of mortuary college, pass a state exam with a score of 70%, and one year of apprenticeship after college.

- Medical examiners are appointed physicians.

- Cash advance items may not be marked up with a commission for the mortuary. They must be billed to the consumer in the same amount the funeral home is billed.

- No mortuary may be operated on cemetery grounds or connected with a cemetery.

- Funeral complaint procedures are spelled out in the statutes, with a time schedule for response. The Funeral Board will accept both written and oral complaints, including anonymous ones.

- "Any licensed funeral director may obtain a duplicate funeral director's certificate upon proof of satisfactory evidence to the Board that the original has been lost or destroyed . . ." How does one "prove" that something has been lost?

- If you have not named a designated agent for body disposition, the written wishes of the deceased are to prevail.

- Disinterment must be done under the direction of a licensed funeral director after obtaining a permit from the state registrar.

This chapter was sent for review to the Delaware Department of Public Health—Vital Statistics and the Department of Banking. It was also sent to the state Funeral Board. No written responses were received, but some information was verified by telephone.

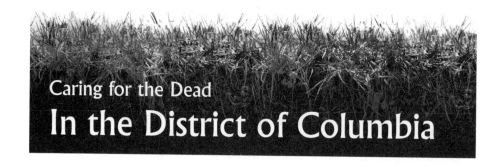

Caring for the Dead
In the District of Columbia

Please refer also to the general introduction to state chapters—"Caring for the Dead: Necessary Information."

Persons in DC may care for their own dead. The legal authority to do so is found in:

> *Title 6-211: The funeral director or person acting as such who first takes custody of the dead body shall file a certificate of death.*

There are no other statutes that might require you to use a funeral director when no embalming is desired.

Death Certificate

The District is now using electronic death registration but a paper copy may also be used. The family doctor or a local medical examiner will supply and sign the death certificate within 48 hours stating the cause of death. The remaining information must be supplied, typewritten or in black ink. The death certificate must be filed with the local registrar within five days and before final disposition.

Fetal Death

A fetal death report is required if death occurs after 20 weeks of gestation or when the weight is 500 grams or more (almost 18 ounces). If there is no family physician involved, the local medical examiner must sign the fetal death certificate.

Transporting and Disposition Permit

A body may be moved within the District with the consent of the physician or medical examiner certifying death. The next-of-kin must authorize final disposition. For out-of-state disposition, the burial transit permit generated by the electronic process will be needed. If a paper death certificate was used, the burial transit permit is one of the four copies.

Burial

Because of the metropolitan nature of the District of Columbia, home burial generally is not feasible. When cemetery burial is arranged, the family member acting as the funeral director must sign the authorization for disposition and file it with the mayor by the end of the month.

Cremation

A permit for cremation must be obtained from the medical examiner. There may be a fee for this. Most crematories insist that a pacemaker be removed, and authorization by next-of-kin usually is required. There are no laws regarding the disposition of cremated remains. You may do as you wish.

Other Requirements

Disposition of a body must occur within one week. Weather and reasonable planning should be considered. There are no embalming requirements.

If the person died of a contagious or infectious disease, disposition must be handled by a licensed funeral director.

Medical Schools for Body Donation

Body donation to a medical school is another option for disposition. Find the information for DC at <www.finalrights.org>.

District Governance

The District of Columbia Funeral Board has five members. Four are funeral directors, and one is a consumer representative.

<http://app.dcra.dc.gov/about/index_bpla_funeral.shtm>

Cemeteries must register with the Department of Human Services. Cemetery land is tax-exempt.

Crematories must be built on cemetery grounds unless permission is granted in writing from more than half the property owners within a radius of 200 feet of the property line.

Prepaid Cemetery and Funeral Funds

There is no protection for prepaid cemetery or funeral transactions in the District although the administrator for the Board says they are working on it.

Consumer Concerns

- The death rate in DC can support approximately 27 full-time mortuaries; there are 40.

- There are no trusting requirements for prepaid funeral contracts. 100% of prepaid funeral money and prepaid cemetery goods and services should be placed in trust, with interest to accrue. (Twenty-nine states require 100% trusting for funeral preneed contracts. Preneed is alive and well in those states.)

- There is no requirement for reporting to the consumer annually where the money is and how much is there, paperwork that would be useful to survivors and which would help to enforce any trusting requirements once they are established.

- There is no provision for an adequate description of funeral goods selected preneed nor for a substitution of equal quality and construction if the selected item is no longer available at the time of death. Any substitution should be approved by the survivors.

- There is no provision for cancellation of prepaid funeral contracts with a full refund of principal and interest, nor for transfer to another funeral home if the agreement is irrevocable.

- Until there is a District effort to regulate preneed sales of cemetery and funeral purchases, it is a terrible idea to prepay for either in the District.

- The coroner or medical examiner's permit for cremation in the case of an anticipated death from natural causes is totally unnecessary and creates an additional burden and charge for families.

- There is no requirement to identify and tag the body at the place of death before removal. Given the regular mix-ups that have been happening at chain-owned establishments with central prep facilities, this should be mandatory.

- There is no requirement that low-cost caskets be included in a casket display.

- The standards for ethical conduct are inadequate and should be strengthened. That would make it easier for a consumer to prevail when filing a complaint.

- There are no detailed procedures available to anyone wishing to file a funeral complaint.

- The FTC Funeral Rule has not been adopted by reference in the regulations which would make it more enforceable by the District.

Miscellaneous Information

- Educational requirements for becoming a funeral director: mortuary college (at least one year), two years of apprenticeship, and an exam. If the applicant has a two-year degree, only one year of apprenticeship is required.

- Cash advance items must be billed in the amount paid. Interest may be charged for a balance unpaid beyond 30 days.

- No person may engage in the practice of funeral directing while employed either part-time or full-time by a nursing home, hospital, morgue, or ambulance service.

- Preference is given to the written wishes of the deceased. A person may also designate an agent to make after-death arrangements.

- Medical examiners are appointed physicians.

- Tissue banks must be accredited by the American Association of Tissue Banks. With new standards for non-transplant tissue banks, there should be good regulation of the body parts business.

- Authorization for disinterment can be obtained from the local registrar.

This chapter was sent for review to the District Funeral Board with no response. Some information was confirmed by telephone with the Department of Vital Records.

Caring for the Dead
In Florida

Please refer also to the general introduction to state chapters—"Caring for the Dead: Necessary Information."

The language typically used to allow families to care for their own dead is a reference to a "funeral director or person acting as such." That language has been removed from Florida statutes, which now read as follows:

> *FS 382.006 Burial-transit permit—(1) The funeral director who first assumes custody of a dead body or fetus must obtain a burial-transit permit . . . . The application for a burial-transit permit must be signed by the funeral director and include the funeral director's license number.*

However, this does not have to be construed restrictively. In checking this chapter prior to publication, the Vital Statistics Administrator, Kenneth Jones, pointed out that the definition of "funeral director" now reads:

> *Chapter 382.002(8) "Funeral Director" means a licensed funeral director or direct disposer licensed pursuant to Chapter 497 or **other person who first assumes custody** [emphasis added] of or effects the final disposition of a dead body or a fetus as described in subsection (6).*

Therefore, next-of-kin and designated death care agents claiming custody of the body may care for their own dead in Florida.

Death Certificate

It is the responsibility of the person acting as a funeral director to prepare a typewritten death certificate with all required information and take to the physician or medical examiner for completion of the medical certification of death. The attending physician or district medical examiner will sign the death certificate within 72 hours after presentation. The death certificate must be filed in the county of death within five days of death and before final disposition.

Florida began electronic death registration in 2010. When that is in full-swing statewide, families caring for their own dead will continue to use the paper procedure. A blank death certificate can be gotten from a county health office.

Fetal Death

A fetal death certificate is required when death occurs after 20 weeks of gestation. If there is no family physician involved, the district medical examiner must sign the fetal death certificate.

Transporting and Disposition Permit

The local registrar or deputy registrar in the county health department will issue the burial-transit permit after you file the death certificate. There is no fee for this permit. The permit must be obtained within five days after death and prior to final disposition of the body. It must be filed in the county where disposition takes place, within ten days.

Burial

Cemeteries of less than five acres do not need to be registered with the state. It is unlikely that there are local zoning regulations regarding home burial, but you should review them before planning a family cemetery. If your land is in a rural area, draw a map of the property showing where the burial ground will be and have it filed with the deed. That may be all you have to do to establish your family cemetery. There must be 12 inches of earth on top. A sensible guideline is 150 feet from a water supply and 25 feet from a power line or neighbor's boundary.

When burial is arranged, the family member acting as the funeral director must sign the burial-transit permit and deliver it to the local registrar within 10 days. If there is no person in charge, the words "no person in charge" must be written across the face of the permit.

Cremation

A medical examiner's authorization on the burial-transit permit is required for cremation. The usual charge for this varies from one county to the next. There is a 48-hour wait before cremation. After the first 24 hours, refrigeration is required. Most large hospitals have refrigeration facilities, but if the storage becomes crowded, removal may be requested. All but a few crematories have refrigerated storage for which a fee is often charged.

Most crematories insist that a pacemaker be removed, and authorization by next-of-kin is required if one did not authorize one's own cremation prior to death. The crematory will sign the disposition permit which must be filed with the local registrar within 10 days. There are no laws regarding the disposition of cremated remains. You may do as you wish.

Other Requirements

Refrigeration or embalming is required after 24 hours. If the person died of a contagious or communicable disease, the doctor in attendance should be consulted.

Medical Schools for Body Donation

Body donation to a medical school is another option for disposition. Find the information for Florida at <www.finalrights.org>.

State Governance

There has been significant reorganization of Florida funeral and cemetery regulation. The current Board of Funeral, Cemetery, and Consumer Services is under the aegis of the Department of Financial Services. There are ten members, one of whom is the state health officer or designee. Two are funeral directors, one other a funeral director with a preneed license and a crematory. Two are cemeterians, and one a monument dealer. Three are public members, at least one of which is 60 years of age or older and another who is a CPA. No two board members may work for the same company. This board regulates funeral homes, funeral directors, direct disposers (the state's unfortunate name for no-frills cremation and burial businesses), refrigeration facilities, body transport services, embalming facilities, crematories, monument dealers, and prepaid funeral and cemetery purchases. As of late 2010, Florida now insists that anybody in the direct disposition service must be a funeral director—an unnecessary and anti-competitive requirement.

<http://www.myfloridacfo.com/FuneralCemetery/>

Prepaid Cemetery and Funeral Funds

Florida has some excellent anti-tying provisions for cemeteries:

497.280 Illegal tying arrangements.—

(1) No person authorized to sell grave space may tie the purchase of any grave space to the purchase of a monument from or through the seller of any other designated person or corporation. . . . No person

who is authorized to sell grave space and no cemetery company or other entity owning and operating a cemetery may:

1. Require the payment of a setting or service charge, by whatever name known, from third party installers for the placement of a monument;

2. Refuse to provide care or maintenance for any portion of a gravesite on which a monument has been placed; or

3. Require waiver of liability with respect to damage caused by cemetery employees or agents to a monument after installation . . .

All cemetery goods and services available must be disclosed on a printed or typewritten price list. 10% of the grave, columbaria, or mausoleum price must be set aside for perpetual care.

All preneed contracts must be on state-approved forms which are sequentially numbered. The contract may be made irrevocable only for people applying for Medicaid. That said, watch out for the lousy refund or transfer provisions.

With so many thoughtful and thorough provisions in Florida's funeral and cemetery laws, it is astonishing that the preneed portions of the laws are among the worst in the country, especially in a state full of retirees and snowbirds. You are at risk of losing a large portion of what you paid if you move or change your mind. Were AARP and other senior groups asleep at the wheel?

100% of all money for cash advance items must be placed in trust. Not counting the cost of interment rights, only 70% of prepaid funeral and cemetery services and 30% of retail or 110% of the wholesale cost of merchandise must be placed in trust. "Constructive delivery" can bypass this requirement for monuments, markers, and outer burial containers. This is accomplished by issuing a certificate of ownership and warehousing the merchandise. Once "delivered," the cemetery is under no obligation to issue a refund even if the items have never been used.

Substitution of merchandise of equal or greater quality is required if the specified items are not available.

A consumer may get a full refund within 30 days of signing any *cemetery* or funeral contract. At any time after that, a consumer may get a full refund of services, facilities and cash advance items—not merchandise—by providing a written request. Since only 70% of services went into trust and the funeral folks must dig into their pockets for the other 30%, this may be a difficult check to receive from a cash-strapped funeral home. One woman had been given the run-around for nearly a year before she was advised to contact the state. The seller keeps all interest.

A consumer is entitled to a full refund of funeral merchandise only if "the pre-need licensee cannot or does not deliver." If your funeral plans have changed from body burial to cremation, you'll have no use for the $2,000 casket. The family of one woman who died in New Jersey on a trip back north was told, "The casket is in our warehouse. Come and get it." The FAQ page on the board's website states: "A licensee that is willing and capable of delivering the purchased merchandise is not required to make a refund." If a purchaser defaults on time payments, the seller may keep all merchandise money.

Trusting requirements can be avoided if a bond or letter of credit has been filed with the state.

The only reporting requirement seems to be from the trustee holding pre-paid funds to the seller. Funds for administrative costs may be withdrawn from the interest earned.

Florida has a Preneed Funeral Contract Consumer Protection Trust Fund to provide restitution in the case of a delinquent provider. The consumer gets an amount equal to what was paid, with no consideration for interest. Any claim must be filed within one year of the going-out-of-business or bankruptcy of the preneed seller. How might consumers be guaranteed notification? The law doesn't say.

Consumer Concerns

- The death rate in Florida can support approximately 674 full-time mortuaries; there are, however, 755. This ratio is not as bad as in many other states, but funeral prices tend to be higher in areas where there are "too many" funeral homes.

- In some areas of Florida almost all funeral homes are owned by one of several large corporations, limiting choices for price-sensitive consumers.

- The rights of families and religious groups to care for their own dead are not clearly defined in the statutes.

- Finance charges are permitted for installment purchases of prepaid cemetery arrangements. This is outrageous. When you finance a car, house, or other retail purchase, you get to use the item. But a finance charge makes no sense on a lay-away plan before they lay you away.

- Trusting requirements are insufficient. All money (100%) for prepaid funeral goods and services should be placed in trust, with better provisions for transfer or refund of monies paid plus interest.

"Constructive Delivery" or warehousing should not be permitted. Preneed is alive and well in the 29 states that require 100% trusting.

- There is no annual reporting requirement to the purchaser of prepaid funeral and cemetery goods and services, paperwork that might be helpful to the family of a deceased to indicate prepayment. Such reporting would help to "enforce" the required trusting, as well.

- Until the Florida laws are changed, it is probably a terrible idea to prepay for a funeral or any cemetery merchandise and services, given the lack of adequate protection for consumers. Your own trust account in a bank will be safer.

- While Florida requires that the least expensive casket be displayed in the same manner as the more expensive caskets, there is no requirement that low-cost caskets be carried by a funeral home. (One woman said she was shown only two caskets—a plain pine box and a $4,000 casket.)

- An escape clause in the regulations says that disclosure of "a discount or rebate" is not necessary even though cash advance items must be listed in the amount charged to the funeral home. Consumers may wish to ask for the invoice for each cash advance item.

- Not all funeral homes include the cost of cremation in a "Direct Cremation" package. To its credit, statutes state that advertising would be misleading if it "makes only a partial disclosure of relevant facts." Apparently, however, the state is not cracking down on this.

- There is no adoption of FTC requirements by reference even though many of the Florida requirements parallel those of the FTC. A few have been omitted (e.g., the timing of when price information must be given), and—without specific reference—any future amendments of the Funeral Rule will have to be acted on separately in Florida, not an efficient use of legislative time.

- There is no law permitting you to name a designated agent to make your final arrangements. In situations where you are estranged or distant from next-of-kin, this could be important. One family complained to Slocum that an SCI funeral home held their mother's body in refrigeration until the family could get consent signatures from siblings in all corners of the US. This, despite the fact that mom had prepaid, and by doing so, had authorized her own cremation in advance according to Florida law.

Miscellaneous Information

- Educational requirements for becoming an embalmer: mortuary college and a passing grade on the national exam; one year of internship after school is also required. An associate's degree (two years) is required for a funeral director's license, plus exam and internship. Alas, the national exam is a total embarrassment, deemed "irrelevant" and "useless" by consumer advocates and industry practitioners alike.

- Direct disposers and body transport services are licensed. An exam is required covering state laws and determination of death. A law passed in 2010 specifies that direct disposers much be funeral directors.

- A body must be identified and tagged at the place of death.

- This is one of the few states with standards for mausoleum construction including "pressure relief ventilation."

- Florida has an excellent list of ethical standards, grounds for disciplinary action.

- Medical examiners are physicians who are appointed to the position.

- Hospices and nursing homes may not own or operate a funeral home.

- Unless reinterment is within the same cemetery, disinterment must be done in the presence of a licensed funeral director and with the permission of the next-of-kin or authorized person.

- Florida has some minimal laws to regulate the body parts business. Organ and tissue procurement companies must be registered with the state.

This chapter was sent for review to the Florida Board of Funeral, Cemetery, and Consumer Services, but no response was received. The Department of Health, Vital Statistics made some minor corrections.

Caring for the Dead
In Georgia

Please refer also to the general introduction to state chapters—"Caring for the Dead: Necessary Information."

Persons in Georgia may care for their own dead. The legal authority to do so is found in:

Title 31-10-15 (b) The funeral director or person acting as such who first assumes custody of the dead body shall file the certificate of death . . .

There are no other statutes that might require you to use a funeral director.

Death Certificate

The family doctor, registered nurse, physician's assistant, or a local medical examiner will supply and sign the death certificate stating the cause of death. The remaining information must be supplied, typewritten or in black ink. The death certificate must be filed with the local registrar (health department) within 72 hours and before final disposition.

Electronic death registration is set to be in place at the time of this writing. Paper documents are still be available for families to use. Contact the local health department prior to death to make sure of the latest procedures.

Fetal Death

A fetal death report is required for each fetal death. If there is no family physician involved, the local medical investigator must sign the certificate.

Transporting and Disposition Permit

A body may be moved with the consent of a physician or county coroner. After receiving the death certificate, the local registrar will issue a final disposition permit if cremation or out-of-state disposition is planned. No burial-transit permit is required by statute for in-state burial, although a local ordinance may require one.

Burial

There are no state statutes that specifically permit or prohibit home burial. It is unlikely that local zoning regulations cover home burial, but you should review them before planning a family cemetery. If your land is in a rural area, draw a map of the property showing where the burial ground will be and have it filed with the deed. That may be all you have to do to establish your family cemetery. There are no state burial statutes or regulations with regard to burial locations or depth. A sensible guideline is 150 feet from a water supply, 25 feet from a power line, and two or three feet of earth on top. Plan your family cemetery away from boundaries with neighbors, too.

That said, Bibb County is an exception. When a local couple planned a green burial ground, county commissioners passed ridiculous restrictive ordinances, including requiring all burials to be made in "leak-proof" containers (there is no such thing), and requiring all burials to be 1,000 feet from any water. That absurd requirement would seem to outlaw any burial at all, as one would probably would hit water before digging down 1,000 feet.

Cremation

The registrar's permit for disposition is required before cremation. There is no fee for this. Most crematories insist that a pacemaker be removed, and authorization by next-of-kin is usually required. The crematory will return the burial-transit permit to the registrar.

Within 50 days, cremated remains may be buried at sea. They must be removed from their container and scattered at least three miles from shore. The statutes don't say why you shouldn't wait, say, 100 days. A "verified statement" must be filed with the local registrar, reporting the deed and the name of the deceased. Note, however, that there are no ashes police, and families routinely scatter ashes along coastlines with no problems. They are sterile and pose no environmental risk. There are no statutes restricting the method, or requiring a report, when disposition occurs on land.

Other Requirements

There are no embalming requirements in Georgia. Weather and reasonable planning should be considered.

If the person died of a contagious or communicable disease, the doctor in attendance or the local health officer should be consulted.

Medical Schools for Body Donation

Body donation to a medical school is another option for disposition. Find the information for Georgia at <www.finalrights.org>.

State Governance

The Georgia Board of Funeral Service has seven members—six funeral directors and embalmers and one consumer representative.

<http://sos.georgia.gov/plb/funeral/>

The Georgia Cemetery Board has seven members—six are cemeterians and one is a consumer representative. Prior to 2006, cemeteries were regulated by the Secretary of State. At that time, Cathy Cox, a funeral director's daughter, was enforcing consumer-friendly regulations that riled the for-profiteers who succeeded in getting legislators to put the foxes in the hen house. The new cemetery board now permits an inspection fee of $150—up from $50— if you purchase your monument elsewhere. Other fees such as the cost to transfer a lot have been raised, too. Fortunately, the Secretary of State still regulates the trust funds.

<www.sos.ga.gov/plb/cemeteries/>

Crematories are licensed and inspected by the Funeral Board. A crematory must be under the supervision of a licensed funeral director.

Sellers of burial and funeral merchandise as well as preneed sales agents must be licensed by the State Cemetery Board.

Prepaid Cemetery and Funeral Funds

Cemeteries must provide a printed copy of prices and regulations on request.

100% of cemetery installation services and 35% of monument or outer burial container merchandise (or 110% of wholesale cost) must be placed in trust unless the monument has been installed. 100% of funeral merchandise must be placed in trust or at least 110% of wholesale. This statute seems totally contradictory [O.C.G.A. 10-14-7 (2)].

Only a funeral director may sell prepaid funeral services. 100% must be deposited in trust and allowed to accrue interest. Consumers have a right of refund for money paid plus interest when cancelling a funeral agreement, less 10% or half of the interest, whichever is less.

Consumer Concerns

- The death rate in Georgia can support approximately 266 full-time mortuaries; there are, however, 686. Funeral prices tend to be higher in areas where there are "too many" funeral homes.

- A consumer loses 10% of prepaid funeral funds or half the interest if there is a need to cancel or transfer the contract.

- There is no provision for substitution of equal quality and construction when selected merchandise is no longer available. Survivors should approve substitutions.

- There is no requirement for an annual report to consumers indicating the institution of deposit and current total of all prepaid funeral monies. Such documentation could be important to survivors who might not otherwise know about prepaid accounts and might help to "enforce" the trusting requirements.

- There is no statutory provision to protect consumers against default of prepaid agreements if funds were never put in trust.

- Until there is better trusting, better reporting, and survivor-approved substitution of merchandise, consumers in Georgia may not want to prepay for their funerals or cemetery arrangements.

- The statute that requires a crematory to be under the supervision of a licensed funeral director is clearly aimed at limiting competition and low-cost funeral alternatives. Cremation costs to consumers are generally higher in the few states where independent crematories are not allowed. The knowledge and skills for running a crematory do not require 3,120 hours as an apprentice funeral director, a college degree, nor training in embalming. Mortuary curricula do not generally cover the running of a crematory, nor is the operation of a crematory covered on the national funeral directors' exam, which further indicates the absurdity of this restriction. Therefore, Title 43-18-71 and related statutes should be amended. Training by the manufacturer and apprenticeship at, say, ten cremations—in-state or out—would be consistent with the task involved. The requirement of seating for 30 and the use of a hearse is also an unfair burden to a crematory business. Many nursing homes, for example, much prefer that removals be done with a service van.

- The regulations require that at least eight adult caskets be on display, but there is no requirement that low-cost caskets be included in that display. Such a requirement is also a financial burden to the funeral home when it can offer much more casket variety with a computer or catalog display.

- There is no provision either forbidding a mark-up on cash advance items or requiring the disclosure of how much the mark-up would be. Consumers may wish to ask for an invoice for such charges.

- This state has no laws regulating the body parts business.

Miscellaneous Information

- Educational requirements for funeral directors and embalmers: mortuary school and an exam on state laws. Apprenticeship of eighteen months is also required—3,120 hours. This seems excessive compared to other states but is undoubtedly a source of cheap labor for the industry.

- The FTC Funeral Rule has been endorsed by statutory reference.

- A body must be tagged with identification prior to burial or cremation.

- The Secretary of State (now via the Cemetery Board) may set minimum standards for vaults and caskets, the only such state that mentions this.

- Strangely, statutes permit next-of-kin to sell a used pacemaker, but the Food and Drug Administration forbids re-use in this country. Some nonprofit organizations are distributing them to the poor in foreign countries, making such a donation a worthy cause.

- Medical examiners are appointed; coroners are elected and may be funeral directors with a conflict of interest. Statutes permit a county to abolish such an office by referendum, and consumers would be well-advised to do so, moving all death investigations to the office of medical examiner.

- It is an unlawful act to hold a body for debt.

- You may name an agent for body disposition. This should be done with a notarized statement.

- A permit for disinterment must be obtained from the local registrar if a body is to be removed from the cemetery.

This chapter was sent for review to the Secretary of State's Office (Cemetery Board, Funeral Board) and the Department of Health—Vital Statistics. Helpful details were provided by the Director for the Cemeteries and Charities division, and state Registrar Kenneth Bramlett.

Caring for the Dead
In Hawaii

Please refer also to the general introduction to state chapters—"Caring for the Dead: Necessary Information."

Persons in Hawaii may care for their own dead. The legal authority to do so is found in:

Chapter 338-1 "Person in charge of disposition of the body" means any person who . . . disposes thereof.

Chapter 338-9 (a) The person in charge of the disposition of the body shall file with the department of health in Honolulu or with the local agent . . . a certificate of death.

There are no other statutes that might require you to use a funeral director.

Death Certificate

Hawaii is now using electronic death registration. Home funeral families must get a worksheet from the local department of health and fill in the demographic information before taking it to the physician to fill out and sign. The death certificate worksheet must be filed with the local registrar or health agent within three days and before final disposition.

Fetal Death

A fetal death report is required if death occurs after 24 weeks of gestation. If there is no family physician involved, the local health officer must be notified. All other procedures apply if disposition is handled by the family.

Transporting and Disposition Permit

A burial-transit permit must be obtained within 72 hours of death from the local registrar or deputy and prior to final disposition of the body. There is a modest charge—$5 as of this writing. The family member acting as funeral director must sign the permit and, within 10 days, file it with the registrar of the district where disposition took place.

Burial

Check with the local registrar for zoning laws regarding home burial. Burial must be on land approved as a cemetery by the county council. A written certificate of dedication exclusively to cemetery purposes must be filed with the registrar along with a map. Burial depth must be sufficient to avoid a public health nuisance and to make it impossible for animals to disturb the grave. A useful guideline is 150 feet from a water supply and at least two feet of earth on top.

Cremation

The burial-transit permit is sufficient for cremation and no additional permit is needed. Most crematories insist that a pacemaker be removed, and authorization by next-of-kin usually is required. There are no laws regarding the disposition of cremated remains. You may do as you wish.

Other Requirements

A body shall be embalmed, cremated, or buried within 30 hours after death, or, according to Health Department regulations, placed in "refrigerated storage in a state-approved hospital." Most mortuaries have their own refrigeration, however.

Home funeral families may want to invest in a supply of dry ice or frozen gel packs if plans will be drawn out at all. This can be a practical step, even though there are no "embalming or refrigeration police."

Bodies dead from the following diseases may not be embalmed: plague, Asiatic cholera, smallpox, epidemic typhus fever, yellow fever, or louse-borne relapsing fever. This is one of only four US states that have recognized the potential hazard from embalming. Delaware as well as Ontario forbid embalming under such circumstances. Ohio and Montana require immediate disposition.

Medical Schools for Body Donation

Body donation to a medical school is another option for disposition. Find the information for Hawaii at <www.finalrights.org>.

State Governance

There is no Hawaii State Funeral Board. Funeral directors are no longer licensed by the Professional & Vocational Licensing Division of the

Department of Commerce and Consumer Affairs (DCCA). The DCCA's Cemetery and Pre-Need Funeral Authority Program regulates and monitors prepaid cemetery and funeral trusts only. Or is supposed to.

<http://hawaii.gov/dcca>

Crematories are regulated by the Department of Health.

Prepaid Cemetery and Funeral Funds

For perpetual care, $1 per square foot of interment space, $50 for each mausoleum crypt, and $15 for each niche must be placed in trust.

Cemetery and funeral preneed sellers may retain the lesser of "acquisition costs" or 30% of the contract, placing in trust at least 70%. Interest may be withdrawn by the seller as long as the Authority deems that sufficient funds are there.

Preneed sellers must make an annual "audited financial statement" to the director of DCCA. One might guess that the state doesn't even check to see if they are being submitted, though, given the Rightstar scandal (see below) where millions went missing. The DCCA may require reports to purchasers but apparently hasn't bothered to do so. That is unfortunate as such reports might help to enforce the trusting requirement as well as being useful documentation for a family handling the funeral.

A general price list must be provided for all cemetery and funeral transactions, signed by the purchaser. Prices must be the same for at-need and preneed purchases. A "clear and concise statement" of all purchases must be included in the preneed contract, but this falls short. There is no provision for a satisfactory substitution of unavailable merchandise (i.e., caskets) without an extra charge.

There is no provision for transfer of irrevocable contracts in the preneed statutes, although the implications are that a consumer may cancel at will. While terms for a refund must be disclosed in the preneed contract, the state does not require a full refund over and above the 70% in trust when the contract is cancelled. The seller gets the interest.

Preneed sellers must carry a $50,000 bond proof of surety. This is a paltry sum, given the aggressive preneed marketing these days. Default on just ten $5,000 funerals would wipe that out, leaving untold numbers uncovered.

In 2005, Rightstar Management owned both cemeteries and funeral homes–50% of the death-care market in Hawaii. Bankruptcy was declared when the Attorney General found that more than $20 million was missing from the trust accounts. The circuit court took over business matters, and the sale of assets was approved in 2007 with few buyers in sight for this debt-ridden company. Although the state is saying that the 50,000 or so consumers whose money is missing will still be served, one has to wonder if that will be at the expense of taxpayers. A mere $9 million is needed to "restore" prepaid funeral funds according to an agreement the state signed with various parties. That would yield only $180 per person, enough to pay for a cardboard cremation container and not much else. Despite this financial meltdown and years of lobbying by the FCA of Hawaii and FCA national, state lawmakers have caved to industry lobbyists each year and have refused to enact more stringent preneed laws.

Consumer Concerns

- The death rate in Hawaii can support approximately 39 full-time mortuaries; there are, in fact, only 18. This is one of the very few states where there is not a significant glut of funeral homes, and prices are competitive in some areas. Consumers will have to shop around, however, as there is a huge difference from one funeral home to the next.

- Constructive delivery (warehousing) is permitted to bypass the trusting requirement for preneed purchases.

- Trusting requirements are inadequate.

- There is no provision for substitution of equal quality and construction when selected merchandise is no longer available. Survivors should approve substitutions.

- There is no statutory provision for transferring an irrevocable preneed account.

- There is insufficient statutory provision to protect consumers against default of prepaid funeral agreements if funds were never put in trust.

- Until the Hawaii laws are changed to require 100% trusting of all money and interest for prepaid funeral and cemetery goods and services and adequate provision for transfer, it is probably a **terrible** idea to prepay for these arrangements. Your own trust account in a bank will be safer.

- There is no requirement that low-cost caskets be included in any display.

- There is no provision either forbidding a mark-up on cash advance items or requiring the disclosure of how much the mark-up would be. Consumers may wish to ask for a copy of the invoice for each cash advance item.

- There is no law that allows you to state your funeral preferences or for naming a designated agent to make your final arrangements. In situations where you are estranged or distant from next-of-kin, this could be important.

- Ethical standards and unprofessional conduct are not clearly defined, which might be necessary for valid consumer complaints to prevail.

- The FTC Funeral Rule has not been adopted.

- There is no requirement to identify and tag a body at the place of death before removal.

- This state has no laws regulating the body parts business.

Miscellaneous Information

- There are several possibilities for qualifying as an embalmer in Hawaii: five years of apprenticeship, or a high school diploma and two years of apprenticeship, or mortuary school and one year of apprenticeship. A written exam is also required. There is no licensing for a funeral director.

- The chief of police and deputies serve as coroners. The medical examiner serves in that capacity for the city of Honolulu.

- Complaints regarding cemetery and funeral trusts may be filed with the Regulated Industries Complaints Office (RICO), DCCA, Suite 600A, 828 Fort Street Mall, Honolulu, HI 96813; 808-587-3222.

- A permit for disinterment must be obtained from the director of the Health Department.

This chapter was sent for review to the Hawaii Health Department's Vital Records and the Department of Commerce and Consumer Affairs but no responses were received. Information on electronic death registration was obtained by telephone. The Department of Sanitation made some minor suggestions.

Caring for the Dead
In Idaho

Please refer also to the general introduction to state chapters—"Caring for the Dead: Necessary Information."

Persons and religious groups in Idaho may care for their own dead. The legal authority to do so is found in:

> *Title 39-260: (re death registration) . . . the person in charge of interment or of removal of the body from the district shall be responsible for obtaining and filing the certificate.*

> *Title 54-1104: Exemptions from provisions of act (re licensing of morticians) . . . Any duly authorized representative of any church, fraternal order or other association or organization honoring the dead who performs a funeral or other religious service . . .*

There are no other statutes that might require you to use a funeral director.

Death Certificate

Idaho has adopted electronic death registration. Funeral directors and physicians have access to the computerized system. Families caring for their own dead will have to resort to the older paper process.

The family can pick up a death certificate form from the local health department registrar Monday through Friday. There is no after-hours or weekend service for a death certificate form. The family member who is in charge must provide all the vital statistics of the deceased. Information must be typed or in black ink. The family member needs to have the cause of death certified by either the family physician, physicians assistant, advanced practice professional nurse, or local coroner.

There are two carbons, so do not use a felt-tip pen. The death certificate must be filed with the local registrar within 5 days.

Fetal Death

A certificate of stillbirth is required when death occurs after 20 weeks of gestation or when a weight of 350 grams is attained, and must be filed as above.

Transporting and Disposition Permit

A body may be moved with medical permission. The second (blue) page serves as the burial-transit permit. It is necessary to have a physician's or coroner's authorization before removing a body from the state.

Burial

Home burial is permissible in Idaho. Check with the county or town clerk for any local zoning laws. There are no state burial statutes or regulations with regard to depth. A sensible guideline is 150 feet from a water supply and three feet of earth on top.

Three or more residents may organize a nonprofit rural cemetery association.

Cremation

A cremation permit from the coroner is required on the blue page of the death certificate. There is no state-set fee for this, although individual coroners may have a fee. Authorization by next-of-kin is usually required, and a pacemaker must be removed. A person may authorize his/her own cremation as part of a preneed plan. There are no laws regarding the disposition of cremated remains. You may do as you wish.

Other Requirements

A regulation of the Board of Morticians requires embalming or refrigeration after 24 hours. That would not apply to families caring for their own dead; only funeral licensees.

If the person died of a contagious or communicable disease, the doctor in attendance should be consulted.

Bodies transported by commercial carrier must be embalmed, an unnecessary requirement that infringes on personal choice and disrespects religious traditions that frown on embalming.

Medical Schools for Body Donation

Body donation to a medical school is another option for disposition. Find the information for Idaho at <www.finalrights.org>.

State Governance

The Idaho Board of Morticians has three members. There are no consumer representatives. It operates within the Bureau of Licensing: <https://secure. ibol.idaho.gov/IBOL/Home.aspx>

Idaho, North Dakota, and Alabama are the only states without a consumer representative on such a board. Therefore, it may not be too surprising that this board seems insulated from and out of touch with recent trends driven by consumer interests, even though green burials and home funerals are being reported in popular media such as AARP's magazine and the *New York Times*. From the minutes of a July 2008 board meeting:

- "Ms. Mac Master reported the Prosecutor's Office was notified about the green burials and unlicensed practice. The definition of green burials and the conduction of green burials must be clarified."

- "The concern of the Board is that there are persons acting as Morticians or Funeral Directors without licensure and the law and rules need to be clarified."

- "Ms. Mac Master is to work with investigators on green burial complaints."

- "Ms. Mac Master is to work on language for future legislative changes for green burials. The Board is to work with the Idaho Funeral Service Association for recommendations on changes."

Ms. Mac Master is an assistant Attorney General. One would have thought that, with that much education, she might have quickly discovered (try the Internet) that a "green burial" simply means no embalming and a biodegradable burial container. Who is filing complaints against that? Jews and Muslims, among others, have been doing that forever. And what does green burial have to do with "unlicensed practices"? Ensuing minutes don't mention the issue again. Did it go away? Or is this a board that eventually intends to take away consumer rights to environmentally-friendly burial practices?

Public cemeteries are generally regulated by county commissioners. Private cemeteries are supposed to be regulated by the Idaho Board of Cemeterians, but the board has never been established.

In 1996 crematories became regulated by the Board of Morticians. Prior to that, the Department of Health and Welfare licensed crematories.

Prepaid Cemetery and Funeral Funds

Only 50% of the funds for prepaid *cemetery* merchandise must be placed in trust. "Constructive delivery" (warehousing) can avoid any trusting requirements at all.

Only 85% of all other preneed funeral and cemetery services and merchandise must be placed in trust. Sellers are forbidden from inflating the price of non-trusted items and reducing others to avoid trusting requirements. The trustee holding the funds may withdraw from the interest "reasonable" expenses for administering the funds, not to exceed 10% of the interest, per Board rule. At the time of death, remaining interest on a guaranteed-price agreement goes to the seller. On a non-guaranteed agreement, excess interest goes to the estate.

A purchaser may cancel a revocable preneed plan and collect "all payments made, plus accrued interest thereon, less reasonable administrative expenses and taxes incurred." Obviously, the purchaser is going to be missing the interest on the 15% that was never deposited. There is no provision for transferring an irrevocable contract.

The preneed seller must make an annual report to the state.

Preneed solicitations at hospitals, rest homes, or similar institutions are forbidden unless specifically invited. Such in-person solicitation is sort of forbidden elsewhere if it "comprises an uninvited invasion of personal privacy at the personal residence." Why didn't the law just come right out and say no in-person or telephone solicitation?

If selected merchandise is not available at the time of death, the seller must supply a substitute equal in quality of material and workmanship satisfactory to the person making the arrangements. If the seller is unable to provide an acceptable substitute, the person handling the arrangements may transfer to another provider all funds in the trust (85% of what was paid, plus interest, less expenses).

Consumer Concerns

- The death rate in Idaho can support approximately 42 full-time mortuaries; there are, however, 73 such establishments. Given the low density of population over a large geographic area, mortuary careers are not likely to be full-time work. Unfortunately, because of the low volume of business per mortuary, funeral prices will tend to be higher than elsewhere.

- No annual report to the consumer is required, paperwork that might be helpful to the family as a record of prepayments by the deceased, and which would help to "enforce" trusting requirements.

- There is no provision for transferring irrevocable preneed accounts.

- There is no state protection in the case of default of prepaid funeral monies. (There have been defaults even in states requiring 100% trusting.)

- Until the Idaho laws are changed to require 100% trusting of both cemetery and funeral purchases, it is probably a terrible idea to pre-pay for any merchandise or services, given the inadequate protection for consumers. Your own trust account in a bank will be safer.

- Only a funeral establishment may now run a crematory in Idaho. This is clearly a restraint of trade effort by undertakers to limit competition and low-cost choices. Cremation costs for consumers are generally higher in the few states where independent crematories are not allowed. The knowledge and skills for running a crematory do not require apprenticeship as a funeral director, a college degree, nor training in embalming. Mortuary curricula do not generally cover the running of a crematory, nor is the operation of a crematory covered by the national funeral directors' exam. Therefore, Title 27-305 and related statutes should be amended. Training by the manufacturer and apprenticeship at, say, ten cremations—in-state or out—would be consistent with the task involved.

- The coroner's permit for cremation in the case of an *anticipated* death from natural causes is totally unnecessary and creates an additional paperwork burden.

- There is no requirement to identify and tag the body at the place of death before removal.

- Embalming laws and regulations do not have exceptions for religious or personal objections. Why? No airline requires embalming, according to a recent report in the trade press.

- There is no requirement to include low-cost caskets in any display.

- There is no provision either forbidding a mark-up on cash advance items or requiring the disclosure of how much the mark-up would be. Consumers may wish to request a copy of each invoice for such.

- The standards for ethical, professional conduct are inadequate. Clear and explicit language would make it easier for a consumer to prevail when filing a valid complaint. (See Appendix A: Ethical Standards for the Funeral Industry.)

- Complaint procedures are unclear and inadequate.
- The FTC Funeral Rule has not been adopted in this state.
- This state has no laws regulating the body parts business.

Miscellaneous Information

- A funeral director's license requires two years of college, 15 mortuary school credits , one year of apprenticeship and passing an exam.
- Coroners are elected. They need not be physicians and in some parts of the state are funeral directors with a conflict of interest.
- Unprofessional conduct includes: "using profane, indecent or obscene language in the presence of a dead human body, or within the immediate hearing of the family or relatives of a deceased, whose body has not yet been interred or otherwise disposed of." (Then watch out?)
- A person may establish funeral preferences in a preneed plan. A person may also delegate disposition authority to a survivor.
- A disposition permit must be obtained from the state registrar, office of Vital Statistics. A licensed funeral director must be in charge.

This chapter was sent for review to the Department of Health—Vital Statistics and the Board of Morticians. No response was received from the Board. Gregory Heitman in Vital Statistics made some minor corrections.

Please refer also to the general introduction to state chapters—"Caring for the Dead: Necessary Information."

In Illinois a dead body becomes a hostage of the funeral industry, one of only eight such states that require the use of a funeral director. (Connecticut, Illinois, Indiana, Louisiana, Michigan, Nebraska, New Jersey, and New York.) In almost no other situation is a private citizen forced to use a for-profit business to fulfill the interests of the state. The statutes and regulations also conflict with each other:

> *55 ILCS 5/3-3021. [Coroner] Public policy—Release of body to next of kin. As a guide to the interpretation and application of this Division it is declared that the public policy of the State is as follows:*
>
> > *That as so as may be consistent with the performance of his duties under this Division the coroner shall release the body of the decedent to the decedent's next of kin, personal representative, friends, or to the person designated in writing by the decedent or to the funeral director selected by such persons, as the case may be, for burial, and none of the duties or powers of coroners enumerated in this Division shall be construed to interfere with or control the right of such persons to the custody and burial of the decedent upon completion of the coroner's investigation. (1990)*
>
> *410 ILCS 535/21(1). The funeral director or person acting as such who first assumes custody of a dead body or fetus shall make a written report to the registrar of the district in which death occurred . . . .*

But the restrictive mischief is found in the Administrative Code:

> *500.10 Definitions — "Funeral director or person acting as such" means a person licensed in the State of Illinois to practice funeral directing, or a person acting under the direction or supervision of an*

Illinois licensed funeral director as an employee or an associate of the funeral director.

A movement is afoot to get the limiting code changed. It shouldn't be hard. In a 1909 federal case, *Wyeth v. Cambridge Board of Health,* the court ruled:

. . . the refusal to permit one to bury the dead body of his relative or friend, except under an unreasonable limitation, is also an interference with a private right that is not allowable under the Constitution of the Commonwealth or the Constitution of the United States.

Parents can file a birth certificate when there is no doctor involved. What's the big deal for the death certificate?

Death Certificate

Illinois is now using electronic death registration (EDR) although it is voluntary and not all doctors and morticians are using it yet. A paper alternative is allowed.

The attending physician, medical examiner, or coroner will enter the cause of death into the system if using it. (The Cook County coroner refuses to use EDR.) The remaining demographic information must be supplied through the funeral home's computer or filled in on the paper form.

Fetal Death

A fetal death report is required when death occurs after 20 weeks of gestation. If there is no family physician involved, the local medical examiner or coroner must generate/sign the fetal death certificate.

Transporting and Disposition Permit

Once the death certificate is complete, the state computer will create a permit for disposition that can be printed by the funeral home. Otherwise, the permit for disposition may be gotten from the registrar at the local health department if the funeral home doesn't already have blank permits.

Burial

Family burial grounds are permitted in Illinois and should be registered with the Comptroller's office. The fee is $5. You will need to provide proof of ownership which might include a tax bill at that address. The advantage of going to the trouble to register with the state is that their database is made available to future developers, and no new road, for example, would be permitted through that spot. Mary Formeller in that office is very helpful.

It is unlikely that there are local zoning regulations regarding home burial, but you should check to be sure. Then draw a map of the property showing where the burial ground will be and have it filed with the deed where such documentation will be readily available to a future landowner. The top of the coffin must be covered by 18 inches of earth if not in a vault. A sensible guideline is 150 feet from a water supply and 25 feet from a power line or neighbor's boundary.

Cremation

There is a 24-hour wait prior to cremation. A permit for cremation must be obtained from the county coroner, and there is likely to be a fee, although it varies from one county to the next. This must be obtained before the permit for disposition. A pacemaker must be removed, and authorization by next-of-kin or other authorizing agent is required. There are no laws regarding the disposition of cremated remains. You may do as you wish.

Other Requirements

Embalming is not required under any circumstances. Illinois has no requirements controlling the time schedule for the disposition of the dead. Weather and reasonable planning should be considered.

Medical Schools for Body Donation

Body donation to a medical school is another option for disposition. Find the information for Illinois at <www.fiinalrights.org>.

State Governance

The Illinois State Funeral Board has six members. There is one consumer representative.

<http://www.idfpr.com/dpr/WHO/fundir.asp>

The Office of the Comptroller regulates cemeteries, crematories, and both cemetery and funeral preneed sales. One does not need to be a funeral director to run a crematory. <http://www.ioc.state.il.us/>

Prepaid Cemetery and Funeral Funds

One has to wonder what the legislators in Springfield were thinking when they let the industry rascals write some of the Illinois laws. In addition to being licensed by the Comptroller, preneed cemetery sales people must have a surety bond of $10,000 or up to 10% of the trust funds. Seems like the state is inviting scoundrels to make off with 90% of the public's money.

However, there is a Cemetery Consumer Protection Fund for reimbursement against loss, funded by a $5 fee for each preneed cemetery contract written. (In 1997, the manager of Valley View Cemetery in Edwardsville was found to have diverted cemetery money into his own account. Similar problems have been found at Mt. Hope Cemetery in Belleville and Warren County Memorial Park Cemetery in Monmouth.) If restitution is not made, consumers will be protected by this fund. As of January 2010, there is a similar Preneed Funeral Consumer Protection Fund to guard against embezzlement or loss of prepaid funeral money. This was precipitated by a major shortfall and mismanagement of a master trust set up by the Illinois Funeral Directors Association.

Only 50% of preneed *cemetery* purchases (and 85% of the vault price) must be placed into trust. "Constructive delivery" can bypass the trusting requirement. "Delivery" is usually accomplished by issuing a certificate of ownership and warehousing the vault or marker, but few states are checking to see if the goods are actually there. Once "delivered," it will be impossible to get a refund even if the items have never been used. If a person opted for cremation at a later date, a burial vault would not be needed, for example.

If installment payments are made to cover both interment rights and cemetery merchandise or services, the payments may be allocated to the lot purchase first. Even when you pay up the full amount, those funds will not be placed in trust and are not required to be refunded if you change your mind. Suppose the cemetery costs you've contracted for were $2,000 for a lot, $1,000 for a vault, $1,000 open-and-closing, and $1,000 for a marker—$5,000 total—the first $2,000 goes directly to the cemetery. After that, only $1,850 of the remaining $3,000 will go into trust . . . maybe. If the merchandise has been delivered to a warehouse and you want a refund because you're moving to Arizona to be with your daughter, you can expect to get back only 50% of the opening-and-closing fee—the grand sum of $500 out of the $5,000 that you paid.

The contract must also disclose all penalties for cancellation or default, but the statutes not only don't limit what those penalties may be, they amount to a give-away to the seller. For example, a consumer wishing to cancel the cemetery contract is entitled to receive the amount in the trust (which isn't likely to be very much anyway), *but only after the last payment is made.* If a consumer can't keep up the payments and defaults on the contract, the cemetery may retain all that was paid as "liquidated damages." Why would the state condone this kind of profiteering on the backs of the poor?

If construction has not begun on undeveloped interment space for which there have been advance sales, the purchaser may, within 12 months of purchase, cancel the agreement and get a full refund. But once the first brick has been laid, the seller may keep all that was paid as "liquidated damages" if the buyer wants to cancel.

The seller may withdraw "a reasonable fee" from the trust fund annually for administrative purposes. Legislation passed in 2010 took out any limit on what would be considered "reasonable," i.e., 3% of the trust or any and all of the interest earned, so there isn't likely to be any "undistributed income" in a requested refund.

A mention of finance charges was deleted in the 2010 legislation, but nowhere does it actually say that finance charges are not permitted on preneed cemetery and funeral purchases. This hits the poor the hardest. Why should anyone pay interest on a lay-away plan before they lay you away?

For preneed *funeral* goods and services, a commission of 5% is permitted, with 95% going into trust or insurance. A 15% commission is permitted on outer burial containers, 85% going into trust or insurance when sold through a funeral home. "Constructive delivery" or warehousing can bypass the trusting requirement.

The initial payments of installment purchases may be allocated entirely to the commission (and finance charges?), rather than making such allocations proportionately. This limits the amount earning interest at the beginning.

Can you get a refund if you change your mind or move? Unless it is irrevocable, a consumer may cancel a preneed funeral arrangement, but *only* after it is fully paid for. That seems an absurd requirement. In that case, the seller may retain the original 5% commission not put in trust, and you will get the rest plus any "undistributed" interest. Well, maybe you will, if the vault or casket isn't in a warehouse.

If you die somewhere else and the funeral home provides no services, it gets to keep everything in the warehouse plus 10% or $300, whichever is less, before sending the balance to your estate. Why isn't there a provision for the funds to be moved to another provider without penalty, without the warehousing sham?

If you never finish paying for your funeral and default on the payments, the seller may retain 25% or $300, whichever is less, as "liquidated damages." If you have paid $1,000 toward a $5,000 funeral, you'll get back only $750.

Funeral insurance or annuities are transferable. However, if you come upon hard times, you won't get back any where near what you paid if you try to cash in your insurance policy.

Sellers of preneed arrangements must report annually to the state Comptroller. Per a new requirement as of 2010, the buyer must also receive a report accounting for the funds and interest.

If merchandise is not available at the time of death, a substitution similar in style and equal in quality of material and workmanship is required.

The Comptroller's office has two booklets, one a consumer guide for prepaid *funeral* purchases and another for preneed *cemetery* purchases. Nothing on the Comptroller's web site mentions these, though perhaps after nudging from Carlson, they'll make them more accessible to the public. Wouldn't hurt to jazz them up a little bit, too, with some meaningful examples. While the purpose of the booklets is to inform you of your "rights" and "protections," the writing style is so pedantic that by the time you get to "no chance of a refund," you almost don't notice that the seller is the one who has all the rights, and you, the consumer, have very few protections.

Consumer Concerns

- The death rate in Illinois can support approximately 422 full-time mortuaries; there are, however, 1,213. Funeral prices tend to be higher in areas where there are "too many" funeral homes.

- It is not clear whether finance charges are permitted for installment purchases of prepaid funeral arrangements.

- Constructive delivery (warehousing) is permitted to avoid trusting. The trusting requirement for preneed purchases should be increased to 100% for all goods and services—both cemetery and funeral expenses. Funeral agreements should be fully transferable, and—in the case of revocable contracts—fully refundable.

- Despite the Cemetery and Funeral Consumer Protection Funds and until the Illinois laws are changed, it is probably a terrible idea to prepay for a funeral or cemetery merchandise and services, given the raw deal a consumer would get in trying to transfer or back out of such a purchase. Your own trust account in a bank will be safer.

- There is no requirement to include low-cost caskets in any display.

- There is no provision either forbidding a mark-up on cash advance items or requiring the disclosure of how much the mark-up would be if there is one. Consumers may want to ask for a copy of the invoice for each cash advance item.

- The FTC Funeral Rule has not been adopted, which would improve consumer protections.

- There is no requirement that the body be identified and tagged at the place of death before removal.

- The coroner's or medical examiner's permit for cremation in the case of an *anticipated* death from natural causes is totally unnecessary and creates an additional burden and charge for families.

- Coroners are elected and are not necessarily physicians. Indeed, some are morticians with a conflict of interest.

- This state has no laws regulating the body parts business.

Miscellaneous Information

- The educational requirements for becoming a funeral director/embalmer in Illinois are one year of college and one year of mortuary school (or two years of mortuary school) plus one year of apprenticeship. All must pass a state-approved exam.

- You may name a designated agent for body disposition. You may state your wishes and require that they not be changed.

- Complaints are handled by a Complaint Intake Unit covering all regulated businesses and professions. (It is difficult to get through on the phone.)

- A disposition permit from the local registrar is required for disinterment.

This chapter was sent for review to the Illinois Department of Health—Vital Records. It was also sent to the Office of the Comptroller and the State Funeral Board. No response was received from the Funeral Board. The others were most helpful in making corrections.

Caring for the Dead
In Indiana

Please refer also to the general introduction to state chapters—"Caring for the Dead: Necessary Information."

In Indiana, a dead body becomes a hostage of the funeral industry, one of only eight states that requires the use of a funeral director. (Connecticut, Illinois, Indiana, Louisiana, Michigan, Nebraska, New Jersey, and New York.) In almost no other situation is a private citizen forced to use a for-profit business to fulfill the interests of the state. While the majority of the statutes in the Indiana Code clearly recognize the rights of families or a designated agent to control the disposition of a body, one statute stands out in conflict, inviting a court challenge. This one was surely passed to benefit the special interests of the mortuary industry and is buried near the end of the Embalmers and Funeral Directors section of the Code:

> *IC 25-15-8-25. A local health officer may issue a [disposition] permit under IC 16-37-3-10 only to a funeral director . . . .*

Another section of the funeral directors code, IC 25-15-2-10, says that clergy are exempt from the mortuary licensing laws if "the funeral is arranged and directly supervised by a funeral director."

Mormons, Muslims, and Orthodox Jews have not always found undertakers to be cooperative in accommodating religious bathing and dressing rituals. The Hmong have also had trouble finding sympathetic services for their extensive family involvement at a time of death.

The public health code has no such restrictions and deals only with the necessary concerns of the state. Indeed, parents may file a birth certificate in Indiana if there is no doctor involved. What's the big deal about a death certificate?

> *IC 16-37-3-2. As used in this chapter, "person in charge of interment" means a person who places or causes to be placed a stillborn child or dead body or the ashes, after cremation, in a grave, vault, urn, or other receptacle, or otherwise disposes of the body or ashes.*

IC 16-37-3-3. The person in charge of interment shall file a certificate of death or of still birth with the local health officer. . . .

IC 16-37-3-10. Upon receipt of a properly executed certificate of death or stillbirth or, when authorized by rule of the state department, a provisional certificate of death, a local health officer in the county in which the death occurred shall issue a permit for the disposal of the body.

Even under the funeral directors' statutes a family's rights are acknowledged:

IC 25-15-9-18. . . .the following persons, in the order of priority indicated, have the authority to designate the manner, type, and selection of the final disposition and interment of human remains:

(1) An individual granted the authority in a funeral planning declaration executed by the decedent under IC 29-2-19.

(2) An individual granted the authority in a health care power of attorney executed by the decedent under IC 30-5-5-16.

(3) The individual who was the spouse of the decedent at the time of the decedent's death.

(4) The decedent's surviving adult child. If more than one (1) adult child is surviving, any adult child who confirms in writing that the other adult children have been notified, unless the licensed funeral director or licensed funeral home receives a written objection from another adult child.

(5) The decedent's surviving parent. If the decedent is survived by both parents, either parent has the authority unless the licensed funeral director or licensed funeral home receives a written objection from the other parent.

It's hard to understand why the legislators did such a half-hearted job on the right of disposition. What if the spouse is estranged? While "any adult child" may make funeral arrangements, who decides if there is a conflict between more than one? Ditto for surviving parents? In some states, such disputes may be settled by the Probate Court. In Indiana, that court seems empowered to deal only with wills and assets. Too bad.

IC 25-15-8-1 Grounds for Discipline . . . A licensee that . . . takes possession of human remains without authorization from the person legally entitled to custody of remains . . . may be disciplined. . . .

With the rapid growth of the home funeral movement, there will likely be efforts to find ethical legislators willing to repeal 25-15-8-25 and related offending language. Funeral directors might even decide that's in their best interests, too, rather than perpetuating an unwanted monopoly. Morticians will always be needed; not everyone will want a home funeral.

Death Certificate

The family doctor or a local health officer will sign the death certificate, stating the cause of death. The remaining information must be supplied, typewritten or in black ink. The death certificate must be filed with the local health officer prior to final disposition.

Indiana is testing electronic death registration that should go into effect some time in 2011. When that is adopted the procedure will change somewhat.

Fetal Death

A death certificate is required in a case of stillbirth after 20 weeks of gestation.

Transporting and Disposition Permit

The local health officer will issue the authorization for disposition upon receipt of a properly executed death certificate. A burial transit permit (two copies) is required if the body is to be transported by common carrier. An out-of-state transit permit, for bodies brought into Indiana, must be filed with the local health officer.

Burial

Burial in Indiana must occur in an "established cemetery" and have a cover of not less than two feet of earth. To establish a family cemetery in a rural area, it must be surveyed, with a plat recorded with the county. Unfortunately, it appears statutes require almost all cemeteries to maintain a $100,000 maintenance trust fund. The legislature clearly intended to regulate commercial cemeteries, not to lay such a burden on private family burial grounds (religious cemeteries, for example, are exempt from the requirement), but until the statute is clarified, some families may have difficulty. As of this writing, one town is citing this statute while it does everything in its power to stop an 82-year-old woman from burying her husband on her rural 300 acres, going so far as to send the sheriff to her house! Perhaps your town or county won't take such a hostile stance (and we certainly wouldn't recommend bringing the maintenance fund law to their attention).

Cemeteries less than an acre are taxed at the rate of $1. If your family cemetery is more than 10 acres, it is required to be registered with the state.

Cremation

There is a 48-hour wait prior to cremation unless waived by the local health officer. (One might wish to seek this waiver if the crematory intends to charge a holding fee.) A pacemaker must be removed, and authorization by next-of-kin or other authorizing agent is required.

An authorizing agent must sign a statement saying that arrangements have been made for viewing the body (or for holding it until other services with the body present have been arranged first). Some funeral homes will interpret this to mean that they can require ID viewing and charge for it. Identification and tagging of the body at the place of death prior to removal would be a more responsible requirement. Indeed, to avoid any such extra charges, you may want to announce to the funeral director that you plan to view the body at the place of death.

The crematory can send cremated remains only to a funeral home or cemetery, a bizarre requirement since they may be retained by the person with legal control. Or they may be disposed of in a crypt or cemetery, on the property of a consenting owner, on uninhabited public land or a waterway. A form recording the disposition must be filed with the county recorder within ten days of the final disposition. There are no cremains police checking to see if they are still on your mantel.

Other Requirements

There are no embalming requirements in Indiana. Disposition must occur within "a reasonable time" after death. When death has occurred from an infectious disease, consult the doctor in attendance.

Medical Schools for Body Donation

Body donation to a medical school is another option for disposition. Find the information for Indiana at <www.finalrights.org>.

State Governance

There are eleven members on the Funeral and Cemetery Board—four funeral directors, four cemeterians, two consumer members, and one member from the public health department. (No more than five may be of the same political party.) However, cemeterians may not vote on funeral issues and funeral directors may not vote on cemetery issues. This seems to negate the positive aspect of having a combined board.

<www.in.gov/pla/funeral.htm>

Crematories are licensed by the Funeral and Cemetery Board and may be operated by anyone so licensed—not necessarily a mortician. Unfortunately, there is no representation on the Board.

Cemetery personnel may not sell markers or monuments for a profit if any public funds are accepted by that cemetery. Cemeteries have the exclusive right to open and close graves or to install markers. This is an unfortunate limitation if one is dealing with a for-profit cemetery and appears to violate the Sherman Anti-trust Act.

Prepaid Cemetery and Funeral Funds

A portion of ground interment rights or crypt sales must be placed in perpetual care: 8% for crypts, 15% for lots. There is a Consumer Protection Fund for Cemetery Maintenance, with 1% for that. That fund is not available to municipal, religious or small cemeteries under ten acres.

100% of all money paid preneed for funeral or cemetery goods and services must be placed in *trust* and the *interest* allowed to accumulate with the funeral home as the sole beneficiary. The seller may *also* take up to 10% for administrative expenses. Perhaps that was a legislative typo that should have been only 1%, a more realistic figure for the actual cost and more in line with what other states allow. In another part of the statutes, "reasonable" administrative expenses are to be paid according to the rules of the department of financial institutions. We wonder what that department thinks about an $800 administrative fee for an $8,000 funeral.

"Constructive delivery" can bypass the trusting requirement. "Delivery" usually is accomplished by issuing a certificate of ownership and warehousing the casket, vault and/or marker, although few states are checking to see if the goods are actually there. Once "delivered," it is almost impossible to get a refund even if the items have never been used. If a person opted for cremation at a later date, a burial vault would not be needed, for example.

All preneed funeral policies are irrevocable after 30 days. (That means it can't be cashed out, but can still be transferred.) At that point, the seller may pocket the 10% permitted for administration. The irrevocable requirement seems a strange limit on consumer choice. Only the "settlor" (the person for whom a preneed was purchased) may transfer a prepaid funeral contract to another funeral home. What does a daughter do if Mom dies while visiting her in Arizona? All contract terms must be fulfilled with any transfer, so constructive delivery mischief and the 10% that got taken out *may* get undone, but it looks, from the wording, like any need to transfer could be riddled with problems.

All prepaid funeral contracts must guarantee to supply goods and services of equal value at the price you originally paid, without additional charge. Current industry literature warns against guaranteeing prices because funeral inflation exceeds the interest usually received on such contracts. Therefore, one must wonder if folks in Indiana have a great deal going or whether funeral homes are finding mischievous ways around the law to collect the difference. The word "value" is an obvious problem. A $795 casket ten years ago would have been far fancier than a $795 casket today.

Finance charges are permitted for installment purchases of prepaid funeral services and merchandise. This is outrageous and should be repealed immediately. When you finance a car or house, you get to use either. But a finance charge on a lay-away plan before they lay you away?

Excess money left over after the contract services have been provided is to be returned to the family, an unlikely event, given funeral inflation.

Sellers of preneed funeral plans must make an annual report to the state board of prepaid funds collected.

Indiana has a preneed Consumer Protection Fund that may accumulate up to $1 million. It is financed by a fee for each preneed contract written—$2.50 for those under $1,000 in value, $5 for those $1,000, and $10 for those $1,500 and more. This fund will be used in the case of default by a funeral provider. Given that several preneed meltdowns have far exceeded $1 million, this cap is inappropriately low today.

Consumer Concerns

- The death rate in Indiana can support approximately 224 full-time mortuaries; there are, however, 649. Funeral prices tend to be higher in areas where there are "too many" funeral homes.

- Finance charges on preneed purchases should not be permitted.

- Substitution of equal value is a problem. There is no guarantee that an adequate description will be listed on the preneed contract. Survivors should be allowed to approve any substitution of equal quality and construction.

- Constructive delivery (warehousing) is permitted to bypass the trusting requirement for preneed purchases.

- There is no annual reporting requirement to the purchaser of pre-paid funeral goods and services, paperwork that might be useful to the family of a deceased and which would help to "enforce" the trusting requirement.

- Given the loopholes and the irrevocable requirement for preneed contracts, it is a **terrible** idea to prepay for cemetery and funeral expenses in Indiana unless one must set aside assets for Medicaid eligibility. Money in your own bank account will be safer, is more transferable, and allows for a change in plans. Twenty-nine other states require 100% trusting. Preneed is alive and well in those states. Why doesn't the legislature want the same protection for Indiana residents?

- There is no requirement to identify and tag the body at the place of death before removal.

- There is no requirement that low-cost caskets be included in any display.

- The statute on mark-up of cash advance items is vague and does not appear to forbid a mark-up or require disclosure of the exact amount of any mark-up if there is one.

- The FTC Funeral Rule has not been adopted in this state, which would give consumers more protection.

- Settling funeral disputes when the deceased has not left specific instructions is difficult without large legal expenses. In other states, that task is assigned to the Probate Court which one may use without hiring a lawyer, while in Indiana, one must go through a Circuit Court.

- Ethical standards are not clearly defined. Clarity in standards may be necessary for valid consumer complaints to prevail. (See Appendix.)

- This state has no laws regulating the body parts business.

Miscellaneous Information

- The educational requirements for becoming a funeral director in Indiana are one year of college and one year of mortuary school (or two years of mortuary school) plus one year of apprenticeship. All must pass a state-approved exam.

- A crematory may not sell inorganic matter (e.g., gold) retrieved from a body.

- A county coroner is elected, many of whom are morticians with a conflict of interest.

- You may name a designated agent for body disposition in a "funeral planning declaration." The state-specific form may be found in the Indiana code 29-2-19-13.

- There is no state assistance for burial of indigents.

- A disinterment order must be obtained from the state Department of Health. A licensed funeral director must be in charge.

This chapter was sent for review to the Funeral and Cemetery Board and the Department of Health—Vital Records, with minor changes offered by each.

Caring for the Dead
In Iowa

Please refer also to the general introduction to state chapters—"Caring for the Dead: Necessary Information."

Families and church groups in Iowa may care for their own dead when no communicable disease is involved. The legal authority to do so is found in:

Title 144.27 (re filing a death certificate) — When a person other than a funeral director assumes custody of a dead body, the person shall be responsible for carrying out the provisions of this section.

Title 156.2 Persons excluded (from the Practice of Funeral Directing and Mortuary Science regulations) 4. Persons who, without compensation, bury their own dead . . . .

Death Certificate

The family doctor or a local medical examiner will supply and sign the death certificate within 24 hours stating the cause of death. The remaining information must be supplied, typewritten or in black ink. The death certificate must be filed with the local registrar within three days and before final disposition.

Iowa is researching electronic death registration but is behind schedule. When that is adopted, paper documents will still be available to home funeral families.

Fetal Death

A fetal death report is required when death occurs after 20 weeks of gestation or over 350 grams in weight (about 12 ounces). If there is no family physician involved, the local medical examiner must sign the fetal death certificate. All other procedures apply if disposition is handled by the family.

Transporting and Disposition Permit

The local registrar, medical examiner, or a funeral director may issue the burial-transit permit. This authorization must be obtained before moving the body from the place of death.

Burial

There are no state statutes that specifically permit or prohibit home burial. It is also unlikely that there are local zoning regulations regarding home burial, but you should review them before planning a family cemetery. If your land is in a rural area, draw a map of the property showing where the burial ground will be and have it filed with the deed. That may be all you have to do to establish your family cemetery. There are no state burial statutes or regulations with regard to burial locations or depth. A sensible guideline is 150 feet from a water supply, 25 feet from a power line, with two or three feet of earth on top. Plan your family cemetery away from boundaries with neighbors, too.

When burial is arranged, the family member acting as the funeral director must sign the burial-transit permit and return it within 10 days to the issuing office.

Cremation

A cremation permit must be obtained from the medical examiner. The cost will not exceed $35. Most crematories insist that a pacemaker be removed, and authorization by next-of-kin or designated agent is required. The crematory will return the disposition authorization to the issuing registrar.

Crematories may not contract directly with the public, a self-serving regulation to protect the high-priced funeral homes, no doubt.

There are no laws regarding the disposition of cremated remains. You may do as you wish.

Other Requirements

According to administrative code, an unembalmed body may be held up to 72 hours, and three days more if refrigerated between 38 and 42 degrees.

Embalming is required if death was from a communicable disease. Because of that the funeral director may start embalming without the family's permission, surely a religious violation in some cases. This is also the worst possible circumstance under which to embalm, putting funeral personnel at risk; it is surprising that the funeral directors have not made an effort to change this law. CDC does not recommend embalming for any reason;

embalming does not protect the public health. Only a funeral director may handle such deaths. Families that care for an ailing AIDS patient or someone with Hepatitis C are at less risk after death than before, yet the right to care for their own dead has been snatched away by this law. Families should object strenuously to having the body taken from them in such cases—enlisting the physician in charge might help. Embalming or a sealed casket is required when shipping a body by common carrier.

Medical Schools for Body Donation

Body donation to a medical school is another option for disposition. Find the information for Iowa at <www.finalrights.org>.

State Governance

The Iowa Board of Mortuary Science Examiners has seven members. Two are consumer representatives, one a crematory operator, and four are morticians. Crematories are regulated by the Mortuary Board but one does not have to be a funeral director to run a crematory.

<www.idph.state.ia.us/licensure/board_home.asp?board=ms>

Cemetery funds are monitored by the Insurance Department. Preneed sellers are licensed by the Insurance Department.

<http://www.iid.state.ia.us/>

Prepaid Cemetery and Funeral Funds

Iowa has both perpetual care cemeteries and non-perpetual care cemeteries, although all cemeteries established after 1995 must provide for perpetual care. A contract with a non-perpetual care cemetery must be clearly marked as such.

Twenty percent of the lot purchase must be put into a guarantee fund when sold by a perpetual care cemetery. A cemetery may not require that you purchase cemetery merchandise only from that cemetery, something to keep in mind as the for-profit companies move in.

Corporate chains are purchasing and building cemeteries in Iowa. Cemeteries are tax-exempt, which gives the corporations a huge incentive to invest in such. The cost of cemetery space and services—when owned by a for-profit corporation—tend to be extremely high.

One has to wonder if legislators were tippling corn liquor when they wrote the prepaid funeral statutes. Dennis Britson in the Department of Insurance was kind enough to translate for us.

Eighty percent of all money prepaid for *funeral* and *cemetery* service and merchandise must be placed in trust in a federally insured institution. A $50,000 fidelity bond (a woefully inadequate amount) is required unless 100% is trusted, as an inducement to trust the full amount. Twenty-nine other states require 100% trusting. Preneed is alive and well in those states. Why doesn't the legislature want the same protection for Iowa residents instead of fooling around with bonds and such?

An annual report of each trust fund must be made to the state Insurance Department every year. Each preneed contract must carry a disclosure indicating that the consumer may contact the Insurance Department to verify the whereabouts and amount of the fund being held.

After pocketing 20%, the seller, with the buyer's permission, may use the funds to purchase an insurance policy, for which the seller undoubtedly collects a commission. One has to hope consumers have the good sense to say "no" to such a conversion; the cash value of insurance will be far less than what was paid if one wants to change plans to a more modest exit and get some money back later.

Some funeral homes don't bother to ask permission about insurance as happened to one Iowa couple. The Zemans each planned a $7,000 funeral but didn't have the funds to pay in advance. They were sold two Homesteaders insurance policies and told they could pay for them over 10 years, at the rate of $230 a month. After four years and $11,000 in payments, they checked to see what the exact balance would be. They were stunned when told that they were committed to making these payments for a full 10 years for a total of $27,900, almost double the actual cost of the funerals. If they stopped paying, which they did, the cash value of their policies amounted to $6,000. They had lost $5,000 and any interest growth. Their son is now working to seek some legislative remedies.

In another statute, the preneed contract must "explain the disposition of the income. . . ." Mr. Britson tells us that because there is no language permitting the withdrawal of interest, one can't. By the same logic, if there's no language saying you can't withdraw it, you would think you could. Other states have solved this problem with three little words: "interest to accrue."

According to several pages of preneed statutes, the trusting requirement does not apply to merchandise that has been "delivered" to the consumer. This usually means the merchandise could be stored by the seller with the buyer's name on it. However, consumers are protected from that practice by a single sentence buried on page 855 (out of 877 pages of various insurance regs), which became effective in 2007: ". . . warehousing is no longer an alternative to the trust requirements. . . ."

Although a prepaid funeral plan must disclose the terms under which substitutions "may" be made, there is *no requirement* for a full description of the merchandise and *no requirement* for the undertaker to supply merchandise of equal quality and construction when it is a guaranteed-price arrangement.

If a trust-funded preneed contract is cancelled or transferred, the seller may keep up to 10% of the purchase price for any expenses incurred (plus the cost of any merchandise that has been delivered prior to July 2007). If the seller initially pocketed 20%, the seller will have to fork over half the loot in order to refund 90%. In the case of an insurance policy, cashing in will bring back far less than what one paid, possibly only about half.

Finance charges are permitted, a practice which targets the poor. If one finances a car, one gets to drive it right away. But finance charges on a layaway plan before they lay you away seem usurious.

Consumer Concerns

- The death rate in Iowa can support approximately 113 full-time mortuaries. There are, however, 476. Funeral prices tend to be higher in areas where there are "too many" funeral homes, and there is likely to be a greater default on prepaid funeral monies.

- There is little or no oversight of cemetery sales practices, although preneed sales are monitored by the Insurance Department.

- The trusting of prepaid funeral money and cemetery merchandise is inadequate and should be increased to 100%, with no withdrawal of interest.

- Rights of transfer and cancellation permit 10% penalties.

- Finance charges exploit the poor.

- There are inadequate provisions for substitution if selected merchandise is not available at the time of death. A full description should be spelled out in prepaid contracts, with an obligation to supply merchandise of equal quality and construction. Survivors should have the right to approve any substitutions.

- There is no requirement to report to the consumer annually on the status of prepaid funeral funds. This would provide a record that may be useful to survivors and would help to enforce the trusting requirements.

- There is no Guarantee Fund to protect consumers against embezzlement of preneed funds.

- Until the laws have been improved for prepaid funeral and cemetery purchases, it is probably a *terrible* idea to prepay for a funeral or for cemetery services and merchandise in Iowa.

- The regulation requiring embalming when death involves communicable diseases puts funeral staff at risk and does not acknowledge religious or personal objections to embalming.

- The laws do not distinguish between "communicable" and "contagious" or "infectious" diseases. Those who have cared for someone dying of AIDS, for example, should not be forbidden from personally handling the funeral arrangements.

- There is no requirement for a display of low-cost caskets.

- There is no required disclosure of how much mark-up will be charged on cash advances nor is a mark-up forbidden.

- The ethical standards for funeral directors are inadequate. They should be more detailed and explicit, with clear procedures available to anyone wishing to file a complaint.

- This state has no laws regulating the body parts business.

Miscellaneous Information

- Two years of college plus a course in mortuary study are required to become a funeral director. One year of internship after school is required, plus a passing score on national, state, and practical exams. Alas, the national exam is an embarrassment, deemed "irrelevant" and "useless" by consumer advocates and industry practitioners alike.

- A county medical examiner must be an MD and is appointed by the medical examining board. A medical examiner may not influence the choice of a mortuary.

- The FTC Funeral Rule has been adopted by reference in the Mortuary Science Board rules.

- One may sign a declaration to appoint a designee for handling funeral arrangements, helpful when estranged from next-of-kin.

- A body must be tagged with identification by the funeral director.

- A public official who is otherwise forbidden from accepting gifts of value may, however, accept funeral flowers and memorial gifts designated for a nonprofit organization.

- Cemetery commissioners may subscribe to cemetery publications paid for by the cemetery fund.

- Coal mining is not suitable if it is within 100 feet of a cemetery.

- A disinterment permit must be obtained from the Department of Public Health. A funeral director must be in charge.

This chapter was sent for review to the Department of Health, the Iowa Board of Mortuary Science Examiners, and the Department of Insurance, all of whom made helpful suggestions.

Caring for the Dead

In Kansas

Please refer also to the general introduction to state chapters—"Caring for the Dead: Necessary Information."

Persons in Kansas may care for their own dead. The legal authority to do so is found in:

> *Title 65-1713b. Every funeral service or interment, or part thereof, hereafter conducted in this state must be in the actual charge and under the supervision of a Kansas licensed funeral director or of the duly licensed assistant funeral director. Provided, however, that this shall not prevent a family from burying its own dead where death did not result from a contagious, infectious or communicable disease, nor shall it prevent a religious group or sect whose religious beliefs require the burial of its own dead from conducting such services where death did not result from a contagious, infectious or communicable disease.*

There are no other statutes that might require you to use a funeral director unless the death is from a contagious disease (See Consumer Concerns.)

Death Certificate

Kansas has started electronic death registration (EDR) but also permits paper filing. The coroner's office will have access to the electronic system, but nothing becomes final until the state registrar's office is open. If you are working on your own, you may get a blank death certificate from the state registrar's office, 785-296-1428. The family doctor (or coroner) will fill out the cause of death. The remaining information must be supplied by the family or agent, typewritten or in black ink. The death certificate must be filed with the state registrar within three days and before final disposition.

Fetal Death

A certificate of stillbirth is required when the weight of the fetus is 350 grams or more and death did not result from an induced termination of pregnancy.

If there is no family physician involved, the local coroner must sign the fetal death certificate.

Transporting and Disposition Permit

A body may be moved with medical permission. If out-of-state disposition is planned, the state registrar will issue a transit permit.

Burial

Home burial is generally permissible in Kansas. If your land is in a rural area, draw a map of the property showing where the burial ground will be and have it filed with the deed. You should review any local zoning laws first, although it is unlikely to be mentioned. A sensible guideline is 150 feet from a water supply, 25 feet from a power line, with two or three feet of earth on top. Plan your family cemetery away from boundaries with neighbors, too.

Cremation

A cremation permit from the local coroner is required. There is no fee for this. Authorization by next-of-kin is usually required, and a pacemaker must be removed. There are no laws regarding the disposition of cremated remains. You may do as you wish.

Other Requirements

If disposition will not take place within 24 hours, embalming or refrigeration is required. A reasonable extension of this may be permitted if no health hazard or nuisance will result.

When death has occurred from meningococcal infection, ebola virus infection, Lassa fever, anthrax, rabies, brucellosis, or any other infectious or contagious disease, the body must be embalmed if cremation or burial cannot be accomplished within 24 hours. In the case of immediate burial for infectious diseases, the body must be in a sealed metal casket, a requirement with no public-health or environmental purpose.

The statutes say that a body to be shipped by common carrier or for burial in a mausoleum must be embalmed, but a regulation states that if the body is in a sealed metal container it may be considered "embalmed" for transportation purposes.

Medical Schools for Body Donation

Body donation to a medical school is another option for disposition. Find the information for Kansas at <www.finalrights.org>.

State Governance

The Kansas State Board of Mortuary Arts has five members. Three are embalmers and two are consumer representatives. This board also regulates funeral directors and crematories, but there is no provision for their representation on the board. The consequence of this bias is obvious: When new legislation passed to regulate the crematories in 2001, it required crematories to be run by funeral directors or embalmers if they were dealing directly with the public. This makes no sense whatsoever. In Europe and many New England states, crematories are found on cemetery grounds run by cemeterians. Furthermore, there is almost nothing on the national funeral directors' study guide about cremation and very little in the mortuary curriculum guide on running a crematory. Now that embalmers and funeral directors have succeeded in hogging the cremation business in Kansas, the prices will likely be much higher than in areas where there is more open competition among diverse practitioners.

<www.kansas.gov/ksbma/>

The Secretary of State regulates cemetery preneed transactions.

Prepaid Cemetery and Funeral Funds

Kansas statutes do not address how prepaid *cemetery service* money should be handled, but there are some pretty wild provisions for what a cemetery can do with the money you prepaid for *cemetery merchandise*—presumably vaults and markers. "Constructive delivery" can bypass any trusting requirements altogether, so the cemetery is likely to give you a certificate of ownership and call it "delivered" (in the warehouse, though few states are checking to see if your vault and marker really are). Otherwise, 110% of the wholesale cost must go into trust. But it doesn't go into trust right away: the cemetery can pocket 35% of your purchase price before allocating any payments to your lay-away trust account. If any of your prepaid money actually ends up in the bank, "reasonable" amounts may be withdrawn from the income to administer the account. How much does it cost to watch the interest grow?

After wading through the legalese of the Kansas statutes we suspect that the state also permits preneed funeral and cemetery installment sales to come under the "actuarial method." That would mean that finance charges are permitted, and your payments will be applied to the carrying charges before they will be applied to the merchandise and services you're purchasing.

There are no provisions for simply cancelling a purchase of cemetery goods and services and getting a refund unless you move 150 miles away. If you can't afford to keep up the payments, you can probably kiss whatever money you've already paid goodbye.

But listen to the statutory plan if you do move more than 150 miles away and the vault and marker have not yet been installed or "delivered": In that case, you may ask the cemetery to send the merchandise to a new cemetery but you'll have to pay the transportation costs. The lid alone on an average vault is 900 pounds. What's will it cost to ship the whole thing to, say, Vermont?

If you do want to cancel—but, remember, you have to be 150 miles away first—you are entitled to—*ta-da!*—85% of what's in trust (if there's anything really there). In case you're feeling muddled, the most that the cemetery ever had to leave in the trust was 110% of the wholesale cost for your vault and marker! If you paid $1,000 for the vault but it cost the cemetery only $350, then $385 might have been put into trust. Not counting interest—which can be withdrawn for "reasonable" expenses—you get 85% of that or $327.25. What a deal the Secretary of State has arranged for you!

All payments for preneed *funeral* goods and services (including vaults sold by a funeral home, but not markers) must be placed in trust, with interest to accumulate. Payment checks must be made out to the depository bank or institution unless the mortuary carries an insurance policy of at least $100,000 against employee dishonesty. The state may audit accounts on a random basis.

A report of preneed arrangements must be made by the funeral home to the Mortuary board every two years.

A prearranged contract may be cancelled by the buyer at any time. An irrevocable policy may be transferred to another provider at any time.

Consumer Concerns

- The death rate in Kansas can support approximately 99 full-time mortuaries; there are, however, 326. Funeral prices tend to be higher in areas where there are "too many" funeral homes.

- There is no state board governing cemeteries.

- Trusting requirements for cemetery merchandise are inadequate. "Constructive delivery" should not be permitted. Trusting requirements should be increased to 100% of cemetery goods and services, with a full right of cancellation and refund including interest.

- If finance charges are permitted for installment purchases of prepaid funeral services and merchandise, this is outrageous. When you finance a car or house, you get to use what you are buying. But a finance charge on a lay-away plan before they lay you away?

- There is no annual reporting requirement to the purchaser of prepaid funeral goods and services, paperwork that might be helpful to the family of a deceased to indicate prepayment and would help to "enforce" trusting requirements.

- There is no guarantee fund to protect prepaid funeral money in case of default. The $100,000 insurance policy against employee dishonesty is not mandatory nor likely adequate.

- There is no requirement that when merchandise is selected for a guaranteed-price preneed agreement that a clear description be given and that merchandise of equal quality and construction must be substituted if the original item selected is not available. Survivors should have a right to approve any substitution.

- Until the laws governing preneed cemetery and funeral purchases have been changed, it is probably a terrible idea to pay for either ahead of time in Kansas.

- The coroner or medical examiner's permit for cremation in the case of an *anticipated* death from natural causes is totally unnecessary and creates an additional burden for families.

- There is no requirement to identify and tag the body at the place of death before removal.

- The embalming laws are unreasonable and irresponsible. When death occurs from a contagious disease, funeral professionals are at risk. Refrigeration is a more reliable method of body preservation and should not be needed for 72 hours under normal circumstances. This would allow for most funeral rituals to occur according to religious preference.

- Those who have cared for someone dying of AIDS, for example, should not be forbidden from personally handling the funeral arrangements. The state should distinguish between "communicable" and "contagious" or "infectious" diseases.

- There is no provision either forbidding a mark-up on cash advance items or requiring the disclosure of the mark-up. Consumers may want to ask for a copy of the invoices for such charges.

- There is no requirement to include low-cost caskets in any display.

- Although complying with the FTC Funeral Rule is required professional conduct, the statutes that describe funeral pricing bundled with the casket price should be eliminated, as the FTC Rule requires itemization of funeral services.

- This state has no laws regulating the body parts business.

Miscellaneous Information

- Educational requirements for becoming an embalmer: mortuary college (2 years), national exam, and one year of apprenticeship. For a funeral director: two years of college, state exam, and one year of apprenticeship prior to exam. Alas, the national exam is an embarrassment, deemed "irrelevant" and "useless" by consumer advocates and industry practitioners alike. This state also licenses assistant funeral directors, the only one to do so. Requirement: 17 years of age and of "good moral character and temperate habits." One must pass a state exam and be employed by a licensed funeral director.

- Ethical standards for morticians are fairly comprehensive, but additional ones will be found in the Appendix.

- Complaint information is spelled out in a pamphlet put out by the Mortuary Board.

- District coroners are licensed physicians who are appointed.

- You may name an agent for body disposition in your durable power of attorney for health care.

- No new permits are required for disinterment but the person with the right to control disposition must authorize it.

This chapter was sent for review to the Kansas Department of Health and Environment—Vital Statistics, the Secretary of State, and the Kansas State Board of Mortuary Arts. The latter supplied helpful corrections. Other information was verified by phone.

Caring for the Dead
In Kentucky

Please refer also to the general introduction to state chapters—"Caring for the Dead: Necessary Information."

Persons in Kentucky may care for their own dead. The legal authority to do so is found in:

> *Title 213.076* **Certificate of Death** *... The funeral director, or person acting as such, who first takes custody of a dead body shall be responsible for filing the death certificate . . . .*

There are no other statutes which might require you to use a funeral director.

Death Certificate

If the deceased was not attended by a physician, dentist, or chiropractor within the prior 36 hours, the death must be reported to the coroner, regardless of the cause of death. The death certificate, obtainable from the health department or a funeral director, must be presented to the physician, dentist, or chiropractor in charge of the patient's care within five days. The nonmedical information must be supplied, typewritten. The physician will return the completed death certificate within five working days to the funeral director or person acting as such. The death certificate must then be filed with the Office of Vital Statistics.

A provisional death certificate will serve as the burial-transit permit. This may be procured from the county coroner or facility releasing the body.

Kentucky began a pilot program for electronic death registration in 2010 and is adding more areas as the training is completed. A paper option is available to families caring for their own dead.

Fetal Death

A fetal death must be reported when death occurs after 20 weeks of gestation or when the weight is 350 grams (about 12 ounces). If no physician is in attendance, the coroner must be notified.

Transporting and Disposition Permit

The local registrar (within the county health department) or a deputy will issue the provisional report of death. The top copy serves as the burial transit permit. This must be obtained prior to final disposition of the body. After disposition, it must be filed with the local registrar within five days.

Burial

There are no state statutes that specifically permit or prohibit home burial. It is also unlikely that there are local zoning regulations regarding home burial, but you should review them before planning a family cemetery. If your land is in a rural area, draw a map of the property showing where the burial ground will be and have it filed with the deed. That may be all you have to do to establish your family cemetery. A sensible guideline is 150 feet from a water supply, 25 feet from a power line, with two or three feet of earth on top. Plan your family cemetery away from boundaries with neighbors, too.

The Attorney General's office has suggested additional considerations such as a survey and fencing, but those are optional, not requirements.

When burial is arranged by the family, the family member acting as the funeral director must sign the authorization for disposition and return it to the registrar of that locale within 10 days.

Cremation

A coroner's signature on the provisional report of death is required for cremation. As of 1996, physicians accounted for only a dozen or so of those serving as coroners. The majority of the rest were associated in some way with funeral homes. This may put a family wishing to care for its own dead in an awkward and difficult position if the mortician doesn't understand a family's rights.

State law requires that a pacemaker be removed. Persons may authorize their own cremation or designate an authorizing agent; otherwise authorization from all next-of-kin of the same order is required. The crematory may offer to file the paperwork. There are no laws regarding the disposition of cremated remains. You may do as you wish.

Other Requirements

There are no embalming requirements in Kentucky. Weather and reasonable planning should be considered.

If the person died of a contagious or communicable disease, the physician or local health officer should be consulted.

Medical Schools for Body Donation

Body donation to a medical school is another option for disposition. Find the information for Kentucky at <www.finalrights.org>.

State Governance

The Kentucky Board of Embalmers and Funeral Directors has five members. One is a consumer representative and four are funeral directors or embalmers.

<http://kbefd.ky.gov/>

A bill passed in 2006 requires all funeral businesses to be affiliated with or owned by a "full-service establishment," with all the expensive overhead that goes with that. A funeral board regulation forbids funeral establishments in strip malls or office buildings, surely aimed to make it difficult for low-cost direct disposition providers.

The Attorney General's office licenses cemetery sales people, preneed sellers, and crematories. Sound crematory practices are well-defined in the statutes passed in 1994. See <http://ag.ky.gov/>.

Prepaid Cemetery and Funeral Funds

A cemetery must deposit 20% of each lot sale, 5% of each crypt sale, and 10% of each niche sale in its perpetual care fund.

100% of preneed *cemetery services* must be placed in trust. 40% of the payments for *cemetery merchandise* must be placed in trust unless the merchandise has been "delivered" (stored in a warehouse) with a certificate of ownership supplied to the purchaser. This is called "constructive delivery." Once the merchandise has been so "delivered," it may not be possible to get a refund. Bonding may be used in lieu of the trust fund. If a purchaser defaults on partial payments, the cemetery may collect the portion paid from the trust.

All (100%) prepaid funeral money must be placed in trust in a federally controlled financial institution. Funds may be co-mingled, but separate accounting must be maintained.

A preneed contract may be cancelled with 15 days notice and all principal and interest returned to the purchaser.

Preneed licensees and cemetery companies must file annual reports of all sales with the state.

A fee of $5 for cemetery sales of $500 or less and $10 for sales over $500 in value must be paid to the Attorney General's office for the "consumer security account" to provide restitution to consumers who have been defrauded by cemetery companies and preneed sellers.

Consumer Concerns

- The death rate in Kentucky can support approximately 160 full-time mortuaries; there are, however, 494. Funeral prices tend to be higher in areas where there are "too many" funeral homes.

- Trusting requirements for cemetery purchases are inadequate. 100% of all prepaid cemetery merchandise should be placed into trust with the right to cancel and receive a refund. Constructive delivery should not be permitted.

- Although the Attorney General's office of Consumer Protection is sensitive to consumer complaints, there is little or no oversight of cemetery sales practices. Reconstructing the make-up of the Funeral Board would be one way to begin. Suggested possibility: two funeral directors, two cemeterians who are not funeral directors or affiliated with a mortuary, one crematory operator who is not a funeral director or affiliated, and two consumer representatives.

- No annual report to the consumer is required for prepaid funeral funds. Such paperwork could be useful to survivors and would help to enforce the trusting requirements.

- There is no requirement that when merchandise is selected on a guaranteed-price, preneed agreement that a clear description be given and that merchandise of equal quality and construction must be substituted, with approval of survivors, if the original item selected is not available at the time of need.

- Until there is better protection for preneed funeral and cemetery funds, it is probably a **terrible** idea to prepay for these in Kentucky.

- There is no requirement to identify and tag the body at the place of death before removal.

- There is no requirement that low-cost caskets be displayed along with others.

- There is no provision to either disclose the mark-up on cash advance items or to forbid such a practice.

- The Funeral Board does not have a clear mandate to set and enforce ethical standards. Clear statutes would make it easier for a consumer to prevail when filing a valid complaint. The $500 limit on fines should be raised a significant amount in order to act as a deterrent.

- The FTC Funeral Rule has not been adopted. Kentucky dies require the FTC-mandated price lists but is silent about other provisions such as misrepresentation and anti-tying.

- There is no requirement that coroners must be medical personnel, and yet a coroner is required for at least preliminary judgment regarding medical investigation. The fact that this is an elected position is demeaning of the role. A medical investigator should not have to run in a popularity contest; the position should be filled via appointment based on medical training and competence. A mortician holding this position is facing a clear conflict of interest. If families and church groups plan to bypass the local funeral establishment, one can only hope that it will not be difficult to obtain cremation permits from the local coroner/funeral director.

- Next-of-kin may challenge in court the wishes of the deceased to be cremated even if there is a preneed authorization, but deference must be given to the deceased "unless extraordinary circumstances exist." Laws to allow for a designated deathcare agent would be helpful, when estranged or distanced from next-of-kin or when dealing with unexpected circumstances.

- If the funeral home drafts the obituary, the name of the funeral director and the name and address of the funeral home must be included, which means you'll be paying for the funeral home's advertising.

- This state has no laws regulating the body parts business.

Miscellaneous Information

- The educational requirements for becoming an embalmer are an associate's degree from a mortuary college plus one year of apprenticeship. For funeral directors, the only requirement is a high school diploma or equivalent plus three years of apprenticeship. One or two years of mortuary college may be substituted for up to two years of apprenticeship. Both must pass an exam approved by the board which may include the national exam. Alas, the national exam is a total embarrassment, deemed "irrelevant" and "useless" by consumer advocates and industry practitioners alike.

- This is the only state where a dentist is authorized to sign a death certificate.

- A permit for disinterment must be obtained from the state registrar.
- Funeral consumer complaints should be filed with:

Consumer Protection Division
Office of the Attorney General
1024 Capital Center Drive
Frankfort, KY 40601
502-696-5395

This section was sent for review to Vital Statistics, the Board of Embalmers, and the Attorney General's Office. The AG's office was very helpful, especially regarding home burial.

Caring for the Dead
In Louisiana

Please refer also to the general introduction to state chapters—"Caring for the Dead: Necessary Information."

In Louisiana, a dead body becomes a hostage of the funeral industry, one of only eight states that requires the use of a funeral director. (Connecticut, Illinois, Indiana, Louisiana, Michigan, Nebraska, New Jersey, and New York.) In almost no other situation is a private citizen forced to use a for-profit business to fulfill the interests of the state.

The laws are contradictory and invite a court challenge.

> *R.S. 8 Chapter 10 Human Remains § 655. Right of disposing of remains—A. The right to control interment . . . of the remains of a deceased person, unless other specific directions have been given by the decedent in the form of a written and notarized declaration, vests in and devolves upon the following in the order named: (1) The surviving spouse, if not judicially separated from the decedent. (2) A majority of the surviving adult children of the decedent . . .*

In the public health statutes, the language is typical of most states:

> *RS 40: 49 A. The funeral director or person acting as such shall prepare and file the certificate of death*

In 1986, however, the funeral industry influenced self-serving legislation to take away the rights granted above—and then some.

> *R.S. 40 Public Health and Safety § 32 Definitions—(17) "Funeral director or person acting as such" is a licensed funeral director or embalmer . . .*

Parents may file a birth certificate if there is no doctor involved. What's the big deal about death certificates?

After reading the Professions and Occupations statutes, one must wonder if clergy are allowed to conduct funerals in Louisiana:

R.S. 37 Chapter 10 Embalming and Funeral Directors § 831. Definitions—(23) "Funeral directing" means the operation of a funeral home, or, by way of illustration and not limitation, any service whatsoever connected with the management of funerals, or the supervision of hearses or funeral cars, the purchase of caskets or other funeral merchandise, and retail sale and display thereof, the cleaning or dressing of dead human bodies for burial, and the performance or supervision of any service or act connected with the management of funerals from time of death until the body or bodies are delivered to the cemetery, crematorium, or other agent for the purpose of disposition.

R.S. 37 Chapter 10 Embalming and Funeral Directors § 848 Unlawful practice— . . . (5) Every dead human body shall be disposed of and prepared through a funeral establishment and under the supervision of a licensed funeral home or embalmer.

What about religious groups that routinely bathe and shroud the dead? Not in Louisiana? With the growing interest in home funerals, there is some work to be done to change the laws.

Death Certificate

The family doctor will sign the death certificate within 24 hours, stating the cause of death. If the death is a coroner's case, the coroner may take 48 hours. The remaining information must be supplied, typewritten or in black ink. The death certificate must be filed with the parish registrar within five days and before final disposition.

Electronic death registration is still being worked on. A paper filing option should be available when that takes place.

Fetal Death

A fetal death report is required if death occurs after 20 weeks of gestation or when the weight is 350 grams or more (about 12 ounces). If there is no family physician involved, the local coroner must sign the fetal death certificate.

Transporting and Disposition Permit

Once the death certificate has been filed, the local registrar will issue a burial-transit permit which is a separate document, not attached to the death certificate, and for which there is a modest fee. This permit must be obtained prior to final disposition of the body.

Burial

Burial must occur in a duly authorized cemetery, so you'll have to jump through some hoops to set up a family burial ground. Check first with the parish registrar for local zoning laws. If there are no restrictions, here are links to the instructions and forms you will need to file with the Louisiana Cemetery Board to register your family burial ground, shared with us by Heath Gault, a helpful Louisiana resident:

<www.lcb.state.la.us/forms/fbg_app_instructions.pdf>

<www.lcb.state.la.us/forms/fbg_app.pdf>

<www.lcb.state.la.us/forms/aod_fbg.pdf>

The casket must have a covering of two feet of soil unless a burial vault or lawn crypt is used. Although not mentioned in the law, burial should be at least 150 feet from a water supply and 25 feet from a power line or neighbor's boundary.

When burial occurs, the burial-transit permit must be filed within ten days with the registrar of the parish where disposition takes place.

Cremation

A permit to cremate must be obtained from the coroner in the parish where death occurred. The charge for this is $50. A pacemaker must be removed, and authorization by next-of-kin is required. The crematory will sign the burial-transit permit. This permit must be filed with the parish registrar within ten days. There are no laws regarding the disposition of cremated remains. You may do as you wish.

Persons with a religious need to witness or participate in the cremation may do so. (Anybody may ask to do so, regardless of religious need.)

Other Requirements

If disposition is not arranged within 30 hours of death, the body must be embalmed or refrigerated below 45°.

If the person died of a contagious or communicable disease, the doctor in attendance should be consulted.

Medical Schools for Body Donation

Body donation to a medical school is another option for disposition. Find the information for Louisiana at <www.finalrights.org>.

State Governance

The Louisiana Board of Embalmers and Funeral Directors has nine members. Four are licensed embalmers, four are licensed funeral directors, and one— over the age of 60—represents the elderly.

The Louisiana Cemetery Board oversees all cemeteries in Louisiana. There are seven members, two of whom shall not have any direct or indirect interest in a cemetery or funeral business.

There is a separate board—the Louisiana Unmarked Burial Sites Board—to preserve historical grave sites.

Crematories are licensed by the Funeral Board, but not represented on the Funeral Board. One does not need to be a funeral director to run a crematory.

Prepaid Cemetery and Funeral Funds

10% of the purchase price of a cemetery lot must go into a perpetual care trust fund. Only 50% of the money for prepaid *cemetery* merchandise, such as a vault or memorial, must be placed in trust. "Constructive Delivery" can bypass the trusting requirement. Therefore, it is highly unlikely that you would get any money back if you were to change your mind.

All prepaid *funeral* monies (100%) must be deposited in a separate savings or trust account for each purchaser with interest to accrue and a report filed annually with the state. Unless the account is made irrevocable, the purchaser may cancel the agreement and withdraw the funds at any time. There is no clear provision for transferring an irrevocable contract.

Substitution must be of "equal quality, value, and workmanship." A full description of funeral merchandise is required. The word "value" might be a problem if the description is not detailed. A $900 casket ten years ago was a pretty swell casket. Today, it might be the low-end casket.

Restrictive Casket Sales and an Attack on the Benedictine Monks

According to the definition in the statutes, retail sales and display of caskets is considered "funeral directing" for which one must be licensed as a funeral director, a little silly since a casket is just a glorified box. The FTC Funeral Rule states that all funeral homes must accept a casket supplied by the consumer, a painful reality for some funeral folks, as many depend on the casket sale for a significant portion of the profit. And while the Funeral Board wishes to make it illegal for retail casket sales in Louisiana, a funeral home must accept any casket that a Louisiana resident orders from another state, driving that money elsewhere if they succeed. Legislators are supposed to look at the fiscal implications of any law and might want to re-think this one.

The Board of Embalmers and Funeral Directors has harassed a Texas monument and casket company that advertises in Louisiana, even though the company is based in Texas. But most offensive of all is the "cease and desist" order sent to St. Joseph Abbey prompted by a complaint filed with the Board by a major Louisiana funeral home chain-owner, Boyd Mothe, Jr. Mr. Mothe's style of doing business is described in a consumer complaint on the FTC site:

<www.ftc.gov/bcp/rulemaking/funeral/comments/Comment063.htm>

Monks at the Abbey in St. Benedict, led by Mark Coudrain, are building and selling attractive cypress wood caskets as a reflection of their commitment to spiritual simplicity: <www.clcabbey.com>. Efforts to change the law failed in 2008, but there will be new efforts in the coming year(s), Mark says. In mid 2010, the Abbey filed suit against the state of Louisiana and its funeral board, represented by the Institute for Justice, which had won a similar suit in Tennessee in 2000.

What does the Funeral Board think of the prisoners at the state penitentiary building (and selling) caskets? Two were purchased by the Billy Graham family for $215 each. From the minutes of the April 28, 2010 Board meeting:

> Discussion ensued in regards to the Board not receiving a response from LA Department of Corrections/LA State Penitentiary with the handling of services for inmates who pass away while incarcerated. A directive for the issuance of a subpoena was given in order to obtain the information requested.

Prisoner volunteers run their own hospice program, too.

Consumer Concerns

- The death rate in Louisiana can support approximately 171 full-time mortuaries; there are, however, 299. Funeral prices tend to be higher in areas where there are "too many" funeral homes.
- Church groups and individuals do not have the right to care for their own dead.
- Trusting requirements for cemetery merchandise are inadequate. The amount going into trust should be increased to 100% to

permit consumers to withdraw the account—as would be needed if one moved to another geographic location and sold or did not use the lot.

- There is no annual report to preneed funeral consumers required. Consumers should get an annual report indicating the institution of deposit and value (purchase price plus interest) of all prepaid funeral monies. Such documents could be important to survivors who might not know about prepaid accounts otherwise and would help to enforce the trusting law.

- There is no statutory provision to protect consumers against default of prepaid funeral agreements if funds were never put in trust. Consumers in other states have experienced a loss of funds in spite of trusting requirements.

- Although Louisiana laws are now better than some, it is probably a terrible idea to prepay for a funeral in this state unless one needs to spend down assets for Medicaid eligibility.

- The restrictive interpretation on who may sell caskets is a restraint of trade which subverts the FTC's provision specifically permitting consumers to purchase *only* the goods and services desired from the funeral provider.

- There is no requirement to identify and tag the body at the place of death before removal.

- The regulations require that at least six adult caskets be on display, but there is no requirement that low-cost caskets be included in that display.

- Cash advance items may be marked up.

- The standards for ethical, professional conduct are inadequate. They should be strengthened to make it easier for a consumer to prevail when filing a valid complaint.

- The FTC Funeral Rule is not clearly adopted by statutory or regulatory reference. Although morticians must follow the laws of "any other federal . . . entity" and submit the required disclosures to consumers, the FTC Funeral Rule should be adopted by reference to make it easier to enforce in this state.

- This state has no laws regulating the body parts business.

- There is no provision for naming a designated agent for body disposition, helpful when one is estranged from next-of-kin or they don't get along.

Miscellaneous Information

- Educational requirements for becoming a funeral director: one year of college (30 hours) and one year of apprenticeship. For an embalmer: mortuary science program (15 months) and one year of apprenticeship.

- When a funeral home changes ownership or more than 50% of the stock is sold, the state Funeral Board must be notified and a new license acquired.

- Wishes of the decedent will prevail if written and notarized.

- The Board of Embalmers and Funeral Directors employs an investigator to handle complaints and violations.

- Coroners must be physicians.

- A funeral home or crematory may not refuse to release a body.

- The written consent of the person with the right to control disposition is required for disinterment.

This chapter was sent for review to the Louisiana Board of Embalmers and Funeral Directors, the Cemetery Board, and the Department of Vital Statistics. No response was received, but some information was checked by telephone.

Caring for the Dead
In Maine

Please refer also to the general introduction to state chapters—"Caring for the Dead: Necessary Information."

Persons in Maine may care for their own dead. The legal authority to do so is found in Chapter 707 of Title 22. The following section is pertinent:

> § 2846—*Authorized person. For the purposes of this chapter, the "authorized person" responsible for obtaining or filing a permit or certificate shall mean a member of the immediate family of the deceased, a person authorized in writing by a member of the immediate family of the deceased if no member of the immediate family of the deceased wishes to assume the responsibility, or in the absence of immediate family, a person authorized in writing by the deceased.*

There are no other statutes that might require you to use a funeral director.

Death Certificate

The family doctor, nurse practitioner, physician's assistant, or a medical examiner will supply and sign the death certificate within 24 hours, stating the cause of death. The remaining information must be supplied, typewritten or in black ink. The death certificate must be filed with the local town or city clerk within three days.

Maine started a pilot area on electronic death registration in 2010 and went statewide shortly after that. A paper alternative is available for home funeral families.

Fetal Death

A fetal death report is required when death occurs after 20 weeks of gestation. If there is no family physician involved, the local medical examiner must sign the fetal death certificate.

Transporting and Disposition Permit

The municipal clerk will issue a permit for disposition of human remains. The fee for this permit is $4. The death certificate must be obtained first, as well as a medical examiner's release if cremation, burial-at-sea, or out-of-state disposition is planned. If a permit is needed when the municipal clerk is not available, one of the clerk's sub-registrars (some of whom are funeral directors) may be asked to issue the permit. For issuance of this permit to an authorized person, the death certificate must indicate that the doctor personally examined the deceased after death.

The disposition permit must be filed, within seven days, with the clerk of the municipality where burial or cremation takes place. If this is in another district, an additional fee may be charged to file the permit.

Burial

Check with the city or town for local zoning laws regarding home burial. Family burial grounds of not more than a quarter of an acre are protected as a "burial place forever." This plot must be recorded in the registry of deeds in the county where burial takes place and enclosed by a fence or other markers to be "exempt from attachment and execution." There are no state burial statutes or regulations with regard to depth. A sensible guideline is 150 feet from a water supply and 25 feet from a power line or neighbor's boundary.

Cremation (or Burial at Sea)

A permit (usually called a "release") for cremation or burial at sea must be signed by a local medical examiner. The usual fee for this is $15. There is a 48-hour waiting period prior to cremation unless waived by the medical examiner due to contagious disease. A rigid combustible container must be used. Authorization by next-of-kin is usually required. A pacemaker and other non-combustible items must be removed prior to cremation. There are no laws regarding the disposition of cremated remains. You may do as you wish.

All cremations must occur in a licensed crematory.

Other Requirements

Embalming is not required in Maine for typical funeral arrangements. Weather and reasonable planning should be considered.

Bodies to be shipped by common carrier must be embalmed or in a sealed Ziegler case.

Death from a "disease" may require the involvement of a medical examiner. Check with the attending physician to be sure.

Medical Schools for Body Donation

Body donation to a medical school is another option for disposition. Find the information for Maine at <www.finalrights.org>.

State Governance

The Maine Board of Funeral Service has eight members. There are three consumer representatives and five funeral practitioners.

<http://maine.gov/pfr/professionallicensing/professions/funeral/index.htm>

Cemeteries are usually owned and operated by municipalities, churches, or voluntary nonprofit associations, although a few are for-profit businesses. There is no state cemetery board.

Crematories must be registered with the Department of Health and Human Services, CDC. One does not have to be a licensed funeral director to run a crematory. Crematories must be built only on cemetery grounds, although the new regulations grandfathered any existing non-cemetery crematories. Crematories must make monthly and annual reports to the Department of Health.

Prepaid Cemetery and Funeral Funds

Preneed sellers may not solicit sales (the consumer must initiate the contact), although advertising is permitted.

All money for prepaid *cemetery products and services* (i.e., cremation or opening-and-closing charges but not the lot) must be placed in trust. If the purchaser cancels the arrangement, the cemetery may keep the interest, but the principal will be refunded.

All money for a prepaid *funeral* contract must be deposited in a separate account, with interest to accrue. The financial institution must send a confirmation of the deposit to the purchaser within 30 days. If funds are transferred to another institution, the purchaser must be notified. Funeral insurance is permitted, but the seller may not be paid a commission.

The preneed agreement may be cancelled for a refund or transferred. A revocation fee of 7% of the trust, not to exceed $250, is permitted. An administrative fee may be withdrawn each year, not to exceed 25% of the annual interest or $125. If selected merchandise is not available, substitution must be of equal quality. There is a standardized trust agreement form that must be used for prepaid funerals. It is in 12-point type and, although lengthy, easy to read. Payments must be made out to the trustee, not the funeral home.

Consumer Concerns

- The death rate in Maine can support approximately 50 full-time mortuaries; there are 125 such establishments. However, given the low density of population over a large geographic area, mortuary careers are not likely to be full-time work. Unfortunately, because of the low volume of business per mortuary, funeral prices will tend to be higher than in busier mortuaries.

- Although there is an initial notification, there is no requirement for an annual report to the purchaser of prepaid funeral goods and services, paperwork that might be useful to the family of a deceased to indicate prepayment and which would help to "enforce" trusting requirements.

- There is no state-administered fund to reimburse consumers in case of default on prepaid funeral funds that were never put into trust if the seller failed to use the state-mandated preneed form.

- There is no provision for an adequate description of funeral goods selected preneed to guide the substitution if the selected item is no longer available at the time of death. Survivors should have the right to approve any substitutions.

- Until there is better reporting and a guarantee fund, it is probably an unwise idea to prepay for a funeral in Maine.

- The 48-hour wait before cremation and the medical examiner's permit are totally unnecessary when the death is anticipated and survivors are in agreement, as this may be causing additional charges to families including "storage."

- There is no requirement to identify and tag the body at the place of death before removal.

- There is no provision either forbidding a mark-up on cash advance items or requiring the disclosure of how much the mark-up would be. Consumers may wish to ask for a copy of such invoices.

- There is no requirement that low-cost caskets be included in any display.

- This state has no laws regulating the body parts business.

Miscellaneous Information

- Educational requirements for becoming a funeral director: one year of college and one year of mortuary college (or two years of mortuary college) plus 2,000 hours of apprenticeship. Applicants must pass a practical exam, a state exam, as well as the National Board Exam, which practitioners and consumer advocates alike claim is irrelevant and severely out of date.

- The 1984 FTC Funeral Rule, as amended, has been adopted by reference.

- The Board of Funeral Service has a nice Code of Ethics in its regulations.

- Prior to death, individuals may designate a person to serve as a legally authorized agent for funeral arrangements and indicate directions for such.

- Medical examiners are physicians appointed to the position.

- A cemetery may not employ a funeral director to arrange funerals. A cemetery may, however, employ a funeral director to be its landscaping foreman or accountant, provided the funeral director is not paid more than $500 per year.

- Next-of-kin can obtain a disinterment permit from a municipal clerk.

This chapter was sent for review to the Department of Health—Vital Statistics and the Board of Funeral Service, all of whom were very helpful. Ernie Marriner, past president of FCA, made some corrections, too.

Caring for the Dead

In Maryland

Please refer also to the general introduction to state chapters—"Caring for the Dead: Necessary Information."

Persons and church groups in Maryland may care for their own dead. In 1987, Charles R. Buck, Jr., Secretary of Health and Mental Hygiene at the time, wrote to Carlson:

> *Under English Common Law, which is carried over in our State law, the immediate families may dispose of their dead either by burial or cremation. They must, however, conform to the laws. . . .*

Nothing has changed in the laws since then.

Death Certificate

When death occurs in a hospital or nursing home, the death certificate will be supplied by the institution. In the case of a home death, contact the office of Vital Records, Division of Field Services, to obtain a blank death certificate: 410-764-3173. On weekends a field rep can be paged at 410-909-4810. Enter the phone number at which you may be called.

The attending or certifying physician—or a local medical examiner—will sign the death certificate within 24 hours, stating the cause of death. The remaining information must be supplied, typewritten or with black ball-point pen. There are two carbons. The first page of the death certificate must be filed with the Department of Health and Mental Hygiene, Division of Vital Statistics, within 72 hours.

Maryland is still developing electronic death registration procedures. A paper option should be available to home funeral families. The person handling the home funeral should sign where it says "Funeral Service Licensee" along with relationship—spouse, designated agent, son, etc.

Fetal Death

A fetal death report is required if death occurs after 20 weeks of gestation or when, gestation unknown, a weight of 500 grams or more (almost 18 ounces). It is also required at any age if the fetus is transported from the place of delivery for cremation or private burial. If there is no family physician involved, the local medical examiner must sign the fetal death certificate.

Transporting and Disposition Permit

Page three of the death certificate serves as the burial transit permit. The physician's or medical examiner's signature is required.

Burial

There are no state statutes that specifically permit or prohibit home burial.

Contact the county health department and zoning board for local ordinances or regulations that may apply to home burial. There are no state burial statutes or regulations with regard to depth. A sensible guideline is 150 feet from a water supply and at least two feet of earth on top.

When burial is arranged, the family member acting as the funeral director must sign the burial-transit permit and return it to the Department of Health and Mental Hygiene, Division of Vital Records, within 10 days.

Cremation

The burial-transit permit serves as the permit for cremation. There is a 12-hour waiting period prior to cremation. The body must be identified and cremation approved by the next-of-kin or other person who is authorized to arrange for final disposition. "ID viewing" is being used as a sales ploy to sell more expensive cremation caskets—"Most families don't want to see their loved-one in a cardboard box." Maryland requires that the body be tagged with identification which should be done at the place of death before removal, not at a separate viewing. That way, there should be fewer mix-ups at the mass-production preparation facilities used by the conglomerates. Remember, you may insist on "viewing" the body at the hospital or home, if practical, to avoid any ID viewing charges.

Most crematories insist that a pacemaker be removed. The crematory may offer to file the burial-transit permit. There are no laws regarding the disposition of cremated remains. You may do as you wish.

Other Requirements

Maryland has no embalming requirements. Weather and reasonable planning should be considered when dealing with an unembalmed body.

If the person died of a contagious disease, the doctor in attendance should be consulted.

Medical Schools for Body Donation

Body donation to a medical school is another option for disposition. Find the information for Maryland at <www.finalrights.org>.

State Governance

The Maryland Board of Morticians has eleven members. Five are consumer representatives and six are funeral directors. The board has the authority to establish a school of mortuary science, a unique-to-Maryland provision, although it has not done so.

<www.dhmh.state.md.us/bom/>

The Office of Cemetery Oversight regulates cemeteries and burial goods businesses including preneed sales. The Office's Advisory Council has eleven members, five of whom are consumer members.

<www.dllr.state.md.us/license/cem/>

Crematories on cemetery grounds are regulated by the Office of Cemetery Oversight. Others are regulated by the Funeral Board.

Prepaid Cemetery and Funeral Funds

One has to wonder what was in the statehouse drinking water when the preneed statutes were passed. Half of the funds for preneed *cemetery merchandise and services* must be placed in trust—but only the "second 50%"—if you are paying by installments. The cemetery may pocket your first payments right away. The statutes go on to say that within 30 days of your last payment, a tad bit more should be deposited to bring the account up to 55% of the contract. Why didn't they just say 55% in the first place? By a process of deduction it would seem that this 55% refers to the cost of a marker, a grave liner or coffin vault, and the opening-and-closing charges because the next statutory paragraph says the trusting requirement for a "casket or casket vault" sold by a cemetery is 80%. (A "casket vault" is a one-piece unit that combines the features of both a casket and a vault. They are in limited usage where cemeteries may sell vaults but not caskets.) However, the trusting requirements apply only if the cemetery hasn't taken advantage of the "constructive delivery" loophole, handing you a certificate that says the merchandise is yours and is in storage—a common ploy to get their hands on all your money now.

That's bad enough, but get this: If the cemetery is dutifully putting your installment payments into trust, it may not charge you interest on the purchase. *However,* if the cemetery plans to put your vault or marker (or even a casket) into its warehouse—to "purchase" it now for you—then the cemetery may levy a *finance charge.* You could also end up with a finance charge if the cemetery sells the contract to a lending institution. If you are offered a contract with a "Notice to Consumers" clause, watch out! You have a right to refuse to sign any such contract or scratch out the parts that are unacceptable and initial them before you sign it.

If you default on your installment payments before getting to the half-way mark, kiss your money goodbye—the first 45% never had to go into trust anyway, remember? After that, the cemetery may withhold "reasonable expenses" before returning what might be in the trust.

And what does happens if you change your mind about needing a vault—if you've decided to be cremated instead? Forget it. In the existing statutes, there is no provision for any such change of heart and a refund. If you move more than 75 miles away, you *might* get 55% of what you paid plus interest that's in the trust—*if* the vault isn't already in the warehouse with your name on it or waiting in the ground; in which case, you won't even get the installation service charges refunded.

A bill that passed in the 1998 legislature requires a 100% refund for the sale of a casket or "casket vault" (80% in trust, plus interest, plus an additional contribution from the seller to bring your refund check up to the amount of your initial payment only—not initial payment plus interest). Of course that is meaningless if the merchandise has already been "delivered" to a warehouse with your name on it.

Each cemetery must make an annual report of its sales, including preneed sales, to the Board of Cemetery Oversight.

Only licensed morticians and funeral directors may sell preneed *funeral* plans in Maryland, a sane limitation as the commissioned sales reps (ex-vacuum cleaner sales people perhaps) in other states have generated a slew of preneed complaints.

Your protection for prepaid *funeral* contracts has been weakened in recent years: 100% of *services* must be placed in trust, but only 80% of the *vault and casket* must be trusted, matching the cemetery mischief. This, of course, reduces the interest to be earned, too. The funeral home must send you an annual report of the interest income for tax purposes, but such a report should also show the total value of the trust, useful information for survivors.

Funeral insurance may be used instead of a trust, but trust funds may not be converted to insurance without the buyer's permission. While insurance is fully portable, you should probably just say "no." You get only a portion of money paid if you come upon hard times and want to cash it in or simply change your mind from an expensive body burial to a more frugal cremation.

Substitution of merchandise must be "comparable," but there is no provision for an adequate description in the preneed contract.

Maryland has an excellent provision seen in only a few other states: When a funeral home is going to be sold, you must be notified and given a choice of either continuing with the new owner or asking for a refund or transfer. Before assuming that you will want to continue with the new owner, you may wish to see what kind of reputation the new one has for honoring preneed arrangements. If you weren't paying attention when you first got a notice—or suddenly discover that you were never notified—you might want to check that out now.

Unless it is an irrevocable agreement, you may cancel a contract and request a refund of all funds paid, plus interest, at any time. Irrevocable funeral trusts may be transferred to a new provider. Let's hope the funeral director doesn't have a problem coming up with the 20% of casket and vault money that may have been pocketed early on.

There is a *Family Security Trust Fund to* protect preneed purchasers against theft. An annual contribution by each funeral establishment will be made until the fund reaches $1 million (a cap that's inadequate today given the multi-million-dollar preneed scandals that have occurred).

$3,500 from a limited estate is given reserve priority for funeral expenses over other debts. The morticians are trying to increase this to $4,500, which would leave even less for rent, utilities, medical bills or other such final expenses.

Consumer Concerns

- The death rate in Maryland can support approximately 179 full-time funeral homes; there are, however, 245. Funeral prices tend to be higher in areas where there are "too many" funeral homes.

- Cemetery trusting requirements are inadequate. "Constructive delivery" and finance charges should not be permitted for cemetery purchases; 100% of all prepaid cemetery merchandise and services should be placed into trust.

- There is no provision for an adequate description of merchandise to make sure that the substitution is, indeed, "comparable"as required, nor for the survivors to approve such a replacement. Savvy consumers should add these provisions to any prepaid contract.

- Trusting for prepaid funeral merchandise is inadequate and should be returned to 100%.

- Although there is supposed to be annual reporting of interest income, not all consumers may be getting this. A 1099 tax form does not give the family a report on the total asset in the prepaid account. This would be useful information for survivors at a time of death and would help to enforce the trusting requirement.

- Until the cemetery and funeral laws are changed, it is probably a terrible idea to prepay for such goods and services in Maryland.

- There is no requirement to identify and tag the body at the place of death before removal.

- There is no provision either forbidding a mark-up on cash advance items or requiring the disclosure of how much the mark-up would be. Consumers may wish to request a copy of the invoices for such items.

- There is no requirement that low-cost caskets be displayed along with others.

- The priority for the right to control disposition is not in one's control. One may state in writing one's funeral wishes which are supposed to be honored, but one's designated agent for final disposition appears fifth in the priority list, after spouse, adult child, parent, adult sibling. So who does have priority?

- There are no ethical standards for funeral directors. These should be detailed and explicit. (See Ethical Standards in the Appendix.)

- The FTC Funeral Rule has not been adopted. (Carlson was told that licensees are given a copy of "Complying with the Funeral Rule," however.)

- The downloadable consumer rights pamphlet available on the Board of Morticians website has only a portion of what you need to know—if you can even read it. It's printed in six or seven point type with very poor contrast in the layout.

- This state has no laws regulating the body parts business.

Miscellaneous Information

- Educational requirements for becoming a mortician (embalmer): associate's degree from a mortuary school (2 years) and 1,000 hours of apprenticeship. A funeral director's license does not require training in embalming. Applicants must pass a practical exam, a state exam, as well as the National Board Exam, which practitioners and consumer advocates alike claim is irrelevant and severely out of date.

- Medical examiners are physicians who are appointed to the job.

- The form suggested in the Health Care Decisions Act, Title 5-603, allows you to name, in your Advance Directive, a designated agent for funeral planning. In spite of the conflicting statute on priority mentioned earlier, we believe the Advance Directive would prevail if it were tested in Probate Court, as most case law sides with the wishes of the deceased.

- A disinterment permit must be obtained from a state or local health officer.

This chapter was sent for review to the Department of Health and Mental Hygiene—Vital Statistics, the Office of Cemetery Oversight, and the Board of Morticians but no responses were received.

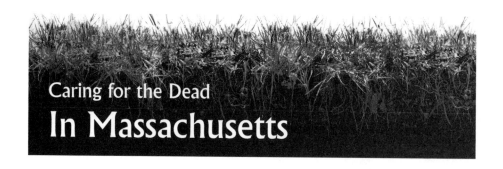

Caring for the Dead
In Massachusetts

Please refer also to the general introduction to state chapters—"Caring for the Dead: Necessary Information."

Persons and church groups in Massachusetts may care for their own dead. The legal authority to do so is found in:

> *Title 46 § 9. Death certificates. A physician . . . shall immediately furnish for registration a standard certificate of death . . . to an undertaker or other authorized person or a member of the family of the deceased. . . .*

There are no other statutes that might require you to use a funeral director.

History

The Board of Registration in Embalming issued a regulation in 1905 stating:

> *No permits for . . . burial . . . shall be issued . . . to any person . . . not registered . . . [by] the state board of registration in embalming.*

That regulation was found invalid by the Supreme Judicial Court of Massachusetts in 1909, *Wyeth v. Thomas*, 200 Mass. 474, 86 NE 925. The court wrote:

> *There is no doubt that the . . . refusal to permit one to bury the dead body of his relative or friend, except under an unreasonable limitation, is also an interference with a private right that is not allowable under the Constitution of the Commonwealth or the Constitution of the United States.*

The regulation remained on the books until 1998, even though it was invalid and unenforceable. The Board of Registration insisted until 1996 that the regulation was valid and even convinced the Vital Statistics department of the Massachusetts Department of Public Health (MDPH) in 1989 to change the wording on one box on the death certificate form to "funeral service licensee" and to tell local boards of health that burial permits could be issued only to undertakers.

A hospice nurse, certain it was illegal, gave Jan Burhman trouble when burying her mother on Martha's Vineyard. Jan found, after a bit of simple research, that the law had *never required* the use of an undertaker. She contacted the Memorial Society, and volunteer Byron Blanchard picked up the cause. The MDPH, on reviewing the court opinion, agreed privately that persons could care for their own dead but was unwilling to say so publicly. The Board of Health of the Town of Lexington, after considering the matter for 13 months, voted in April 1996 to issue burial permits to non-undertakers. The Board of Registration went to the MDPH seeking its support in opposing the Lexington decision, but the MDPH said that Lexington was correct. Two days later the Board of Registration agreed to drop their opposition to issuance of burial permits to non-undertakers.

The MDPH in August 1996 sent a memo to all 351 towns telling them it *is* legal to issue burial permits to non-undertakers. With the memo was a set of guidelines to be given to persons caring for their own dead, explaining the law and suggesting appropriate precautions. In 1998, the Board of Registration modified its regulation. Byron Blanchard, a long-time member of the Memorial Society in Boston (now Funeral Consumers Alliance of Eastern Mass.), handled the negotiation with the MDPH and Lexington.

Death Certificate

The family doctor or a medical examiner will "immediately" supply and sign the death certificate, stating the cause of death. The remaining information must be supplied, typewritten or in black ink. The death certificate must be filed, within five days, with the Board of Health in the town where death occurred in order to obtain the burial permit. Electronic death registration has not yet been implemented, but it is expected that a paper alternative will be available for home funerals as it is for home births.

Fetal Death

A fetal death report is required when death occurs after 20 weeks of gestation or when the weight is 350 grams or more (about 12 ounces). If there is no family physician involved, the local medical examiner must sign the fetal death certificate.

Transporting and Disposition Permit

The local board of health (or town clerk if there is no board of health) will issue the burial permit. (This is actually a transportation and disposition permit.) This authorization must be obtained prior to moving a body or final disposition. After normal business hours, check with the local police to determine who the after-hours agent is.

Although most boards of health are now willing to work with those caring for their own dead, there are a few recalcitrant ones. If you run into difficulty, suggest that the clerk contact the Department of Health in Boston. On-line, go to www.mass.gov/dph/ then search within the site for "burial." The top option should get your clerk all kinds of pertinent information.

Burial

The board of health in each town regulates burial grounds, whether on private land or established cemeteries. There are no state burial statutes or regulations with regard to depth. A sensible guideline is 150 feet from a water supply and at least two feet of earth on top. If you are doing a home burial, it would be a good idea to draw a map of the land showing where the family cemetery will be and pay to have it recorded with the deed.

When burial is arranged, the sexton or family member acting as the funeral director must sign the coupon on the burial-transit permit and return it to the issuing registrar.

Cremation

A cremation permit from the medical examiner is required. The fee for this is $100. There is a 48-hour waiting period prior to cremation unless the death was due to a contagious or infectious disease. Authorization by next-of-kin or designated agent is required, and a pacemaker must be removed.

Where there is no spouse or next-of-kin and the decedent did not appoint an agent to authorize cremation, the crematory may demand that a court-appointed guardian sign the authorization to cremate. Where there is an estranged or separated spouse or there are next-of-kin opposed to cremation, it is essential for the decedent to have appointed an agent in writing. The form to appoint an agent is called a Declaration of Intent for Cremation and is available from the crematory; it should be witnessed and notarized.

Regulations permit a funeral home to require that the next-of-kin view a body *at the funeral home* prior to cremation if identification was not done earlier. This is a blatant ploy to sell cremation caskets. As one funeral director told a niece, "You'll probably want to upgrade to a cremation casket. Most families don't want to see their loved one in a cardboard box." A more responsible requirement would be identification and tagging at the place of death prior to removal, especially with all the body mix-ups that are becoming endemic at chain-owned mortuaries. For them, it is standard practice to send bodies to a central location for embalming and preparation, and the incidence of negligent body-swapping has spawned a rash of expensive lawsuits that continue afresh as of this writing.

There are no laws regarding the disposition of cremated remains. You may do as you wish.

Other Requirements

Embalming is not required in Massachusetts. Weather and reasonable planning should be considered when arranging final disposition.

If the person died of a contagious or communicable disease, the doctor in attendance should be consulted.

Regulations—which apply only to the bodies handled by undertakers—require that, if there will be no embalming, all orifices must be stuffed with treated cotton, the body washed, then wrapped in a sheet. Off the record, funeral directors say this is rarely done unless there is to be a private family viewing. But by having such a requirement in the regulations, mortuaries may charge for this service, and none is the wiser if it's never done prior to an immediate burial or cremation. (Anyone who considers the cotton-stuffing an indignity may wish to skip the use of a funeral home altogether.)

Medical Schools for Body Donation

Body donation to a medical school is another option for disposition. Find the information for Massachusetts at <www.finalrights.org>.

State Governance

The Massachusetts Board of Registration in Embalming and Funeral Directing has five members. One is supposed to be a consumer representative but phone inquiries to the office are not returned, so it seems impossible to find out which one it is. What good is a consumer rep if consumers don't know who the rep is or how to reach him or her? All must be from different counties, and no more than three may be of the same political party, but that last has been ignored, we're told.

For many years, Byron Blanchard of the local Funeral Consumers Alliance (formerly the Memorial Society) attended board meetings to monitor what was going on . . . or not. Apparently the undertakers didn't like such close scrutiny and started going into executive session for the majority of their meeting time.

The Massachusetts web designer must be sniffing formaldehyde too. Here is the website link for the Board of Registration of Embalming and Funeral Directing. Easy to remember?

<http://www.mass.gov/?pageID=ocasubtopic&L=4&L0=Home&L1=Licens ee&L2=Division+of+Professional+Licensure+Boards&L3=Board+of+Regis tration+of+Funeral+Directors+and+Embalmers&sid=Eoca>

How does one even find this Board's site? The list of state agencies, A to Z, has a Board of Registration of Hazardous Site Cleanup Professionals but nothing for embalmers or funeral directors. That's hidden under "C"— Consumer Affairs and Business Regulation. And where might one find the "Funeral Directors Consumer Fact Sheet"? Under the "For Government" tab, but only if you knew what to search for in the first place. That page refers to a "Buyer's Guide to Pre-Need Funeral Contracts," but that's nowhere to be found. The web page does, however, have the kind of information one might expect in such a Guide.

In 1996, after mailing compliance information to every funeral home in this state, the FTC did undercover test shopping at random establishments. One quarter of them failed to give out a price list to the consumer on both a first and second visit. In 2009, another undercover test showed that still a quarter of Massachusetts funeral homes are failing to meet this basic requirement to allow informed consumer choice. A regulation passed by the Board of Registration requires only that the funeral director give a price list if the consumer "requests one in person."

And just where is the link on how to file a complaint against a funeral director? Guess they're expecting morticians to tattle on each other. It's in a section labeled "For Licensees."

Most cemeteries are town or city cemeteries and are regulated by their municipalities. The Board of Health must approve new cemeteries and crematories.

Crematories are generally considered part of a cemetery's operation, and those on cemetery grounds are not licensed separately. The statutes permit, however, that an independent, nonprofit crematory could be established elsewhere with the permission of the local health department. One does not need to be a funeral director to run a crematory.

Prepaid Cemetery and Funeral Funds

Cemeteries (and crematories) in Massachusetts established after 1936 must be run by not-for-profit corporations. They may not sell monuments. Several have set up separate companies to sell markers but have been caught making sales on cemetery grounds. Funeral directors may not be employed by a cemetery or crematory. There are no statutes regulating prepaid *cemetery* purchases.

Preneed sellers may not solicit sales in a nursing home, hospital, or other care facility unless invited by the prospective customer or a representative. One may market preneed by telephone, however, but there is no requirement to see if the consumer's phone number is on the Do Not Call list.

Preneed regulations were significantly improved in 2004. Alas, any preneed arrangements paid prior to that may be missing funds because of huge loopholes.

Only funeral directors may sell preneed funeral arrangements. The consumer must be given "A Buyer's Guide to Pre-need Funeral Contracts" prior to signing any contract. One funeral director mailed Carlson the pamphlet that he has, put out by a bank that manages the Massachusetts Funeral Trust. This wordy, vague and incomplete pamphlet was approved by the Board of Registration back in 1993. It mentions that a funeral home may keep 10% if you cancel or transfer your arrangements, no longer true. One has to wonder why the Board hasn't written its own such guide and kept it up-to-date.

A buyer may cancel a preneed contract for a full refund within a ten-day cooling off period. Actually, 100% must be placed in trust and, on request, the full trust account refunded or transferred without penalty. So it is strange that there is any reference to a cooling off period at all. There is no mention of interest in the regs, but the trust must remain intact until claimed or transferred, and one can assume that the interest will accrue.

The name of the trustee where the money will be deposited must be disclosed to the buyer. Since 2004, all such trustees are federal or state-chartered banking institutions located in Massachusetts. Before that, some funeral homes had been using a Connecticut outfit that promised a higher-than-could-be-believed rate of interest and refused to submit any audit documentation.

Preneed sellers must make an annual report of all preneed accounts to the state Board of Registration. The requirement of an annual report to the beneficiary was unfortunately dropped in 2004, a report that would help to enforce the trusting requirement and provide useful paperwork to families.

If selected merchandise is not available at the time of death, substitution must be of "fair market value" equal or greater. This could be a problem if there isn't an adequate description in the contract. After all, a $995 casket ten years ago was pretty snazzy. Today, for $995 an undertaker might show you the "welfare casket."

Preneed funeral arrangements—whether revocable or irrevocable—may not be altered after death, even at the request of the family. The regs do not anticipate what should happen if insufficient funds are available to complete the arrangements (or there's no one around to come to the wake).

If the preneed contract is a guaranteed-price agreement, the seller may retain any excess funds. That means that if your prepaid money is worth more than the actual retail price of the funeral at your death, the funeral home still gets all of it. In this way, you've actually paid *more* by prepaying. On a non-guaranteed agreement, the estate gets a refund if funds exceed the actual cost (highly unlikely with the rate of funeral inflation). If the cost exceeds what's in the trust, the estate (or survivors) are liable for the additional costs. If a family may not alter the arrangements as mentioned above, the funeral director may try to stick the family with a funeral bill that wasn't expected.

A funeral establishment must notify preneed customers no later than ten days after a change in ownership.

A preneed seller may amend the funeral contract "at any time"—just let the buyer know ten days prior to the effective date and get the buyer to agree. Do not assume that any such amendment is in your best interest. If, for example, trust funds are being converted to insurance, be sure you decline such a change. Insurance has diddly-squat cash value if you want to change your mind and turn it in.

If funeral directors want to sell funeral insurance, they must be licensed by the Division of Insurance.

Consumer Concerns

- The death rate in Massachusetts can support approximately 223 full-time funeral homes; there are, however, 628. Funeral prices tend to be higher in areas where there are "too many."

- There is no requirement that a clear description of merchandise is given and that merchandise of equal quality and construction must be substituted—to the satisfaction of survivors—if the original item selected is not available.

- There is no state protection to reimburse consumers in case of default on prepaid funeral funds that were never put into trust. One Massachusetts funeral director managed to spend $200,000 of his preneed funds before he landed in jail.

- Until there are statutory protections for preneed funeral consumers that eliminate the mischief cited, it is a terrible mistake to prepay for a funeral in Massachusetts unless you absolutely must for Medicaid eligibility.

- The 48-hour wait before cremation is unnecessary when survivors are in agreement, resulting in extra costs to such families for "storage."

- The medical examiner's permit for cremation in the case of an *anticipated* death from natural causes is unnecessary and creates an additional burden and charge for families. This became a major scandal several years ago when the examiners were not checking bodies, simply collecting money for signing cremation permits.

- There is no requirement to identify and tag the body at the place of death before removal.

- There is no requirement that low-cost caskets be included in any display.

- The FTC Funeral Rule has not been adopted.

- Complaint procedures are unclear and inadequate.

- While case law will give preference to the written wishes of the deceased, there is no law that allows you designate an agent for death care. In situations where you are estranged or distant from next-of-kin, this could be important.

- Funeral homes may not provide food or beverages, a ridiculously outmoded and consumer-unfriendly policy.

- This state has no laws regulating the body parts business.

Miscellaneous Information

- Educational requirements for becoming a registered funeral director or embalmer: high school diploma, mortuary college (9 months), an exam, and two years of apprenticeship. This apprenticeship period seems excessive compared to other states, and we suspect it was more likely imposed as a source of cheap labor for the industry. The national exam required has been deemed irrelevant and out-dated by critics.

- The Board of Registration by statute "registers" funeral directors annually. The local Boards of Health are the ones who issue "licenses"to funeral directors who are on the list of registered funeral directors that the Board of Examiners is supposed to send out each year. "I've never seen it," says one Board of Health staffer regarding such a list. In practice, towns typically renew the license for any funeral director who fills out an application, whether they're "registered" with the state or not.

- From the regulations for the Examining Board, some bizarre distinctions among which kind of funeral director one might be: Registered Funeral Director means any funeral director registered with the Board. Registered Certified Funeral Director means a funeral director registered with the Board and licensed by a city or town who is employed on a full-time basis at a licensed funeral establishment but who does not hold a 10% controlling interest in a licensed funeral establishment. Registered Licensed Funeral Director means a funeral director registered with the Board licensed by a city or town who holds an ownership interest of at least ten percent in one or more licensed funeral establishments.

- But it doesn't stop there. The information from Professional Credential Services, the company that does the testing for the state, shows a great many "license types" which Carlson was told came from the Board. (Apparently the Board has forgotten that only towns may give out licenses.) The types are as follows:

  Type A: *Apprentice* (intern embalmer)

  Type 1 & Type 4: *Registered Embalmer & Registered Unlicensed Funeral Director* (can perform embalming, but cannot do preneed and cannot conduct funeral)

  Type 5: *Certified Funeral Director* (can perform licensed Funeral Director activities, but cannot advertise name; can sign death certificate only in the Funeral Director's absence)

  Type 4: *Downgrade* (Applies to candidate who previously has a Type 5 *Certified Funeral License* and needs to downgrade it to Type 4 *Registered Unlicensed Funeral Director*)

  Type 3: *Registered Embalmer and Licensed Funeral Director* (can embalm and also owns at least 10% of a funeral home business)

  Type 1 & Type 4: *Downgrade* (Applies to candidate who previously has a Type 3 License and needs to downgrade to Type 1 & Type 4 *Registered Embalmer & Registered Unlicensed Funeral Director*)

Type 1 & Type 5: *Downgrade* (Applies to candidate who previously has a Type 3 License and needs to downgrade it to Type 5 & Type 1 *Registered Embalmer & Certified Funeral Director*)

- Like many states, Massachusetts requires Continuing Education. The Board's website has 298 listings from which to choose, including eight credits for attending the National Funeral Directors Association conference, typically held in places like Las Vegas with golf a major activity planned. Of course, the industry suppliers like Batesville Casket and Pierce Chemicals are handing out "education," too.

- Medical examiners are physicians who are appointed.

- Cash advance items must be billed in the same amount as is billed to the funeral director.

- Unprofessional conduct includes: "the use of profane, indecent or obscene language in the presence of a dead human body, or within the immediate hearing of the family or relatives of a deceased, whose body has not yet been interred or otherwise disposed of." Then watch out?

- Each funeral home must have a "chapel"of at least 300 sq. feet—a for-profit church blessed by the Board of Registration?

- Ownership of a funeral home must be disclosed on all stationery and advertising materials.

- A funeral business may not represent itself as a society, fund, trust or other not-for-profit unless it is, in fact, not-for-profit.

- Undertakers registered with the board "shall be fair with present or prospective customers with respect to quality of merchandise, freedom of choice, quality of service, and reasonableness of price, and shall not misrepresent any material fact with respect to such matters." Perhaps consumers should start filing complaints against funeral homes that do not have "reasonable" prices!

- One may not picket within 500 feet of a funeral home when a funeral is in progress.

- Rendering funeral services may not be made contingent on payment or expectation of payment.

- The Commonwealth will pay $1,100 toward the burial of indigents, provided the total cost is not more than $1,500.

- The town board of health regulates burials and should be consulted for disinterment.

Board Secrecy

The following article by Byron Blanchard appeared in a 2010 FCAEM newsletter:

Open Meeting and Public Record Law Violations

The Board of Registration in Embalming and Funeral Directing flouts the Open Meeting law in several ways. Their minutes omit many topics discussed and decisions taken. They deny access to minutes and agendas. Meetings are held in a small room that often lacks any extra chairs. The Board denies licensees administrative due process in the way they discuss disciplinary cases. The Board excludes the accused person (and the public) while they discuss how best to present the case to themselves when later, wearing a different hat, they act as judges to decide on his/her guilt. This eliminates any pretense that they will judge fairly. They go into Executive Session using the Litigation Strategy Exemption. But this isn't litigation as meant by the law. The Board Members Manual explains why using this exemption is not legal. But they do it anyway.

Properly, Executive Session is used to consider the discipline or hear complaints or charges brought against an individual. Executive sessions held for this purpose require special procedural safeguards for the licensee (i.e. the licensee has the right to be present, to have counsel, to speak, or to request the meeting be held in open session). A licensee must also be given written notice 48 hours in advance of such a session. Such notice, while not legally required, should also be given to those who will be discussed in open meeting—it's the right way to treat people.

Board meeting minutes and agendas are no longer available. I attended almost all Board meetings from 1997 thru 2005. They sent me the agenda and draft minutes via e-mail prior to each meeting. They stopped sending them in January 2006, and then wouldn't even give me paper copies at the meetings. Because of that and the increasing time I had to spend sitting in the waiting room during executive session it is no longer fruitful for me to attend their meetings.

In October 2009 I made a public records request for copies of all the minutes from May 1996 to the present as .DOC files delivered on a compact disc. The request was acknowledged in writing, but the files were never delivered. The case is now on appeal in the office of the Supervisor of Public Records. In October 2009 I also requested copies of the current listing of Open Complaints and a listing of all closed complaints from 1993 to present. A closed complaint printout was promptly furnished. It didn't list the final decision or the closing date, and many of the names and registration numbers were redacted, with no explanation. The open complaint listing was never provided.

Another area where the Board has been obstructive is with regard to Pre-need Annual Reports, which show the number of new contracts and who holds the money. I was the only person who ever looked at them. The Board got a new attorney, Kathe Mullaly, who took the position that I could only look at them if they, at my expense, photocopied each page, redacted exempt information, and then photocopied it again.

The Board is composed of five funeral directors and one "public" member (currently a Vital Records employee at Boston City Hall) all appointed by the governor. They are unpaid and rely on paid staff of the Division of Professional Licensure. The Board and its staff has shown its contempt for the public it is charged with protecting, and particularly for representatives of a consumer group that actually tries to monitor its activities.

This chapter was sent for review to the Massachusetts Department of Public Health—Vital Records, Office of Consumer Affairs and Business Regulation, and the Board of Registration in Embalming and Funeral Directing, as well as the Massachusetts Funeral Directors Association.

In response, Carlson received a letter from Charles Kilb, Board Counsel for the Board of Registration in Embalming and Funeral Directing, ". . . There do appear to be several factual inaccuracies in your article regarding board procedures under public records and open meeting laws . . ." Carlson replied, "Are you saying that the Board did indeed provide Mr. Blanchard with the minutes he requested? Are you saying that the Board did indeed provide Mr. Blanchard the list of open cases? Are you saying the Board does not go into executive session except when there is a hearing on complaints? Are you saying the staff returns phone calls requesting an agenda? I will look forward to your response." There wasn't any.

Caring for the Dead
In Michigan

Please refer also to the general introduction to state chapters—"Caring for the Dead: Necessary Information."

In Michigan a dead body becomes a hostage of the funeral industry, one of only eight such states that require the use of a funeral director. (Connecticut, Illinois, Indiana, Louisiana, Michigan, Nebraska, New Jersey, and New York.) In almost no other situation is a private citizen forced to use a for-profit business to fulfill the interests of the state. The restricting laws were enacted in 2003 and 2006.

> *MCL 700.3206 Right and power to make decisions about funeral arrangements . . . .(1) . . .The handling, disposition, or disinterment of a body shall be under the supervision of a person licensed to practice mortuary science in this state.*

Under the title, "What is a License For," Phil Douma, Executive Director of the Michigan Funeral Directors Association, wrote in the association's journal of July 2007, "The Michigan legislature and the Attorney General understand that the citizens of the state need to be protected . . . ." From themselves? (It was a funeral home, not "the citizens" or family, that left a body in the funeral home garage waiting for cremation, a body that was collected by the trash removal folks and ended up in the landfill instead, never to be found.) Douma goes on to question a funeral director who is willing to assist families with home funerals: "Perhaps he needs to ask himself why he has this license in the first place." If Mr. Douma's attitude reflects that of the morticians he represents, it is clear that funeral directors in Michigan are using that license not as a testament to formal education and skilled compassion but as a license to limit consumer choice and protect a business monopoly. To require a family to use a licensee puts the funeral director in a position of authority and creates an obligation that may cost the family thousands of dollars. . . and sometimes heartache.

MCL 333.2843 Report of death by funeral director . . .(1) A funeral director who first assumes custody of a dead body, either personally or through his or her authorized agent, shall report the death. . . . (3) A death record shall be certified by a funeral director licensed under article 18 of the occupational code . . .

Parents may file a birth certificate if no doctor is involved. What's the big deal about a death certificate?

Vital Records says that "certifying" the death certificate means attesting that the demographic information supplied by the family is correct, then readily admits that there are often errors.

The restrictive statutes are in conflict with those that recognize a family's rights to act as their own funeral director:

MCL 52.205(5) . . . The county medical examiner shall, after any required examination or autopsy, promptly deliver or return the body to relatives or representatives of the deceased . . . .

MCL 333.2848(1) . . . a funeral director or person acting as a funeral director, who first assumes custody of a dead body, . . . shall obtain authorization for the final disposition.

MCL 339.1810 Prohibited conduct. (n) . . .sending or causing to be sent to a person or establishment licensed under this article the remains of a deceased person without having first made inquiry as to the desires of the person with authority over the disposal of the remains of the decedent under section 3206 of the estates and protected individuals code, 1998 PA 386, MCL 700.3206, and of the person who may be chargeable with the funeral expenses of the decedent. If a person with authority over the disposal of the remains of the decedent under section 3206 of the estates and protected individuals code, 1998 PA 386, MCL 700.3206, is found, the person's authority and directions shall govern the disposal of the remains of the decedent.

Disposal?

A summary in Michigan Civil Jurisprudence, 1984 Revised Volume 7, states: ". . . The generally accepted rule now is that the right to the possession of a dead human body for the purposes of decent burial belongs to those most intimately and closely connected with the deceased by domestic ties. . . . A person whose duty it is to care for the body of a decedent is entitled to its possession and control . . . ." A 1995 federal court decision, *Whaley v. County of Tuscola* [58 F.3d 1111 (C.A. 6 1995) (applying Michigan law), denied,

116 S.Ct. 475, 133 L.Ed.2d 404, *on remand* 941 F. Supp.1483.], reaffirmed the right of next-of-kin to possess a body "for the purpose of preparation, mourning and burial."

In a 1909 federal case, *Wyeth v. Cambridge Board of Health*, the court ruled:

> *. . . the refusal to permit one to bury the dead body of his relative or friend, except under an unreasonable limitation, is also an interference with a private right that is not allowable under the Constitution of the Commonwealth or the Constitution of the United States.*

If the home funeral people are not successful in getting legislative changes, a court case may be the next alternative.

Death Certificate

The attending physician, registered nurse, or county medical examiner must sign the death certificate within 48 hours, stating the cause of death. The remaining information must be supplied, typewritten or in black ink. The death certificate must be filed with the local registrar within 72 hours.

Michigan is testing electronic death registration in pilot counties, and, if there aren't too many bugs, hopes to have it statewide by the end of 2011. A paper alternative is available for home births, so—if the laws get changed—a paper alternative is likely to be available for home deaths.

Fetal Death

A fetal death report is required after 20 weeks of gestation or when the weight is at least 400 grams (about 14 ounces). It must be filed with the state registrar within five days. A physician or medical examiner must fill out the cause of death.

Transporting and Disposition Permit

A body may be moved with the consent of the physician or medical examiner who certifies the cause of death. The local registrar will issue the authorization for disposition in the form of a burial-transit permit. This authorization must be obtained within 72 hours of death and prior to final disposition.

Burial

Family graveyards under one acre outside city or village limits are permissible. Such land is exempt from taxation and must be surveyed and recorded with the county clerk. Permission from the local health department is required to establish a private cemetery. There are no state burial statutes or regulations with regard to depth. A sensible guideline is 150 feet from a water supply and at least two feet of earth on top. A private family cemetery can be recorded with the state Cemetery Commissioner's office.

Cremation

A signature of the medical examiner in the county where death occurred is required on the burial-transit permit for cremation. The fee for this ranges by county, from $0 to $75. Authorization by next-of-kin is usually required, and a pacemaker must be removed. There are no laws regarding the disposition of cremated remains. You may do as you wish.

Other Requirements

The Bureau of Epidemiology has a regulation—not a statute—in the Administrative Code that says a body of one who has died of diphtheria, meningococcic infections, plague, poliomyelitis, scarlet fever, or small pox must be embalmed, the worst possible circumstances under which to embalm. Fortunately, those diseases are almost nonexistent now, thanks to medical progress. To their credit, Hawaii and Ontario forbid embalming under these circumstances. Ohio and Montana require immediate disposition.

The next immediate paragraph in that code is totally garbled as to its intent, stating that bodies that will reach their destination within 48 hours "may be received for transportation when encased in a sound shipping case." It's hard to imagine that a funeral director transporting Granny to the Upper Peninsula will worry about a "sound shipping case" if he's sold Granny's family a typical casket at a price much higher than a "shipping case."

The next sentence says that if the body won't reach its destination within 48 hours, it must be "prepared for shipment" as if it had died from the plague and other diseases mentioned above; in other words, it must be embalmed. But if the funeral director is merely waiting for the doctor to finish the death certificate details or the cemetery to open the grave before driving to the Upper Peninsula for burial in a local cemetery there (not exactly "shipment"), did the regulators really mean to impose such harsh strictures that might violate the religious beliefs of some without allowing for alternatives such as refrigeration? That seems unlikely. Furthermore, are there any "embalming police" in Michigan, or just funeral directors who will try to sell you an expensive and invasive procedure whether you want it or not? Let's hope the legislature will clarify and protect consumer rights soon. In the meantime, if you don't want Granny embalmed, just say no.

Medical Schools for Body Donation

Body donation to a medical school is another option for disposition. Find the information for Michigan at <www.finalrights.org>.

State Governance

The Michigan Board of Mortuary Science has nine members. There are three consumer representatives.

<www.michigan.gov/dleg/0,1607,7-154-35299_35414_35464---,00.html>

Preneed sellers are licensed by the Department of Energy, Labor, and Economic Growth.

The director of the Department of Energy, Labor, and Economic Growth serves as the cemetery commissioner and governs crematories and cemeteries (other than municipal or religious cemeteries). Or is supposed to. The state got stuck with running 28 cemeteries after a real rascal, Clayton Smart, emptied the trust accounts. (See Chapter 6 for details.)

Amazingly, they found an investor, David Shipper, who replenished the funds and took over operations in 2007. One can guess that prices at these cemeteries will now skyrocket given Mr. Shipper's previous cemetery endeavors. From the on-line profile of the company that bought these cemeteries, "David was a vice president of corporate development for The Loewen Group, Inc., a multi-national, publicly traded funeral and cemetery corporation. While at Loewen, David led cemetery and combination acquisition activities, and was involved in the purchase of over 450 locations." According to consumer surveys done during that time, funeral and cemetery prices quickly escalated after a purchase by Loewen. Their prices were among the highest on these surveys, and hard-sell or deceptive sales tactics generated numerous complaints.

<www.michigan.gov/cemetery>

Prepaid Cemetery and Funeral Funds

For *cemetery merchandise*—vaults and markers—80% must be placed in trust. Alas, "A burial vault shall be installed only at need or by separate written authorization of the purchaser. The cemetery shall have the right to withdraw the amount on deposit for the delivered vault or outside container." So if the cemetery asks permission to install your vault, it's best to say no in case you move or want to change your mind to cremation. For cemetery services (opening and closing or cremation), 100% must be placed in trust.

Finance charges are permitted for installment sales—for both cemetery and funeral purchases—at a rate of interest not to exceed 10.5%. This is absurd. Consumers would be wise to demand an adjustment to any contract, deleting finance charges before signing an agreement. Tell the sales person it would be silly to pay interest on a layaway plan before they lay you away.

All prepaid funeral funds must be placed in trust. (For those wishing to make an irrevocable plan—to be eligible for social services, the amount may not exceed $2,000.) A preneed seller may charge an additional 10% in commission. Yes, ladies and gentlemen, step right up. Pay now, and it will cost you only 10% more than if you wait and pay later. We wonder if only 90% goes into trust, with the 10% taken from the contract price and the paperwork adjusted to keep everyone happy. Two checks would do the trick: one for 90% of the charges of which all (100%) goes into trust, and another for 10%—the commission.

To its credit, Michigan has required since 1986 that an annual report of preneed funds be sent to the purchaser unless waived in writing. One can only hope that slick sales people haven't convinced unwitting purchasers to sign away their rights with a simple, "Just sign here, and here, and here."

Although Michigan has no guarantee fund to protect against default by a preneed seller, the annual reporting requirement to the purchaser should be a compelling factor for keeping funds properly invested and for reducing the chance of consumer loss. Any consumer *not getting an annual report,* however, should immediately demand one, even if—or perhaps especially if—the agreement was made prior to 1986.

Every year preneed sellers must make audited reports to the state. Records must be open for inspection any time.

Fees not to exceed 1% of the trust may be withdrawn (or accumulated to the credit of the fund trustee) for "reasonable fees and expenses."

If excess funds remain after services have been provided, there is a complicated formula for how much gets refunded to the heirs or estate, ranging from 0% to 100%—varying with how big the initial commission was and whether or not it was a guaranteed-price funeral. In practice—with funeral inflation generally exceeding bank interest, one shouldn't fret about how big a refund you might get on grandma's funeral. There isn't likely to be one.

You are entitled to a full refund if you cancel within 10 days of purchase. If you want to cancel a preneed contract later (30 days notice), you should pay attention to the issue of "commission." If no commission was acknowledged on the preneed agreement, the seller may retain 10% before issuing a refund. You may transfer an irrevocable contract.

If you've been making only intermittent payments, a seller may cancel an installment contract that is more than 90 days in default and retain 10% of the amount in escrow.

Consumer Concerns

- The death rate in Michigan can support approximately 334 full-time mortuaries; there are, however, 805. Funeral prices tend to be higher in areas where there are "too many" funeral homes.

- Trusting requirements for cemetery preneed contracts is inadequate. 100% of all cemetery merchandise should be placed in trust; a purchaser should have a full right of refund at any time, along with the interest.

- Finance charges are permitted for installment sales of prepaid funeral and cemetery arrangements. This should be repealed. When you finance a car or house, you get to use either. But a finance charge on a lay-away plan before they lay you away?

- There is no statutory requirement that when merchandise is selected on a guaranteed-price preneed contract that a clear description is given and that merchandise of "equal quality and construction" must be offered if the merchandise selected is not available (although this provision *may* appear on individual contracts). Survivors should be allowed to approve any substitutions.

- Signing away he right to an annual report on a consumer's preneed account should not be allowed.

- Until the Michigan laws are changed to require 100% trusting of all money and interest for prepaid goods and services and adequate substitution of funeral merchandise that meets the approval of survivors, it is probably a *very unwise* idea to prepay for these arrangements. Your own trust account in a bank will be safer and will be transferable.

- The coroner or medical examiner's permit for cremation in the case of an *anticipated* death from natural causes is unnecessary and creates an additional burden and charge for families.

- There is no requirement to identify and tag the body at the place of death before removal.

- The regulation requiring embalming when death occurs from a communicable disease is unreasonable. Besides being offensive to some religious groups, it also puts the funeral professionals at risk. Refrigeration is a more reliable means of body preservation.

- There is no provision either forbidding a mark-up on cash advance items or requiring the disclosure of how much the mark-up would be. Consumers may wish to ask for a copy of those invoices.

- There is no requirement that low-cost caskets be included in any display.

- Casket-funeral-package pricing is still permitted by administrative rules in violation of the FTC's itemization requirements.

- Although there is reference to using FTC pricing methods when selling preneed arrangements, the full FTC Funeral Rule has not been adopted.

- The standards for ethical, professional conduct are inadequate and should be strengthened. That would make it easier for a consumer to prevail when filing a valid complaint. (See Ethical Standards in the Appendix.)

- This state has no laws regulating the body parts business.

Miscellaneous Information

- Educational requirements for a license in mortuary science: mortuary college (3 years), one year of apprenticeship, and a national and state exam. Alas, practitioners and consumer advocates alike have deemed the National Board Exam out-dated and irrelevant.

- Funeral directors may not own or have an interest in a cemetery or a crematory (which is considered part of a cemetery function). Someone who is not a mortician may, however, be licensed to run an independent crematory if zoning and environmental concerns are met.

- In a strangely conflicting statute found in 339.1811: "(1) The purchase of a vault or similar receptacle . . . shall not be required as a condition to burial in a cemetery in this state. There shall not be a discrimination by price, burial fee, or otherwise by reason of a failure to purchase the vault or similar receptacle. . . . (2) This section shall not limit the right of a cemetery to require the use of a vault in a burial in the cemetery." Which is it?

- One may name a personal representative in a will to carry out written instructions for funeral arrangements and body disposition. Michigan should amend this by adopting a modern designated-agent law.

- From the mortician statutes, prohibited conduct includes: "using profane, indecent or obscene language in the presence of a dead human body, or within the immediate hearing of the family or relatives of a deceased, whose body has not yet been interred or otherwise disposed of." Then watch out?

- From the "Rural Cemetery" statutes: ". . . no saloon or place of entertainment shall thereafter be set up or established for the sale of intoxicating drinks, and no sporting festival shall be held within ¼ of a mile of the entrance to the grounds" . . . "No person shall use firearms . . . or hunt game . . . or enter into such inclosed cemetery by climbing or leaping over or through any fence or wall" . . . "nor cause any animal to enter. . . ." So much for walking your dog at the cemetery.

- Failure to maintain a cemetery plot in a public cemetery is at the risk of losing one's burial rights there. This does not apply once you're buried in it. After all, how could they expect you to mow it then.

- Cemetery regulations provide that a disinterested party must be present when interment rights are being promoted to someone who doesn't speak the language the seller is using.

- One office handles complaints for more than 27 different occupations. The complaint form is relatively easy to fill out.

- Coroners are no longer elected. County medical examiners must be licensed physicians and are appointed.

- A disinterment permit may be obtained from the local health department.

This chapter was sent for review to the Department of Public Health, the Cemetery Commission, the Board of Examiners in Mortuary Science, and the Michigan Funeral Directors Association. Helpful corrections were received from the Cemetery Commissioner's office and the licensing office. Vital Records information was verified by telephone. MFDA thanked us for the courtesy.

Caring for the Dead
In Minnesota

Please refer also to the general introduction to state chapters—"Caring for the Dead: Necessary Information."

Families and church groups in Minnesota may care for their own dead. The legal authority to do so is found in:

> *Chapter 149A [re disposition of bodies and funeral directing] Subd. 3 Exceptions to licensure . . .(b) This chapter does not apply to or interfere with the recognized customs or rites of any culture or recognized religion in the ceremonial washing, dressing, and casketing of their dead, to the extent that all other provisions of this chapter are complied with.*

> *(c) Noncompensated persons with the right to control the dead human body may remove a body from the place of death; transport the body; prepare the body for disposition, except embalming; or arrange for final disposition of the body, provided that all actions are in compliance with this chapter.*

One paragraph in this statute might require you to use a funeral director:

> *(e) Notwithstanding this subdivision, nothing in this section shall be construed to prohibit an institution or entity from establishing, implementing, or enforcing a policy that permits only persons licensed by the commissioner to remove or cause to be removed a dead body or body part from the institution or entity.*

If hospitals have no problem letting you take home a live patient, why would they not let you take the body of someone you love? The hospital certainly has a lot less liability when releasing a body to the person with the right to control disposition compared to someone who may be a complete stranger.

Death Certificate

Minnesota has been using electronic death registration since 2002. Physicians and medical examiners have access to the system to enter the cause of death as do most morticians. For those not on the system, a "Documentation of Death Worksheet" must be completed for the demographic information and with the cause of death verified by a physician, coroner or medical examiner.<www.health.state.mn.us/divs/chs/osr/deathreg/04deathworksheet.pdf> Once completely filled out, the documentation of death worksheet is filed with the State Registrar to the attention of the supervisor of Death Record Processing using fax number 651-201-5750.

Fetal Death

A fetal death report is required when death occurs after 20 weeks of gestation or more and must be filed as above.

Transporting and Disposition Permit

When a body is to be moved from one location to another, a certificate of removal must be filled out with one copy retained at the place of death and the other kept by the person doing the removal. The form can be downloaded on-line: <http://www.health.state.mn.us/divs/hpsc/mortsci/certrem.pdf>. The body must be wrapped in a nonporous or plastic sheet and placed on on a rigid carrier. The vehicle used to move the body must be enclosed.

Once the death certificate information is complete, the state system will generate a burial transit permit.

Burial

Any person and any religious corporation may establish a cemetery on their own land. The land must be surveyed and a plat recorded with the county recorder. Family graveyards are exempt from taxation. Check with the county or town registrar for local zoning laws regarding home burial. There are no state burial statutes or regulations with regard to depth. A sensible guideline is 150 feet from a water supply and at least two feet of earth on top.

The original copy of the burial-transit permit is to be filed with the place of disposition. In the case of home burial, the original should be retained with your deed unless the clerk of the court requires it to be recorded with official land records. The second copy must be filed with the Department of Health.

Cremation

A permit for cremation must be obtained from the coroner or medical examiner. There is no fee for this. Authorization by next-of-kin is usually required, and a pacemaker must be removed. There are no laws regarding the disposition of cremated remains. You may do as you wish.

Other Requirements

Disposition must be within a "reasonable time." The body must be embalmed or refrigerated if disposition will not be accomplished within 72 hours. Refrigeration is limited to six days; use of dry ice is limited to four days. Embalming can be ordered by the Commissioner of Health in the case of infectious diseases, the worst possible circumstances for embalming.

A body must be embalmed prior to shipping via public transportation, even though most airlines are willing to make exceptions for religious reasons if the casket is tightly closed.

A new statute can be interpreted to mean that embalming is required for public viewing in a funeral home. Representative Carolyn Laine shepherded through a bill that rolled back many of Minnesota's consumer-unfriendly restrictions, but left open to interpretation whether an exemption to an embalming requirement for viewings on "private property" includes funeral homes, churches, etc. This should be clarified as soon as possible.

The right of a family or designated agent to be in the preparation room was deleted in 2007. What on earth are they trying to hide? Why can't the family dress Granny and do her hair there? The 2010 change to the laws says that funeral directors can work out ways to let the family dress the body elsewhere but not in the prep room.

Medical Schools for Body Donation

Body donation to a medical school is another option for disposition. Find the information for Minnesota at <www.finalrights.org>.

State Governance

Minnesota no longer has an Advisory Council in Mortuary Science. All regulation goes through a Mortuary Section of the Health Department. That office licenses morticians, funeral homes, and crematories. One does not need to be a mortician to run a crematory.

<www.health.state.mn.us/divs/hpsc/mortsci/mortsci.htm>

The Mortuary Science Section has published a bulky, 21-page consumer guide, "A Time for Choices: Making Decisions About Death Arrangements," that one can download from its website. The most glaring omission from this wordy "pamphlet" is the failure to tell families that they may care for their own dead, unlike the excellent and detailed website put up by the Vermont Department of Health. It also reports, erroneously, that a funeral director may charge a fee for writing your preneed contract, or that price lists must be given *"when requested"* [emphasis added.]. Yes, they must give prices if someone is merely funeral shopping or doing a price survey, but the FTC requires a funeral director to give the price lists prior to any discussion of funeral arrangements or the showing of caskets and vaults, *without* the consumer having to "request" them. It states that earth burials "are the most common type of disposition." While technically correct, nearly 45% of Minnesota residents opt for cremation, at a growing rate, clearly reversing the trend of earth burial.

There is no state board governing cemeteries.

Prepaid Cemetery and Funeral Funds

Cemeteries larger than ten acres must send a report of perpetual care funds annually to the county auditor.

There are no statutes governing or protecting other portions of a cemetery purchase such as opening-and-closing charges, vaults, and markers—no trusting requirements whatsoever. That means the cemetery can spend your money the minute you pay it, and you'll have to hope they're still in business when you need what you've paid for. There is no provision for changing your mind and getting a refund, either. With the for-profit cemeteries moving into Minnesota, this should be of considerable concern.

All of the money paid preneed for a funeral purchase must be placed into trust. The purchaser must be given the name of the financial institution and the account number where the money will be deposited.

A purchaser may get a full refund, including interest, of a revocable plan. Although the statutes are a little vague, it would appear that one has a full right to transfer an irrevocable agreement, as well.

Under the disbursement of funds portion of the statute is an interesting provision: "The funds shall be distributed for the payment of the *actual at-need value* [emphasis added] of the funeral goods and/or services selected with any excess funds distributed to the estate of the decedent." This would imply that funeral homes may not sell a guaranteed-price funeral, because price guarantees entitle the seller to all money deposited, not just the "at-need price." The general sales lure to buyers, however, is to select a casket and all other details of the funeral service now, to lock in prices. We fear that the "at-need value" clause leaves a funeral home free to imply that a family must honor a particular casket choice, for example, even if there is not sufficient money to pay for it at today's prices. With the rate of funeral inflation, excess funds are unlikely, and survivors would—presumably—be billed for an additional amount if they felt such arrangements were binding. A more responsible provision would be for the substitution of equal quality merchandise at no extra cost (and with the approval of the survivors).

When a funeral home has been sold to a new owner—especially a funeral chain, the at-need prices are likely to increase dramatically. Because the state guarantees a full right of refund, you may want to move any prepaid account to another funeral home if what is in the account will not cover the new prices—even if the body is already at the funeral home.

The funeral home must make an annual report to the commissioner of all prepaid accounts.

Consumer Concerns

- The death rate in Minnesota can support approximately 150 full-time mortuaries; there are, however, 430. Funeral prices tend to be higher in areas where there are "too many" funeral homes.

- There is no provision for placing preneed cemetery services and merchandise in trust.

- There is no annual reporting requirement to the purchaser of pre-paid funeral goods and services, paperwork that might be useful to the family to show what was prepaid and which would help to enforce trusting requirements.

- There is no state protection for consumers in case of default on pre-paid funeral funds that were never put into trust.

- With no adequate provision for cemetery trusting or for substitution of funeral merchandise selected preneed, it is probably a terrible idea to prepay for cemetery and funeral arrangements in Minnesota until the laws are changed.

- The coroner or medical examiner's permit for cremation in the case of an *anticipated* death from natural causes is totally unnecessary and creates an additional burden for families.

- There is no requirement to identify and tag the body at the place of death before removal.

- The laws requiring embalming for any purpose are offensive to some and should be repealed.

- There is no provision either forbidding a mark-up on cash advance items or requiring disclosure of how much the mark-up would be

- There is no requirement to include low-cost caskets in any display.

- Minnesota requires separate price lists for alternative containers, cremation containers, and caskets, in violation of the FTC requirement that these be all on the same list to allow consumers to readily choose. Unethical funeral directors have told families they need a "burial" casket, rather than a less-expensive "cremation" casket.

- Current statutes permit hospitals and other facilities to require that only a funeral director may pick up a body, an especially troubling requirement when parents are faced with the death of a child.

- This state has no laws regulating the body parts business. Legislation failed to pass in 2010.

Miscellaneous Information

- Educational requirements for a funeral director or embalmer: bachelor's degree (4 years) in mortuary science, or bachelor's degree plus mortuary course of study, or number of credits equivalent to a degree program plus mortuary studies, plus the national and state exams, and one year of internship. Practitioners and consumer advocates alike deem the National Board Exam outdated and irrelevant.

- The language of the FTC Funeral Rule has been largely adopted in the statutes. Too bad it wasn't done by reference so that any improvements in the Rule would automatically take effect in Minnesota.

- Rental caskets are specifically permitted by law.

- Medical examiners are appointed physicians. Coroners are elected and may be funeral directors, but there has been, in practice, a shift of coroner's duties to medical examiners.

- It is a misdemeanor to hold a body for debt.

- You may state your funeral wishes in writing or name an agent for body disposition.

- A disinterment permit may be obtained from the Health Commissioner or a licensed mortician. The casket may not be opened without a court order.

This chapter was sent for review to the Minnesota Department of Health Mortuary Science Section and Vital Records. Vital Records did not respond to comment, but information had been verified by telephone.

Caring for the Dead

In Mississippi

Please refer also to the general introduction to state chapters: "Caring for the Dead: Necessary Information."

Persons and church groups in Mississippi may care for their own dead. The legal authority to do so is found in:

> *Health Department Rule 41: Filing of death certificate (a) The funeral director, or person acting as such, who first assumes custody of a dead body, shall review and correct any items completed by an institution or the medical examiner, complete the death certificate and file it with the Office of Vital Records . . . .*
>
> *MS Code 73-11-63 . . . nothing in this chapter shall be construed to prevent or interfere with the ceremonies, customs, religious rites or religion of any people, denomination, or sect, or to prevent or interfere with any religious denomination, sect or anybody composed of persons of a denomination, or to prevent or interfere with any church or synagogue from having its committee or committees prepare human bodies for burial or the families, friends or neighbors of deceased persons who prepare and bury their dead without charge.*
>
> *MS Code 73-11-65 Every funeral service or interment, or part thereof, that is conducted in Mississippi must be in the actual charge and under the supervision of a funeral director or funeral service licensee who is licensed under this chapter. However, this section shall not prevent a family from burying its own dead without charge.*

There are no other statutes that might require you to use a funeral director.

Death Certificate

The attending physician or local medical examiner will sign the death certificate within 72 hours, stating the cause of death. The remaining information must be supplied, and the use of a typewriter is preferred. There are three carbons. The original (white copy) must be filed with the Office of Vital Records within five days and before final disposition. The third page may be retained by a hospital or nursing home and the fourth page by the physician.

The medical examiner will certify the cause of death in violent or unexpected circumstances and when a physician was not in attendance within 36 hours, except in cases where terminal illness has been diagnosed.

Mississippi is just beginning to study electronic registration. A paper alternative will be available for home funerals.

Fetal Death

A fetal death report is required when death occurs after 20 weeks of gestation or when weight is 350 grams or more. If there is no family physician involved and the death is not subject to the jurisdiction of the coroner or medical examiner, the person attending or the parents may file the fetal death report with the State Registrar within five days. A fetal death report may be obtained from a physician, hospital, or the county health department.

Transporting and Disposition Permit

A body may be moved with the consent of a physician, coroner, or medical examiner. If the body is moved out of state, it must be accompanied by a burial-transit permit signed by the doctor or medical examiner certifying the death. This is the yellow page of the four-copy death certificate.

Burial

Draw a map of your land showing where a family cemetery will be and check with the county Board of Supervisors if home burial is planned outside the corporate limits of a municipality. Inside the city limits, one must deal with the "governing authorities." There is likely to be a modest fee to record your map with the deed. A cemetery must be at least 500 feet from a hospital or other medical facility. A good practice is 150 feet from a water supply and 25 feet from a power line or neighbor's boundary. The top of the coffin must be 24 inches below the natural surface of the earth.

When burial is arranged, the family member acting as the funeral director must sign the death certificate and file it with the Office of Vital Records within five days.

Cremation

The death certificate must be filed with the Office of Vital Records before cremation. Most crematories insist that a pacemaker be removed, and authorization by next-of-kin usually is required. There are no laws regarding the disposition of cremated remains. You may do as you wish.

Other Requirements

When the destination cannot be reached within 24 hours or disposition does not take place within 48 hours, a body must be embalmed or refrigerated.

When death is from a contagious disease that may constitute a public hazard, the matter must be referred to a medical examiner.

Medical Schools for Body Donation

Body donation to a medical school is another option for disposition. Find the information for Mississippi at <www.finalrights.org>.

State Governance

The Mississippi State Board of Funeral Service has seven members. One is a consumer representative, the others are all funeral directors or funeral service practitioners. In addition to funeral business, the Board licenses and regulates casket retailers and crematories. Unfortunately, the latter two have no representation on the Board. The legislature's Performance Evaluation and Expenditure Review (PEER) was conducted in 2004. It found that "Board members' investigations and board actions to resolve complaints are poorly documented in the board's investigative files and meeting minutes." . . . "When the board and OSHA conduct inspections of the same establishments and OSHA finds multiple violations and the board finds none, the board's effectiveness in conducting inspections is called into question." . . . "The board does not utilize disciplinary actions consistently to deter violators and, in at least one case, has administered a disciplinary action not authorized by statute." The full embarrassing report is on-line at <www.peer.state.ms.us/469.html>.

Don't expect much information from the Board's website. It erroneously claims that embalming "preserves" a body and that embalming is required for a public viewing when no such statute exists. The link to laws and regs goes to an out-dated legislative bill long since passed.

The Secretary of State regulates preneed contracts and licenses preneed sellers.

<www.sos.state.ms.us/REnf/pre-need.asp>

There is no state cemetery board, but the Secretary of State and the Attorney General's Office go after anyone who tries to raid the cemetery trust funds, as one rascal extradited from his hide-out in Pennsylvania discovered.

Prepaid Cemetery and Funeral Funds

All cemetery land is exempt from taxation per MS Code 27-31-1. Carlson found at least two for-profit cemeteries that were not paying property taxes in 2010. Why would the state exempt for-profit companies, owned by out-of-state Wall Street corporations that charge outrageous prices, putting a larger tax burden on local folks?

All *cemeteries*, unless exempt, must maintain a perpetual care trust fund. Exempt entities are religious-affiliated cemeteries; family cemeteries; community cemeteries; fraternal-affiliated, and government-operated cemeteries. A "perpetual care cemetery" must put 15% of all lot sales, and 5% of crypt and niche sales must be placed in trust.

Prepaid funds for vaults, urns, memorials, scrolls, vases, foundations, and bases are exempt from any trusting requirements if the seller has delivered "a valid warehouse receipt." This "constructive delivery" makes a refund nearly impossible if you were to move or change your mind.

Only 85% of prepaid *cemetery and funeral* money must be placed in trust, and—from the income—the trustee may withdraw funds to cover "reasonable" expenses and taxes. Although this is a big improvement over the laws ten years ago when only 50% went into trust, the legislators were extremely irresponsible in the rest of the preneed laws. For example, § 75-63-63 states, "If the preneed contract contains a revocation clause, the contract insured or his representatives may name a substitute provider . . . ." So maybe your preneed contract will have a clause in it that lets you transfer the contract and maybe it won't. Nothing is said about cancelling it entirely and getting your money back. The state couldn't be bothered to protect your interests. And how much will get transferred? No mention of the interest, but "not less than the amount put into trust," 85% . . . unless they've engraved and installed your marker or put your casket in a warehouse with a warehouse receipt attached to your paperwork. In which case, they will have claimed payment for those already.

Mississippi Code still contains statutes (dated mostly in the 1930s) for "burial associations" that are governed by the state insurance commissioner. As of 1996, no new burial associations may be established. On certain policies, there is a restriction as to which funeral home may be used or a limit on benefits, the maximum being $500. As the elderly owning these contracts die, there will be a rude shock: there was no provision for the interest on the amount paid to cover inflation. On the other hand, if the policy was supposed to cover a casket and all services and if survivors select a more expensive casket than the flimsy one that is usually shown (a blatant bait and switch tactic), any substitution may void the policy altogether or yield only the face value, not the full funeral cost as intended. If a person stops making payments on one of these burial policies, there will be no refund. Either way, the seller benefits while the consumer is cheated.

Unless you have only six months or so to live and don't mind being buried in something not much better than a giant shoe-box, it's probably a good idea to stop making any more payments to a burial association. Put your money in the bank with a next-of-kin on your account. There it will be readily available at a time of death along with all the interest.

Finance charges are permitted on payment plans. Interest on a layaway plan before they lay you away? Outrageous.

Preneed sellers must make an annual report to the Secretary of State, but there is no reporting requirement to the purchaser, paperwork that might be helpful to next-of-kin.

The Secretary of State oversees the *Preneed Contracts Loss Recovery Fund*. It is funded by a $10 fee for each preneed contract sold, to be used in the case of a provider embezzlement or other default.

Consumer Concerns

- The death rate in Mississippi can support approximately 116 full-time mortuaries; there are, however, 293. Funeral prices tend to be higher in areas where there are "too many" funeral homes.

- Cemeteries run by for-profit corporations have not been paying property taxes. This places an unfair burden on the local taxpayers.

- Trusting requirements are inadequate. The law should require 100% trusting of all prepaid funeral and cemetery funds—to allow interest to build against inflation and for a full refund if the consumer were to move to another location or simply change funeral plans. (Twenty nine other states require 100% trusting. Preneed is alive and well in those states.)

- There is no requirement providing for substitution of funeral merchandise of equal quality and construction, with an adequate description—to allow for the satisfaction of the family. A common ploy of morticians—especially on a "guaranteed" or "inflation protected" funeral package—is to announce that the selected casket is no longer available or to display a particularly shoddy model as the one that comes with the package. Family members then pay additional funds for a better casket.

- There is no requirement for an annual report to the consumer indicating the institution of deposit and value (purchase price plus interest) of all prepaid funeral monies. Such documents could be important to survivors and would help to enforce the trusting requirements.

- Until the preneed laws are strengthened in Mississippi, it is probably a terrible idea to prepay for any funeral or cemetery arrangements (except perhaps a plot). A personal bank account is much safer.

- There is no requirement to identify and tag the body at the place of death before removal.

- There is no requirement to include low-cost caskets in any display.

- There is no restriction on taking a mark-up on cash advance nor a requirement to disclose how much it is if a mark-up is taken.

- The ethical standards for funeral directors are inadequate and need to be defined and expanded. That would make it easier for a consumer to prevail when filing a valid complaint. (See Ethical Standards in the Appendix.)

- Complaint procedures are unclear and inadequate, although preneed contracts must list contact information for the Secretary of State's office for the purpose of filing a complaint.

- Coroners are elected, and—while they must attend State Medical Examiner Death Investigation Training School—a potential conflict of interest is raised when the person holding a coroner's job is also a funeral director rather than a physician.

- Although provisions of the FTC Funeral Rule regarding price lists are adopted by statute, the statute omits any reference to misrepresentations or the anti-tying provisions of the Rule.

- Although the written wishes of the deceased are to prevail, especially if the funeral is prepaid, there is no provision for naming a designated agent for body disposition. This would be helpful when one is estranged from next-of-kin or they don't get along.

- This state has no laws regulating the body parts business.

Miscellaneous Information

- The educational requirements for becoming a funeral director in Mississippi are: a high school diploma, two years of apprenticeship, and passing a state-approved written or oral exam. For being licensed in funeral service (as an embalmer) the requirements are: high school, one year of mortuary school, one year of apprenticeship, and passing a state-approved written or oral exam or the National Board Exam. Alas, practitioners and industry critics alike have deemed this exam out-of-date and irrelevant.

- No funeral home may accept a body from a hospital, nursing home, or public agency without first ascertaining the wishes of the person with the right to control disposition. If a funeral home gains custody of a body in violation of that provision, no charges may be made until the person with the right to control disposition has made arrangements. We have not seen this excellent provision in any other state.

- The body of a person with an infectious or communicable disease must be tagged. These diseases include infectious hepatitis, tuberculosis, AIDS, and any venereal disease, although CDC says universal precautions should be used with all bodies.

- An order for disinterment or exhumation must be obtained from a circuit court.

This chapter was sent for review to the Mississippi Secretary of State, the Attorney General's Office, the Department of Public Health—Vital Statistics, and the State Board of Funeral Service. Some helpful corrections came from the Secretary of State's office, but no response was received from the others.

Caring for the Dead
In Missouri

Please refer also to the general introduction to state chapters—"Caring for the Dead: Necessary Information."

Persons in Missouri may care for their own dead. The legal authority to do so is found in:

> *Title 193.145 . . . . 4. The funeral director or person in charge of final disposition of the dead body shall file the certificate of death.*

> *CSR 2120-2.060 (29) (A) No person shall be deemed by the board to be engaged in the practice of funeral directing or to be operating a funeral establishment if the person prepares, arranges, or carries out the burial of the dead human body of a member of one's own family or next of kin . . . (B) The board shall not deem a person to be engaged in the practice of funeral directing or to be operating a funeral establishment if the person prepares, arranges, or carries out the burial of a dead human body pursuant to the religious beliefs, tenets, or practices of a religious group, sect, or organization . . .*

There are no other statutes that might require you to use a funeral director.

Death Certificate

The family doctor or a local medical examiner will supply and sign the death certificate within 72 hours, stating the cause of death. The remaining information must be supplied, typewritten or in black ink. The death certificate must be filed with the local registrar within five days. A "notification of death" must be filed with or mailed to the local registrar prior to disposition if the death certificate has not been completed. This form can be obtained from the registrar or a funeral director.

Although Vital Records has started electronic birth registration, electronic death registration has been delayed for more testing. A paper alternative should be available for home funeral people once it's in place, however.

Fetal Death

A fetal death report is required when death occurs after 20 weeks of gestation or when the weight is 350 grams or more (about 12 ounces). If there is no family physician involved, the local medical examiner must sign the fetal death certificate. The fetal death certificate must be filed within seven days.

Transporting and Disposition Permit

A body may be moved with the consent of a physician, medical examiner, or coroner. An out-of-state disposition permit can be obtained from a funeral director or the Bureau of Vital Records if the body will be removed from the state.

Burial

Home burial is permissible in Missouri. Land, not to exceed one acre, must be deeded in trust to the county commission and the deed filed with the county court within 60 days. Check with the county or town registrar for local zoning laws regarding home burial. There are no state burial statutes or regulations with regard to depth. A sensible guideline is 150 feet from a water supply and at least two feet of earth on top. There is no permit required for burial if the notification of death or death certificate has been filed.

Cremation

All cremations must be in a licensed facility. The death certificate must be completed and filed with the registrar prior to cremation. The physician completing the death certificate will authorize cremation. Authorization by next-of-kin is also required, and a pacemaker must be removed.

One may authorize one's own cremation prior to death.

There are no laws regarding the disposition of cremated remains. You may do as you wish.

Other Requirements

A sturdy capsule with the name of the deceased, social security number, and dates of birth and death must be placed in each casket or container for cremated remains.

For families handling a "normal" death on their own, there are no statutory embalming requirements.

Regulations promulgated by the Board of Embalmers and Funeral Directors, however, require embalming or refrigeration after 24 hours. If next-of-kin have not yet been located or if waiting any longer would make the embalming job more difficult, the mortuary may go ahead and embalm the body after six hours. This seems outrageously presumptive, with such disparate religious or personal views on embalming and when refrigeration is a more reliable method of body preservation.

If a person dies of a communicable disease, the body must be tagged and labeled with the disease. This seems at odds with the advice from the Centers for Disease Control which says **all bodies** should be handled with universal precautions. And given the constant mix-ups at mortuaries with mass-preparation facilities, all bodies should be tagged at the place of death anyway, prior to removal.

When death is due to an infectious disease, burial or cremation must occur within 24 hours unless the body is embalmed. Embalming under such circumstances is the worst possible thing to do as it puts funeral personnel at risk. To their credit, Hawaii, Delaware, North Carolina and Ontario forbid embalming in those situations; Ohio and Montana require immediate disposition.

If shipping by common carrier, a body which will not reach its destination within 24 hours must be embalmed or encased in a sealed casket. If death is due to Asiatic cholera, typhus, typhoid or ship fever, yellow fever, bubonic plague, diphtheria, scarlet fever, glanders, anthrax, leprosy, small pox, TB, puerperal fever, erysipelas, measles or "other dangerous or communicable diseases," embalming is required prior to shipping. Alternatively, the body may be wrapped in a disinfectant-saturated sheet before being placed in a sealed casket.

Medical Schools for Body Donation

Body donation to a medical school is another option for disposition. Find the information for Missouri at <www.finalrights.org>.

State Governance

The Missouri Board of Embalmers and Funeral Directors has ten members. One is a consumer representative; the others are embalmers and funeral directors. The board is overseen by the Department of Professional Regulation.

<www.pr.mo.gov/embalmers.asp>

It would appear that embalmers have a special place in the hearts of state officials in Missouri. In addition to the website above, the e-mail for the Funeral Board is <embalm@pr.mo.gov>.

Crematories are licensed, regulated, and inspected by the Board of Funeral Directors and Embalmers but not represented on the Board. One does not need to be a funeral director to run a crematory. A limited license is given.

Casket retailers do not need to be licensed by the Funeral Board, per a consent agreement with the FTC. The need for this came about when Larry Gegner, a Missouri man who sold caskets from a flea market, encountered harassment from the Board when they found out he was telling citizens they had the right to bypass funeral homes and bury their own dead. In 2005, the Board (then made up of five funeral directors or embalmers, and only one public member) took Gegner to court and filed a laundry list of charges against him. Astonishingly, these included "unlicensed activities" such as selling caskets to the public, even though Missouri Law specifically allows retail casket sales. The Board also charged Gegner with vague "violations" such as "arranging" funerals without a license.

The Institute for Justice and FCA stepped in to protest, which provoked a complaint against the Board by the FTC. The settlement with the FTC required the Board to revoke any regulations barring the sale of caskets by non-funeral directors, and required the Board to promise it would write no such regulations in the future. Before the affair concluded, though, the Board floated proposed rules that would have put families' rights to home funerals in jeopardy. Once again, FCA objected, noting the Board had no statutory authority to do so. The Board finally relented, and actually clarified the rights of families to perform their own funerals in subsequent regulations.

While the Board's actions in 2005 and 2006 were outrageous, it's only fair to note that newly elected members changed its character and the Board became far more consumer-friendly. During debate over reforming preneed laws, funeral directors on the board (and its staff) actively reached out to FCA for help. They invited Slocum to testify as part of a working committee, and the board backed a bill that would have required 100 percent trusting for prepaid funeral money (sadly, that provision failed).

The Division of Professional Registration is responsible for regulating cemeteries as well, but there is no state cemetery board.

Prepaid Cemetery and Funeral Funds

Only 110% of the wholesale cost for prepaid *cemetery merchandise* must be placed in trust. "Constructive delivery" can bypass the trusting requirement, but the chances are that the state isn't checking to see what's in the warehouse. There is no trusting requirement for prepaid *cemetery services* such as the opening-and-closing fee. If there is anything in trust, the interest may be withdrawn by the cemetery. This is piddley protection for consumers who are unlikely to get any refund if they were to change their minds. For example, if you decide on cremation later, a coffin vault would not be needed, but you'd get no refund.

The cemetery must make an annual report to the Division of Registration.

100% of prepaid *funeral funds* must be placed into trust. The seller may then obtain from the trustee a 5% "origination fee." On top of that, the seller may also request a 10% payment. If you are purchasing an installment plan, the seller gets to keep the first 15% right off. The seller is entitled to all income from guaranteed preneed trusts and may withdraw the interest annually. Administrative fees must be taken from the interest. In 29 other states, 100% trusting is required. Preneed is alive and well in all those states. Commissioned sales reps have been a major source of preneed hard-sell complaints.

A purchaser may cancel a preneed contract, but if done so after 30 days, the refund will be only 95% of the total contract (the seller gets to keep only the 5% origination fee), without any interest if guaranteed or minimal interest if not guaranteed. Likewise, for anyone wishing to transfer an irrevocable contract, all that likely gets moved is 95%. Let's hope there won't be a problem putting the 10% back in if it's already been spent.

On the other hand, a seller may suggest, in lieu of a trust, a joint deposit account—in the names of both the seller and the purchaser. In this case, 100% must be placed in the account. The "deposited funds" in such an account are fully refundable if it has not been made irrevocable. (Whether that includes interest "deposited" is questionable. Read the fine-print in your contract.) Why a preneed seller would suggest this plan over the 85% plan, one can only speculate. Perhaps to avoid annual interest-reporting paperwork.

A seller must report preneed sales to the state funeral board annually. A consumer may request in writing a report of all deposits made by the seller.

Consumer Concerns

- The death rate in Missouri can support approximately 221 full-time mortuaries; there are, however, 595. Funeral prices tend to be higher in areas where there are "too many" funeral homes.

- Trusting requirements are still inadequate. All (100%) money prepaid for cemetery and funeral goods and services should be placed into trust, with full right of refund or transfer.

- There is no provision for an adequate description of funeral goods selected preneed nor for a substitution of equal quality and construction if the selected item is no longer available at the time of death. Substitution should require the approval of survivors.

- There is no annual reporting requirement to the purchaser of pre-paid funeral goods and services, paperwork that might be useful to the family of a deceased to indicate prepayment and which would help to "enforce" trusting requirements.

- There is no state protection for consumers in case of default on pre-paid funeral funds that were never put into trust.

- Until the laws are changed to require 100% trusting for preneed cemetery and funeral purchases and other loopholes are closed, it is probably a terrible idea to prepay for any such arrangements other than perhaps a plot. A personal bank account is much safer and can easily be transferred.

- There is no requirement to identify and tag a body at the place of death before removal.

- The embalming laws are unsafe and excessive. All laws and regulations requiring embalming should be repealed, especially those for when the death has occurred from a communicable or contagious disease. This is not only an offense to some religious groups, it puts the funeral professionals at risk.

- There is no requirement that low-cost caskets be included in any display.

- The standards for ethical, professional conduct are inadequate and should be strengthened. That would make it easier for a consumer to prevail when filing a valid complaint. (See Ethical Standards in the Appendix.)

- Complaints against funeral establishments are kept secret.

- The limitation on cremation providers will keep the cost high to the general public.

- The FTC Funeral Rule has not been adopted in this state.

- Coroners are elected and may be funeral directors with a conflict of interest.

- This state has no laws regulating the body parts business.

Miscellaneous Information

- Educational requirements for becoming a funeral director: high school, one year of apprenticeship, and a state and practical exam.

For an embalmer: mortuary college (2 years), one year of apprenticeship, a state and National Board Exam. Alas, practitioners and consumer critics alike deem the NBE out-dated and irrelevant. A person running a crematory must get a limited license: high school and a state law exam, plus a criminal background check.

- Missouri has some weird establishment licenses: Function A—embalming only, Function B—cremation only and may not deal directly with the public, Function C—may make arrangements as well as having visitations and funerals (in other words a full-service establishment), Function D—visitations and funerals only and operated under C (a branch).

- Cash-advance items must be billed to the customer in the same amount as they were billed to the funeral home.

- You may name in a power of attorney a person to handle your funeral arrangements, helpful if you are estranged from next-of-kin.

- The county coroner or medical examiner and next-of-kin must be notified prior to a disinterment, but the statutes don't say how much prior.

This chapter was sent for review to the Department of Public Health, the Board of Embalmers and Funeral Directors, and the Division of Professional Registration, but no responses were received.

Caring for the Dead
In Montana

Please refer also to the general introduction to state chapters—"Caring for the Dead: Necessary Information."

Persons in Montana may care for their own dead. The legal authority to do so is found in:

> *50-15-403. Preparation and filing of death or fetal death certificate. (2) . . . The person in charge of disposition shall obtain the completed certification of the cause of death from the physician, the advanced practice registered nurse, or the coroner and shall, within the time that the department may prescribe by rule, file the death or fetal death certificate with the local registrar in the registration area where the death occurred*

There are no other statutes that might require you to use a funeral director.

Death Certificate

The clerk and recorder's office or the local registrar can supply a blank death certificate. (Ask for the authorization for disposition form at the same time.) The person in charge of disposition of the dead body or fetus shall present the death certificate to the certifying physician, the certifying advanced practice registered nurse, or the coroner to obtain the medical cause of death. (You will also need a signature on the authorization form.) The remaining information must be supplied, typewritten with no errors. The death certificate must be filed with the local registrar within ten days.

Montana has started electronic death registration, but a paper alternative is still available for home funeral people.

Fetal Death

A fetal death certificate is required when a weight of 350 grams (about 12 ounces) or after 20 weeks of gestation if weight is unknown. It is handled the same as a death certificate.

Transporting and Disposition Permit

A body may be moved with medical permission, but a "Dead Body Removal Authorization" must be signed by the medical people or a mortician within 24 hours. There are four copies, with one each going to the registrar of the district where the death occurred, the coroner, and the person in charge of disposition. The fourth copy stays with the body until burial or cremation.

Burial

There are no state statutes that specifically permit home burial, but private family graveyards are mentioned and exempt from regulation by the Funeral Board. It is also unlikely that there are local zoning regulations regarding home burial, but you should review them before planning a family cemetery. If your land is in a rural area, draw a map of the property showing where the burial ground will be and have it filed with the deed. That may be all you have to do to establish your family cemetery. There are no state burial statutes or regulations with regard to burial locations or depth. A sensible guideline is 150 feet from a water supply, 25 feet from a power line, with two or three feet of earth on top. Plan your family cemetery away from boundaries with neighbors, too.

There must be 18 inches of earth on top of any vault or casket, but only 12 inches if it's a double-depth burial.

Cremation

The Dead Body Removal Authorization is sufficient for cremation, but there is a 24-hour wait prior to cremation. Authorization by next-of-kin (or the deceased prior to death) is also required, and a pacemaker must be removed. Cremation must be in a licensed crematory. There are no laws regarding the disposition of cremated remains. You may do as you wish.

Other Requirements

Persons dying from an infectious disease must be buried or cremated as soon as is reasonably possible with the least amount of handling. A body that will not reach its destination within 48 hours must be embalmed or refrigerated.

Medical Schools for Body Donation

Body donation to a college anatomy program is another option for disposition. Find the information for Montana at <www.finalrights.org>.

State Governance

The Montana Board of Funeral Service has six members: one consumer representative, one crematory operator, one cemeterian, and three morticians. Crematories and for-profit cemeteries are governed by the Board of Funeral Service. One does not have to be a funeral director to run a crematory.
    <http://bsd.dli.mt.gov/license/bsd_boards/fnr_board/board_page.asp>

Prepaid Cemetery and Funeral Funds

Most of Montana's cemetery laws deal with municipal or county cemeteries and are relatively mundane. Another set of laws governs private cemetery associations, with an implication that these are not-for-profit. A few newer laws address for-profit cemeteries, a growing concern if conglomerate funeral chains buy up any of the private associations or start any new cemeteries. No laws deal with prepaid cemetery funds.

A lot owner selling a lot must offer it to the cemetery first, at the going rate.

All money (100%) prepaid for *funeral* arrangements must go into trust with interest to accrue. The buyer should receive confirmation of the deposit from the trust institution within 30 days. A buyer may cancel or transfer the preneed arrangement at any time without penalty. A preneed contract may be made irrevocable only within six months of applying for Medicaid and other social benefits. If merchandise is not available at the time of death, substitution must be of "equal quality, value and workmanship." Value can be problematic. A $1,200 casket was a pretty swell casket ten years ago. Ten years from now it's likely to be considered "the welfare casket."

Consumer Concerns

- The death rate in Montana can support approximately 33 full-time mortuaries; there are, however, 77. This may be understandable because of the wide geographic area. Unfortunately, because of the low volume of business per mortuary, funeral prices may tend to be high given their expensive overhead.

- There is no provision for an adequate description of funeral goods selected preneed. Substitution of equal quality and construction— not value— should be allowed with the approval of persons making the arrangements.

- There is no annual reporting requirement to the purchaser of prepaid funeral goods and services, paperwork that might be useful to the family of a deceased to indicate prepayment and which would help to "enforce" trusting requirements.

- There is no state protection for consumers in case of default on pre-paid funeral funds that were never put into trust.

- Despite better protections than in some other states, prepaying for cemetery and funeral purchases may be unwise, given the loopholes.

- There is no requirement to identify and tag the body at the place of death before removal.

- There is no provision either forbidding a mark-up on cash advance items or requiring the disclosure of how much it would be.

- There is no provision that the least expensive casket be displayed with equal prominence as other caskets.

- Coroners may be funeral directors, with a conflict of interest.

- This state has no laws regulating the body parts business.

Unlike most other states, Montana has eliminated more than half the "consumer concerns" Carlson reported in her 1998 book.

Miscellaneous Information

- Educational requirements for a funeral director: two years of college plus mortuary school, one year of apprenticeship, and a state exam plus the National Board Exam. Practitioners and consumer critics alike have deemed the NBE out-of-date and irrelevant.

- You may name in a power of attorney a person to handle your funeral arrangements, helpful if you are estranged from next-of-kin.

- A body may not be held for debt.

- The FTC Funeral Rule has been incorporated by reference in the regulations.

- Hospitals and others may not send a body to a funeral home without first checking with the next-of-kin or person making arrangements.

- A disinterment permit must be obtained from the local registrar.

This chapter was sent for review to the Department of Public Health, which gave helpful suggestions. No response was received from the Board of Funeral Service.

Caring for the Dead

In Nebraska

Please refer also to the general introduction to state chapters: "Caring for the Dead: Necessary Information."

In Nebraska a dead body becomes a hostage of the funeral industry, one of only eight such states that require the use of a funeral director (Connecticut, Illinois, Indiana, Louisiana, Michigan, Nebraska, New Jersey, and New York). In almost no other situation is a private citizen forced to use a for-profit business to fulfill the interests of the state. Given the conflicting laws and the growing interest in home funerals, a court case may be necessary if legislative changes can't be made.

> *Chapter 71-605(1)—The funeral director and embalmer in charge of the funeral of any person dying in the State of Nebraska shall cause a certificate of death to be filled out . . . (7) No dead human body shall be removed from the state for final disposition without a transit permit issued by the funeral director and embalmer having charge of the body . . . (8) The interment . . . shall be performed under the direct supervision of a licensed funeral director and embalmer . . . (9) All transit permits . . . shall be signed by the funeral director and embalmer in charge . . .*

Parents may file a birth certificate if no doctor is involved. What's the big deal about a death certificate?

Other statutes appear to give rights to next-of-kin or a designated agent:

> *23-1816. Inquest; body of deceased; disposition.*
>
> *The coroner shall cause the body of each deceased person which the coroner is caused to view, to be delivered to the friends of the deceased, if there be any . . . .*
>
> *38-1425. Deceased persons; control of remains; interment; liability.*

(1) . . . the right to control the disposition of the remains of a deceased person . . . unless other directions have been given by the decedent in the form of a testamentary disposition or a pre-need contract, vests in the following persons in the order named:

(a) Any person authorized to direct the disposition of the decedent's body pursuant to a notarized affidavit authorizing such disposition and signed and sworn to by the decedent. . . ;

(b) The surviving spouse of the decedent;

(c) If the surviving spouse is incompetent or not available or if there is no surviving spouse, the decedent's surviving adult children. . . .;

(d) The decedent's surviving parents;

(e) The persons in the next degree of kinship under the laws . . .

(3) The liability for the reasonable cost of the final disposition of the remains of the deceased person devolves jointly and severally upon all kin of the decedent in the same degree of kindred and upon the estate of the decedent . . .

The primary concern of 38-1425 seems to be an effort to nail down who will pay for the "reasonable cost of interment." What if the cost isn't "reasonable" (and by whose standards is "reasonable" measured)? What remedy do families have then? Certainly not caring for their own dead, if these conflicting laws are allowed to stand. There is also no provision for estrangement.

A pediatric oncology nurse has noted there is often a dramatic difference in the healing for parents who have had a hands-on funeral experience— a sentiment reported by home funeral families themselves. But people in Nebraska do not have this meaningful and therapeutic choice. Nor do religious groups wishing to play an active role at a time of death. And Native Americans will be at the mercy of a mortician before heading back to the reservation. A court challenge would certainly be decided in favor of a family's rights, according to legal precedents. In a 1909 federal case, Wyeth v. Cambridge Board of Health, the court ruled:

. . . the refusal to permit one to bury the dead body of his relative or friend, except under an unreasonable limitation, is also an interference with a private right that is not allowable under the Constitution of the Commonwealth or the Constitution of the United States.

One other curious law—71-609—appears in the statutes. Casket retailers must include a copy of the laws and a blank death certificate. Doesn't that give the impression that families have the right to care for their own dead?

Death Certificate

The family doctor or a local medical examiner will sign the death certificate within 24 hours, stating the cause of death. The remaining information must be supplied by the family, typewritten or in permanent ink. The death certificate must be filed with the Bureau of Vital Statistics within five business days—by a funeral director.

Nebraska is using electronic death registration for about 60% of the deaths, but some paper records are still used.

Fetal Death

A fetal death report is required if death occurs after 20 weeks of gestation. If there is no family physician involved, the county attorney must be notified.

Transporting and Disposition Permit

A transit permit is required only for a body shipped out of state. A funeral director will issue this permit. You may have difficulty getting the funeral director to grant the permit if you are driving the body to another state, but you do have a legal right to do so; no statutes in Nebraska restrict who may transport a body. You may not need a mortician at the receiving end if delivering a body to a medical school, cemetery, or crematory but you should check. Unfortunately some may not accept the body from the family.

Burial

Check with the county registrar for local zoning laws regarding home burial. Family graveyards are exempt from taxation and must be registered with the county clerk. When burial is arranged—even on private land—it must be under the direct supervision of a licensed funeral director.

There are no state burial statutes or regulations with regard to depth. A sensible guideline is 150 feet from a water supply and two or three feet of earth on top.

Cremation

A permit for cremation must be obtained from the county attorney. There is no fee for this. Most crematories insist that a pacemaker be removed, and authorization by next-of-kin is usually required unless authorized by the decedent prior to death. There are no laws regarding the disposition of cremated remains. You may do as you wish.

Other Requirements

Embalming is not routinely required in Nebraska. Weather and reasonable planning should be considered.

If the person died of a contagious or communicable disease, the doctor in attendance should be consulted.

A body shipped by common carrier must be embalmed, an affront to some with religious objections to embalming. Airlines and most other states permit shipping in a sealed casket or shipping case.

Medical Schools for Body Donation

Body donation to a medical school is another option for disposition. Find the information for Nebraska at <www.finalrights.org>.

State Governance

The Nebraska State Board of Embalmers and Funeral Directors has four members. There is one consumer representative.

<http://www.dhhs.ne.gov/crl/mhcs/fun/funeraldirecting.htm>

The Department of Health and Human Services also regulates crematories. One does not need to be a mortician to run a crematory.

The Department of Insurance regulates preneed funeral and cemetery purchases even though not all preneed arrangements are funded through insurance. Their website, <www.doi.ne.gov/>, isn't a lot of help. But Carlson did stumble on a consumer brochure put out by the Department:

<www.doi.ne.gov/brochure/out93027.pdf>

Alas, it says that irrevocable preneed contracts are for services and revocable contracts are for merchandise. Not the case at all. Both services and merchandise can be part of either preneed contract.

Prepaid Cemetery and Funeral Funds

Nebraska statutes provide that cemeteries must be operated "in nowise with a view to profit." Only municipalities, churches, and nonprofit cemetery associations may operate cemeteries. "The establishment of a cemetery by any agency other than those enumerated herein shall constitute a nuisance, and its operation may be enjoined at the suit of any taxpayer in the state." With corporate funeral chains finding greater profits in cemetery operations than in mortuaries, Nebraskans need to be alert. An operation that is technically nonprofit on the surface can easily siphon off exorbitant sums—to a holding company for rent of the land, perhaps—or in management fees. A definite nuisance, indeed.

Preneed marketing agents are not necessarily morticians but must be working for a preneed seller, the one who will be providing funeral or cemetery services.

A seller may charge and pocket interest on installment purchases. This is absurd—finance fees for a lay-away plan before they lay you away.

Only 85% of prepaid money for funeral and cemetery merchandise (i.e., markers and vaults) must be placed in trust, reducing the amount that otherwise might generate interest against inflation. "Constructive delivery" can bypass trusting requirements. This is usually accomplished with a title showing ownership or a document stating that the marker or vault is in the cemetery warehouse with your name on it. Carlson was unable to find out if Nebraska was checking the warehouses. Few states do.

Only 85% of your service dollars must be placed in trust. The seller may pocket 15% right away, payment for doing nothing more than running a sales pitch—before you die. Even car dealers don't get to collect a commission until you actually buy the car. Twenty nine other states require 100% trusting. Preneed is alive and well in those states.

The seller may withdraw annually any income (interest) in excess of the National Consumer Price Index. That is, if the national inflation rate is 2%, then an amount of the income equal to 2% of the trust must be left in the account to cover inflation or "cost of living" increases. Anything over that can be withdrawn by the seller. Obviously, Nebraska legislators are out of touch with what's really happening in the industry: funeral inflation is running between 3% and 4% a year; much more for low-cost funeral selections, and more still if "your" funeral home has been purchased by a chain. Interest on CDs or money market and stock investments aren't keeping up. With some of the interest having been sapped out of these accounts earlier by such ill-conceived bookkeeping, there will be less at the time of need, a situation that invites manipulative sales tactics. "Gee, Mrs. Brown. The casket your father picked out is no longer available. You'll have to pick out another, and, by the way, the price has gone up."

The financial trustee may also withdraw "reasonable costs incurred in the administration of the trusts." This little statement is a sneaky one, as many state trade organizations have set up "master" trusts through which to invest preneed funeral funds. The state funeral directors association usually gets a monthly commission as does the funeral director who sold the preneed arrangement. The state is not aware of any such master trust at this time, but the idea may catch on later.

Anyone seeking to cancel or transfer a preneed agreement can throw 15% of the initial payment to the prairie winds. What you get will also be depleted by the price of whatever has already been "delivered" and the annual "excess" income or administrative fees withdrawn. Oh, yes, don't expect a refund or transfer for 90 days—less a permitted service charge from the bank. (Any financial institution taking that long to process a transaction shouldn't be allowed to charge for it.)

An irrevocable funeral trust is limited to $4,000.

There is no provision for an adequate description of merchandise selected preneed. While the seller *"may"* substitute merchandise of like or better quality if the item selected is not available, this is not a requirement.

The preneed seller must make an annual report to the director of the Insurance Department.

Consumer Concerns

- The death rate in Nebraska can support approximately 62 full-time mortuaries; there are, however, 232. With the low density of population over a wide geographic area, mortuary careers are not likely to be full-time work. Unfortunately, because of the low volume of business per mortuary, funeral prices may tend to be high given their expensive overhead.

- There is no provision for an adequate description of funeral goods selected preneed nor a requirement for the substitution—approved by survivors—of equal quality and construction if the selected item is no longer available at the time of death.

- Warehousing is permitted. Trusting requirements should be increased to 100%, with all interest to accrue. The consumer should get full benefit of all interest and amounts paid when cancelling or transferring an arrangement.

- There is no requirement for an annual report to funeral consumers indicating the institution of deposit and value (purchase price plus interest) of all prepaid funeral monies. Such documents could be important to survivors who might not otherwise know about prepaid accounts and could serve to enforce the trusting requirements.

- There is no state protection for consumers in case of default on prepaid funeral funds that were never put into trust.

- Until the preneed loopholes and omissions have been fixed, it is probably a terrible idea to prepay for a funeral or cemetery goods and services in this state. Money in the bank will be safer.

- There is no requirement to have low-cost caskets on display.

- There is no requirement to disclose how much a cash advance item may be marked up or forbidding such a mark-up.

- There is no requirement to identify and tag the body at the place of death before removal.

- The cremation permit from the county attorney is an unnecessary burden on families in the case of an anticipated death.

- Not everyone wants the funeral director to call the shots. The definition of "funeral directing" in the statutes sounds as if morticians were clergy, "counseling families or next of kin in regard to the conduct of a funeral service for a dead human body. . . ."

- Ethical standards are inadequate and should be expanded and clearly defined in order for valid consumer complaints to prevail.

- The FTC Funeral Rule has not been adopted in this state.

- This state has no laws regulating the body parts business.

- The Funeral Board no longer approves Continuing Ed courses. A practitioner merely has to "attest" that he or she spent 16 hours (every two years) in the following areas of "Continuing Competency":
  a. Communication/Media
  b. Counseling/Arbitration
  c. Customer relations
  d. Disaster training
  e. Embalming practice
  f. Funeral directing practice
  g. Management (stress/personnel/business)
  h. Marketing/advertising
  i. Personal development
  j. Pre-need.

And one can get these hours by attending tours, exhibits, or association meetings, typically held in places like Las Vegas or Orlando where golf is also a major activity.

Miscellaneous Information

- The educational requirements for becoming an embalmer/funeral director are 60 semester hours of college (two years), plus mortuary "college" (could be one year), and one year of apprenticeship. Also required is a state exam, an exam on vital records forms, and a "national standardized exam." Alas, practitioners and consumer critics alike deem the National Board Exam out-of-date and irrelevant.

- Under standards for funeral directors and embalmers, no "indecent, profane, or obscene language" may be used in the presence of the body or family and friends "prior to the burial." After that, watch out?

- You may name someone to handle your funeral arrangements in a notarized affidavit.

- There are no restrictions on who may sell caskets at retail. The casket retailer, however, must keep a record of each sale including the name, place, and date of death.

- Coroners are elected. They must be attorneys.

- A disinterment permit request must be filed with the health department.

This chapter was sent for review to the Nebraska Department of Health and Human Services, the Nebraska Board of Examiners in Funeral Directing and Embalming, and the Department of Insurance. No written responses were received, but some information was verified by telephone.

Caring for the Dead
In Nevada

Please refer also to the general introduction to state chapters: "Caring for the Dead: Necessary Information."

Persons in Nevada may care for their own dead. The Office of Vital Statistics (Department of Human Resources, Health Division) accepts a liberal interpretation of the statutes. According to 1986 correspondence, "The funeral industry has hotly contested this viewpoint. . . ." Nothing has changed since then. The relevant statutes are found in:

> *NRS 440.370: Signature of statements as to disposition of the body. The statement of facts relating to the disposition of the body must be signed by the funeral director or person acting as undertaker. . . .*

> *NRS 642.550: Applicability of chapter (re funeral directors and embalmers). Nothing in this chapter shall be construed to apply: 1. To persons engaged as layers-out or to those who shroud the dead.*

A surviving spouse or the parents of minor children are "responsible for the decent burial or cremation of his or her spouse or such child within a reasonable time after death."

Death Certificate

Nevada has been using electronic death registration since 2006. A paper alternative is still available for home funeral folks.

The family doctor will sign the cause of death. In an anticipated death, he or she may delegate this to a physician's assistant or registered nurse. If the death is unattended, the local health officer, or coroner will sign the death certificate. The remaining information must be supplied, typewritten or in black ink. The death certificate must be filed with the local registrar within 72 hours and before final disposition.

Fetal Death

A fetal death report is required for each fetal death of 20 weeks gestation. If there is no family physician involved, the local health officer or coroner must sign the fetal death certificate.

Transporting and Disposition Permit

A body may be moved with the permission of the person certifying death. The local health officer will issue the final burial or removal permit. This must be obtained within 72 hours of death. It should be filed with the registrar in the district of burial. In the Administrative Code promulgated by the Funeral Board is a regulation that implies only a funeral director may transport a body: " A licensed funeral director, or a person who holds a license to conduct direct cremations or immediate burials, may transport a dead human body . . . ." However, the Funeral Board has authority only over licensees, not private citizens, and there is a clear exemption for the layers out of the dead.

Burial

Family cemeteries are allowed by statute:

> The board of county commissioners of a county whose population is less than 50,000 may adopt an ordinance . . . allowing a family cemetery. . . . Before the first interment in a family cemetery . . . a member of the family or a representative of the family shall notify the Health Division of the Department of Health and Human Services of the designation of the family cemetery and its specific location on the land owned by the family.

If you are thinking of home burial, plan ahead to make sure your county has such an ordinance. It would then be a good idea to draw a map of the property showing where the burial ground will be and have it filed with the deed once your family cemetery is approved. There are no state burial statutes or regulations with regard to burial locations or depth. A sensible guideline is 150 feet from a water supply, 25 feet from a power line, with two or three feet of earth on top. Plan your family cemetery away from boundaries with neighbors, too.

When burial is arranged, the family member acting as funeral director must sign the burial permit and file it with the local health officer within 10 days.

Cremation

No additional permit is required for cremation. Authorization by next-of-kin or designated agent is required unless a cremation order is signed prior to death by the deceased. A pacemaker must be removed. Cremation must be in a licensed crematory. There are no laws regarding the disposition of cremated remains. You may do as you wish.

Other Requirements

Funeral homes may not require embalming for the first 72 hours unless ordered by the board of health. If the person died of a contagious or communicable disease, the doctor in attendance should be consulted for state health guidelines. In this case, embalming may be required, the worst possible circumstances under which to require it. To their credit, Ontario, Delaware, North Carolina, and Hawaii forbid embalming in the case of infectious diseases. Ohio and Montana require immediate disposition. Bodies held for cremation must be refrigerated after 24 hours if not embalmed.

A body to be shipped by common carrier must "be prepared" by an embalmer. But most airlines will accept a sealed casket if there are objections to embalming.

Administrative code generated by the Board of Health reads as if a body may not be transported at all unless it has been embalmed, clearly a violation of some religious practices and an affront to some personal beliefs.

Medical Schools for Body Donation

Body donation to a medical school is another option for disposition. Find the information for Nevada at <www.finalrights.org>.

State Governance

The Nevada State Funeral Board has five members: one funeral director, one cemeterian, one crematory operator, and two consumer representatives. What a comprehensive, well-balanced board! Furthermore, this is the only state that requires that the chairman of the Board must be chosen from the members who are representatives of the general public.

<http://funeral.state.nv.us/>

The Board's website has an easy-to-use complaint form but is missing an active link for the FAQ item or mission. While there are links to the administrative code and funeral director statutes, a link to the preneed statutes is missing, a strange oversight even if the Insurance Department regulates preneed. Most unfortunately, there is no mention of the guide that the statutes say the Board "may" publish, one that would list all funeral, cemetery, and cremation providers with their prices.

Crematories are licensed and regulated by the funeral board. One does not need to be a funeral director to run a crematory.

The Commissioner of Insurance is supposed to regulate preneed cemetery and funeral purchases, as well as pet cemeteries and pet crematories. There is absolutely nothing—zilch—on their website about any of these.

<http://doi.state.nv.us/>

The State Board of Health sets the standards for mausoleum construction.

Prepaid Cemetery and Funeral Funds

There are statutory provisions for moving a cemetery—with the consent of known heirs.

Cemeteries, including pet cemeteries, must be eleemosynary (charitable), not-for-profit organizations. Funeral conglomerates are finding ways around this, and SCI (the largest funeral home and cemetery chain in the world) owns at least one cemetery as of this writing.

Preneed sellers (funeral homes and cemeteries) and preneed agents (commissioned sales reps) must be registered with the Department of Insurance. The sellers must post a surety bond of $50,000 or enough to cover the "aggregate liability" of the trust which is *not* 100% of what the consumer paid. At least 10 states have some sort of guarantee fund to protect consumers against default or embezzlement of preneed funds.

Boy, is Nevada generous to its preneed sellers. Preneed must be a booming business in this state. Only 60% of preneed cemetery goods and services must be placed in trust. 60% of the income may be withdrawn annually by the seller after administrative fees are paid.

If you paid $1,000 for a vault, $1,000 for opening-and-closing, and $1,000 for a marker, for a total of $3,000, only $1,800 will go into the trust. If you change your mind and decide on cremation and won't need the expensive vault or hefty opening-and-closing, there's no telling what provision for cancellation there might be. On the other hand, if you move, the statutes do allow the cemetery to transfer the $1,800 or so that's left in the trust from your original $3,000.

But wait. Somebody really has it in for the struggling buyer. If you are paying on an installment plan, statutes provide that the 40% commission *may* be retained before any money is put into trust. In 1998, Carlson was told by one of the Insurance Department staffers that the commissioner was preparing a regulation that would require a proportionate share of each payment to be placed into trust. More than a dozen years later, it's not there yet.

If you default on "any" payment, the cemetery may terminate the contract and keep "as damages not more than 40% of the total purchase price." Not 40% of what is paid, but 40% of what you *would* have paid. In plain talk, if you have paid $1,000 of the $3,000 and hit a month of hard times missing a payment, you'll get back nothing, not one red cent. If you've paid $2,000, you'll get back $800. What a deal!

Only 75% of preneed *funeral* expenses must be placed in trust. If you are paying on an installment plan, the 25% commission may be retained before any is put in trust. That is, if you have negotiated for a $6,000 funeral, the seller may keep the first $1,500 you pay before the remaining $4,500 is put aside for your funeral. But the seller's preneed income doesn't stop there. Let's say your trust earns 3% interest each year. After the trust institution has deducted any administrative fees, the seller may withdraw 75% of the income from the trust annually. Suppose the trustee takes 1% for administration; that leaves 2% of which the seller may claim three-quarters of that, leaving only a small bit of interest added to the account. With funeral inflation running about 3–4% a year, 1% isn't even enough to keep up let alone half a percent. Once the account has built up to 125% of the initial amount (which was only $4,500, not $6,000), the trust will be capped—at the grand sum of $5,625 in this case—and the seller may withdraw all income after that.

Although the preneed contract must carry a "clear and unambiguous statement of the services and property to be supplied," there is no provision for substitution of merchandise equal in quality and construction if the item selected is not available. This has been a source of some mischief around the country. Typical ploy: "I'm sorry, we no longer have that model. You'll have to pick another casket. And, oh, yes, the price has gone up."

You may cancel a preneed arrangement within the first 10 days for a full refund. After that, you'll only get "all the money in the trust fund"—75% of what you initially paid plus whatever piddley interest has been left in the account. There is a strange provision that if you die and your account is all paid up, your survivors could transfer the contract to another provider and expect "all money paid"—$6,000 in the case above. That won't include the interest, but it's more than you'd get if you moved and cancelled the agreement yourself.

Trustees for preneed funeral and cemetery accounts must make quarterly reports to the insurance commissioner.

There is one interesting provision in the Nevada statutes that doesn't seem to appear anywhere else in the country except California: The funeral director or cemetery authority must give a copy of any preneed agreement to the person making final arrangements. Failure to do so may result in a fine three times the amount of the preneed sales agreement. This seems like a great idea if there weren't already so many loopholes.

Consumer Concerns

- The death rate in Nevada can support approximately 71 full-time mortuaries; there are 43 such establishments. This is one of the few states where there is not a significant glut of funeral homes, and prices are competitive in some areas. Consumers will have to shop around, however, as there are huge differences from one funeral home to the next.

- There is no provision for an adequate description of funeral goods selected preneed nor for a substitution of equal quality and construction if the selected item is no longer available at the time of death. Survivors should have a right to approve any substitution.

- Trusting requirements are inadequate and should be increased to 100%. Twenty nine other states require 100% trusting. Preneed is alive and well in those states.

- There is no required annual report indicating the institution of deposit and value (purchase price plus interest) of all prepaid funeral monies. Such documents could be important to survivors who might not otherwise know about prepaid accounts. This report would also help to enforce the trusting requirements.

- Until trusting requirements are increased to 100% with interest income kept intact and adequate provisions for cancellation or transfer, it is probably a terrible idea to prepay for a funeral or any cemetery services and merchandise in Nevada.

- There is no requirement to identify and tag the body at the place of death before removal.

- There is no provision either forbidding a mark-up on cash advance items or requiring the disclosure of how much any mark-up is.

- There is no requirement to have low-cost caskets in any display.

- Ethical standards are insufficient and should be expanded as well as clearly defined in order for valid consumer complaints to prevail.

- This state has no laws regulating the body parts business.

Miscellaneous Information

- Educational requirements for becoming an embalmer: two years of college, one year of mortuary school, one year of apprenticeship, an exam on state laws and the National Board Exam. Alas, practitioners and consumer critics alike have deem this out-dated and irrelevant. Requirements for a funeral director or direct disposition provider: 18 years of age and passing scores on the above-mentioned exams.

- Unless it is run by a society for the purpose of preventing cruelty to animals, only a cemetery may operate a pet crematory.

- The FTC Funeral Rule has been adopted by reference.

- Livestock may not be pastured in a cemetery.

- It is unprofessional conduct to use "profane, indecent or obscene language in the presence of a dead human body, or within the immediate hearing of the family or relatives of a deceased whose body has not yet been interred or otherwise disposed of." After that, watch out?

- It is a misdemeanor to hold a body for debt.

- You may name an agent in an affidavit to carry out your funeral wishes; that person will take precedence over next-of-kin.

- A disinterment permit must be obtained from the local health officer.

This chapter sent for review to the Department of Insurance, the Department of Health—Vital Records, and to the State Funeral Board, but no responses were received.

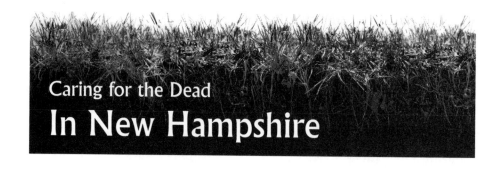

Please refer also to the general introduction to state chapters: "Caring for the Dead: Necessary Information."

Families in New Hampshire may care for their own dead. It took nearly ten years and three legislative tries before the restrictive laws were changed in 1999.

> *290:17 Custody and Control Generally. —The custody and control of the remains of deceased residents of this state are governed by the following provisions:*
>
> *I. If the subject has designated a person to have custody and control in a written and signed document, custody and control belong to that person. The person designated by the subject shall be entitled to no compensation or reimbursement of expenses related to the custody and control of the subject's body.*
>
> *II. If the subject has not left a written signed document designating a person to have custody and control, or if the person designated by the subject refuses custody and control, custody and control belong to the next of kin. [An estranged spouse may not make arrangements.]*
>
> *III. If the next of kin is 2 or more persons with the same relationship to the subject, the majority of the next of kin have custody and control. If the next of kin cannot, by majority vote, make a decision regarding the subject's remains, the court shall make the decision upon petition under RSA 290:19, IV.*

Death Certificate

The family doctor, advanced practice registered nurse, or a local medical examiner will supply and sign the death certificate, stating the cause of death. The remaining information must be supplied by the family, and all information "immediately" filed with the Bureau of Vital Records and Health Statistics electronically via computer. Town clerks have the appropriate computer program as do many funeral directors. The state's computer will generate a burial-transit permit and return it to the sending computer.

Fetal Death

A fetal death report is required for stillbirths of 20 weeks gestation or when a weight of 350 grams (about 12 ounces). It must be filed in the same manner as a death certificate if death is outside a hospital.

Transporting and Disposition Permit

The burial-transit permit that was furnished by the state must be returned to the town clerk or board of health where death occurred within six days after burial.

Burial

Check with the town clerk for zoning laws regarding home burial. A few cities, including Keene, do not allow home burial. The location of private burial sites must be recorded with the deed. No cemetery can be laid out within 100 feet of any dwelling or school, store or other place of business without the consent of the owner, and may not be laid out within 50 feet of the right-of-way of highways. There are no burial statutes with regard to depth. A sensible guideline is 150 feet from a water supply and three feet of earth on top.

Cremation

A cremation permit from the medical examiner is required. The fee for this is $60. There is a 48-hour waiting period prior to cremation unless the person died of a communicable disease. Authorization by next-of-kin or a designated agent is required, and a pacemaker must be removed. The cremation may be witnessed. There are no laws regarding the disposition of cremated remains. You may do as you wish.

Other Requirements

New Hampshire requirements controlling the schedule for disposition of unembalmed bodies are vague. Weather and reasonable planning should be considered. There is one curious statute and the only place where an embalming requirement is mentioned:

> 325:40-a: No dead human body shall be exposed to the public for a period in excess of 24 hours unless said body is properly embalmed.

This law was passed in 1971 at a time when two- and three-day wakes were more usual—sometimes all-day affairs well into the evening. By the third day on a hot July afternoon, there's no doubt that some effort to retard decomposition was appreciated. In current practice, viewings and visitations are most commonly held for a couple of hours in the afternoon and/or evening (or maybe just for an hour prior to the service), "exposing" the body for a total of four hours, possibly five—not anywhere near 24.

Although we've heard NH funeral directors cite this statute as requiring embalming if there is to be a viewing any time after the body has been dead for 24 hours, that simply isn't what the law says. Use good common sense and don't be concerned about that law unless you're planning to "expose" the body to the public for more than 24 hours total. Certainly the time when close friends and relatives are paying their respects at home during *unpublished hours* shouldn't be counted the same as time open "to the public."

If the person died of a contagious or communicable disease, the doctor in attendance should be consulted.

Medical Schools for Body Donation

Body donation to a medical school is another option for disposition. Find the information for New Hampshire at <www.finalrights.org>. Also check Boston University in Massachusetts which will pay for transportation in all six New England states.

State Governance

The New Hampshire Board of Registration of Funeral Directors and Embalmers has five members. One is a consumer representative; the others are funeral directors.

<www.nh.gov/funeral/>

Crematories are regulated by the Department of Health and Human Services. One does not need to be a funeral director to run a crematory.

Public cemeteries are governed by the trustees of the municipality in which they are located. Private cemeteries are not regulated. Funeral directors may serve as trustees of a cemetery but may not receive more than $500 a year in payment from a cemetery.

Prepaid Cemetery and Funeral Funds

All money paid for a preneed *funeral* arrangement must be placed in trust, with interest to accrue or in a licensed insurance company. There are no laws protecting prepaid *cemetery* services.

ACA Assurance, a fraternal benefit society that sold a fair amount of funeral insurance, was put in "rehabilitation" by the NH Department of Insurance in September 2008, apparently for the second time. Policies were stripped of their value by 25% because of ACA's poor financial condition, and a moratorium was placed on any cash surrender payments. Because of its nonprofit status, ACA was not a member of any guarantee fund that would otherwise protect insurance policy holders.

A purchaser may cancel a preneed contract for a full refund.

There is no annual report to the consumer being required and no guarantee fund to protect against embezzlement. Although the New Hampshire Funeral Directors Association has publicly promised this assistance, such social obligations of a trade organization cannot be enforced. Would NHFDA provide the same resources if the defaulter were not an NHFDA member or if the funeral consumer wished to spend the reimbursement with other than an NHFDA member? A similar promise made in a neighboring state— by the Vermont Funeral Directors Association—was not honored when the Calderwood Funeral Home in St. Johnsbury was closed in 1995 with $150,000 in preneed money missing. Two nearby morticians who came to the aid of shafted consumers—at their own expense—saw not a penny from VFDA. But then, they were not VFDA members.

Consumer Concerns

- The death rate in New Hampshire can support approximately 37 full-time mortuaries; there are, however, 103. Funeral prices tend to be higher in areas where there are "too many" funeral homes.

- There is no annual reporting requirement to account for prepaid funeral investments. Such paperwork might be helpful to the family of a deceased, to indicate prepayment and might help to "enforce" the trusting requirements.

- There is no state protection in the case of default of prepaid funeral monies.

- There is no requirement that when merchandise is selected on a guaranteed-price, preneed agreement that a clear description is given and that merchandise of equal quality and construction must be substituted if the original item selected is not available. Survivors should have a right to approve any substitution.

- There are no laws allowing for a transfer of an irrevocable preneed arrangement to another provider.

- Until there is better protection for preneed arrangements, it is probably a terrible idea to prepay for a funeral in New Hampshire. Your own trust account in a bank will be safer and may be made irrevocable if you need to shelter assets.

- The 48-hour wait before cremation is totally unnecessary when survivors are in agreement and is causing additional charges to families for "storage."

- The coroner or medical examiner's permit for cremation in the case of an *anticipated* death from natural causes is totally unnecessary and creates an additional burden and charge for families.

- There is no requirement to identify and tag the body at the place of death before removal.

- There is no provision either forbidding a mark-up on cash advance items or requiring the disclosure of how much the mark-up would be. Consumers may wish to request a copy of the invoices for these charges.

- There is no requirement that low-cost caskets be included in a casket display.

- The standards for ethical, professional conduct are weak and should be more well-defined. That would make it easier for a consumer to prevail when filing a complaint. (See the Appendix.)

- Complaint procedures are unclear and inadequate.

- The FTC Funeral Rule has not been adopted in this state.

- This state has no laws regulating the body parts business.

Miscellaneous Information

- Educational requirements for becoming a funeral director or embalmer: one year of college, one year of mortuary college, and one year of apprenticeship plus any exam required by the Board. Let's hope the Board doesn't accept the National Board Exam which has been deemed out-of-date and irrelevant by practitioners and consumer critics alike.

- Crematories are regulated by the Department of Health. They may be erected on the grounds of a cemetery or other location approved by the selectmen. In practice, there are no cemeteries currently operating crematories. One does not need to be a funeral director to run a crematory. The funeral board inspects crematories.

- The owner of any livestock found trespassing on public or private graveyards is guilty of "a violation." Ironically, in Vermont, sheep were tried for reducing the cemetery's mowing costs.

- You may name a designated agent to carry out your funeral wishes.

- Medical examiners are physicians who are appointed.

- Anyone wishing to make grave rubbings must get the permission of the selectmen or mayor first.

- A disinterment permit must be obtained from the state health department and signed by the local health officer.

This chapter was sent for review to the State Board of Funeral Directors and Embalmers the Department of Health and Human Services, and the Department of Insurance, all of which verified the information as factual.

Caring for the Dead
In New Jersey

Please refer also to the general introduction to state chapters: "Caring for the Dead: Necessary Information."

In New Jersey a dead body becomes a hostage of the funeral industry, one of only eight such states that require the use of a funeral director (Connecticut, Illinois, Indiana, Louisiana, Michigan, Nebraska, New Jersey, and New York). In almost no other situation is a private citizen forced to use a for-profit business to fulfill the interests of the state. The statutes also conflict with each other:

> *45:27-22 Control of funeral, disposition of remains.*
>
> *22. a. If a decedent, in a will . . . appoints a person to control the funeral and disposition of the human remains, the funeral and disposition shall be in accordance with the instructions of the person so appointed. . . . If the decedent has not left a will appointing a person to control the funeral and disposition of the remains, the right to control the funeral and disposition of the human remains shall be in the following order, unless other directions have been given by a court of competent jurisdiction:*
>
> > *(1) The surviving spouse of the decedent or the surviving domestic partner.*
> >
> > *(2) A majority of the surviving adult children of the decedent.*
> >
> > *(3) The surviving parent or parents of the decedent.*
> >
> > *(4) A majority of the brothers and sisters of the decedent.*
> >
> > *(5) Other next of kin of the decedent according to the degree of consanguinity.*

Alas, the control evaporates with the requirements to use a funeral director for filing the death certificate.

26:6-6 Execution of death certificate. (2003) a. The funeral director in charge of the funeral or disposition of the body of any person dying in this State shall be responsible for the proper execution of a death certificate in a legible manner, or by means of the NJ-EDRS, and filed in exchange for a burial or removal or transit permit with the local registrar . . .

26:6-8 Duty to furnish particulars; verification. In the execution of a death certificate, the personal particulars shall be obtained by the funeral director from the person best qualified to supply them. . . .

If the laws cannot be repealed given the growing interest in home funerals, they will likely generate a court case contesting their constitutionality. In a 1909 federal case, *Wyeth v. Cambridge Board of Health,* the court ruled:

. . . the refusal to permit one to bury the dead body of his relative or friend, except under an unreasonable limitation, is also an interference with a private right that is not allowable under the Constitution of the Commonwealth or the Constitution of the United States.

Death Certificate

New Jersey is now using electronic death registration. Within 24 hours, the doctor in attendance, a registered professional nurse, or the county medical examiner must initiate the death certificate, stating the cause of death. The remaining information must be supplied and "verified" by a funeral director. How exactly is a funeral director supposed be able to verify information that could only come from the family themselves? In other states, a paper worksheet is available to home funeral families and the data is entered by a state or local registrar. Parents may file a birth certificate if no doctor is involved.

Fetal Death

A fetal death certificate is required if death occurs after 20 weeks of gestation. If there is no physician involved, the medical examiner must sign the certificate.

Transporting and Disposition Permit

The electronic death registration will generate a burial or removal permit, once the death certificate information is complete. The fee for this is $5, back down from $15, thanks to a veto from the Governor. This permit is to be given to the cemetery, crematory, or other place of disposition and then filed with the registrar of that district within 10 days.

Burial

There are no state statutes that specifically permit or prohibit home burial. It is also unlikely that there are local zoning regulations regarding home burial, but you should review them before planning a family cemetery. If your land is in a rural area, draw a map of the property showing where the burial ground will be and have it filed with the deed. That may be all you have to do to establish your family cemetery. There are no state burial statutes or regulations with regard to burial locations. A sensible guideline is 150 feet from a water supply, 25 feet from a power line. Plan your family cemetery away from boundaries with neighbors, too. The top of an adult casket must be covered by four feet of earth; a child's casket by three and a half feet of earth. When a vault is used, the depth requirement is reduced to six inches.

Unlike other states where burial constitutes a permanent easement on the land, the New Jersey cemetery statutes provide, "Human remains buried on property that is not part of a cemetery may be removed by the owner of the property provided that removal is in compliance with applicable law and the remains are then properly re-buried in a cemetery."

When burial is arranged, the burial permit must be filed with the local registrar within 10 days. When there is no person in charge of the burial ground, "No Person in Charge" must be written across the face of the permit.

Cremation

The burial permit is sufficient for cremation. (The New Jersey legislature had the good sense in 1983 to eliminate the requirement for a medical examiner's permit.) There is a 24-hour waiting period prior to cremation. Authorization by next-of-kin is required, and a pacemaker must be removed. There are no laws regarding the disposition of cremated remains. You may do as you wish.

Other Requirements

A body to be shipped by common carrier must be embalmed unless the destination will be reached within 24 hours, an unfortunate requirement as most airlines will accept a body in a sealed casket when honoring religious objections to embalming. There are no other embalming requirements in this state.

Medical Schools for Body Donation

Body donation to a medical school is another option for disposition. Find the information for New Jersey at <www.finalrights.org>.

State Governance

There are thirteen members of the state Board of Mortuary Science; four of those are public members, one is a government member, and the remaining eight are morticians. The Mortuary Science Board has some unique powers. It is authorized to make rules ". . . for and in the interest, preservation, and improvement of the public health, morals, safety and welfare." Morals?

<www.njconsumeraffairs.gov/mort/>

The New Jersey Cemetery Board oversees the cemetery business. The board has ten members—five cemeterians, two public members, one is the Commissioner of Community Affairs or the commissioner's designee serving ex-officio, one member is the Attorney General or his designee serving ex-officio, and one member is the designee of the Commissioner of Health and Senior Services.

<www.njconsumeraffairs.gov/cemetery/>

Crematories are licensed, regulated, and inspected by the Department of Health. One does not need to be a funeral director to run a crematory.

Prepaid Cemetery and Funeral Funds

As of 1971, all newly established New Jersey cemeteries must be run by non-profit organizations. "Plenty" of private, for-profit cemeteries had been established prior to that, Carlson was told by a Cemetery Board office staffer. Cemeteries are tax-exempt, which means the taxpayers are subsidizing for-profit cemetery companies.

Cemeteries may not be affiliated with a funeral home or sell vaults and markers. In spite of that, Loewen (which went bankrupt, reemerged as The Alderwoods Group, and was then purchased by Service Corporation International) managed to get into the cemetery business back in the 1990s. Somehow the lawmakers were conned into making it legit by 2004, grandfathering it as existing for-profit that can run cemeteries:

> *45:27-7.1 Certificate of authority to provide management services for a cemetery, issuance to certain for-profit entities.*
>
> *1. a. A for-profit corporation, partnership, association or other private entity that managed or operated a cemetery in this State prior to January 14, 2004, shall be issued a certificate of authority to manage or operate a cemetery by the New Jersey Cemetery Board and may continue to manage or operate that cemetery on or after that date, notwithstanding its for-profit status and shall be subject to all the applicable provisions of the "New Jersey Cemetery Act, 2003," P.L.2003,*

c.261 (C.45:27-1 et seq.). A for-profit corporation, partnership, asso-
ciation or other private entity that managed or operated more than
one cemetery in this State prior to January 14, 2004, shall be issued
one certificate of authority pursuant to this subsection covering all
such cemeteries.

There may be a plus side to this. Many of the old cemeteries are run by volunteers, with no perpetual care funds. The cemeteries are deteriorating and at risk of being abandoned. It may be the for-profit folks who take over but will necessarily raise prices.

Cemeteries must have a posted price list.

In-person soliciting for the purpose of selling funeral services is not permitted. Prices charged for preneed purchases may not exceed those on the current price list.

Unless one is purchasing funeral insurance, all prepaid *funeral* money must be placed in trust with the interest to accumulate. If the money is to be deposited in a pooled trust account, the trustee (financial manager) may withdraw a 1% commission annually. In the case of these "master trusts"—which are heavily promoted by morticians—the commission is often shared with morticians or with their state associations. The purchaser has a right to an annual report reflecting the amount and interest accrued. This does not seem to be mandatory, and there appear to be no reporting requirements for individually trusted accounts.

If a provider converts a trust account to funeral insurance, the commission and any other differences must be disclosed to the purchaser. The law is not clear whether the purchaser's permission is required for such a conversion.

A person may transfer or cancel a prepaid arrangement at any time, for a full refund including interest (less the 1% annual commission that probably has been withdrawn). "Constructive delivery" is not permitted.

If merchandise selected preneed is no longer available at the time of death, the provider may substitute "goods of equal quality, value and workmanship." The word "value" may be a problem, however. A casket that cost $950 ten years ago was quite a fancy casket. For $950 today, many funeral homes would offer up a gray cloth-covered "minimum" casket with the goal of getting the survivors to ante up some extra dollars for something "nicer."

Consumer Concerns

- The death rate in New Jersey can support approximately 294 full-time mortuaries; there are, however, 729. Funeral prices tend to be higher in areas where there are "too many" funeral homes.

- There is no provision for an adequate description of funeral goods selected preneed nor for a substitution of equal quality if the selected item is no longer available at the time of death.

- There is no annual reporting requirement to the purchaser of pre-paid funeral goods and services, paperwork that might be helpful to the family of a deceased to indicate prepayment and would help to "enforce" trusting requirements.

- There is no guarantee fund or other protection against default of prepaid funeral funds.

- While the preneed regulation in New Jersey is not too bad, it may be unwise to prepay for a funeral until there are adequate provision for substitution and reporting.

- The requirement to embalm when shipping by common carrier is offensive to some religions or personal beliefs and should be repealed.

- There is no requirement that low-cost caskets be included in any display.

- There is no requirement to identify and tag the body at the place of death before removal.

- The standards for ethical, professional conduct are weak and should be more well-defined. That would make it easier for a consumer to prevail when filing a valid complaint. (See Ethical Standards in the Appendix.)

- The language of the 1984 Funeral Rule was incorporated into the regulations, but that has not been updated to reflect the changes of 1994. Adopting the Rule by reference would save the state from having to update its own laws every time there's a change.

- Funeral homes may not provide food or beverages, a ridiculously outmoded and consumer-unfriendly policy.

Miscellaneous Information

- Educational requirements for becoming a mortuary science practitioner: two years of college, one year of mortuary school, and two years of apprenticeship. Three years of college reduces the apprenticeship requirement to one year. A state exam and practical exam are also required.

- Cash advance items must be billed at the actual cost to the funeral director.

- You may name an agent in your will to handle your funeral arrangements but be sure a copy of that will is easily accessible; never leave only one copy in a safety deposit box that may not be easy to access as soon as the will is needed.

- Any organization operating as a tissue and organ procurement outfit must be run not-for-profit and be registered with the state. New Jersey is one of the few states with such regulation of the body parts business.

- No special permit is required for disinterment but must be done at the direction of the person with the right to control disposition.

This chapter was sent for review to the Board of Mortuary Science, the state Cemetery Board and the Department of Public Health. The Cemetery Board staffer didn't seem to think prices would go up or that legislators had been "conned." No response came from the Mortuary Board. Vital record information was verified by telephone.

Caring for the Dead
In New Mexico

Please refer also to the general introduction to state chapters: "Caring for the Dead: Necessary Information."

Persons in New Mexico may care for their own dead. The legal authority to do so is found in:

> *Title 24-14-20: Death Registration. The funeral service practitioner or person acting as a funeral service practitioner who first assumes custody of the dead body shall file the death certificate.*
>
> *Title 24-14-23: Permits; authorization for final disposition . . . A burial-transit permit shall be issued by the state registrar or a local registrar for those bodies which are to be transported out of the state for final disposition or when final disposition is being made by a person other than a funeral service practitioner or direct disposer.*

There are no other statutes which might require you to use a funeral director.

Death Certificate

New Mexico is now using electronic death registration (EDR). A paper alternative is also available for families caring for their own dead.

The family doctor or a medical investigator will sign the death certificate within 48 hours, stating the cause of death. The remaining information must be supplied, typewritten or in black ink. Do not use a felt-tip pen; there are five copies. The death certificate must be filed with any registrar within five days and before final disposition.

Fetal Death

A fetal death report is required when death occurs and the weight is 500 grams or more (almost 18 ounces). If there is no family physician involved, the state medical investigator must sign the fetal death certificate. The fetal death certificate must be filed with the state registrar within ten days.

Transporting and Disposition Permit

A body may be moved with medical permission. No burial-transit permit is required if disposition is under the direction of a funeral service practitioner or direct disposer *and* disposition occurs within the state. In other cases, the local registrar must sign the burial-transit permit (page four of the death certificate) before final disposition.

Burial

Check with the county registrar for local zoning laws regarding home burial in rural areas. Prior arrangements must be made with the county clerk's office to record a map designating the burial site. Burial must be 50 yards from a stream or other body of water and five feet from the property line; minimum depth is six feet. Unless the registrar in the district of disposition requests the burial-transit permit, persons acting as the sexton should retain it for their records.

Cremation

A permit for cremation must be obtained from the state medical investigator. There is no charge for this when a family is handling arrangements. Most crematories insist that a pacemaker be removed, and authorization by next-of-kin usually is required. There are no laws regarding the disposition of cremated remains. You may do as you wish.

Other Requirements

Bodies must be embalmed or refrigerated to a temperature below 40° if disposition has not occurred within 24 hours.

If the person died of a contagious or communicable disease, the Office of the Medical Investigator should be consulted. A sealed casket or embalming may be required, an inappropriate and potentially hazardous requirement.

Medical Schools for Body Donation

Body donation to a medical school is another option for disposition. Find the information for New Mexico at <www.finalrights.org>.

State Governance

The New Mexico Board of Thanatopractice has six members. Three are funeral directors, two are consumer representatives, and one is a direct disposer (the state's unfortunate and insensitive name for simple burial and cremation businesses).

<www.rld.state.nm.us/Thanatopractice/>

Endowed cemeteries must register with and report on their endowment funds to the Director of Financial Institutions.

<www.rld.state.nm.us/FID/index.html>

The Superintendent of Insurance regulates preneed sales.

<www.nmprc.state.nm.us/id.htm>

Prepaid Cemetery and Funeral Funds

25% of cemetery lot sales and 10% of crypt, vault, or niche sales shall be set aside in trust (presumably for endowed care, but the law doesn't say).

Only the "special care" fund for *cemetery* markers must be placed in trust, which essentially means that a cemetery can spend all other income from marker sales and—presumably—declare a memorial "delivered" with a certificate of ownership. Just 10% of vault sales must be placed in trust, which makes the possibility of cancellation and a refund bleak. There is no statutory mention to protect other prepaid cemetery service charges, such as the opening-and-closing fee, often a significant expense.

Funeral directors may not sell funeral prearrangements unless also licensed as insurance agents. Prearranged funerals can be financed with a trust or through insurance. Anything labeled "insurance" usually means that someone is getting a commission. Consequently, there is likely to be fine-print denoting limitations on the policy, such as reduced benefits if death occurred within two years. About the only good thing about funeral insurance is that it can usually be easily transferred, assuming that it is not a policy that is restricted to "approved providers."

Funeral insurance isn't really "insurance" at all. There is no risk for the insurance company such as with fire insurance or auto insurance. If you want a $7,000 funeral, you'll usually pay at least $7,000 to let the insurance company play with your funeral money before you die. Alas, if you decide to opt for a simple cremation and want to cancel the expensive funeral you paid for a few years ago, the cash value on your insurance policy is likely to be only about half of what you paid. Safer to put your funeral money in a pay-on-death account or CD at the bank with a next-of-kin or designated agent on the account.

If your funeral funds go into a trust, the interest is to accrue. This must be a New Mexico bank which most likely sends an annual or quarterly report to the buyer. Even though there is no statutory provision for cancellation or transfer of an irrevocable trust, the trust must be in the name of the buyer, not the funeral home, which leaves the buyer in charge.

The laws are silent about any substitution if selected funeral merchandise is not available at the time of death.

An annual report to the superintendent may be required of all prearranged funeral sellers, but that statute has never been utilized. There is no guarantee fund to protect consumers against embezzlement of prepaid funds.

Consumer Concerns

- The death rate in New Mexico can support approximately 59 full-time mortuaries; there are, however, 75. Funeral prices tend to be higher in areas where there are "too many" funeral homes, although this is a modest number to cover such a large geographic area.

- There is no requirement that—when merchandise is selected as a part of a guaranteed-price, preneed agreement—a clear description be given and that merchandise of equal quality and construction be substituted if the original item selected is not available. Survivors should have the right to approve substitutions.

- Without better preneed laws, it is probably an unwise idea to prepay for a funeral in New Mexico. With no state protection for prepaid cemetery expenses, it is definitely a terrible idea to prepay for these.

- There is no requirement to identify and tag the body at the place of death before removal.

- There is no provision either forbidding a mark-up on cash advance items or requiring the disclosure of how much the mark-up is.

- A casket display of at least 12 caskets "in a range of models and prices" is required, but "range" is not defined to include low-cost caskets. Many funeral homes now prefer to display caskets by computer, as there can be a much greater variety shown.

- Funeral establishments must have a 600-sq.-ft. chapel, totally unnecessary for a business that wants to offer "affordable" low-overhead options.

- There is no mandate for the Board of Thanatopractice to set ethical standards. Such practices need to be clearly defined in order for valid consumer complaints to prevail. (See Appendix.)

- The FTC Funeral Rule has not been adopted in this state.

- A funeral home may hold a body if the bill has not yet been paid. This could incur unnecessary "storage" charges over a weekend, for example, before insurance or social benefits are received. Such tactics should not be permitted, let alone endorsed by state law.

- This state has no laws regulating the body parts business.

Miscellaneous Information

- Educational requirements for funeral director: two years of college (60 semester hours) plus mortuary school, a written exam including state law, a practical exam, and one year of apprenticeship.

- Direct disposers are licensed by the Board of Thanatopractice and do not have to be funeral directors or embalmers. They may not conduct funerals (which seems like an illegitimate, anti-competitive restriction). New Mexico has excellent statutory provisions for this low-cost option for body disposition. However, there have been an increasing number of complaints filed against the existing direct disposers (not by consumers, mind you, but by competitors)—complaints that appear to be frivolous. Consumer vigilance will be necessary to keep this affordable option available in the future.

- Crematories are licensed by the Board of Thanatopractice. They do not need to be operated by a funeral director.

- Medical investigators are licensed physicians and are appointed.

- There is a statutory duty to comply with the written wishes of the decedent. Any adult may authorize his own cremation and disposition of cremated remains. In situations where you are estranged or distant from next-of-kin, you may wish to also indicate a personal representative in your will to act as an agent for body disposition.

- General Assistance will pay $200 toward the burial or cremation of indigents.

- A disinterment permit will be issued to a funeral service practitioner or direct disposer by the state registrar or state medical examiner.

This chapter was sent for review to the Board of Thanatopractice, Superintendent of Insurance, and the Registrar of Vital Records. Helpful information was received from the Insurance Department. Vital Records information was verified over the telephone. No response was received from the Board of Thanatopractice.

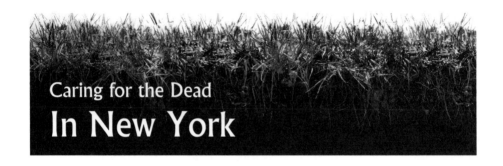

Caring for the Dead

In New York

Please refer also to the general introduction to state chapters: "Caring for the Dead: Necessary Information."

In New York a dead body becomes a hostage of the funeral industry, one of only eight such states that require the use of a funeral director (Connecticut, Illinois, Indiana, Louisiana, Michigan, Nebraska, New Jersey, and New York.). In almost no other situation is a private citizen forced to use a for-profit business to fulfill the interests of the state. Until there is a court challenge or other change in the laws, families and church groups in New York will be limited in caring for their own dead. Some statutes seem contradictory or defy logic; others are restrictive and intrusive.

> *Article 41 Vital Statistics Sec. 4140. Deaths; registration 2. . . . the registrar of the district in which the death occurred shall then issue a burial or removal permit to the funeral director or undertaker.*

Parents may file a birth certificate if no doctor is involved. What's the big deal about a death certificate?

In addition, the Sanitary Code—"Practice of Funeral Directing" states:

> *77.7 (b)(1) In no case shall a dead human body be released from any hospital, institution or other place where the death occurred or from the place where the body is held by legal authority to any person not a duly licensed and registered funeral director or undertaker.*

Later in the same code, however, is found:

> *77.7(f) Nothing contained in this section shall be deemed to require that a mere transporter, to whom or to which a dead human body has been duly released for the sole purpose of transportation or transfer, shall be a duly licensed and registered funeral director or undertaker.*

So the State has determined that there is no health problem with someone other than a funeral director transporting bodies. What, then, is the rationale that would require a licensee to pick up the accompanying paperwork and add his/her signature? The doctor fills out the medical portion; the family supplies the personal data. But the undertaker's signature might cost the family a nondeclinable basic service fee of maybe $2,000. Just for a signature!

But back to the statutes in 77.7 to see more promotions of the industry:

> *(a)(2) A licensed funeral director or undertaker shall be present and personally supervise the conduct of each funeral service.*
>
> *(a)(3) Nothing herein shall be construed as prohibiting religious supervision of the funeral service by a member or members of the clergy designated by the family of the deceased person.*

What about the Orthodox Jewish groups such as the Chevra Kadisha or the Muslims or Amish who wish to bathe and shroud their dead? They aren't "clergy." It takes a stunning amount of arrogance to write a law—we're certain it was penned by industry—noting that clergy are not prohibited from supervising funerals. There will, of course, be an attending charge for the funeral director's services, regardless of whether or not the presence of a funeral director is wanted.

Apparently, New York funeral directors—with a mere two years of mortuary school (that most likely did not include any training on religious funeral rituals and services other than some cursory Christian components)—have now become pseudo-clergy, usurping a role that traditionally was religious in nature. From an e-mail to Carlson: "I am a Catholic priest. About three years ago, while still a seminarian, I was doing a feature story on the most prominent mortician in the diocese, a Catholic active in just about everything. In the interview, I asked him if the curriculum at mortuary school included courses about religious practices. I was floored when he said 'No'."

And an undertaker can keep the meter running with another statute:

> *77.7(a)(4) A licensed funeral director or undertaker shall be present and personally supervise the interment or cremation . . . .*

The undertaker, though not needed to transport the body, must be at a crematory when that method of disposition has been chosen. Rather strange. Crematory operation is not included in most mortuary curricula or even mentioned in the study guide for the national exam for funeral directors. What kind of supervision is the undertaker qualified to do at the crematory?

If you are planning home burial as permitted in New York, you'll have to pay a funeral director to hang around under the apple tree. A Bruderhof Christian community in New York handles all aspects of the funeral for a member—the preparation and bathing of the body, as well as conducting the service and burial. "Oh, yes, the funeral director comes out and spends the day with us, has lunch with us, and sort of hangs around," one member told Carlson, but she had no idea what the charge was, if any.

A movement is afoot to get the limiting statutes changed—through legislation or court action. In a 1909 federal case, *Wyeth v. Cambridge Board of Health,* the court ruled:

> . . . the refusal to permit one to bury the dead body of his relative or friend, except under an unreasonable limitation, is also an interference with a private right that is not allowable under the Constitution of the Commonwealth or the Constitution of the United States.

Death Certificate

New York State is not yet using electronic death registration although New York City is. The doctor last in attendance, county coroner, or medical examiner will supply and sign the death certificate, stating the cause of death. The remaining information must be supplied, typewritten or in black ink. The death certificate must be filed with the local registrar within 72 hours and before final disposition.

Fetal Death

A fetal death report is required for each fetal death and must be filed as above. If there is no family physician involved, the local medical examiner must sign the fetal death certificate. If gestation is more than 20 weeks, a disposition permit and the involvement of a funeral director will be needed.

Transporting and Disposition Permit

The local registrar will issue the burial and removal permit to a licensed funeral director only (until the statute has been successfully challenged). New York City charges $40. This authorization must be obtained within 72 hours of death and prior to final disposition. Once this permit has been obtained, a family may handle the moving of a body, although you will need a mortician at the other end to oversee disposition if burial or cremation will occur in New York. Make sure that the undertaker you initially use will be willing to relinquish custody, however; more than one family has had difficulty when the undertaker did not understand the law. During transportation, the body must be obscured from public view.

Burial

Any person may dedicate land to be used as a family cemetery provided that it is less than three acres and not closer than 100 rods (1,650 feet) to a dwelling. Such land must be registered with the county clerk. Check with the county or town for local zoning laws regarding home burial. There are no state burial statutes or regulations with regard to depth. A sensible guideline is 250 feet from a water supply and at least two feet of earth on top. (Two towns do have the 250-foot distance from a water supply written into law.)

When a person is buried in a cemetery or other burial place where no person is in charge, the undertaker will sign the permit and write across the face of the permit, "No person in charge." The permit must be filed within three days with the registrar of the district in which burial took place.

Cremation

No additional permit is needed for cremation. Authorization by next-of-kin or designated agent is required, and a pacemaker must be removed. One may not be cremated with a radioactive implant or battery. The crematory will file the disposition permit with the local registrar. If there is no licensed funeral director on the crematory staff, the family must arrange for a funeral director to be present at the time of delivery, a totally unnecessary and burdensome requirement. There are no laws regarding the disposition of cremated remains. You may do as you wish.

Other Requirements

New York has no embalming requirements. A body must be buried or cremated within a "reasonable time after death." Weather and reasonable planning should be considered.

If the person died of a contagious disease, the doctor in attendance should be consulted.

Medical Schools for Body Donation

Body donation to a medical school is another option for disposition. Find the information for New York at <www.finalrights.org>.

State Governance

The Funeral Directing Advisory Board, under the Department of Health, has ten members. There are three consumer representatives, one cemetery operator, and six undertakers.

The Bureau of Funeral Directing has two helpful web pages on preneed and funeral planning as well as the form for naming an agent for disposition of remains:

<www.nyhealth.gov/professionals/patients/patient_rights/>

Cemeteries are governed by the Cemetery Board and the Division of Cemeteries. The board is made up of the Secretary of State, the Attorney General, and the Commissioner of Health or their designees. There is also a citizens advisory council composed of a member designated by the secretary of state, a member designated by the attorney general, a member designated by the commissioner of health, a member designated by the comptroller and a member designated by the commissioner of taxation and finance.

Cemetery Customer's Bill of Rights

The Cemetery Board has been working with FCA of Long Island to establish a Bill of Rights for consumers making cemetery purchases. The current draft, as of this writing, could serve as a model for other states as well:

All New York Cemeteries are not-for-profit. This cemetery (name, address, telephone) is regulated by the NYS Division of Cemeteries. The nearest office is located at: (address, telephone number, e-mail address).

When you buy cemetery property, you are buying the right to interment, not an actual piece of land. When you sell cemetery property, it must first be offered back to the cemetery. The minimum price the cemetery must pay to buy back the property is set by law. You can also give your right to interment if you are the lot owner.

You can be denied the right to interment only for non-payment of the total purchase price, non-payment of interment price or non-payment of a tax authorized by the Cemetery Board.

Though New York law DOES require that a container or wrappings used for cremation be non-metal, it does NOT require embalming for interment (burial, entombment or placement of cremains in a niche or grave). New York law does NOT limit the number of cremation urns that can be placed in a grave. New York law also does NOT require any particular type of casket or external wrappings for burial or placement in a mausoleum crypt. Nor does it restrict the type of container used to place ashes in a niche or grave.

New York law requires that rules and regulations of a cemetery be reasonable and that they have written Cemetery Board approval. [Any restrictions by the cemetery must be disclosed to the consumer prior to any sale.]

<http://www.dos.state.ny.us/cmty/cemetery.html>

Crematories are regulated by the Cemetery Board. One does not need to be a funeral director to run a crematory, but a funeral director must be present for cremation. Why?

Prior to 1998, a few funeral homes were permitted by the Cemetery Board to construct what are supposed to be not-for-profit crematories. That practice is no longer allowed.

Prepaid Cemetery and Funeral Funds

Cemeteries must be run not-for-profit and may not have any business ties with a funeral home. In the 1990s, both Service Corporation International (SCI) and Loewen (a now bankrupt chain bought up later by SCI) tried to get into the cemetery business in New York by purchasing cemetery mortgage certificates for which they have paid wildly-inflated sums compared to the face value. The Cemetery Board found that financial practices at these cemeteries had not always stayed within the law. Thanks to tight regulations and vigilant oversight, those practices were quickly corrected, and the corporations were finally booted out.

If a lot-owner wishes to sell a lot, it must first be offered back to the cemetery at the original sale price plus 4% per year.

Cemeteries may not sell monuments or vaults; they may sell grave-liners. If there is a religious objection to the use of a liner or vault, the cemetery may not require one but it may impose a "reasonable" maintenance fee for refilling a settling grave. The cemetery's schedule of fees must be approved by the Cemetery Board. Cemeteries must be available for interments six days a week and must now perform burials in winter according to state law. Cemeteries may charge you the actual costs of snow removal or penetration of frozen ground.

100% of all prepaid *funeral and cemetery* purchases must be placed in trust, with the interest to accrue. The purchaser must be notified within 30 days of the institution where the funds have been deposited.

The seller must report annually to the purchaser where the funds are held, along with the current total. Administrative fees may not exceed .75 of 1%. Although there is no guarantee fund to protect funeral consumers against default, the annual reporting should go far in enforcing the trusting requirement.

Prepaid funds are considered the property of the purchaser and may be withdrawn at any time for a full refund if it is a revocable contract. An irrevocable agreement may be transferred. The only time when the contract can be made irrevocable is for Medicaid eligibility.

If a funeral home changes ownership, the owner of a preneed agreement must be notified. With the mad scramble of chains to purchase funeral homes, it would be interesting to see if they are obliging. The Bureau of Funeral Directing should be able to tell you who owns the one where you prepaid for your funeral: 518-402-0785. Be sure to file a complaint if you were not notified.

A preneed contract must specify whether or not it is a guaranteed-price agreement. It must "fully describe" the services and merchandise selected, but there is no clear provision for how detailed that should be. There might be a $1,000 difference between the least expensive "20-gauge steel" and the highest. There is no statutory directive for substitution when selected merchandise is no longer available. If it is not a guaranteed-price arrangement excess funds must be returned to the estate or the purchaser.

A funeral home may not sell or be the beneficiary of funeral insurance. However, some funeral homes may ask you to sign over such a policy to cover the deceased's funeral expenses at a time of need. It's better not to let the funeral home even know how much the policy is worth. Otherwise, if there is a surplus of funds, you may not get a refund. The cost of the funeral has a strange way of rising to the amount of insurance available. Get the bill from the funeral home and then have the insurance company mail any check to you so you can pay the funeral bill from that.

Consumer Concerns

- The death rate in New York can support approximately 629 full-time mortuaries; there are, however, 1,850. Funeral prices tend to be higher in areas where there are "too many" funeral homes.

- Until the laws are changed, families and church groups may not care for their own dead without the use of a funeral director.

- There is no provision for an adequate description of funeral goods selected on a guaranteed-price agreement nor for a substitution of equal quality if the selected item is no longer available at the time of death. Substitutions should meet the approval of survivors.

- There is no requirement that low-cost caskets be included in any display.

- The format for pricing is in conflict with FTC requirements. New York requires a separate charge for *supervision* and another for *facilities* for viewing, for example. The FTC requires a single fee— *facilities and staff for viewing.* Consequently, many funeral homes list prices both ways in order to be in compliance with both state and federal requirements. This clutters the General Price List (GPL) and is definitely confusing to consumers. New York may *certainly* require that additional options be offered on the price list—as does Vermont—but the standard pricing format of the FTC should be adopted.

- The New York GPLs are now required to include a statement, "The direct cremation prices do not include the crematory charge," probably because most crematories are on the grounds of cemeteries and are not owned by funeral homes. This should be changed to require the inclusion of the crematory fee. How can you have a "direct cremation" without cremation? Who would think to ask if it were extra? For someone shopping over the phone, the disclosure will never be seen. If a funeral home uses more than one area crematory, and prices differ from one to the next, an appropriate disclosure would be, "There will be an additional $50 charge if the crematory at Mt. Such-and-Such is used."

- There is no requirement to identify and tag the body at the place of death before removal.

- Complaint procedures are unclear and inadequate.

- New York has some excellent laws for governing the body parts business but is not enforcing them for lack of staff and money. Companies are not being asked for prices or financial statements. A form for informed consent has not been developed.

- A New York State legislator helped defeat a 2008 bill that would have made alkaline hydrolysis—dissolving the body in an alkaline solution—a legal option for final disposition by branding it the "Hannibal Lecter Bill," a reference to the serial killer from the popular book and movie, *The Silence of the Lambs.* Alkaline hydrolysis is touted as a more environmentally friendly option than cremation, as it produces no gaseous emissions. This kind of irrational sensationalism is just a modern re-enactment of the hysterical protests and legal bans that occurred when cremation was first introduced in the US in the 1870s.

Miscellaneous Information

- Educational requirements for becoming a funeral director or embalmer: mortuary college (60 semester credits) and one year of apprenticeship plus an exam on state laws.

- The law states, "Upon receipt of satisfactory evidence that a license or certificate has been lost, mutilated or destroyed, the department may issue a duplicate license. . . ." How does one prove something is lost?

- Cash advance items must be billed at the actual cost to the funeral director.

- Misconduct in funeral directing is defined in a fairly comprehensive listing, although additional factors will be found in the Appendix of this book.

- It is a misdemeanor to hold a body for debt.

- Although the Funeral Rule was not adopted by reference, statutes include almost identical requirements.

- Medical examiners are physicians who are appointed. Coroners are elected.

- You may name an agent for body disposition, helpful if you are estranged from next-of-kin.

- A disinterment permit must be obtained from the local registrar.

This chapter was sent for review to the New York Division of Cemeteries and the Bureau of Funeral Directing. Both provided helpful corrections or information.

Caring for the Dead
In North Carolina

Please refer also to the general introduction to state chapters: "Caring for the Dead: Necessary Information."

Persons in North Carolina may care for their own dead. The legal authority to do so is found in:

> *Title 130A-420. Authority to dispose of body or body parts. (b) If a decedent has left no written authorization for the disposal of the decedent's body as permitted under subsection (a) of this section, the following competent persons in the order listed may authorize the type, method, place, and disposition of the decedent's body:*
>
> *(1) The surviving spouse.*
> *(2) A majority of surviving children.*
> *(3) The surviving parents . . . .*

There are no other statutes that might require you to use a funeral director.

Death Certificate

A Notification of Death must be obtained from the local registrar and completed within 24 hours. The registrar will keep one copy; you keep the other.

Within three days, the family doctor or a local medical examiner will supply and sign the death certificate, stating the cause of death. The remaining information must be supplied, typewritten or in black ink. The death certificate must be filed with the local registrar in the county health department within five days and before final disposition.

North Carolina has not yet implemented electronic death registration. A paper alternative should be available when that happens.

Fetal Death

A fetal death report is required when death occurs after 20 weeks of gestation and must be filed as above. If there is no family physician involved, the local medical examiner must sign the fetal death certificate.

Transporting and Disposition Permit

The physician or local medical examiner will authorize disposition. A burial-transit permit is required only if the death is under the jurisdiction of the medical examiner or if the body is to be removed from the state. It is the third copy of the medical examiner's death certificate. In other cases, the burial-transit permit may be obtained from the local registrar at no cost.

Burial

There are no state statutes that specifically permit or prohibit home burial. It is also unlikely that there are local zoning regulations regarding home burial, but you should review them or check with the county health department. If your land is in a rural area, draw a map of the property showing where the burial ground will be. If you get the county's approval, have that filed with the deed. A cemetery must be 300 feet from a public water supply. Plan your family cemetery away from power lines and boundaries with neighbors, too. There must be 18 inches of earth on top of the casket.

Cremation

A permit from the medical examiner is required before cremation (or burial at sea) unless the death was attended by a physician or hospice staff and is considered a natural death. The fee for this may not exceed $50. There is a 24-hour waiting period prior to cremation that may be waived in case of death from an infectious disease. A pacemaker must be removed. Unless you have authorized your own cremation prior to death, authorization by next-of-kin will be required. The Board of Funeral Service has generated a form for authorization: <www.ncbfs.org/1CRemReqAuth.pdf>.

Families and authorized agents may witness a cremation. There are no laws regarding the disposition of cremated remains. You may do as you wish.

Other Requirements

North Carolina has no embalming requirements. Weather and reasonable planning should be considered.

If the person died of a contagious disease, the doctor or medical examiner should be consulted. In that situation, the body must be encased in a sealed casket. If the death was due to smallpox, plague or acute respiratory disease, the body may not be embalmed.

Medical Schools for Body Donation

Body donation to a medical school is another option for disposition. Find the information for North Carolina at <www.finalrights.org>.

State Governance

The North Carolina Board of Funeral Service has nine members. Three are consumer representatives (including one from FCA) and six are morticians.

In March of 2007, a family added to an obituary, "Funeral Consumers Alliance of Central Carolinas has assisted the family," in gratitude for the educational information this nonprofit organization provides through its volunteers. Responding to that, the lawyer for the Funeral Board sent a certified letter to Mary Brack, president of FCACC, stating: "North Carolina law provides clear criminal liability for anyone who practices funeral directing without a license. . . . Any further instance of this conduct could be referred to the local district attorney for criminal prosecution. . . ." But Mrs. Brack had nothing to do with writing the obituary. After several letters from Slocum and a lawyer at the Institute for Justice to both the executive director and the board counsel, Mrs. Brack has yet to receive an apology.

A Crematory Authority functions as a committee of the board and recommends rules for running crematories. It has five members, two of which are Board members. The other three are elected by licensed crematory operators. One does not need to be a funeral director to run a crematory.

The Board of Funeral Service also licenses body transporters. One does not need to be a funeral director to transport bodies for a fee.

<http://www.ncbfs.org/>

Cemeteries are regulated by the North Carolina Cemetery Commission. It has nine members, two of which are public members. Unlike the Funeral Board, you won't find much information on their website, which is at: <http://www.nccemetery.com/>.

Prepaid Cemetery and Funeral Funds

Only 60% of *cemetery* services and goods must be placed in trust. A performance bond can avoid the trusting requirement. "Constructive delivery" can also bypass the trusting requirement. "Delivery" usually is accomplished by issuing a certificate of ownership and warehousing the vault and/or marker. Once "delivered," it is almost impossible to get a refund even if the items have never been used. Actually, a purchaser has only 30 days in which to cancel a contract. The law is a little vague as to exactly how much one would get back then, what's in trust being only 60% if none of the merchandise has been "delivered." If the purchaser defaults on payments, the seller may cancel the contract and refund the 60% in trust—less anything "delivered." Interest on installment payments is limited to the interest earned in the trust.

Interest on the cemetery trust account may be withdrawn by the seller.

An annual report of the perpetual care fund must be made to the cemetery commission.

Only 90% of prepaid funeral funds must be placed in trust, which must be stated on the contract. The purchaser should also expect to get, within 30 days, a confirmation that the preneed contract has been filed with the state, and a notice to that effect must appear on the preneed contract. Sellers must send annually to the board a report of their preneed accounts. If funded by insurance, 100% of what the consumer pays must be sent to the insurance company, but it's the buyer's choice—trust or insurance.

Funeral insurance isn't "insurance" at all, and it may be a very bad deal. There is usually no risk for the insurance company such as with fire insurance or auto insurance. If you want a $7,000 funeral, you'll almost always pay $7,000 to let the insurance company play with your funeral money before you die. And if you're paying over time, it may cost you twice as much.

With the buyer's permission, the preneed seller may withdraw trust funds and purchase insurance. Be sure to say "no" to this deal, as the seller already took 10% of your money before it went into trust and may just be looking for a commission on top of that. More worrisome, if you changed your mind from body burial to cremation and didn't want an expensive funeral, you might get back only half of what you paid in if you tried to cancel the policy.

A preneed contract may be modified with the "mutual consent" of the licensee and the buyer or a representative. What if the mortician didn't want to see the services reduced?

A consumer may cancel a preneed contract and get a refund—less the permitted 10% that can be retained. Irrevocable preneed funeral contracts may be transferred, with only the 90% in trust available for transfer.

Unless the contract was made at a guaranteed price, excess funds at the time of death are to be returned to the estate. With a 10% commission permitted, and funeral inflation exceeding most bank interest, this is an unlikely event.

A Preneed Recovery Fund is fed by $2 of the $18 fee collected for each preneed contract. This will be used to reimburse consumers in the event of a preneed supplier in default.

Consumer Concerns

- The death rate in North Carolina can support approximately 294 full-time mortuaries; there are, however, 750 such establishments. Funeral prices tend to be higher in areas where there are "too many" funeral homes.

- Finance charges are permitted for installment purchases of prepaid cemetery services and merchandise. This is outrageous and should be repealed. When you finance a car or house, you get to use either. But a finance charge on a lay-away plan before they lay you away?

- There is no annual reporting requirement to the purchaser of prepaid funeral goods and services, paperwork that might be useful to the family of a deceased to indicate prepayment and which would help to "enforce" trusting requirements.

- There is no provision for an adequate description of funeral goods selected preneed nor a requirement for the substitution—approved by survivors—of equal quality and construction if the selected item is no longer available at the time of death.

- Irrevocable preneed arrangements may not be altered. A provision should be added, "provided that the deceased left sufficient financing to carry out the stated wishes."

- "Constructive delivery" (warehousing) can avoid trusting requirements and should not be permitted.

- Until the laws are changed to require 100% trusting of all money and interest for prepaid funeral and cemetery goods and services, it is probably a *terrible* idea to prepay for these arrangements in North Carolina. Your own trust account in a bank will be safer.

- There is no provision either forbidding a mark-up on cash advance items or requiring the disclosure of the amount of the mark-up. Consumers may wish to ask for a copy of the invoice for such items.

- North Carolina appears to still permit casket-price bundling, with all costs presented as one and attached to the casket. This would be in violation of the FTC Funeral Rule, which permits only the non-declinable "basic" fee to be so included, along with a disclosure that must use specific wording.

- There is no requirement to include low-cost caskets in any display.

- The 24-hour wait before cremation is unnecessary when survivors are in agreement and may be causing additional charges to families for "storage."

- The coroner or medical examiner's permit for cremation in the case of an *anticipated* death from natural causes is unnecessary and creates an additional burden and charge for families.

- There appear to be no ethical standards for funeral directors. They should be adopted and unethical conduct clearly defined in order for valid consumer complaints to prevail. (See Appendix.)
- This state has minimal laws regulating the body parts business.

Miscellaneous Information

- Educational requirements for becoming a funeral director or an embalmer: mortuary college (1 year), one year of apprenticeship, plus a state and the appropriate portion of the National Board Exam. A funeral service practitioner (which covers directing and embalming) requires two years of mortuary college, plus apprenticeship and exams. Alas, practitioners and consumer advocates alike have deemed the National Board Exam out-dated and irrelevant.

- A crematory operator's license may be revoked if guilty of "using profane, indecent or obscene language in the presence of a dead human body, and within the immediate hearing of the family or relatives of a deceased, whose body has not yet been cremated or otherwise disposed of." After that watch out?

- Medical examiners are physicians who are appointed, not elected.

- Complying with the FTC Funeral Rule is required by statute.

- Preference is given to the expressed wishes of the deceased in a pre-need contract. Or you may name a designated death-care agent for your final arrangements. In situations where you are estranged or distant from next-of-kin, this could be important.

- A funeral home facility may not be used for harvesting bone and tissue.

- A disinterment permit is issued by the local registrar.

This chapter was sent for review to the North Carolina Board of Funeral Service, the Cemetery Commission, and the Department of Health. Helpful corrections were made by the Cemetery Commission, and the executive director for the Funeral Board answered questions. No response was received from the Health Department.

In North Dakota

Caring for the Dead

Please refer also to the general introduction to state chapters: "Caring for the Dead: Necessary Information."

Persons in North Dakota may care for their own dead. The legal authority to do so is found in the Health Code:

> *Title 23-06-02. Who is entitled to custody of body. The person charged with the duty of burying the body of a deceased person is entitled to the custody of such body for the purpose of burying it.*

> *Title 23-06-03. Duty of burial. The duty of burying the body of a deceased person devolves upon the following persons: 1. . . . upon the surviving husband or wife. 2. If the deceased was not married but left kindred, upon the person or persons in the same degree, of adult age, nearest of kin to the deceased living within the state . . . .*

Death Certificate

North Dakota has used electronic death registration—EDR—since 2008. A paper worksheet can be obtained from the state department of Vital Records for families managing a home funeral. After filling in the demographic information, a staffer in the Vital Records office will enter it into the system. Most doctors and coroners are already on the system and will fill out the cause of death portion electronically.

Fetal Death

A fetal death report is required when death occurs after 20 weeks of gestation. If there is no family physician involved, the county coroner must sign the fetal death certificate.

Transporting and Disposition Permit

The state EDR system will generate a burial transit permit. It must be filed with the county recorder in the county of disposition.

Burial

It is unlikely that family burial grounds are mentioned in local zoning laws, but you should check. Burial must be in a "properly registered cemetery or in some other place requested by the relatives and friends of the deceased if the same is authorized by the state department of health."You will need to hire a licensed surveyor to map out the cemetery area on your property. That plat will need to be recorded with the county before registering your family cemetery with the state. A good practice is 150 feet from a water supply and 25 feet from a power line or neighbor's boundary. The top of the casket must be 3½ feet below the natural surface of the earth if there is no vault.

When burial is arranged, the family member acting as the funeral director must sign the burial-transit permit and file it with the county recorder in the county of disposition within 10 days.

Cremation

No additional permit is needed for cremation. Most crematories insist that a pacemaker be removed, and authorization by next-of-kin or an agent of the deceased is required. A disposition plan for the cremated remains must be indicated, but there are no restrictions on what that may be. The crematory will sign the burial-transit permit, which must be filed with the county recorder in that district within 10 days. There are no laws regarding the disposition of cremated remains. You may do as you wish.

Other Requirements

Disposition must be made within eight days. By law, a body must be embalmed if it will not reach its destination within 24 hours or if disposition is not accomplished within 48 hours, an unfortunate requirement when refrigeration is a more sensible alternative, especially when there is a religious objection. Families who wish to perform a home funeral should remember there are no embalming police with a stopwatch going door to door to check. If preservation is a concern, a cold room, dry ice, or frozen gelpacks do a good job. When death is due to viral hepatitis, TB, AIDS, plague, Creutzfeldt-Jakob, rabies, or meningitis, the body must be tagged: "Blood and body fluids precautions should be observed." The Centers for Disease Control, however, recommend such precautions for all deaths.

If death is due to anthrax, small pox, cholera, plague, TB, meningococcus, or meningitis, the body must be embalmed, the worst possible circumstances under which to embalm. Delaware, Hawaii, North Carolina, and Ontario forbid embalming under this conditions. Montana and Ohio require immediate disposition.

Medical Schools for Body Donation

Body donation to a medical school is another option for disposition. Find the information for North Dakota at <www.finalrights.org>.

State Governance

The North Dakota State Board of Funeral Service has three members plus the state health officer. There are no consumer representatives.

<http://www.nd.gov/funeral/>

Crematories are licensed by the Board of Funeral Service but there is no representation on the Funeral Board. One does not need to be a funeral director to run a crematory. A crematory used for human remains may not be used to cremate animals or pets.

The state Department of Health regulates cemeteries.

<http://www.ndhealth.gov/DoH/contact.htm>

The Securities Commissioner regulates preneed funeral sales.

<http://www.ndsecurities.com/department-info/default.asp>

Prepaid Cemetery and Funeral Funds

A cemetery lot unused for 60 years may be reclaimed by the cemetery if the owner cannot be located or expresses no interest in retaining ownership.

20% of the cost of a lot, mausoleum, or niche space must be put into the perpetual care fund. Not all cemeteries are perpetual care cemeteries and, if not, must so note on signs and paperwork.

50% of *cemetery merchandise* must be placed in trust. There is no trusting requirement for cemetery services such as the opening-and-closing charge. "Constructive delivery" can bypass the trust requirement. That means you will be given title to the merchandise, and it will be placed in a warehouse marked as yours. Few states are checking to see if it is actually there. If you were to change your mind and want a refund, forget it—your money has already been spent. Even if it hasn't, all you'll get back is 50%.

100% of prepaid funeral expenses must be placed in trust. However, trusting can be avoided with "constructive delivery" of funeral merchandise, too. A person may request in writing a refund or transfer of any preneed account. If the casket is in "storage," the refund will be reduced accordingly.

The preneed seller must report all preneed sales annually to the Securities Commissioner. Within 90 days, the commissioner will verify the deposits.

A preneed seller must carry a bond in an amount deemed "adequate" by the commissioner. Because the cost of bonding in the full amount of preneed accounts being carried is quite expensive, there is motivation to avoid reporting all preneed sales.

Consumer Concerns

- The death rate in North Dakota can support approximately 24 full-time mortuaries; there are 100 such establishments. However, given the low density of population over a vast geographic area, mortuary careers are not likely to be full-time work. Unfortunately, because of the low volume of business per mortuary, funeral prices will tend to be higher than elsewhere.

- Trusting requirements for cemetery merchandise and services are inadequate and should be raised to 100% with right to full refund.

- Constructive delivery of cemetery merchandise avoids the trusting requirement and should be repealed.

- There is no provision for an adequate description of funeral goods selected on a guaranteed-price preneed contract nor for a substitution of equal quality and construction if the selected item is no longer available at the time of death. Any substitution should be with the approval of survivors.

- There is no annual reporting requirement to the purchaser of prepaid funeral goods and services, paperwork that might be useful to the family of a deceased to indicate prepayment and which would help to "enforce" trusting requirements. Consumers have lost money even in other states requiring 100% trusting.

- There is no guarantee fund to protect consumers against default of preneed cemetery and funeral purchases.

- Until better trusting is required and other loopholes are closed, it is probably a terrible idea to prepay for a funeral in North Dakota.

- There is no requirement to identify and tag the body at the place of death before removal.

- Requiring embalming when death occurs from a communicable disease is not only an offense to some religious groups, it puts the funeral professionals at risk.

- The time requirements for disposition without embalming are unnecessarily restrictive and pose an unreasonable burden on those who find this procedure repugnant.

- There is no requirement that low-cost caskets be included in any display.
- There is no provision either forbidding a mark-up on cash advance items or requiring disclosure of how much the mark-up would be.
- The standards for ethical, professional conduct are weak and should be strengthened. That would make it easier for a consumer to prevail when filing a valid complaint.
- Complaint procedures are unclear and inadequate. License revocation is the only penalty; there is no provision for a fine.
- There is no law that allows you to state your funeral preferences or for naming a designated agent to make your final arrangements. In situations where you are estranged or distant from next-of-kin, this could be important.
- This state has no laws regulating the body parts business.

Miscellaneous Information

- Educational requirements for becoming a funeral director or embalmer: two years of college, mortuary school, one year of apprenticeship, and an exam that may include the National Board Exam. Alas, practitioners and consumer advocates alike have deemed this exam irrelevant and out-of-date.
- A funeral home may not be located on tax-exempt property.
- The 1984 FTC Funeral Rule has been adopted by reference.
- It is a misdemeanor to hold a body for debt.
- The county social services department will provide up to $1,500 for burial expenses for those with insufficient means.
- A disinterment permit must be obtained from the state registrar.

This chapter was sent for review to the Securities Commissioner, the North Dakota State Board of Funeral Service, and to the North Dakota Department of Health. No response was received from the first two. Surprisingly, the staffer in the Health Department thought we shouldn't mention the 150 feet away from water in the burial section because that's not in the law. Be so advised.

Caring for the Dead
In Ohio

Please refer also to the general introduction to state chapters: "Caring for the Dead: Necessary Information."

Persons and religious groups in Ohio may care for their own dead. The legal authority to do so is found in:

> *RC 3705.16—Registration of death with local registrar; certificate of death. Each death which occurs in Ohio shall be registered with the local registrar of vital statistics of the district in which the death occurred by the funeral director or other person in charge of interment or cremation of the remains.*

> *RC 4717.12—Exceptions to provisions [for licensing] . . . (B) This chapter does not prevent or interfere with any of the following:*

> *(1) The ceremonies, customs, religious rights, or religion of any people, denomination, or sect;*

> *(2) Any religious denomination or sect, or any body composed of members of a denomination;*

> *(3) Any church or synagogue committee in preparing dead human bodies for burial;*

> *(4) The conducting of funerals and the burial of dead human bodies in accordance with the ceremonies or rights described in division (B) of this section without the use, employment, or supervision of a licensed embalmer or funeral director, except when the body is that of a person whose death was caused by a virulent communicable disease, in which case the rules of the department of health or board of health having territorial jurisdiction shall apply.*

There are no other statutes that might require you to use a funeral director.

Death Certificate

Ohio has been using electronic death registration (EDR) since 2007. All funeral directors and coroners are on the system, and some doctors and hospitals in large cities are, too.

No one in the vital records office in Columbus was willing to talk to Carlson about how families could record a death without a funeral director, so she started calling local registrars in the county health departments. One told Carlson she could print off a data form for the family to fill out before getting the medical input. When Carlson checked with a county office in another part of the state, the local registrar had no idea how to print out that form or which form to print, saying she'd have to call the help desk in Columbus (the same number where a woman told Carlson she couldn't talk to "the media").

Frustrated by the difficulty in getting accurate information, Carlson sent e-mails to various other Department of Health people including the director. She finally got a call from someone at the help desk for EDR who was marginally helpful, followed by another call from an administrator who had a somewhat better grasp of the issues. The local registrar would indeed print off a three-page data form found on the EDR support site, <http://vitalsupport.odh.ohio.gov/gd/gd.aspx>. Actually, a family may print this off ahead of time, too. The form includes both demographic information and medical confirmation that a death has occurred including a place for the doctor's signature and license number.

Once that is filled out, the form must be faxed by the registrar to the state for entry into the system which, Carlson was assured, would be "the same day." The local registrar would then be notified by fax when the information is accepted and a blank death certificate can be printed out, allowing the doctor to sign the actual "certificate," not just a form. This can happen only on a weekday during business hours. Do-it-yourselfers will be well-advised to walk through this procedure *way* ahead of time. We are wondering how long it will take the Ohio medical profession to get the law changed so that an actual quill-and-ink signature is no longer required.

Families caring for their own dead may find working with a coroner or funeral director helpful or necessary to deal with this awkward process. County coroners are listed here:

<www.osca.net/ohio_coroners.php>

When funeral directors or coroners enter the demographic information into the system, they don't have to wait for it to be "accepted." The death certificate can be printed off right away and given to the doctor to fill in and sign.

It's hard to understand why local registrars are not also allowed to do this as they are in other states.

Fetal Death

A fetal death certificate is required when gestation is 20 weeks or more.

Transporting and Disposition Permit

The local health department or sub-registrar will issue the burial permit once the death certificate has been generated. The charge for this is $3.00. This permit must be filed with the registrar in the district of disposition. (Some funeral directors may serve as sub-registrars.)

When a body is brought into the state, a certificate of service must be filed with the local registrar after disposition.

Burial

There are no state statutes that specifically permit or prohibit home burial. It is also unlikely that there are local zoning regulations regarding home burial, but you should review them before planning a family cemetery. If your land is in a rural area, draw a map of the property showing where the burial ground will be and have it filed with the deed. That may be all you have to do to establish your family cemetery. There are no state burial statutes or regulations with regard to burial locations or depth. A sensible guideline is 150 feet from a water supply, 25 feet from a power line, with two or three feet of earth on top. Plan your family cemetery away from boundaries with neighbors, too.

When burial is arranged, the family member acting as the funeral director must sign the burial-transit permit and file it with the registrar where the disposition takes place.

Cremation

The local health department issues the cremation permit. There is a 24-hour wait prior to cremation. Authorization by next-of-kin or your designated agent is required, and a pacemaker must be removed. The crematory may offer to file the permit with the health department.

A person may authorize his/her own cremation. The form must indicate the final disposition of the cremated remains, but there is no restriction on what that may be. The wishes of a spouse or other next-of-kin may over-ride such authorization if you have not otherwise named a designated agent for disposition.

There are no laws regarding the disposition of cremated remains. You may do as you wish.

Other Requirements

Ohio has no embalming requirements. Weather and reasonable planning should be considered.

The body of a person who has died from a communicable disease must be buried or cremated within 24 hours.

Medical Schools for Body Donation

Body donation to a medical school is another option for disposition. Find the information for Ohio at <www.finalrights.org>.

State Governance

The Board of Embalmers and Funeral Directors has seven members. Two are consumer representatives, at least one of whom must be at least 60 years old. Of the five funeral directors, one must be knowledgeable about crematories.

Although crematories are licensed by the Funeral Board, one does not have to be a funeral director to run one, and many are found on cemetery grounds. A separate Crematory Review Board adjudicates complaints. Three of the board are members of the Funeral Board and three are nominated from the Cemetery Dispute Committee. A seventh member to the committee must have no affiliation with a cemetery or funeral home.

The Ohio Cemetery Dispute Resolution Commission, under the Real Estate and Professional Licensing Division of Commerce, regulates cemeteries. There are nine members, two of whom represent the public. It has a helpful brochure for consumers. Most Ohio cemeteries are municipal or religious ones.

<www.com.ohio.gov/real/CeMain.aspx>

Prepaid Cemetery and Funeral Funds

Seventy per cent of *cemetery services* must go into trust. For *cemetery merchandise*, 110% of cost or 30% of retail—whichever is greater—must be placed into trust. "Constructive delivery" (warehousing) can bypass trusting requirements. If you wish to cancel this purchase after the first week, your refund will be 60% of whatever you paid, plus 80% of the interest, less the cost of any merchandise that has been delivered to a warehouse.

Many cemeteries are making their contracts irrevocable, but the cemetery must get your signature giving up your right to revoke the contract. You probably should not agree to do so unless qualifying for Medicaid.

100% of prepaid *funeral* goods and services must be placed into trust with interest to accrue. If you do want to cancel your preneed arrangement, how much you get will depend: Was it a guaranteed-price arrangement? If so, you'll get back only 90% of the principal. Otherwise, you'll get back all you paid plus interest.

You may transfer an irrevocable preneed plan.

If the casket you picked out is not available, the funeral director may substitute one of equal "quality, value and workmanship." The word "value" is a problem without a clear description. A $900 casket ten years ago was a pretty nice casket. Today it might be bottom-of-the-line.

Consumer Concerns

- The death rate in Ohio can support approximately 439 full-time mortuaries; there are, however, 1,132. Funeral prices tend to be higher in areas where there are "too many" funeral homes.

- Cemetery trusting requirements are inadequate. All purchase money for burial vaults should be placed in trust, with provision for cancellation and refund; "constructive delivery" should be forbidden.

- There is no annual reporting requirement to the purchaser of prepaid funeral goods and services, paperwork that might be helpful to the family of a deceased to indicate prepayment and which would help to "enforce" trusting requirements.

- There is no state protection from default of prepaid funeral monies.

- There is no provision for an adequate description of funeral goods selected preneed nor for a substitution of equal quality if the selected item is no longer available at the time of death. Survivors should be permitted to approve any substitution.

- Until "constructive delivery" is eliminated and adequate provisions for refund or transfer of all prepaid funeral money plus interest are enacted, it is probably a *terrible* idea to prepay for a funeral in Ohio.

- There is no requirement to identify and tag the body at the place of death before removal.

- There is no provision either forbidding a mark-up on cash advance items or requiring disclosure of how much the mark-up would be.

- There is no requirement to include low-cost caskets in any display.

- The standards for professional conduct are weak and should be better defined. That would make it easier for a consumer to prevail when filing a valid complaint.

- Complaint procedures are unclear and inadequate.

- If you die with limited funds and no prepaid funeral arrangements, look who gets your money and in what order:

  —the lawyers handling your estate
  —$4,000 to the funeral director and $3,000 for the cemetery
  —support for surviving spouse and minor children
  —"debts entitled to a preference" under US law
  —the doctor and hospital, medical
  —another $2,000 for the funeral director if more is owed . . .
  —taxes and Medicaid claims
  —debts for manual labor not to exceed $300 (home health aides gets shafted if not considered a medical expense)
  —other debts

- Funeral directors are exempt from the telephone solicitation laws and may make cold calls for preneed sales.

Miscellaneous Information

- Educational requirements for an embalmer: a four-year college degree, one year of mortuary college, and one year of apprenticeship. For a funeral director: bachelor's degree and two years of apprenticeship. A four-year degree plus one additional year of mortuary school can reduce the apprenticeship to one year. All must pass an exam on state laws and a "nationally recognized" exam. Typically, this is the National Board Exam which practitioners and consumer advocates alike have deemed out-of-date and irrelevant. (Minnesota is the only other state that requires funeral directors to have a four-year degree.)

- Coroners are elected. They must be licensed physicians.

- No person may picket a funeral home, church, or cemetery within 300 feet or one hour before and during a funeral, nor may one picket a funeral procession.

- A commercial pet cemetery must be at least three acres, with a beginning endowment fund of $12,000. Fifty dollars from each lot sale must be added to the fund.

- Coal mining is not allowed within 100 feet of a cemetery.

- If no other resources exist, adults who are already receiving state aid can receive $750 toward their funeral expenses. For children under the age of 11, the amount is $500. A family may contribute up to the same amount to help defray either cost.

- You may name a designated agent for body disposition, helpful if you are estranged from your legal next-of-kin.

- The administrative code requires funeral homes to abide by the FTC Funeral Rule.

- A permit for disinterment must be obtained from the Probate Court.

- Tissue banks must be accredited by the American Association of Tissue Banks. With new standards for non-transplant tissue banks, there should be good regulation of the body parts business.

This chapter was sent for review to the Ohio Department of Health, the Ohio Cemetery Dispute Resolution Commission, and the Board of Embalmers and Funeral Directors. A small correction was made by the cemetery committee. No other responses were received when the chapter was finished, but there had been much communication during the research process.

Caring for the Dead

In Oklahoma

Please refer also to the general introduction to state chapters: "Caring for the Dead: Necessary Information."

Persons in Oklahoma may care for their own dead. The legal authority to do so is found in:

Title 59 § 396.12b Conduct of Funeral Services . . . A. Each funeral conducted within this state shall be under the personal supervision of a duly-licensed funeral director. . . .

C. Nothing in this section regarding the conduct of funerals or personal supervision of a licensed director . . . shall apply to persons related to the deceased by blood or marriage.

§63-1-317. Death certificate . . .(b) The funeral director or person acting as such who first assumes custody of a dead body shall file the death certificate.

While the statutes are pretty clear about your rights as next-of-kin, it may come as a surprise to clergy that those in the funeral business apparently aspire to a role of spiritual leadership, as the rules promulgated by the Funeral Board read:

235:10-1-2 . . . "Funeral Service" means a ritual or ceremony conducted with a body or bodies present with said ritual or ceremony conducted prior to final disposition. A funeral service shall be conducted by a licensed funeral director . . .

At the risk of meddling with religion even further, the Funeral Board has decided that those who care for their own dead should skip any funeral or prayers over the dead altogether, for the rules go on:

235:10-1-3 When Board rules are not applicable . . . Board rules shall not apply where an individual related to the deceased by blood or marriage provides a burial receptacle and buries the related deceased without embalming or **conducting a funeral service.** *[Emphasis added.]*

Our advice? Go ahead anyway. The courts would surely affirm your right to freely engage in the religious or spiritual activity of your choice—at a time of death or any other time.

Death Certificate

Oklahoma is not yet using electronic death registration (EDR) although they are for births. Once EDR is started, a paper worksheet will be available from the office of Vital Records or possibly on-line.

The family doctor or a local medical examiner will sign the death certificate within 48 hours, stating the cause of death. The remaining information must be supplied, typewritten or in black ink. The death certificate must be filed with the local registrar within three days and before final disposition.

Fetal Death

A fetal death report is required for each fetal death.

Transporting and Disposition Permit

The medical examiner will issue a burial-transit permit if the body is to be moved out of state. The fee for this is $100.

Burial

There are no state statutes that specifically permit or prohibit home burial. It is also unlikely that there are local zoning regulations regarding home burial, but you should review them before planning a family cemetery. If your land is in a rural area, draw a map of the property showing where the burial ground will be and have it filed with the deed. That may be all you have to do to establish your family cemetery. There are no state burial statutes or regulations with regard to burial locations or depth. A sensible guideline is 150 feet from a water supply, 25 feet from a power line, with two or three feet of earth on top. Plan your family cemetery away from boundaries with neighbors, too.

Cremation

A permit for cremation must be obtained from the medical examiner. The fee for this is $150, the highest in the country. Most crematories insist that a pacemaker be removed, and authorization by next-of-kin is required. The crematory will return the disposition authorization to the issuing registrar.

There are no laws regarding the disposition of cremated remains. You may do as you wish.

Other Requirements

Regulations—which apply only to funeral directors—require embalming or refrigeration after 24 hours. Weather and reasonable planning should be considered. If the person died of a contagious or communicable disease, the doctor in attendance should be consulted.

Medical Schools for Body Donation

Body donation to a medical school is another option for disposition. Find the information for Oklahoma at <www.finalrights.org>.

State Governance

The Oklahoma Funeral Board has seven members. Two are consumer representatives one of which should be from the health care field. The five funeral director members are recommended to the governor by the trade association, an unfortunate political ploy. There are no crematory operators specified to be on this board, even though crematories are now licensed by the Funeral Board as a "funeral establishment." They must be run by a funeral director, an unreasonable requirement that closes out any low-cost cremation providers for consumers. Furthermore, there is almost nothing in the mortuary school curricula on running a crematory and nothing in the study guide for the national exam about cremation. The change in the law put one cemetery-owned crematory out of business.

Prepaid funeral arrangements are governed by the Insurance Department.

<www.ok.gov/oid/>

Prepaid cemetery transactions are monitored by the Banking Commissioner.

Prepaid Cemetery and Funeral Funds

Ten per cent of cemetery lot prices must go to perpetual care. When purchased preneed, 65% of *cemetery services* and 65% of the retail price of an outer burial container and 110% of the wholesale cost of other *cemetery merchandise* (i.e., markers) must be placed in trust, although "constructive delivery"—a certificate saying it's in the warehouse—can avoid this requirement. A refund would be nearly impossible if you were to change your mind or move. The seller may withdraw the interest after administrative fees have been paid. A surety bond can avoid trusting requirements entirely. An annual report must be made to the Banking commissioner. Cemeteries run by religious and benevolent organizations are exempt from these requirements.

Finance charges are permitted for cemetery sales. It is outrageous to permit such charges on a layaway plan before they lay you away.

When a vault is sold by a *funeral* establishment, only 65% must go into trust, as is required when sold by a cemetery. 90% of the remaining funds must be placed in an insured trust fund. Sellers may withdraw up to 1.146% a year for administration. An annual report to the commissioner is required.

A consumer may cancel a funeral contract and claim a refund of the "net value"—money paid plus interest, less the 10% "commission" and administrative fees.

Insurance is permitted as an alternative to trusting. The consumer must give permission to convert a trust to insurance. Just say "no." The seller already took 10% of your money before putting it in trust. The seller may simply be looking for a commission on the insurance which may have limitations on benefits in the first few years and in any event would give back perhaps half of what you paid if you wanted to cash it in.

Those selling preneed funeral arrangements must supply a bond or letter of credit in the amount of $300,000 or 15% of the funds collected, whichever is less. Fifteen percent is hardly adequate protection against default.

Restrictive Casket Sales

This heading shows up in only three state chapters: Louisiana, Oklahoma, and Virginia.

The statutory definition of a "funeral director" in Title 59 § 396.2 -2.(d) indicates that funeral directors sell funeral service merchandise. Well, of course. The statute goes on to define "funeral service merchandise or funeral services" as "those products and services normally provided by funeral establishments." If one were to ask what *normal* was 100 years ago (when local artisans made the caskets and a group of women came in to lay out the dead), it would be very different from what is in practice today.

When the Stone Casket Company in Oklahoma City began to lose its funeral home clients to large corporations, the folks there decided to sell caskets directly to the public. The state Board of Embalmers and Funeral Directors promptly requested an injunction and restraining order.

District Court Judge Amick, however, found that the mortuary board had overstepped its bounds in trying to limit the casket trade and that the state had no compelling interest in restricting who may sell a casket.

Undaunted, the Board of Embalmers and Funeral Directors pressed on, and, on October 2, 1998, the Court of Civil Appeals granted the injunction.

One has to wonder what Judges Garrett and Joplin—two of the three judges who sit on the Court of Appeals—were thinking. (Judge Jones had the good sense to dissent.) The decision reads in part:

> *The State has a legitimate interest in regulating funeral services because those services relate to the preparation and disposal of human remains. Such laws protect the public health and safety of the citizens of Oklahoma. Caskets are directly involved in the burial of human remains. A casket is a part of the funeral service business and cannot be separated as an independent item. The casket, in which human remains are buried, directly impacts sanitation.*
>
> *(Footnote 4) Theoretically, the Oklahoma public could obtain the same casket sold by Casket Company from telephone sales by out of state casket sellers or sales via the Internet without either of these sellers being licensed by the State of Oklahoma. It is apparent to this Court that the State of Oklahoma may prohibit the importation into this state of contraband property. This certainly includes caskets which may not comply with construction requirements and fail to prevent contamination of the environment. Licensing is a proper method for enforcement of safety and health rules.*

Caskets as contraband property? Casket police? And what construction requirements has any state established for the building of caskets? None, not even Oklahoma. Actually, Oklahoma may not interfere with interstate trade; only the US Congress has that power.

But there's a striking new philosophy being put forward by the judges for the use of a casket: "to prevent contamination of the environment." In many countries, Muslims and Jews bury a body directly in the soil. If there is a sweeping and rampant environmental crisis caused by such burials, it's a well-kept secret. And what about the rancher who buries a dead steer with his backhoe? Will Garrett and Joplin suggest they use a cow casket the next time? For the public health, of course.

In 2001, the Institute for Justice filed a challenge to the Oklahoma law in the US District Court for the Western District of Oklahoma. Unfortunately, the court deemed it a legislative issue, not proper for the court to decide, and dismissed the case.

Clearly, any restriction on who may sell caskets or other funeral supplies is a restraint of trade that subverts the FTC's provision specifically permitting consumers to purchase from the funeral provider *only* the goods and services desired. While the Funeral Board wishes to make it illegal for retail casket sales in Oklahoma, a funeral home must accept any casket that an Oklahoma resident orders from another state, driving that money elsewhere. Legislators are supposed to look at the fiscal implications of any law and might want to re-think this one. Until legislators change the laws, you may want to order your casket via the Internet or get directions for building your own.

Consumer Concerns

- The death rate in Oklahoma can support approximately 141 full-time mortuaries; there are, however, 379. Funeral prices tend to be higher in areas where there are "too many" funeral homes.

- The laws which appear to limit church groups and next-of-kin in caring for the dead or holding funeral ceremonies should be amended to clarify their rights.

- Only funeral directors can sell caskets retail. (Any high school graduates, though, may sell caskets preneed via telephone, as long as they are hired by a funeral director to do so.)

- Trusting requirements for prepaid funerals are inadequate. All prepaid funeral and cemetery money (100%) should be placed in trust. If an elderly parent needed to move to another state—perhaps to be cared for by an adult child—a more reasonable amount would be available. (Twenty-nine other states require 100% trusting. Preneed is alive and well in those states.)

- There is no annual reporting requirement to the purchaser of prepaid funeral goods and services, paperwork that might be helpful to the family of a deceased to indicate prepayment and that would help to enforce trusting requirements.

- There is no requirement that when merchandise is selected on a guaranteed-price, preneed agreement that a clear description is given and that merchandise of equal quality and construction must be substituted if the original item selected is not available. Survivors should have the right to approve any substitution.

- There is insufficient statutory protection against default of prepaid funeral agreements if funds were never put in trust. A guarantee fund should be established.

- Until better preneed laws are passed that increase trusting and include adequate provisions for substitution, transfer and cancellation, it is probably a terrible idea to prepay for a funeral in Oklahoma.

- There is no requirement to identify and tag the body at the place of death before removal.

- There is a requirement to display at least five caskets but no requirement that low-cost caskets be included in that display.

- There is no restriction on taking a mark-up on cash advance items nor any requirement to disclose how much it is if a mark-up is taken. Consumers may wish to request an invoice for such charges.

- The ethical standards for funeral directors are weak and need to be well-defined and expanded. (See Appendix.)

- Procedures for handling funeral complaints seem totally inadequate. Initially, only one funeral board member, along with the executive secretary, examine the complaint to determine if the complaint should be referred to the full board. According to Rule 235:10-9-5, "After a complaint has been filed, all interested persons are prohibited from discussing the complaint with any member of the Board or the hearing officer, if one has been designated." If one of the consumer representatives was not the initial investigating board member, a complainant presumably may not contact the consumer rep in an effort to bring the complaint before the full board. "Resolutions" of complaints do not require the consent of the complainant.

Miscellaneous Information

- The educational requirements for becoming a funeral director/embalmer in Oklahoma are: an associate's degree (60 credits or about 2 years) in mortuary science, one year of apprenticeship, and a passing score on the state exam and the National Board Exam. Alas, practitioners and consumer advocates alike have deemed the exam irrelevant and out-dated.

- Medical examiners are appointed, not elected.

- You may name a designated agent for body disposition in an affidavit, helpful if you are estranged from next-of-kin. Written wishes of the deceased are to prevail.

- The FTC Funeral Rule has been adopted by statute.

- Tissue banks must be accredited by the American Association of Tissue Banks. With new standards for non-transplant tissue banks, there should be good regulation of the body parts business.
- A permit from the state Commissioner of Health is required for disinterment.

This chapter was sent for review to the Oklahoma Department of Banking, the Department of Insurance, the Department of Public Health, and the State Funeral Board. Telephone correspondence with the health department was very helpful. No response was received from the others.

Caring for the Dead
In Oregon

Please refer also to the general introduction to state chapters: "Caring for the Dead: Necessary Information."

Persons in Oregon may care for their own dead. The legal authority to do so is found in:

> *ORS 432.005 Definitions . . . "Person acting as a funeral service practitioner" means: (a) A person other than a funeral service practitioner licensed under ORS 692.045, including but not limited to a relative, friend, or other interested party, who performs the duties of a funeral service practitioner without payment. . . .*
>
> *97.130 Right to control disposition of remains; delegation. (1) Any individual of sound mind who is 18 years of age or older, by completion of a written signed instrument [97.130 (7)] or by preparing or pre-arranging with any funeral service practitioner licensed under ORS chapter 692, may direct any lawful manner of disposition of the individual's remains. Except as provided under subsection (6) of this section, disposition directions or disposition prearrangements that are prepaid or that are filed with a funeral service practitioner licensed under ORS chapter 692 shall not be subject to cancellation or substantial revision.*
>
> *(2) A person within the first applicable listed class among the following listed classes that is available at the time of death or, in the absence of actual notice of a contrary direction by the decedent as described under subsection (1) of this section or actual notice of opposition by completion of a written instrument by a member of the same class or a member of a prior class, may direct any lawful manner of disposition of a decedent's remains by completion of a written instrument:*
>
> *(a) The spouse of the decedent.*

(b) A son or daughter of the decedent 18 years of age or older.

(c) Either parent of the decedent. . . .[and so on.]

Alas, it doesn't mention a "majority" of children or how to handle disputes in the case of divorce or an even number of children, nor is estrangement considered. Fortunately, one can name a designated agent for body disposition.

Death Certificate

Oregon started Electronic Death Registration (EDR) in 2006 and most funeral directors and medical examiners are using it. Physicians have balked, so the state uses a hybrid system that may be part electronic and part paper. A home-funeral family may use either an all-paper system or the hybrid.

A home funeral information packet is available from the state Center for Health Statistics. Call 971-673-1180 to request information. Included in the packet will be a blank death certificate, a metal ID tag, a report of death form, and instructions for filling out the report of death. Or you may be able to get these from the county registrar. Be sure to do this in advance of need. Instructions for completing the death certificate are at the following website:

<www.oregon.gov/DHS/ph/chs/registration/instructions.shtml>

The report of death must be filed with the local registrar within 24 hours. This provides the county with information about who has control of the body and states that a death certificate will follow shortly.

If using an all-paper system, the family doctor, certified nurse practitioner, physician's assistant, or a local medical examiner can be asked to sign the death certificate (within 48 hours), stating the cause of death.

The remaining demographic information must be supplied, typewritten or in black ink. Do not use a felt-tip pen; the information must carry through to the third page. The death certificate must be filed with the county registrar within five days and usually prior to final disposition. If the physician has indicated that there is no need to hold the body for medical reasons, the disposition may continue as planned by the family.

There is a $20 charge for filing the death certificate. This fee goes to the Mortuary and Cemetery Board and the Indigent Burial fund and is usually billed to the person listed as funeral director after the record is registered with the state.

The metal ID tag is to stay with the body throughout disposition. If death has occurred when it would be unwise to wait for the next working day, one of the required tags might be obtained from a funeral home if you have not already gotten one from the Health Statistics folks.

If the physician is on the EDR system , or the cause of death is investigated by the medical examiner, the death certificate may be initiated electronically and a "drop to paper" copy then printed. The family would then complete the demographic information before filing it with the local registrar.

Fetal Death

A fetal death report is required when the fetus weighs 350 grams or more (about 12 ounces), or, if weight is unknown, after 20 weeks of gestation. If there is no family physician involved or delivery was not in a hospital institution, the local medical examiner must sign the fetal death certificate. If the parents wish to request a commemorative certificate of stillbirth, a fetal death report must be filed even if not otherwise required by law.

Transporting and Disposition Permit

A body may be moved with the consent of a physician or medical examiner. The family member acting as the funeral director must fill in the parts under "disposition" on the first page of the death certificate. One of the attached carbons, after the medical signature has been obtained, serves as an authorization for disposition and may be retained by the cemetery or crematory. The other must be signed and returned to the issuing registrar within 10 days.

Burial

ORS 97.460 allows for the use of property for cemeteries or burial parks if:

- You are the owner of the property;

- You have the written consent of the planning commission of the county or city or, if there is no commission, the governing body of such county or city;

- You agree to maintain accurate, permanent records of the burial if required to do so by the planning commission, and;

- You agree to disclose the burial upon sale of the property.

The Mortuary and Cemetery Board cites this as authority for home burials. There are no state burial statutes or regulations with regard to burial locations or depth. A sensible guideline is 150 feet from a water supply, 25 feet from a power line, with two or three feet of earth on top. Plan your family cemetery away from boundaries with neighbors, too. Draw a map of the property and plan to have it recorded with the deed after jumping through the local zoning hoops if there are any.

The person in charge must sign the burial-transit permit and return it within ten days to the registrar of the county in which death occurred.

Cremation

No additional permit for cremation is needed. If a person has not authorized cremation prior to his or her own death, authorization by next-of-kin or designated agent is required. Any pacemaker must be removed. The crematory will sign the burial-transit permit, which must then be returned to the registrar of the county in which death occurred. There are no laws regarding the disposition of cremated remains. You may do as you wish. If scattering on public land, don't ask, don't tell.

Other Requirements

Administrative rules for funeral service practitioners require that a body that will not reach its destination within 24 hours be embalmed, refrigerated to 36 degrees, or placed in a sealed casket. Families caring for their own dead would not be bound by such a regulation, but reasonable planning and weather should be considered.

Administrative rules also require: "If a public or private funeral service and/or public viewing is desired over an unembalmed refrigerated human remains, the unembalmed human remains shall not be removed from refrigeration for longer than a total of six hours. No public or private funeral service or public viewing shall be held over the remains of an unwashed human remains. . . . No public viewing shall be held over the remains of persons dead from any of the communicable diseases unless embalmed."

The regulation that requires bathing is another excuse to mandate charges that consumers are unable to decline, as only a licensed embalmer may bathe a body. While bathing may be desirable, it should not be required and certainly exceeds the authority of the board. Again, this is a regulation that applies to licensees, not to private families caring for their own dead. The statute reads: "692.320 Powers and duties; rules. (1) The State Mortuary and Cemetery Board may adopt and enforce rules for the protection of the public health, safety and welfare *relating to the following* . . ." [emphasis added] What follows is the list of licensees governed by this Board. In no place does the statute say that the Board has powers over private citizens as well.

If the person died of a communicable disease, the body must be embalmed. This makes no sense, as it is the worst possible circumstance under which to embalm. To their credit, other jurisdictions such as Hawaii, Delaware, North Carolina, and Ontario forbid embalming under these circumstances. Ohio and Montana require immediate disposition.

If religious custom prohibits embalming when shipping by common carrier, a sealed casket must be used.

If disposition does not occur within ten days, the Mortuary Board must be notified.

Medical Schools for Body Donation

Body donation to a medical school is another option for disposition. Find the information for Oregon at <www.finalrights.org>.

State Governance

The Oregon State Mortuary and Cemetery Board has eleven members. Three are morticians, three are cemeterians, one is a crematory operator, and four are public members, one of whom must be a senior citizen. Crematories are licensed, regulated, and inspected by the Mortuary and Cemetery Board. One does not need to be a funeral director to run a crematory.

Preneed funeral and cemetery sales are regulated by the Department of Consumer and Business Services. A preneed seller must be "registered" with the Mortuary/Cemetery Board before being "certified" as doing preneed business by the DCBS, a strange and confusing mixture between two state agencies. Furthermore, the relevant statutes are badly organized, lumping funeral preneed in with pre-construction cemetery sales, creating a wordy mishmash that makes it hard to find consumer information. It certainly mocks the intent of ORS 180.545 which requires "plain language" for consumer contracts.

<www.oregon.gov/MortCem/index.shtml>

Death Care Consultants

As of 2010, "death care consultants" (DCCs) are now also regulated by this board if they ply their work "for payment." There are maybe a dozen ladies in Oregon—yes, all women at the time of this writing—who are interested in helping families with home funerals, many of whom have taken Jerrigrace Lyons's course in family-directed funerals <finalpassages.org>. Although there have been no complaints that might justify such legislation, apparently the mere idea of it had the funeral industry up in arms, sufficiently so that they managed to wind up one legislator over the thought that unlicensed folks might be doing god-knows-what to someone's dead Granny, maybe even out in the back yard.

There was no input sought from any of the home funeral guides, and any attempts to shape the legislation by consumer advocates were repeatedly spurned. (Oregon has a voluntary licensing program for birth midwives that could have provided a model to follow.) Perhaps the most blatant offense in the legislation was the failure to provide representation on the Mortuary-Cemetery Board, a right granted to all other licensees.

The relatively new Executive Director of the Board, Michelle Gaines, expressed grand plans of her own in an e-mail to Carlson:

> As we discussed, in my personal opinion, SB796 is a landmark opportunity for Oregon to address the needs and impacts of death on Oregonians, on our communities, on the workforce and economy, and on the environment. Further, I think it is an opportunity to focus national attention on the evolution of death care, and the wide spectrum of choice and practice that is emerging.

Once the legislation passed, she put together a rule-making advisory committee and then, ignoring what they had recommended, gave her own version of the draft rules to the Board for approval.

The definition: "A 'death care consultant' means an individual who provides consultations related to funeral or final disposition arrangements, for payment, to the person or persons who are acting as a funeral service practitioner . . ." (These families want a home funeral. They aren't funeral director wannabes.) The new rule requires an exam on "Oregon and federal laws and rules relating to the care, preparation, disposition and transportation of dead human bodies," identical terminology for what is required of funeral directors. In fact, one funeral director suggested that the DCCs should have to pass the same test. Might the DCC get stuck with irrelevant questions about preneed trusts or establishment licenses? There won't be any DCC on the Board that decides what questions will be asked on this exam.

Unlike the bar exam, the real estate exam, or a driver's test, after taking this test one may not look at the exam afterward to see what answers are wrong, per "Chapter 162," confidentiality being the only operative function in that statute. They'll simply tell you the general section of statutes you need to study a little more . . . like telling kids to memorize the times tables without telling them which ones they need to work on. Furthermore, in a state dedicated to high educational standards, no training is required for this license, even though that had been a strong recommendation of at least one of the advisory committee people, Nancy Ward, herself a home funeral guide.

The certification is not needed by lawyers, authors, or people giving workshops or speaking engagements, thank goodness, but the regulation is so badly worded that one has to wonder if clergy and hospice people will be allowed to discuss funeral arrangements with a patient or family.

Among other provisions, a DCC may not provide any "direct physical assistance" or "supervision" of the bathing of the dead unless licensed as an embalmer. (A lot of hospice nurses are going to be in trouble now!) Some of the ladies quickly figured out how that bizarre requirement can be avoided. They aren't going to charge for their hands-on services and will operate like the layers-out-of-the-dead did in years past. So much for "landmark" opportunities—with a law that may not have anybody to license after all.

Well, almost nobody. When the first exam for the DCC license was scheduled for October 2010, Carlson decided it needed investigation, as she had little trust in the motives of the Mortuary Board and staff. There were no residency requirements to bar her application, and after paying $160 for a two-year license and $100 to take the exam, Carlson was sent a one-inch-thick study guide, at least 75% being irrelevant to the work of home funeral guides. There was a booklet from the FTC on the Funeral Rule, but these women don't fit the definition of "funeral provider" under the rule if they're only DCCs with no hands-on funeral activities.

There were 33 pages of OSHA requirements that kick in for embalmers and those exposed to blood. Again, not these women. A bunch of pages on death benefits in worker comp cases, but nothing on veterans benefits or Social Security. Pages and pages on prepaid funerals, running a crematory, running a cemetery, mutilation of bodies or monuments, access to historical cemeteries, and probate. And, of course, the relevant Vital Statistics and licensing statutes. Carlson was also sent a pamphlet of "Facts About Funeral and Cemetery Arrangements: Consumer Information" printed in hard-to-read nine-point type. The pamphlet erroneously states that there is a law that requires embalming or refrigeration after 24 hours. That's a regulation, not a law. Nowhere in the pamphlet does it mention that families have the right to care for their own dead. In discussing prepaying for a funeral or cemetery space, none of the pitfalls are mentioned. There is no mention of naming a designated agent for body disposition if the next-of-kin might not all be agreeable. The wordy text rambles badly, with information of questionable usefulness crammed into the tiny type.

That October, Carlson was the only one in the large room taking the exam, 100 true-or-false and multiple-choice questions. Many appeared to be trick questions with the right answer hinging on a single misplaced word rather than a professional test for functional knowledge. For example, by the process of elimination, only one answer is factually true below but not at all relevant to the situation posed:

The person who died wanted to be buried in a shroud without a casket or outer burial container. Which of the following is true:

a. To be buried without a casket or outer burial container is illegal in Oregon. [False, it's perfectly legal.]

b. Cemeteries may not prohibit green burial but may charge extra for it. [They may charge extra if they permit green burial, but there is no law saying that a cemetery must not prohibit green burial. False.]

c. Cemeteries have the right to require a casket and an outer burial container. [Yes, that's true, but how does that meet the needs of a family that wants a green burial?]

d. The planning commission where the cemetery is located must give permission. [No, that's only for burial on your own property.]

Of the 100 questions, Carlson deemed at least 40 and probably closer to 50 were irrelevant to DCC licensure as they were questions on funeral establishment requirements or cemetery or crematory operations, OSHA, and FTC, among others. And just why is it important to know how long the Vital Records office keeps a death certificate confidential? Carlson passed the test but sent her license back as soon as she received it, as she had no plan to use it and every intention of exposing the exam and DCC licensing process for what it was.

The home funeral guides in Oregon are now planning their own certification program, one with a code of ethics, an educational requirement, and practical experience, all missing from the less-than-professional efforts of the Mortuary Board.

Prepaid Cemetery and Funeral Funds

Door-to-door or telephone solicitations are not permitted for preneed sales.

90% of a guaranteed-price "prearrangement" contract (both *funeral* and *cemetery*) and 100% of a non-guaranteed contract must be placed in **trust**, not counting interment rights. "Constructive delivery" (warehousing with your name on it) of the casket, vault, or marker can avoid the trusting requirement for any merchandise, which would be a real problem if you were to change your mind from body burial to cremation or move to another state. The service money could be transferred, but the other funeral director might be told to come pick up your casket and vault.

An amount not to exceed 2% of the trust may be withdrawn each year for the expense of maintaining the account or for taxes. If you wish to cancel the contract, it is not clear how much of a refund you will get. One part of the statute says that "all amounts paid" plus interest in the trust is fully refundable if the contract is not irrevocable. Does the provider have to pony up the 10% pocketed for a guaranteed-price agreement? It doesn't say. But the constructive delivery has a much greater impact on any possible refund: If you spent $6,000 on a funeral and of that $3,000 went for the casket and vault, the only refund you might get would be half of what you paid or $3,000 plus a little interest, if they don't get to keep 10%. The only provision for a transfer (of an irrevocable trust) says that your funeral director "may appoint a successor provider" if you've submitted a written request but doesn't say he has to.

The preneed seller must make an annual report to the Department of Consumer and Business Services showing the total preneed activity and an inventory of any "delivered" merchandise. Facilities are inspected every two years, to check inventory, among other things, Carlson was told.

If a person is making installment payments on a mausoleum not yet constructed and is in default, the seller, after notifying the buyer of the default, may—30 days later—keep all that was paid as "liquidated damages." What a dirty deal the state has handed the poor.

A Funeral and Cemetery Consumer Protection Fund is financed by a $5 assessment for each prepaid contract. Unfortunately, it is not available to anyone who prepaid prior to establishment of the fund in the 1980s. There has been at least one claim on this fund since its inception.

Consumer Concerns

- The death rate in Oregon can support approximately 124 full-time mortuaries; there are 193 such establishments. Given the low density of population over a large geographic area, mortuary careers are not likely to be full-time work. Unfortunately, because of the low volume of business at some mortuaries, funeral prices will tend to be higher than elsewhere.

- Constructive delivery (warehousing with your name on it) can be used to avoid the trusting requirements.

- Transfer and refund rights are not clearly spelled out.

- There is no annual reporting requirement to the purchaser of prepaid funeral goods and services, paperwork that might be helpful to the family of a deceased to indicate prepayment and that would help to "enforce" trusting requirements.

- There is no provision for an adequate description of funeral goods selected preneed nor for a substitution of equal quality if the selected item is no longer available at the time of death.

- In spite of the Consumer Protection Fund and until the Oregon laws are changed to eliminate the loopholes, it is probably a terrible idea to prepay for a funeral or any cemetery merchandise and services in this state, given the raw deal a consumer would get in trying to transfer or back out of such a purchase. Your own trust account in a bank will be safer.

- The regulation requiring embalming or refrigeration after 24 hours is excessive and should be eliminated to avoid unnecessary charges for the first 72 hours or so.

- The regulation requiring embalming when death occurs from a contagious or communicable disease is unwise and should be repealed. This is not only an offense to some religious groups, it puts the funeral professionals at risk. Immediate disposition would be a more responsible option for deaths caused by infectious diseases.

- According to the regulations, only an embalmer may bathe a body, certainly an affront to the religious groups that might want to work with a funeral home while preserving religious bathing rituals, or to parents wanting to bathe and dress a child.

- If a family wants limited body preparation prior to an "identification viewing" (or private family goodbye time) at an immediate disposition establishment, they must be referred to a full-service outfit instead—just to wash the face, comb the hair, and button up a nightie. Somebody wants a monopoly on soap and washcloths.

- There is no provision either forbidding a mark-up on cash advance items or requiring the disclosure of how much the mark-up would be.

- There is no requirement that low-cost caskets be included in any display.

- Complaint procedures seem unclear and inadequate.

- Although all tissue banks must register with the state, there are no statutory standards. A requirement that they be accredited by the American Association of Tissue Banks would save the state any staff or budget, as AATB has good standards for regulating the body parts business.

Miscellaneous Information

- Educational requirements for becoming a funeral practitioner: associate's degree, a state exam, and one year of apprenticeship. For embalmers: mortuary school, both the national and state exams, and one year of apprenticeship

- Regulations require that "free" offers to veterans and others disclose all conditions and not be misleading (such as conditioning a "free" item on the purchase of another or marking up prices over the usual price before promoting a "discount").

- A body may not be detained before payment of the funeral bill.

- Given the poorly-written right-to-control statute, it may be important to name an agent for body disposition in a written document. The form and wording of the document can be found in 97.130 (7).

- Hospitals are required to make an effort to contact the next-of-kin before sending a body to a mortuary.

- Medical examiners are physicians who are appointed to the position.

- The FTC Funeral Rule has been adopted by reference.

- Authorization for disinterment must be obtained from the state registrar by the next-of-kin or person with the right to control disposition.

This chapter was sent for review to the State Mortuary and Cemetery Board, the Department of Consumer and Business Services, and the Oregon Health Division of the Oregon Health Authority. Health Division folks were very helpful. Mortuary Board staff made useful corrections. No response was received from the Consumer Services.

Caring for the Dead

In Pennsylvania

Please refer also to the general introduction to state chapters: "Caring for the Dead: Necessary Information."

Pennsylvania families may care for their own dead. One relevant law states:

> *Chapter 35 Title 450.504. . . . The funeral director or the person in charge of interment or removal shall, within ninety-six (96) hours after the death or fetal death or within ninety-six (96) hours after the finding of a dead body or fetal remains, file with the local registrar a certificate of death or fetal death.*

There are no other statutes that might require you to use a funeral director. However, home-funeral families have been harassed by the state Funeral Board with threats of $10,000 fines. In the Pittsburgh area, funeral directors reportedly have received threats of losing their licenses if they help families or religious groups who bypass commercial funeral establishments. So consumers may face heavy-handed opposition, even with the law on their side.

Death Certificate

The family doctor, county coroner, or a local medical examiner will sign the death certificate stating the cause of death. The remaining information must be supplied, typewritten or in black ink. The death certificate must be filed with the local registrar within 96 hours of death and before final disposition.

There is no projected time for employing electronic death registration. Presumably when that does happen there will be a paper alternative.

Fetal Death

A fetal death certificate is required if death occurs after 16 weeks gestation. If no family physician is involved, the local coroner must sign the certificate.

Transporting and Disposition Permit

The local registrar will issue the authorization for disposition. The death certificate must be obtained first.

Burial

There are no state statutes that specifically permit or prohibit home burial. It is also unlikely that there are local zoning regulations regarding home burial, but you should review them before planning a family cemetery. If your land is in a rural area, draw a map of the property showing where the burial ground will be and have it filed with the deed. That may be all you have to do to establish your family cemetery. Although not mentioned, it is a good idea to pick a site that is at least 150 feet from a water supply and 25 feet from a power line or neighbor's boundary. Pennsylvania law prohibits burial of the dead on any land draining into a stream which furnishes any part of the water supply of a municipality unless at least one mile from the city. The top of the coffin must be two feet below the surface of the earth.

When burial is arranged, the family member in charge must sign the authorization for disposition and file the second copy with the Division of Vital Statistics within 10 days. The first copy is to be retained by the crematory, cemetery, property owner (if home burial), or the Humanity Gifts Registry (if anatomical donation).

Pennsylvania has a number of statutes permitting cemeteries to be moved if the land has been abandoned, ill-kept, or needed for growth and development, a sad provision for some of us. The old Trinity Church cemetery in the middle of the financial district in New York City is a breath of fresh air in more ways than one.

Cremation

The county coroner must receive notice prior to cremation and have an opportunity to view the body if there are any questions. In the case of anticipated deaths, coroner authorization may be granted by telephone. There is a 24-hour wait before cremation. Most crematories insist that a pacemaker be removed, and authorization by next-of-kin or a designated agent is required. The crematory will file the disposition authorization with the local registrar. No laws restrict disposition of cremated remains. You may do as you wish.

Other Requirements

Under the standards of practice and professional responsibilities of funeral directors, the statutes require embalming, a sealed casket, or refrigeration (35°–40°) after 24 hours. So you're stuck with paying for one or the other when you use a funeral home. No such requirements are mentioned in the Public Health statutes, and no one's likely to be running around with a stopwatch when families are caring for their own dead. Weather and reasonable planning should be considered.

Medical Schools for Body Donation

Body donation to a medical school is another option for disposition. Find the information for Pennsylvania at <www.finalrights.org>.

State Governance

The Pennsylvania State Board of Funeral Directors has nine members. Two are public representatives, five are funeral directors, plus one commissioner and one from the attorney general's office.

<www.dos.state.pa.us/portal/server.pt/community/
state_board_of_funeral_directors/12496>

Cemeteries are supposedly regulated by the Real Estate Commission. (The form for renewing one's license as a cemetery salesperson or broker is on the same form used for a timeshare salesperson, builder-owner salesperson, and campground salesperson.) There is no information for consumers regarding cemetery purchases on their website.

<www.dos.state.pa.us/portal/server.pt/community/
state_real_estate_commission/12523>

Other than environmental compliance, crematories are not regulated in Pennsylvania. Anyone may run a crematory.

Prepaid Cemetery and Funeral Funds

Although there is a requirement to put 15% of lot sales into the perpetual care fund, there are few consumer protection laws for *cemetery* transactions.

Statutes in the Cemetery and Funeral Merchandise Trust Fund Act require that 70% of the retail price for *funeral and cemetery merchandise and services* must be placed in trust. (But regulations promulgated by the Funeral Board require 100% trusting.) Once the contract is fully paid and if a consumer moves out of state, the consumer may cancel a preneed contract, but the seller gets to keep the interest. The law doesn't say what happens if you are still paying and/or move from Philly to Pittsburgh. If the buyer defaults on preneed payments, the seller may keep 30% of the contract price, not 30% of what you've paid. So if you have arranged for a $10,000 send-off and have paid $3,000 toward it before changing your mind to a simple cremation, you won't get one red cent back.

Nothing—absolutely nothing—is said in the Funeral Board regulations about transfer rights or refundability or interest or substitutions, all serious omissions. In fact, one Pittsburgh funeral home refused to transfer the "irrevocable" prepaid funds of a woman who moved and was upheld by a court. Such a decision has set a terribly harmful precedent for all other preneed buyers . . . until the laws are changed. *This state is probably one of the worst in the nation for preneed consumer protection laws.*

Consumer Concerns

- The death rate in Pennsylvania can support approximately 506 full-time mortuaries; there are, however, 1,801. Funeral prices tend to be higher in areas where there are "too many" funeral homes.

- Until the conflicting laws and statutes are straightened out to require 100% trusting and 100% portability for all preneed cemetery and funeral purchases—both revocable and irrevocable, it is a terrible idea to prepay for a funeral in this state.

- There is insufficient statutory provision to protect consumers against default of prepaid funeral agreements if funds were never put in trust. A guarantee fund should be established.

- There is no requirement to include low-cost caskets in any display.

- There is no restriction on taking a mark-up on cash advance items nor a requirement to disclose the extent of any mark-up taken.

- Identification and tagging of the body at the place of death before removal should be required.

- The embalming or refrigeration requirement should be changed to 72 hours or eliminated—to permit greater family choice. At 24 hours, it allows a funeral home to make an unnecessary extra charge, even for the most minimal of arrangements. There has been no public health problem in the states without such a requirement.

- The statute requiring embalming when death involves communicable diseases should be repealed. The requirement puts at risk funeral staff and possibly the public health, and overrides religious or personal objections to embalming. The state should also distinguish between "communicable" and "contagious." Requiring immediate disposition is appropriate for contagious or infectious diseases.

- The ethical standards for funeral directors need to be defined and expanded. See Appendix.

- Food may not be served to the public in a funeral home, a consumer-unfriendly stipulation.

- Coroners are elected (or appointed in selected areas) and need not be physicians. More than half of the 67 counties have coroners or deputies who are affiliated with a funeral home. Complaints to the

Funeral Ethics Organization indicate that at least some of these are abusing their public office for personal gain, especially in Luzerne County. There is no code of ethics on the state association's web site. A consumer should feel free to have a body moved to a funeral home of choice.

- This state has no laws regulating the body parts business.

Miscellaneous Information

- Educational requirements for becoming a funeral director in Pennsylvania: two years of college plus one year of mortuary college, one year of internship after college, plus a state exam and the national exam. Alas, the National Board Exam has been deemed out-dated and irrelevant by practitioners and consumer advocates alike.

- Inquiries regarding the interment, transportation, and disinterment of dead bodies and fetal remains may be directed to the Division of Vital Records at 724-656-3121.

- It is "unlawful to erect or establish any slaughter house, manure or bone dust factory, soap factory, distillery or tannery within two hundred yards" of a cemetery.

- A body may not be held for debt.

- Regulations require compliance with the FTC Funeral Rule.

- You may name an agent for body disposition, helpful if you are estranged from your next-of-kin.

- A disinterment permit is required from the local registrar along with a new burial permit. The casket may not be opened without a court order.

This chapter was sent for review to the Pennsylvania Department of Health, Funeral Board, and Real Estate Commission. No responses were received.

Caring for the Dead

In Rhode Island

Please refer also to the general introduction to state chapters: "Caring for the Dead: Necessary Information."

Persons in Rhode Island may care for their own dead. The legal authority to do so is found in:

Title 23-3-16 Death registration . . . . (b) The funeral director, his or her duly authorized agent, or person acting as agent, who first assumes custody of a dead body, shall file the death certificate

Title 23-4-10 Disposition of deceased bodies. The office of state medical examiners shall, after any postmortem examination or autopsy, promptly release the deceased body to the relatives or representatives of the deceased.

There are no other statutes that might require you to use a funeral director.

Death Certificate

The family doctor will furnish and sign the death certificate "immediately" (or a medical examiner within 48 hours), stating the cause of death. The remaining information must be supplied, typewritten or in black ink. The death certificate must be filed with the local registrar within seven days.

Rhode Island lacks funds for electronic death registration. If and when that goes in, there will presumably be a paper alternative for home funeral people.

Fetal Death

A fetal death report is required when death occurs after 20 weeks of gestation. If there is no family physician involved when a death occurs, the local medical examiner must sign the fetal death certificate.

Transporting and Disposition Permit

The funeral director or person acting as such prepares the burial-transit permit which is attached to the death certificate. It must be given to the cemetery or crematory where disposition takes place. It must subsequently be filed with the registrar of that town. Medical donations are reported to the state registrar after final disposition.

Burial

Cities and towns have the authority to regulate burials. If you are in a heavily-populated town, it is unlikely to permit home burial. There are no state burial statutes or regulations with regard to depth. A sensible guideline is 150 feet from a water supply and three feet of earth on top.

Cremation

A cremation permit from the medical examiner is required. There may be a charge of no more than $20 for this. There is a 24-hour waiting period prior to cremation unless the deceased died of a contagious or infectious disease. Authorization by next-of-kin is required unless a prepaid contract for cremation was made by the deceased, and a pacemaker must be removed. There are no laws regarding the disposition of cremated remains. You may do as you wish.

Other Requirements

According to Funeral Board regulations, a body must be embalmed or refrigerated within 48 hours of death. This regulation would not apply to home funeral families. Rhode Island has no other requirements controlling the time schedule for the disposition of unembalmed bodies. Weather and reasonable planning should be considered.

A body shipped by common carrier must be embalmed or in a sealed casket.

If the person died of a contagious or communicable disease, the doctor in attendance should be consulted.

Medical Schools for Body Donation

Body donation to a medical school is another option for disposition. Find the information for Rhode Island at <www.finalrights.org>.

Also check Boston University in Massachusetts that will pay for transportation in all six New England states.

State Governance

The Rhode Island Board of Funeral Directors and Embalmers has five members. Two are consumer representatives, and three are embalmers.

<www.health.ri.gov/hsr/professions/emb_fun_dir.php>

The majority of cemeteries in Rhode Island are operated by towns or churches, with towns having the ultimate authority to regulate burial grounds.

Crematories are licensed, regulated, and inspected by the Board of Health. One does not need to be a funeral director to run a crematory.

Prepaid Cemetery and Funeral Funds

Sale of cemetery lots may not be for profit. 20% of the lot price must be put into the perpetual care fund. There are no laws or regulations giving you specific protections or rights when buying cemetery services and merchandise preneed

100% of prepaid *funeral* money must be placed in escrow, with the interest and income to accrue.

If a purchaser defaults on installment payments, the seller may retain, as liquidated damages, 5% of the amount in escrow or $200—whichever is greater. If you have already paid $5,000 toward a $7,000 funeral contract, it would be better to cancel. Why? If a purchaser wishes to cancel a prepaid funeral contract, the seller may retain the greater of $200 or only 2.5% of the amount in escrow, not 5%. Of course, if you have arranged a modest exit and were planning on spending only $1,200 for an immediate cremation, the $200 cancellation or liquidation fee seems exorbitant.

A funeral contract may be transferred, apparently without penalty. If selected merchandise is not available at the time of death, the funeral service provider must substitute items equal or superior in quality of material and workmanship. If excess funds remain after calculating goods and services at today's prices, the remainder must be returned to the estate, unlikely given the high rate of funeral inflation. Prices at the time of death must not exceed what is in the trust, essentially a guaranteed-price funeral, a practice discouraged by industry advisors.

Prepaid funeral contracts may not be amended by next-of-kin or a funeral planning agent. Since circumstances may change the desired arrangements, this is a good reason to plan but not prepay.

Consumer Concerns

- The death rate in Rhode Island can support approximately 40 full-time mortuaries; there are 102. Funeral prices tend to be much higher in an area where there are "too many" funeral homes.
- There is no annual reporting requirement to the purchaser of prepaid funeral goods and services, paperwork that might be helpful to

the family of a deceased to indicate prepayment and would help to enforce trusting requirements.

- There is no clear description mandated for preneed merchandise, although the statutes do provide for substitution if not available at death. Any change should be made on approval of survivors.

- A penalty for cancelling or defaulting on a prepaid funeral plan is permitted and should be eliminated.

- There is no state protection for consumers in the event that a provider defaults on a prepaid funeral. In other states that required 100% trusting, consumers were without funeral funds when funeral homes there went out of business.

- Until there is better protection for preneed funeral consumers, it is probably unwise to prepay for a funeral in Rhode Island.

- The 24-hour wait before cremation is unnecessary when survivors are in agreement and may be causing additional charges to families for storage.

- The coroner or medical examiner's permit for cremation in the case of an *anticipated* death from natural causes is unnecessary and creates an additional burden and charge for families.

- There is no requirement to identify and tag the body at the place of death before removal.

- There is no requirement that low-cost caskets be included in any display.

- There is no provision either forbidding a mark-up on cash advance items or requiring disclosure of how much the mark-up would be.

- The standards for ethical, professional conduct are weak should be more well-defined. That would make it easier for a consumer to prevail when filing a valid complaint.

- Punishment for violating statutes or regulations include the possibility of six months in prison or a fine limited to $500, an incongruously paltry amount compared to prison time. It's double that for embezzling preneed money—one year or $1,000. If you're holding $50,000 in prepaid funeral money, what's a mere $1,000.

- This state has no laws regulating the body parts business.

Miscellaneous Information

- Educational requirements for becoming a funeral director or embalmer: associate's degree, mortuary college, the national board exam, a practical exam, and one year of internship with the embalming of at least 50 bodies. This is quickly going to become a problem with a 33% cremation rate as of 2008 and an average of just under 100 calls a year. Furthermore, the national board exam is deemed out-dated and irrelevant by industry practitioners.

- Embalmers are exempt from penalties for "the necessary mutilation incident to embalming a dead human body."

- No funeral home may operate on the grounds of or contiguous to a cemetery. Cemetery operators may not be in the business of funeral directing.

- Violation of the FTC Funeral Rule is referenced under the regulations as an example of "unprofessional conduct."

- Medical examiners are physicians who are appointed to the job.

- The town in which death occurred shall see that a body is "decently buried," if the family is without funds. Costs may be recovered from the town of residence.

- You may name a funeral planning agent, helpful if you are estranged from next-of-kin.

- A body may not be held for debt.

- Public assistance for funerals is capped at $900. Friends, not immediate family, may contribute up to $1,600 more.

- A disinterment permit can be obtained from a local registrar.

This chapter was sent for review to the Department of Health and the Board of Funeral Directors and Embalmers, but no responses were received.

Caring for the Dead
In South Carolina

Please refer also to the general introduction to state chapters: "Caring for the Dead: Necessary Information."

Persons in South Carolina may care for their own dead. The legal authority to do so is found in:

> *Title 40-19-280 (B): No public officer or employee, the official of any public institution, physician, surgeon, or any other person having a professional relationship with any decedent shall send or cause to be sent to any funeral establishment or to any person licensed for the practice of funeral service the remains of any deceased person without having first made due inquiry as to the desires of the next of kin and of the persons who may be chargeable with the funeral and expenses of the decedent. If any kin is found, his authority and directions shall govern except in those instances where the deceased made his prior arrangements in writing.*

There are no other statutes that might require you to use a funeral director.

Death Certificate

South Carolina is now using electronic death registration, although it is not yet quite state-wide. A paper alternative is available.

A blank death certificate (Form 0670) and worksheet (Form 0670C) can be obtained from the county vital records office in the county where death occurred, but you will need to get the disposition permit first. Contact the doctor (or coroner or medical examiner) for the cause of death and to sign the death certificate. The remaining information must be supplied, typewritten or printed in black ink. Do not use white-out or strike through items to make changes. Both documents must be unaltered with no extraneous markings.

The death certificate must be filed with the county vital records office within five days of death.

Fetal Death

A fetal death report is required when death occurs after 20 weeks of gestation or when the weight is 350 grams or more (about 12 ounces); the report must be filed by the facility where delivery occurred or the coroner if delivery was outside a facility.

Transporting and Disposition Permit

A body may be moved with the consent of a physician or medical examiner. The local registrar, deputy, or sub-registrar will issue the authorization for disposition. When death has occurred in a hospital, the subregistrar from whom to obtain the permit will be located there. If death occurred outside of an institution, the coroner of the county serves as sub-registrar. This authorization must be obtained within 72 hours of death and prior to final disposition of the body.

Burial

There are no state statutes that specifically permit or prohibit home burial. It is also unlikely that there are local zoning regulations regarding home burial, but you should review them before planning a family cemetery. If your land is in a rural area, draw a map of the property showing where the burial ground will be and have it filed with the deed. That may be all you have to do to establish your family cemetery. There are no state burial statutes or regulations with regard to burial locations or depth. A sensible guideline is 150 feet from a water supply, 25 feet from a power line, with two or three feet of earth on top. Plan your family cemetery away from boundaries with neighbors, too. The top of the casket must be at least ten inches below the surface of the earth.

Cremation

There is a 24-hour wait prior to cremation unless the death was from infectious disease, in which case the waiting period can be waived by the doctor or medical examiner. A cremation permit must be obtained from the medical examiner or county coroner. A certified copy of the death certificate must accompany the burial-removal-transit permit when requesting this. There is no fee for the permit to cremate. Authorization by next-of-kin is required, and a pacemaker must be removed. There are no laws regarding the disposition of cremated remains. You may do as you wish.

Other Requirements

South Carolina has no embalming requirements. Weather and reasonable planning should be considered. If the person died of a contagious or communicable disease, the doctor in attendance should be consulted.

Medical Schools for Body Donation

Body donation to a medical school is another option for disposition. Find the information for South Carolina at <www.finalrights.org>.

State Governance

The South Carolina Board of Funeral Service has eleven members. Two are consumer representatives. Six of the remaining members may be recommended to the governor by the South Carolina Funeral Directors Association. Three may be recommended by the South Carolina Morticians Association. Only a funeral establishment may run a crematory in South Carolina. In addition to crematories, the board also licenses retail casket stores.

<www.llr.state.sc.us/POL/Funeral/>

Preneed funeral transactions are regulated by the state Department of Consumer Affairs. There is no consumer information about preneed funerals on their website, however, though we're told it's coming soon.

<www.scconsumer.gov/licensing/preneed_funeral.htm>

The Perpetual Care Cemetery Board does not regulate municipal, religious (unless selling interment rights to nonmembers), or nonprofit cemeteries, or nature preserves and family burial grounds. There are seven board members, three of whom are public members.

<www.llr.state.sc.us/POL/Cemetery/>

Prepaid Cemetery and Funeral Funds

Cemeteries must have their prices conspicuously posted. They may not restrict one from purchasing a monument from an outside vendor nor charge an unreasonable fee if you do so, only for actual supervision.

Only the wholesale cost for prepaid *cemetery merchandise* such as vaults and markers must be placed into trust. There is no trusting requirement for prepaid services such as opening-and-closing or installation charges. The seller may withdraw from the interest sufficient funds to cover the cost of operating the trust; one has to wonder what that means, as there is little cost to letting money sit in the bank. "Constructive delivery" can bypass the trusting requirements. This is accomplished by putting it in a warehouse with your name on it, but few states are actually auditing the warehouses.

Only after a cemetery contract is fully paid may a purchaser cancel the contract. And what can you expect to get back in a refund? Only the wholesale cost—if the item hasn't been "delivered"—and the interest, less administrative costs.

The cemetery must make an annual report to the Cemetery Board of all prepaid trust funds.

In-person or telephone solicitations for preneed funeral sales are not permitted. The consumer must invite the contact. There is no such restriction for cemetery sales, which surely will be noted by companies with funeral/cemetery combo operations.

Since 1989, 100% of all prepaid funeral money must be placed into trust. If a funeral director has sold a vault, 100% of that, too, must be placed into trust. The seller may withdraw 10% of the interest to cover administrative costs. Insurance is an alternative to trusting but usually not a good deal for consumers, as you might get back only half of what you paid if you cashed it in before death.

If the contract is a guaranteed-price agreement and selected merchandise is not available at the time of death, "the provider shall make available to the purchaser or his representative merchandise of equal or greater value. The purchaser or his representative is entitled to approve any substitutions." While the approval of survivors is commendable in this statute, there is a problem with the wording "equal or greater value." A casket that cost $750 ten years ago might cost $1,750 today. For a $750 "value" today, undertakers are likely to exhibit what many call their "welfare caskets." Carlson was told by one state official that preneed contracts will include a detailed description of the merchandise selected and that there is an obligation to offer substitutes of equal quality and construction. But a consumer may need to be wary; "Windsor 482B" is not a sufficient casket description.

A purchaser may cancel a revocable contract at any time. The seller has a right to retain 10% of the earnings in the final year before termination. If the contract is irrevocable, the purchaser has a 30-day period in which it may be cancelled. After that, it may be transferred, but the seller may retain 10% of the contract amount and 10% of the earnings in the final year.

If a purchaser fails to make installment payments in a timely way, the seller may retain 10% of what was paid and cancel the arrangement for a refund of the remaining amount. If it is not irrevocable, it makes more sense to simply cancel the contract and get all your money back rather than default or transfer.

Five dollars of each preneed contract sold goes to the South Carolina *Preneed Funeral Loss Reimbursement Fund* to protect consumers against embezzlement of funeral money.

Consumer Concerns

- The death rate in South Carolina can support approximately 152 full-time mortuaries; there are, however, 405. Funeral prices tend to be higher in areas where there are "too many" funeral homes.

- Trusting requirements are inadequate, and warehousing can avoid trusting entirely for merchandise. 100% of all cemetery merchandise and services should be placed in trust; a purchaser should have a full right of refund at any time, along with the interest. "Constructive delivery" should not be permitted.

- There is no annual reporting requirement to the purchaser of prepaid funeral goods and services, paperwork that might be useful to the family to indicate prepayment and would help to "enforce" trusting requirements.

- Until the South Carolina laws are changed to require 100% trusting of all money and interest for prepaid cemetery goods and services, it is probably a terrible idea to prepay for these arrangements. Your own trust account in a bank will be safer.

- Only a funeral establishment may run a crematory in South Carolina, which is clearly a restraint of trade, instigated by the undertakers to limit competition and low-cost choices. Cremation costs for a consumer are generally higher in the few states where independent crematories are not allowed. In England and in many US states, a crematory has been traditionally situated on or near cemetery grounds and run by a cemeterian. The knowledge and skills for running a crematory do not require apprenticeship as a funeral director, a college degree, nor training in embalming. Mortuary curricula do not generally cover the running of a crematory, nor is the operation of a crematory covered by the study guide for the national funeral directors' exam, which further indicates the absurdity of this restriction. Therefore, South Carolina statutes should be amended to allow others to offer this service to the public. A requirement for training by the manufacturer would be consistent with the task involved and is, indeed, already included in the South Carolina statutes. One does not need to be a funeral director to be so trained.

- The coroner or medical examiner's permit for cremation in the case of an *anticipated* death from natural causes is totally unnecessary and creates an additional burden for families.

- There is no requirement to identify and tag the body at the place of death before removal.

- There is no provision either forbidding a mark-up on cash advance items or requiring the disclosure of how much the mark-up would be. Consumers may wish to ask for a copy of the invoice for these items.

- There is no requirement that low-cost caskets be included in the required display of six caskets. Many funeral directors prefer to show caskets via catalog or computer, with much more variety available. The casket showroom might be better used for services.

- Provisions of Chapter 19 (re embalmers and funeral directors) do not apply to the burial of paupers, according to 40-19-240. One is hard-put to figure out what this meant unless perhaps one doesn't have to worry about "unprofessional conduct" with the poor.

- This state has no laws regulating the body parts business.

Miscellaneous Information

- Educational requirements for becoming an embalmer: one year of mortuary school, two years of apprenticeship, and a passing grade on an embalming exam and state law exam. Two years of apprenticeship—instead of the more usual one year—provide a cheap source of labor for the industry. To its credit, South Carolina has some innovative ways to license funeral directors. One year of mortuary school *or* a four-year degree *or* 60 semester hours (2 years) in specified fields of general study including psychology, biology, and English. Two years of apprenticeship and two exams are required, funeral directing and South Carolina law. Unfortunately, the funeral directing exam is put out by the International Conference of Funeral Service Examining Boards and is deemed out-dated and irrelevant by many industry practitioners.

- Preference is given to the written wishes of the deceased. You may authorize your own cremation prior to death. You may designate a death-care agent for your final arrangements. In situations where you are estranged or distant from next-of-kin, this could be important.

- A crematory operator may not remove dental gold or any other item of value, including body parts.

- Coroners are elected and need not be MDs. The Attorney General has deemed it unethical for a funeral director to run for coroner. Medical examiners are appointed and are licensed physicians.

- It is considered unprofessional conduct to fail to follow federal laws, which presumably includes the FTC Funeral Rule. The Guide to Complying with the Rule is on the Board's web site.

- There is a nice code of ethics in the Board regulations.

- A dance hall may not be closer than a quarter mile to a cemetery.

- A permit for disinterment must be obtained from the state registrar and will be issued only to a funeral director.

This chapter was sent for review to the Department of Health—Vital Statistics, the Board of Funeral Service, the Department of Consumer Affairs, and the Perpetual Care Cemetery Board. Vital Statistics and Consumer Affairs made some minor corrections.

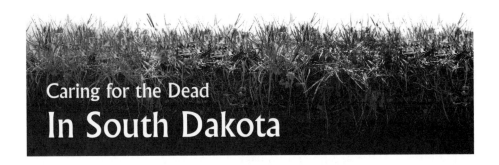

Caring for the Dead
In South Dakota

Please refer also to the general introduction to state chapters: "Caring for the Dead: Necessary Information."

Persons in South Dakota may care for their own dead. The legal authority to do so is found in:

Title 34-25-25: . . . The funeral director or person acting as such who first assumes custody of a dead body shall file a fact of death record.

Title 34-26-14: The person charged by law with the duty of burying the body of a deceased person is entitled to the custody of such body . . . .

There are no other statutes that might require you to use a funeral director.

Title 34-26-16: The duty of burying the body of a deceased person . . . devolves upon the persons hereinafter specified: (1) . . . the husband or wife; (2) . . . person or persons in the same degree nearest of kin to the decedent, being of adult age . . . .

This one obligates you for the costs as well as control.

Death Certificate

South Dakota is using electronic death registration (EDR), since 2004, for about 85% of the deaths. A paper alternative is also available.

The county registrar will supply the Fact of Death form for the demographic portion of the death certificate. You must also name the person who certified the death. The registrar then mails that form to the state Vital Records office. The state will contact the doctor or other certifier for the medical portion of the death certificate.

Fetal Death

A fetal death report is required when death after a gestation of 20 weeks or more. If there is no family physician involved, the local coroner must sign the fetal death certificate.

Transporting and Disposition Permit

Once the Fact of Death report has been filed, the local registrar will issue the disposition permit if the state has not issued one electronically. It must be filed with the registrar of the district in which disposition occurs.

Burial

Check with the county or town registrar for local zoning laws regarding home burial. There are no state burial statutes or regulations with regard to depth. The burial site should be 150 feet or more from a water supply. If burial is on private land, a map designating the burial ground must be recorded with the land records.

When burial is arranged, the family member acting as the funeral director must sign the burial permit and file the original with the registrar (Health Department) within ten days. The second copy is for family records, and the third copy is retained by the cemetery. In the case of home burial, the county registrar may request this copy for recording.

Cremation

Cremation must be in a licensed crematory. There is a 24-hour wait prior to cremation; this can be waived when death is due to infectious disease. No additional permit for cremation is required. A pacemaker must be removed, and authorization by next-of-kin or agent is required if the deceased did not authorize cremation prior to death. The crematory will sign the permit for disposition, which then must be filed with the local registrar within ten days.

The authorizing agent must specify the planned disposition for the cremated remains. If disposition is not in a designated cemetery or public waterway, they may be "disposed of in any manner on the private property of a consenting owner." That written consent, along with a "legal description of the property" (a deed perhaps?), must be given to the crematory prior to release. What a waste of paper and file space. If you simply want to keep them on your mantel, there are no "cremains police" checking to see if they are still there in, say, 25 years.

If you tell the crematory that the cremated remains are to be scattered, the crematory may not release the cremated remains for 30 days and must be given proof that the planned scattering has been recorded with the local registrar. This is totally absurd. If a family from out-of-state has gathered at the time of Granddad's death and wants to scatter the ashes on his ranch before returning home, it will be a class two misdemeanor if they don't record it with the county and wait 30 days. Apparently, any other disposition of cremated remains (i.e., in a cemetery) doesn't have to be recorded with the registrar. Maybe you should say they are being shipped or taken out of state. You will have to give the name and address of the recipient.

This is the only state with such outlandish requirements for cremated remains. One South Dakota funeral director agreed that the laws were silly. His philosophy: "Don't ask, don't tell." Furthermore, he was pretty sure that if someone asked the registrar for a scattering permit, she'd say, "What is that?"

Other Requirements

The Board of Funeral Service has a regulation requiring embalming or refrigeration after 24 hours if disposition has not occurred. This would apply to any body in the possession of a mortician, but the Board of Funeral Service has no jurisdiction over private individuals.

If the person died of a contagious or communicable disease, the doctor in attendance should be consulted.

Medical Schools for Body Donation

Body donation to a medical school is another option for disposition. Find the information for South Dakota at <www.finalrights.org>.

State Governance

The South Dakota Board of Funeral Services has seven members, two of whom are consumer representatives and five funeral directors. The Secretary of Health also serves on the board, making a total of eight.

<http://doh.sd.gov/boards/funeralboard/>

Crematories are licensed and inspected by the Board of Funeral Service. One does not need to be a funeral director to run a crematory. It seems inappropriate not to have a crematory operator represented on the Board. If a crematory wants to deal directly with the public by filing the paperwork and transporting bodies, a funeral director must be hired. This is an unnecessary requirement that drives up cremation prices and helps preserve the funeral directors' undeserved monopoly.

Most cemeteries in South Dakota are operated by municipalities. There is no cemetery board.

Prepaid Cemetery and Funeral Funds

Cemeteries must not be run for-profit. If a cemetery is not a perpetual care cemetery, all printed material must state that fact. Otherwise, 20% of the lot or interment space price must be placed in perpetual care.

Only 70% of prepaid *cemetery* goods and services must be placed in trust. That would make it difficult to get a full refund on a vault, for example, if you changed your mind about body burial and were choosing cremation instead. In fact, there is no statutory provision for cancellation and refunds.

If the contract was for a guaranteed price, 85% of the cost for *funeral* goods and services purchased preneed must be placed in trust. If it was not at a guaranteed price, 100% must be placed in trust.

A purchaser, on 30 days notice, may cancel a preneed funeral contract. The amount of refund will be determined by what was placed in trust—either 85% or 100%—plus all interest. If a purchaser moves, the preneed funds can be transferred or refunded, at the seller's option, a rather strange provision.

Funeral directors and cemeteries must make an annual report to the state Board of Funeral Service for all preneed sales.

Consumer Concerns

- The death rate in South Dakota can support approximately 29 full-time mortuaries; there are 107. However, given the low density of population over a vast geographic area, mortuary careers are not likely to be full-time work. Because of the low volume of business per mortuary, funeral prices will tend to be higher than elsewhere.

- Trusting laws for cemetery and funeral purchases are inadequate and should be increased to 100% for all contracts.

- There is no provision for a detailed description of funeral goods selected preneed nor for a substitution of equal quality and construction if the selected item is no longer available at the time of death. Survivors should have the right to approve any substitution.

- There is no annual reporting requirement to the purchaser of prepaid funeral goods and services, paperwork that might be useful to the family to indicate prepayment and would help to "enforce" trusting requirements.

- There is no state protection for consumers in case of default on prepaid funeral funds that were never put into trust.

- Until the preneed cemetery and funeral laws are improved, it is probably a **terrible** idea to prepay for a funeral in South Dakota.

- There is no requirement that low-cost caskets be included in any display.

- There is no provision either forbidding a mark-up on cash advance items or requiring the disclosure of how much the mark-up would be. Consumers may wish to request a copy of the invoice for these purchases.

- There is no requirement to identify and tag the body at the place of death before removal.

- The standards for ethical, professional conduct are weak should be more well-defined. That would make it easier for a consumer to prevail when filing a complaint. (See Appendix.)

- Complaint procedures are unclear and inadequate. There is no provision for levying a fine when regulations or statutes are violated, only revocation of a license—something rarely done.

- The statutes provide that the Board of Funeral Services may comply *or exempt* themselves from the 1984 FTC Funeral Rule. Note, however, that any state wanting to exempt itself from the Rule has to show the FTC that its own laws are at least as protective. There are no such exemptions for any state. Why wouldn't they want South Dakota residents to have this consumer protection? The Funeral Rule should be adopted by reference.

- The requirements for disposition of cremated remains are unreasonable and should be repealed.

- This state has no laws regulating the body parts business.

Miscellaneous Information

- Educational requirements for funeral service practitioner: two years (60 semester credits) of mortuary school, one year of traineeship, plus state and national exams. Alas, the National Board Exam is deemed out-dated and irrelevant by some industry practitioners. To South Dakota's credit, there is a provision in the statutes to question the validity of this exam: "In order to accept the results of the National Board Examination, the State Board of Funeral Service shall first determine that the knowledge and skills assessed by the examination adequately and accurately evaluate the knowledge and skills needed for actual job performance."

- There is a statutory duty to comply with the disposition wishes of the decedent. You may want to designate a death-care agent for your final arrangements. In situations where you are estranged or distant from next-of-kin, this could be important. You may authorize your own cremation prior to death.

- Coroners are elected and many are funeral directors with a conflict of interest. The Department of Health may appoint death investigators—physicians and nurse practitioners who are trained in forensic pathology.

- The health department will issue a disinterment permit to a funeral director or upon court order.

This chapter was sent for review to the South Dakota Board of Funeral Services and the Department of Vital Records, but no responses were received.

Caring for the Dead
In Tennessee

Please refer also to the general introduction to state chapters: "Caring for the Dead: Necessary Information."

Persons in Tennessee may care for their own dead. The legal authority to do so is found in:

Title 68-3-502: (3b) The funeral director or person acting as such who first assumes custody of the dead body shall file the death certificate.

Title 62-5-102 (b): Nothing herein shall be constituted to prevent or interfere with the ceremonies, customs, religious rites, or religion of any people, denomination, or sect, or to prevent or interfere with any church or synagogue from having their own committee or committees prepare human bodies for burial or to the families, friends or neighbors of deceased persons who prepare and bury their dead without charge.

There are no other statutes that might require you to use a funeral director.

Death Certificate

Tennessee has not yet implemented electronic death registration (EDR), but it's in the works. Presumably a paper alternative will still be available when that happens.

The family doctor or a local medical examiner will sign the death certificate within 48 hours, stating the cause of death. The remaining information must be supplied, typewritten or in unfading black ink. The death certificate must be filed with the local registrar of vital records within five days and usually before final disposition.

Fetal Death

A fetal death report is required when death occurs after 22 weeks of gestation or when the weight is 500 grams or more (almost 18 ounces). If there is no family physician involved, the local medical examiner must sign the fetal death report. The report must be filed with the Department of Health within ten days.

Transporting and Disposition Permit

A body may be moved with the consent of a physician or medical examiner. The registrar where the death certificate is to be filed can issue a burial-transit permit for cremation or removal from the state if the certificate is not yet complete. However, persons handling arrangements without use of a funeral director should try to obtain the death certificate before disposition.

Burial

Family burial grounds are permitted and protected if included in the deed. Check with the local registrar for zoning laws regarding home burial. There are no state burial statutes regarding depth. A sensible guideline is 150 feet from a water supply and 25 feet from a power line or neighbor's boundary. A good practice is at least two feet of earth on top.

Cremation

No additional permit for cremation is required. Most crematories insist that a pacemaker be removed, and authorization from next-of-kin or an agent is required. There are no laws regarding the disposition of cremated remains. You may do as you wish.

Other Requirements

Tennessee has no embalming requirements. Weather and reasonable planning should be considered.

If the person died of a contagious or communicable disease, the doctor in attendance should be consulted.

Medical Schools for Body Donation

Body donation to a medical school is another option for disposition. Find the information for Tennessee at <www.finalrights.org>.

State Governance

The Tennessee State Board of Funeral Directors and Embalmers has seven members. There is one consumer representative. Members must constitute a geographic representation, at least one must be 60 years of age or older, and at least one must be of a racial minority.

<http://tennessee.gov/commerce/boards/funeral/index.shtml>

Crematories must be licensed as a funeral establishment according to regulations promulgated by the Funeral Board. Although the statutes refer to the requirement for funeral directors to use a "licensed crematory," there is no statutory provision for who should license or regulate crematories. The Funeral Board may be exceeding its statutory authority by doing so. Tennessee Code reads:

> The board has the power to select from its members a president and to adopt, promulgate and enforce rules and regulations for the transaction of its business and the management of its affairs, the standards of service and practice to be followed in the profession of **funeral directing** and the betterment and promotion of the educational standards of the profession of funeral directors and embalmers in this state, as it may deem expedient, consistent with the laws of this state.[Emphasis added.]

There is nothing in the study guide for the national funeral directors' exam about running a crematory. There are only two pages on cremation out of 432 in the curriculum guide for mortuary schools, none of which is on actually running a crematory. In Europe, and traditionally in early America, crematories were on the grounds of cemeteries run by cemeterians, not funeral directors. Only Alabama, Alaska, Georgia, Idaho, Oklahoma, South Carolina, and Tennessee require a crematory to be run by a funeral director. In Michigan, a funeral director may not own a crematory. In New York, a crematory must be run by a cemetery. How running a crematory can be considered "funeral directing" seems a stretch. Perhaps the Institute for Justice (a law firm that takes cases against excessive state powers) will take on Tennessee again if an independent operator wants to open a crematory. When Tennessee tried to limit retail casket sales to funeral directors only, IJ came to the rescue of a would-be casket retailer, in the cause for economic freedom and the right to earn a living. Consumers benefit from this kind of economic competition.

Cemeteries and preneed funeral arrangements, including those for cemeteries, are regulated by the commissioner of Commerce and Insurance, Burial Services Division, according to statutes. There is nothing on that website about cemeteries, and all links point back to the Funeral Board website which also reads "Burial Services."

Prepaid Cemetery and Funeral Funds

By law 20% of the lot purchase price and 10% of the cost for mausoleum, crypt, and niche space must be put into an endowment care fund. Cemeteries may charge a maintenance fee ("memorial care") for markers, which will be at the same rate for all regardless of where the marker was purchased. Prices for installation and care are set by the state, based on the consumer price index, which must be a bitter pill for the for-profit companies. Cemeteries must be maintained "so as to reflect respect for the memory of the dead in keeping with the reasonable sensibilities of survivors."

Unless "delivered," 120% of the wholesale cost of *cemetery* goods (markers and urns) and services must be placed in trust when sold preneed. A certificate of delivery (with storage in a warehouse, for example) can bypass the trusting requirement. This is called "constructive delivery," and a refund is not likely should you change your mind. Although the law provides for a substitution of merchandise if you want to change plans, with credit for what was paid, that provision is meaningless if your merchandise is already in the warehouse with your name on it. A vault is considered funeral merchandise for which 100% must be trusted.

In the case of default by a purchaser of 12 months, a cemetery may retain all payments as liquidated damages.

There is now a *Cemetery Consumer Protection Account,* funded by $20 from each preneed contract. This was established after one rascal emptied his cemetery trust accounts of millions of dollars.

Burial *insurance* may not name a specific funeral home as the provider, but a new law in 2008 will allow assignment of an insurance policy for Medicaid eligibility. Insurance is not usually a good way to pay for a funeral. If you were to change your mind from body burial to a more modest cremation and want to cash it in, you might get back only half of what you paid as cash value.

Discounted preneed arrangements are not permitted. Preneed contract forms must be approved by the Division.

100% of prepaid *funeral* money must be placed in trust in a federally insured institution. This would include money for the purchase of vault.

Even if the prepaid arrangement is irrevocable, funds may be transferred to any licensed funeral home. Revocable arrangements may be cancelled with full return of payments and interest.

A Preneed Funeral Protection Account was started in 2008, funded by a $20 fee for each preneed contract written.

Consumer Concerns

- The death rate in Tennessee can support approximately 228 full-time mortuaries; there are, however, 456. Funeral prices tend to be higher in areas where there are "too many" funeral homes.

- Trusting requirements for cemetery merchandise are inadequate. All prepaid funds for cemetery services and merchandise should be placed into trust with a full right of refund with interest. "Constructive delivery" should not be permitted. Until the laws are changed, it is probably a terrible idea to prepay for these cemetery items.

- When a prepaid funeral policy specifies particular merchandise, there is no protection for consumers if that item is no longer available. Consumers should be guaranteed a substitution of equal quality and construction, with an accurate description on the original agreement. Survivors should approve any substitution.

- There is no annual reporting requirement to the purchaser of prepaid funeral goods and services. Such documents could be important to survivors who might not know about prepaid accounts otherwise and are a deterrent against default. Although the original preneed contract must name the institution where monies will be deposited, the seller is free to move the funds without notice.

- Without an adequate provision for substitution of funeral merchandise and better reporting and protection for trust funds, it is probably an *unwise* idea to prepay for funeral services in this state.

- There is no requirement that low-cost caskets be included in a casket display.

- The regulation regarding cash advance items from a third-party vendor such as a florist is somewhat vague. While it appears that a *mark-up* on cash advance items is not permitted, retaining a regular discount *is* permitted, provided that the funeral home reveals that it gets a discount. The amount of the discount may not necessarily be disclosed, however.

- Crematories must be licensed as a funeral establishment, run by a funeral director. This is unnecessarily restrictive and burdensome and increases the cost of cremation for consumers.

- Ethical standards are weak. They should be expanded and clearly defined in order for valid consumer complaints to prevail. (See Appendix.)

- Complaint procedures are not adequately documented in law or regulation. The Department of Consumer Affairs works primarily to mediate complaints. Formal action is brought only if Tennessee law has been violated.

- This state has no laws regulating the body parts business.

Miscellaneous Information

- The educational requirements for becoming a funeral director in Tennessee are one year of mortuary school and two years of apprenticeship (rather than the more typical one year). That provides cheap labor for established funeral homes. For embalmers, two years of mortuary school and one year of apprenticeship are required. All must pass a state-approved exam with a score of 75% or better. While it does have a state exam, Tennessee also accepts the National Board Exam. Too bad, as that is deemed out-dated and irrelevant by some industry practitioners.

- Each body must be tagged with identification.

- Funeral establishments must abide by the FTC Funeral Rule.

- You may name an agent in a power of attorney (TC 34-6-204) to handle your funeral arrangements, helpful if you are estranged from next-of-kin.

- A permit for disinterment must be obtained from the state registrar.

This chapter was sent for review to the Tennessee Department of Public Health, Burial Services, and the State Funeral Board. Burial Services provided some helpful information. The Funeral Board had no comments.

Caring for the Dead

In Texas

Please refer also to the general introduction to state chapters: "Caring for the Dead: Necessary Information."

Persons in Texas may care for their own dead. The legal authority to do so is found in the Health and Safety Code:

> *Sec. 711.002. DISPOSITION OF REMAINS; DUTY TO INTER. (a) Unless a decedent has left directions in writing for the disposition of the decedent's remains as provided in Subsection (g), the following persons, in the priority listed, have the right to control the disposition, including cremation, of the decedent's remains, shall inter the remains, and are liable for the reasonable cost of interment:*
>
> *(1) the person designated in a written instrument signed by the decedent;*
>
> *(2) the decedent's surviving spouse;*
>
> *(3) any one of the decedent's surviving adult children;*
>
> *(4) either one of the decedent's surviving parents . . .*

There are no other statutes which might require you to use a funeral director.

Death Certificate; Report of Death

Texas now uses electronic death registration (EDR), also called Texas Electronic Registrar (TER), although not all physicians and funeral directors are on the system yet. A death record can be initiated three ways: by the physician (or if the death was unexpected by the medical examiner or justice of the peace), the funeral director, or the registrar of the jurisdiction where the death occurred. (This may be different from the residence of the deceased.)

The funeral director or person acting as such must file a *report of death* form with the local registrar within 24 hours. This form is prescribed by the Department of Health, one copy of which serves as the authority to transport a body within the state. The form (VS-115) is available from the local registrar or on the vital statistics unit website:

< http://www.dshs.state.tx.us/vs/field/>

Go to "Forms," then "Funeral/Mortuary Services." Print off two copies. The local registrar can then initiate the death certificate process and forward the record to the medical certifier if the doctor is using the system.

If not, the registrar will print out the drop-to-paper *death certificate* which must be carried to the physician for the cause of death and a signature. The remaining information must be supplied, typewritten or in black ink. The death certificate must be returned to the local registrar within ten days for the remaining entries into the system.

Fetal Death

A certificate of stillbirth (fetal death) is required if weight is 350 grams or more (about 12 ounces); if weight is unknown, it is required after 20 weeks of gestation. A fetal death certificate must be filed as the paper alternative described above. There is no EDR provision for fetal deaths.

Transporting and Disposition Permit

A copy of the Report of Death serves as a burial transit permit within the state. If the body is to be transported out of the state or cremated, the local registrar may be asked for a separate Burial Transit Permit.

Burial

The 2006 Attorney General's opinion (GA-0448) states that a family may bury on their own property without the survey and filing requirements of an incorporated cemetery. The Texas Funeral Service Commission has a page on-line regarding family cemeteries and home burial. Few cities, if any, will allow burials within their city limits outside of a designated cemetery. In a rural area, a sensible guideline is 150 feet from a water supply and 25 feet from a power line. Draw a map of your land showing where the family burial ground will be and pay to have it recorded with the deed. The top of the casket must be not less than two feet below the surface of the earth.

Cremation

A Burial Transit Permit is required for cremation. There is a 48-hour wait before cremation unless the person died of a contagious disease. The local medical examiner, or—if none—a justice of the peace, may waive the waiting period. A pacemaker must be removed, and authorization by next-of-kin or designated agent is required. Persons may authorize their own cremations prior to death.

A person may scatter cremated remains over uninhabited public land, over a public waterway or sea, or on the private property of a consenting owner.

Other Requirements

One portion of the Health and Safety Code says a body must be embalmed or refrigerated (to 34°–40°) after 24 hours unless it is in a sealed container. Another part of the code—relating to body donation—says an "unclaimed" body must be embalmed within 24 hours. Why not refrigeration? It may be an impossible task in a scattered society to determine whether a body will be "claimed" within 24 hours and whether embalming would be approved. Refrigeration is a far more effective method of body preservation.

If the person died of a contagious or communicable disease, the doctor in attendance should be consulted.

Medical Schools for Body Donation

Body donation to a medical school is another option for disposition. Find the information for Texas at <www.finalrights.org>.

State Governance

The Texas Funeral Service Commission has seven members: four public members, two funeral directors, and one cemeterian. In addition to funeral homes, the Commission regulates crematories and cemeteries. Before taking office, Commission members must go through a training program on open-meeting laws as well as funeral and cemetery law, administrative law, and disciplinary procedures among others. How remarkably responsible!

The Department of Banking regulates perpetual-care cemetery trust funds and preneed funeral trust transactions.

also see <www.prepaidfunerals.state.tx.us>

The Insurance Department regulates funeral insurance.

It also has a mess on its hands, as Lincoln Memorial Life Insurance, Memorial Service Life Insurance, and National Prearranged Services are all in liquidation after mismanagement by their owners, the Cassity family. Guaranty funds may cover some of the shortages but not all.

Prepaid Cemetery and Funeral Funds

A portion of each lot sale, usually 15%, must be dedicated to perpetual care in all perpetual care cemeteries. Most municipal, religious, fraternal, and association cemeteries are not perpetual care cemeteries, though some may have funds set aside for care and maintenance of their cemeteries. There are few other laws or regulations giving you specific protections or rights when buying cemetery services and merchandise preneed

The cemetery laws have a very peculiar exclusion buried in Chapter 715—"Certain Historic Cemeteries." A nonprofit corporation may petition the district court to take over and restore a cemetery that's more than 75 years old if there is no existing organization actively maintaining the cemetery. Unlike other cemeteries, however, these may not establish crematories.

Both funeral directors and insurance people may be given a permit to sell preneed funeral contracts. Obviously, the insurance folks won't offer funeral trusts as a funding vehicle, but they must pass out an information brochure during any sales pitch. It's okay as far as it goes but doesn't clearly spell out the degree of risk for consumers, such as getting only about half your money back if you cash in an insurance policy ahead of time. The Department of Banking is required by statute to have an informational web site which is listed on the brochure. (There is life insurance and funeral insurance, among others. With funeral insurance it's not really insurance at all, with no risk to the insurance company as there is with life insurance. If you plan an $8,000 funeral, you'll likely pay $8,000 to let the insurance company play with your money until you die. Maybe double that if you pay over time.)

There are Department-approved forms for preneed purchases, one for trust-funded ones and one for insurance. If paying by installments, a total cost must be given, an excellent consumer protection provision. Thanks to Jim Bates, a board member of both the Funeral Consumers Alliance of North Texas and the national FCA board, the department recently rewrote these forms in straightforward plain language. The staff members he worked with were genuinely concerned about doing right by the public, and should be commended for their enthusiasm about working with consumer advocates.

90% of your preneed *funeral* money is supposed to be placed in trust. The seller gets to keep a 10% commission right away. If you are making installment payments, however, the mortician doesn't get just 10% of each payment; undertakers can keep 50% of what is paid until the commission is in their pockets. (There are 29 states that require 100% trusting. Preneed is alive and well in those states. Why wouldn't Texas want the best consumer protection, too?)

The preneed purchases of *cemetery* services and vaults are treated like other preneed *funeral* purchases, with 90% trusting required. Advance purchase of markers and monuments, however, is not protected. That is, there are no trusting requirements and no provision for a refund if you were to change your mind. (To its credit, Texas does not permit "constructive delivery," a warehousing mechanism by which trusting requirements are avoided in some other states.)

Funeral homes may add finance charges to installment preneed sales. When you finance a car, house, or other retail purchase, you get to use the item. But a finance charge on a lay-away plan before they lay you away? The undertaker gets a commission, the undertaker gets the interest even if you cancel, and the undertaker now wants you to pay a little extra for the bother of cashing more than one check! (As of 2001, the seller gets only half the interest.)

A purchaser may cancel a revocable agreement, but kiss half of the interest and the 10% commission good-bye. By the way, if your family didn't know about a prepaid irrevocable account and used another provider at the time of your death, there is no statutory provision for a refund.

You may irrevocably assign an insurance policy to a funeral provider only for Medicaid eligibility purposes, a sensible provision.

If you are paying on installment and still owe a balance, let the funeral home know if you have moved. If the funeral home can't find you for three years, it can take the interest and declare your prepaid funeral funds "abandoned" (if the Banking Commissioner agrees). Although the principal goes to the state, the state will owe you nothing—*nada*—unlike the practice in Canadian provinces that protects a consumer's interest under such circumstances.

A guaranty fund of sorts was established (as of 1988) to protect consumers from mortuary default on prepaid funeral accounts sold by licensed establishments—not cemetery purchases. In most states, that's to help out if a rascal took off with your money and it was never put into trust, but it wouldn't cover situations in which your funeral funds might have been turned over to the state. In Texas, however, it doesn't cover you if you have the misfortune of purchasing a preneed agreement from someone who is not licensed by the state to sell preneed. Preneed sellers need a license to steal?

What about funeral insurance? About the only good thing that can be said for insurance is that it's relatively portable from one funeral home to another. However, it may not appreciate as quickly as money in a trust. Insurance companies decide at the end of each year how much to share with their customers, depending on how much money their investments have made after paying commissions and the money brokers.

Watch out for the greedy double-dippers. Once an undertaker has collected an initial 10% on a trust account, your 90% can be used to purchase funeral insurance. *Voilà!* A second commission for the mortician. Yes, you will get a right-of-refusal letter, but if you ignore the deadline on this "negative notice" and don't say "no" in time, your account will automatically be moved—a little or a lot lighter than before.

As of December 2008, there were $2.928 billion dollars in prepaid funeral contracts; 55% are insurance-funded; 45% trust-funded.

Consumer Concerns

- The death rate in Texas can support approximately 616 full-time mortuaries; there are, however, over 1,201. Funeral prices tend to be higher in areas where there are "too many" funeral homes.

- Finance charges are permitted for installment purchases of prepaid funeral and cemetery arrangements. This should be repealed.

- Trusting requirements are inadequate. 100% of prepaid cemetery goods and services should be placed in trust, with a provision for cancellation and refund. The trusting requirement for preneed funeral purchases also should be increased to 100%, with all interest retained in the account until need.

- Sellers get to keep half the interest and 10% if the preneed contract is cancelled or transferred.

- There is no annual reporting requirement to the purchaser of prepaid funeral goods and services. This paperwork would not only help you to keep track of how much you will actually pay, and also give an accounting to your family at time of death.

- Substitution provisions are inadequate. Survivors should have the right to approve the substitution of any merchandise if what was selected in a preneed contract is no longer available.

- In spite of the Guaranty Fund and until the Texas laws are changed, it is probably a terrible idea to prepay for a funeral or any cemetery merchandise and services in this state. Your own trust account in a bank will be safer, will be portable, and will accumulate interest regularly. You may be able to make it irrevocable if assets need to be sheltered for Medicaid eligibility.

- The 48-hour wait before cremation is unnecessary when survivors are in agreement and is causing additional charges to families for refrigerated storage or embalming.

- Identification and tagging of the body at the place of death before removal should be required.

- The standards for ethical, professional conduct should be strengthened. That would make it easier for a consumer to prevail when filing a valid complaint. (See Ethical Standards in the Appendix.)

- The Funeral Commission has prepared an information brochure for consumers that funeral directors must give to persons inquiring about funeral arrangements. It spells out the procedure for filing complaints. It is vague and weak in explaining the pitfalls of prepaying for a funeral in Texas; that portion should be rewritten.

- Crematories may be owned only by funeral establishments or cemeteries. This kind of business restriction should be either changed in the legislature or challenged in court. Generally, states have a right to make limiting laws only for the public good. There is no justification for effectively limiting crematory operation to these businesses.

- Crematories must place a label on a non-permanent container for cremated remains that discloses: "The temporary container is not intended for the permanent storage of cremated remains in a niche, crypt, cremation interment container, or interment space." This serves nobody except the greedy funeral director who wants an excuse to sell you a more expensive box. (Carlson's father-in-law, Charlie, donated his body to the local medical school. When the family received the cremated remains some months after his death, the cardboard container was marked, "Temporary," a ploy Carlson had read about in *Funeral Service Insider* to get families to purchase expensive urns. Charlie was a great believer in education and his box has now become a traveling display of sleazy sales tactics, displayed in talks by both both Slocum and Carlson.)

- This state has no laws regulating the body parts business.

Miscellaneous Information

- Educational requirements for funeral directors: high school plus mortuary college, national exam, state exam, and one year of apprenticeship. Unfortunately, the National Board Exam put out by the International Conference of Funeral Service Examining Boards has been deemed out-of-date and irrelevant by some industry practitioners.

- There is a statutory duty to comply with the written wishes of the decedent. If you are estranged from next-of-kin, one may use the

"Appointment of Agent to Control Disposition of Remains," down-loadable on the Commission web site.

- A casket display must include a reasonable selection of at least five adult caskets, with the least expensive one visibly displayed in the same general manner as all other caskets.

- If there is a fee for obtaining cash advance items, it must be disclosed in advance.

- The language of the FTC Funeral Rule is included in the Funeral Service Commission rules, making it more enforceable in Texas.

- Medical examiners are appointed physicians. Justices of the peace are elected.

- A person who has killed another may not be buried in the same cemetery as that person's victim.

- Disinterment may be done with the permission of the cemetery, of the lot owner, and the person with the right to control disposition. If there is no agreement, then permission must be gotten from a county court. Notice must be given.

This chapter was sent for fact-checking and review to the Texas Department of Banking, the Texas Funeral Service Commission, The Texas Insurance Department, and the Texas Department of Health—Vital Statistics Unit.

Russell Reese, Director of Special Audits in the Department of Banking, wrote back. "The Texas Department of Banking is not able to review and edit the document you forwarded. The content of the document has not been reviewed by the Department and its accuracy is not confirmed. Representations in your book that the Texas Department of Banking in any way approved or reviewed its content must be removed." One has to wonder why Mr. Reese's agency is "not able" to review this chapter or why he would not be eager to have input on consumer information. The people who will benefit would be the ones paying his salary.

Lamar Hankins, an Austin attorney and past president of FCA, has an eagle eye for corrections and added information that was not in the original draft.

Caring for the Dead
In Utah

Please refer also to the general introduction to state chapters: "Caring for the Dead: Necessary Information."

Persons in Utah may care for their own dead. The legal authority to do so is found in:

Title 26-2-13 (4): The funeral director or person acting as the funeral director who first assumes custody of the dead body shall file the certificate of death.

Title 26-2-16 . . . . (6) The state registrar shall post information on the state registrar's website, providing instructions to a dispositioner for complying with the requirements of law relating to the dispositioner's responsibilities for:

(a) completing and filing a certificate of death; and

(b) possessing, transporting, and disposing of a dead body or dead fetus.

Title 26-2-17 (3): A burial-transit permit shall be issued by the registrar of the district where the certificate of death or fetal death is filed, for bodies to be transported out of the state for final disposition and when disposition is made by a person other than a licensed funeral director.

Thanks to amazing advocacy by Joyce Mitchell, President of the FCA of Utah, lawmakers repealed a 2006 law that had made Utah families' deceased loved ones the property of the funeral industry. The 2006 law made it illegal for anyone but a commercial funeral director to sign and file a death certificate, forcing families to pay whatever the funeral home demanded. In 2009 consumer advocates and casket makers David and Marcia Robles joined Mitchell to successfully lobby for a bill to preserve citizens' rights to conduct a funeral without interference from the mortuary industry. A non-funeral director handling a death is called a "dispositioner."

Death Certificate

Vital Records has been using electronic death registration since 2006. Its website has instructions for filing a death certificate manually:

<http://health.utah.gov/vitalrecords/fileadeath/fileadeath.htm>

We thought the barriers to family-directed funerals were gone, until we discovered that county health departments across Utah are charging outrageous "dispositioner" fees to type in the demographic information, a data entry task of maybe 20 minutes or so for a slow typist. These fees range from $25 in Salt Lake City to $300 in Wasach County and Southeast Utah, with an average of at least $100 elsewhere . . .with the exception of one saintly registrar in Vernal, Utah who has no intention of charging for this public service because there simply won't be that many of them anyway. Some registrars do make themselves available nights and on weekends—for a $300 fee, but, at that rate, most families will wait. Not all doctors are on the new EDR system, but they haven't been hit with these outrageous fees. This is the **only** state where Health Department employees are punishing home funeral families with exorbitant fees for filing a death certificate. Home births are not being financially punished in this way.

There is contact information in a list of local registrars in the "How to File a Death Certificate" document on the above website.

Once the demographic information has been entered, the registrar can then check to see if the family doctor is on the system. If so, the doctor is required to fill out the medical certification within 72 hours, stating the cause of death. Make sure your doctor knows if you are planning to have a home funeral without a funeral director so the doctor doesn't delay in filling out his part. (Maybe your doctor's office would even fill in the demographic information for you, too.)

If your doctor is not on EDR, the registrar will print out a "drop-to-paper" death certificate form for the doctor to fill out and sign. That must be filed with the local registrar within five days of death and prior to final disposition.

Fetal Death

A fetal death report is required for each fetal death. If there is no family physician involved, the local medical examiner must sign the fetal death certificate.

Transporting and Disposition Permit

The local registrar will issue the disposition permit. The fee for this is $47. This will be required before a body can be released from a hospital. After usual business hours, a law enforcement officer or someone "on call" will supply the permit. Unless moved by a funeral director, a body must be encased in a container or plastic pouch.

Burial

There are no state statutes that specifically permit or prohibit home burial. It is also unlikely that there are local zoning regulations regarding home burial, but you should review them before planning a family cemetery. If your land is in a rural area, draw a map of the property showing where the burial ground will be and have it filed with the deed. That may be all you have to do to establish your family cemetery. There are no state burial statutes or regulations with regard to burial locations or depth. A sensible guideline is 150 feet from a water supply, 25 feet from a power line, with two or three feet of earth on top. Plan your family cemetery away from boundaries with neighbors, too.

After burial, the family member acting as the funeral director must sign the disposition permit and file it with the registrar where disposition takes place, by the 10th of the following month.

Cremation

A medical examiner must review the death record. There is a fee of $52 which the registrar will collect. Once released by the medical examiner, a cremation transit permit will be issued. Authorization by next-of-kin or the designated agent is required, and a pacemaker must be removed. The crematory will file the disposition permit.

Other Requirements

Utah has no embalming requirements. Weather and reasonable planning should be considered. If the person died of a contagious or communicable disease, the doctor in attendance should be consulted.

Medical Schools for Body Donation

Body donation to a medical school is another option for disposition. Find the information for Utah at <www.finalrights.org>.

State Governance

The Utah Board of Funeral Service has seven members. Four are funeral directors, one is a preneed seller not affiliated with a funeral home, and two are consumer representatives.

<www.dopl.utah.gov/licensing/funeral_service.html>

The Preneed Funeral Arrangement Licensing Board consists of three funeral establishment representatives, one preneed sales agent, one owner of an endowment care cemetery, and two public members. Preneed sellers funding preneed with insurance must also be licensed by the Insurance Department.

There is no cemetery board. A small section of the statutes covers endowment care and the recording of cemetery plots.

Crematories are not regulated. One does not need to be a funeral director to run a crematory.

Prepaid Cemetery and Funeral Funds

Cemetery lots that have not been used or cared for in 60 years are considered abandoned and may be reclaimed by the cemetery.

There is no statutory protection for preneed *cemetery* transactions. Therefore, money you spend for vaults, markers, and cemetery services may be spent by the cemetery right away. If you later change your mine, or if the cemetery goes out of business, you're out of luck.

Any preneed *funeral* contract must be a "guaranteed product contract," a lousy deal for funeral directors, as funeral inflation has been exceeding interest rates for the last five or more years. Under such circumstances, there is likely to be manipulative mischief. "Gee, Mrs. Brown, we no longer have the casket your mother selected. You'll have to pick out another, and the prices have gone up." There are no statutory provisions for substitution of like quality and construction.

100% of preneed funeral funds must be placed into trust. Interest may be withdrawn for "reasonable" expenses for administering the trust by the institution holding funds and by the seller of the prepaid funeral plan for expenses associated with the sale of the plan, accounting, and reporting. The seller gets to keep any remaining interest if the buyer cancels.

Statutes imply that a purchaser may revoke the contract and get a refund *if* the contract permits it, but how much one might get is not spelled out in the law. The consumer may be at the mercy of the contract fine-print, as the administrative code promulgated by the Funeral Board permits an outrageous revocation fee of 25%—as long as that's what the contract says.

Insurance is a permitted alternative to trusting but not usually a good deal for the consumer. If you are paying over time, you may pay double what the funeral actually costs, and if you change your mind and want your money back, you'll be lucky if the cash value is equal to half of what you paid. Insurance growth usually lags behind that of trust investments, as the company has commissions to pay.

A trust-funded contract may be converted to an insurance-funded contract with the consent of the buyer, after "full disclosure of the consequences" and without "undue influence" or "coercion." Consumers should just say no.

A seller of preneed funeral arrangements must make an annual report to the state.

Consumer Concerns

- The death rate in Utah can support approximately 54 full-time mortuaries; there are 85 such establishments. Given the low density of population over a vast geographic area, mortuary careers are not likely to be full-time work in most areas. Unfortunately, because of the low volume of business per mortuary, funeral prices will tend to be higher than elsewhere.

- There is no provision for irrevocable contracts to be transferred in case the beneficiary were to move.

- There is no provision for an adequate description of funeral goods selected in a guaranteed-price preneed contract nor for a substitution of equal quality if an item is no longer available at the time of death. Survivors should be permitted to approve any substitution.

- There is no annual reporting requirement to the purchaser of prepaid funeral goods and services, paperwork that might be helpful to the family of a deceased to indicate prepayment and which would help to "enforce" trusting requirements.

- There is no state protection from default of prepaid funeral monies.

- Until there is better protection, it is probably a terrible idea to prepay for a funeral in Utah.

- There is no requirement to include low-cost caskets in any display.

- There is no requirement to identify and tag the body at the place of death before removal.

- The standards for ethical, professional conduct are almost nonexistent. These should be spelled out to make it easier for a consumer to prevail when filing a valid complaint.

- A body may be held for funeral expenses. If a mortician has sold a family more of a funeral than it can afford, this provision allows the body to become a hostage until more money can be found.

- This state has no laws regulating the body parts business.

Miscellaneous Information

- Educational requirements for becoming a funeral director: associate's degree in mortuary science (2 years), the National Board Exam, and one year (and 50 embalmings) of apprenticeship. Alas, the National Board Exam is deemed 40 years out of date and irrelevant by many.

- A personal representative may be named to carry out the wishes of a decedent.

- A next-of-kin who is estranged from the deceased loses the right to control disposition.

- Cash advance items must be billed in the actual amount of charges paid by the funeral home including discounts and rebates.

- There is a statutory obligation to abide by the FTC Funeral Rule.

- No surface coal mining is permitted within 100 feet of a cemetery.

- A permit for disinterment must be obtained from the local registrar.

This chapter was sent for review to the Utah Department of Health, the Preneed Funeral Arrangement Licensing Board, and the Board of Funeral Service, but no written comments were received. Vital Records was somewhat helpful over the telephone.

Caring for the Dead
In Vermont

Please refer also to the general introduction to state chapters: "Caring for the Dead: Necessary Information."

Persons in Vermont may care for their own dead. The legal authority to do so is found in:

> *Title 18, Section 5207. Certificate furnished family; burial permit. The physician or person filling out the certificate of death, within thirty-six hours after death, shall deliver the same to the family of the deceased, if any, or the undertaker or person who has charge of the body. Such certificate shall be filed with the person issuing the certificate of permission for burial, entombment or removal obtained by the person who has charge of the body before such dead body shall be buried, entombed or removed from the town. . . .*

There are no other statutes that might require you to use a funeral director.

Death Certificate

Vermont is now using Electronic Death Registration. Home funeral families may use a paper option, however, starting with the Preliminary Report of Death (PROD). That can be found on the Health Department website:

<http://healthvermont.gov/vadr/burial/home.aspx>

The doctor last in attendance or a medical examiner will state the cause of death and sign the medical portion of the PROD. The remaining information must be supplied, typewritten or in black ink. The PROD must be filed with the Office of Vital Records within 48 hours: by fax, (802) 651-1787; by mail, Vital Records, VT Dept. of Health, P.O. Box 70, Burlington, VT 05402, or at 108 Cherry Street, Room 303, Burlington. State staff will enter information from the PROD into the EDR system, after which a certified copy of the death certificate can be obtained.

Fetal Death

A fetal death report is required when death occurs at 20 or more weeks of gestation or when the weight is 400 grams or more (about 14 ounces).

Transporting and Disposition Permit

The town clerk (or any law enforcement officer after hours) will issue a burial-transit permit once the PROD has been filled out. Funeral directors often serve as deputies and sign their own burial-transit permits. The burial-transit permit must be filed with the town clerk in the town of disposition.

Burial

If burial is planned for private land set aside for the use of the immediate family, the town clerk will need a map of the location to record in the land records. (A hand-drawn map will usually suffice.) The local health officer may be asked to check the location. Burial must be at least 150 feet from a water supply (100 from a drilled well). The burial site must be at least 25 feet from a power line. The bottom (not the top) of the casket must be five feet below the natural surface of the earth (three-and-a-half feet for infants).

When burial is arranged, the family member acting as the funeral director must sign the burial-transit permit and file it with the clerk of the town in which burial occurs.

Cremation

A cremation permit ($25) from the medical examiner or an assistant medical examiner is required. Authorization by next-of-kin or designated agent is also required, and a pacemaker must be removed. The crematory will file the burial-transit permit. There are no laws regarding the disposition of cremated remains. You may do as you wish.

Other Requirements

Vermont has no embalming requirements. Weather and reasonable planning should be considered.

If the person died of a contagious or communicable disease, the doctor in attendance should be consulted. Disposition may be under the instructions of the local health officer.

Medical Schools for Body Donation

Body donation to a medical school is another option for disposition. Find the information for Vermont at <www.finalrights.org>.

State Governance

The Vermont Board of Funeral Service has five members. Two are consumer representatives.

<http://vtprofessionals.org/opr1/funeral/>

Crematories are regulated by the Office of Professional Regulation in the Secretary of State's office. One does not have to be a funeral director to run a crematory.

Cemeteries may not be operated for private gain. Almost all Vermont cemeteries are run by local towns or churches.

Disposition of the dead must be by burial in a cemetery, interment in a mausoleum, or by cremation unless buried on one's private property. This statute has stymied folks in Bristol that wish to use conservation land for green burials without constructing a "cemetery" with plats and numbered lots or a perpetual care fund.

Cemetery bylaws may not interfere with religious burial customs. The Vermont Cemetery Association supports the interpretation that a vault may not be required for Jewish, Muslim, or other religious burial practices. That said, most cemeteries do require a vault for maintenance purposes and seem unaware of this statute. There has been some difficulty at Lakeside Cemetery in Burlington in gaining earth burial for Muslims, for example, but consumer advocates are still working to gain a remedy for this.

It seems unfortunate that there is statutory provision for moving a cemetery, "when it is impracticable [for a town] to preserve a burial ground in proper condition." And the Windsor County Probate Court permitted a new owner to move a family cemetery that was at the top of a hill where the view was ideal for a new house.

Although each cemetery must have the lots mapped out and numbered, many old town cemeteries are poorly recorded. In a Bridgewater cemetery, one man's grave was accidently unearthed when excavation began for his wife's. The town Cemetery Commission denied any wrong-doing, but that seemed like a white-wash to the daughter, who'd been given three different stories as to whether there was damage to her dad's casket or not. When the whereabouts of a lot owner has been unknown for 20 years, the cemetery may, through the probate court, regain title. If a claim from one entitled to the lot arises within 17 years after that, the lot will be made available, or, if sold, the proceeds of the sale will go to the claimant.

Prepaid Cemetery and Funeral Funds

100% of prepaid *funeral* money must be placed in trust with interest to accrue. Administrative fees—the lesser of one-half the earnings or 2% of the account—may be withdrawn each year.

A purchaser may transfer an irrevocable contract to a new provider, but the seller may retain 5% of the assets.

Although a funeral provider "may" substitute merchandise of equal quality if the selected item is no longer available, it is not a requirement. Survivors must be "notified" when a substitution is made, but survivor approval is not mandated.

A funeral seller must instruct the escrow agent to send a report annually to the purchaser showing all transactions and the balance of the account. Annual reports must be issued by the institution or escrow agent holding the money. The first year such reports were required, one Vermont funeral director simply cranked out reports on his own computer. Troubled by the $100 administrative fee that had been subtracted, one elderly gentleman contacted an advocate with the Council on Aging. Irregularities were quickly apparent: Instead of posting the last quarter of 1996 interest as of December 31, 1996, it was posted January 1, 1997 in order to qualify for a $100 service fee rather than a mere $50. There were also such outrageously generous interest "deposits" for some years (23.2%) that one had to wonder if the funeral director was playing the ponies with this money, or if the whole report was bogus.

There is a Funeral Services Trust Account to protect preneed consumers against default of the funeral provider. The first claim on it was filed in 2010 after a bankrupt funeral home went out of business.

There are no laws or regulations giving you specific protections or rights when buying cemetery services and merchandise preneed.

Consumer Concerns

- The death rate in Vermont can support approximately 20 full-time mortuaries; there are 70 such establishments. Funeral prices tend to be higher in areas where there are "too many" funeral homes.

- There is no requirement for a detailed description of selected funeral merchandise nor adequate terms for providing a substitute of equal quality and construction, with approval of survivors.

- Administrative fees may be withdrawn from the interest of a preneed account, and a penalty of 5% is permitted for a cancellation or transfer. Administrative fees should be eliminated or drastically reduced. Such withdrawals significantly reduce the amount available against inflation. Transfer or cancellation penalty should be eliminated.

- Although Vermont now has annual reporting and a protection fund, it may be *unwise* to prepay for a funeral until penalties and fees are abolished and substitution issues are improved.

- The medical examiner's permit for cremation in the case of an *anticipated* death from natural causes is unnecessary and creates an additional burden and charge for families.

- There is no requirement to identify and tag the body at the place of death before removal.

- There is no provision either forbidding a mark-up on cash advance items or requiring the disclosure of how much the mark-up would be. Consumers may wish to ask for receipts for these charges.

- Complaints are being white-washed by the Office of Professional Regulation, with little or no oversight by the Board of Funeral Service. One consumer, billed after-the-fact in violation of the Funeral Rule, had to go the Attorney General's office to get the balance of the funeral bill canceled.

- This state has no laws regulating the body parts business.

Miscellaneous Information

- Educational requirements for becoming a funeral director: national exam and assisting at 30 funerals. For embalmer: two years of college (at least one of which is mortuary study), one year of apprenticeship, and a national exam. Unfortunately, the ICFSEB exam is deemed out of date and irrelevant by some industry practitioners. Furthermore, while ICFSEB is supposed to test state-specific items for Vermont, the staff in the Office of Professional Regulation can't get a copy of that exam to see what it covers. Why should the state require an exam it knows nothing about?

- Regulations require that the least expensive casket be shown on display or by photograph. (This is not always the done, according to some reports.)

- Medical examiners are appointed physicians.

- The FTC Funeral Rule has been adopted by reference. In addition, the General Price List (GPL) must include the costs for private family viewing and body donation. The address and phone number for registering a complaint must be on the GPL, along with a statement that state help with funeral expenses may be available to those who qualify.

- You may name a person other than a next-of-kin to manage your funeral arrangements, in section four of the Vermont Advance Directives.

- If a person without funds has no headstone after three years, the town must erect one.

- Cemeteries must be fenced. "If a person or estate is damaged by cattle, horses, sheep or swine breaking into a public burial ground and injuring a grave, headstone, monument, shrubbery or flowers, for want of a legal fence around such burial ground, such person or estate may recover of the town double the amount of damages."

- A removal permit must be obtained from the town clerk to move a body from one cemetery to another.

This chapter was sent for review to the Board of Funeral Service and the Department of Health—Vital Records, but no response was received from the Funeral Board or Office of Professional Regulation. Vital Records staff were very helpful.

Caring for the Dead
In Virginia

Please refer also to the general introduction to state chapters: "Caring for the Dead: Necessary Information."

Persons in Virginia may care for their own dead. The legal authority to do so is found in:

> *Title 32.1-263-B. The licensed funeral director, funeral service licensee, office of the state anatomical program, or next of kin as defined in § 54.1-2800 who first assumes custody of a dead body shall file the certificate of death with the registrar.*

There are no other statutes that might require you to use a funeral director.

Death Certificate

The family doctor or a medical examiner will sign the death certificate within 24 hours, stating the cause of death. The remaining information must be supplied, typewritten or in black ink. The death certificate (two copies) must be filed with the local registrar within three days and before final disposition or removal from the state.

Virginia hopes to start a pilot for electronic death registration soon. When that is adopted state-wide, home funeral folks will still be able to use a paper alternative. A blank death certificate may be obtained from a physician, hospital, medical examiner, or local health department.

Fetal Death

A fetal death report is required for each fetal death. If there is no family physician involved, the local medical examiner must sign the fetal death certificate.

Transporting and Disposition Permit

A body may be moved with medical permission. A burial-transit permit is required only for out-of-state disposition. The death certificate must be obtained first. In all cases the local registrar must sign line 30 of the death certificate before disposition.

Burial

The state requires no additional permit for disposition by burial.

Although family graveyards are mentioned in the laws, there are no state statutes that specifically permit or prohibit home burial. It is also unlikely that there are local zoning regulations regarding home burial, but you should review them before planning a family cemetery. If your land is in a rural area, draw a map of the property showing where the burial ground will be and have it filed with the deed. That may be all you have to do to establish your family cemetery. There are no state burial statutes or regulations with regard to burial locations or depth. A sensible guideline is 150 feet from a water supply, 25 feet from a power line, with two or three feet of earth on top. Plan your family cemetery away from boundaries with neighbors, too.

Family graveyards, abandoned after 25 years, may be moved with the permission of the circuit court if there is no objection. That's too bad. In many other states, a burial site becomes a permanent easement on the land.

Cremation

A permit for cremation or burial at sea must be obtained from the medical examiner. The usual fee for this is $50. There is a 24-hour wait before cremation or burial at sea unless visual identification is made by next-of-kin. A pacemaker must be removed, and authorization by next-of-kin or a designated agent is required. There are no laws regarding the disposition of cremated remains. You may do as you wish.

Other Requirements

Virginia requires embalming or refrigeration after 48 hours. The funeral director may not embalm without the family's permission.

If the person died of a contagious or communicable disease, the doctor in attendance should be consulted.

Medical Schools for Body Donation

Body donation to a medical school is another option for disposition. Find the information for Virginia at <www.finalrights.org>.

State Governance

The Virginia State Board of Funeral Directors and Embalmers has nine members. There are two consumer representatives.

<www.dhp.virginia.gov/funeral/default.htm>

Crematories are licensed by the Board of Funeral Directors and Embalmers. One does not need to be a funeral director to run a crematory, but only those crematories affiliated with a funeral home may deal directly with the public. Virginia also licenses body transport services.

A state Cemetery Board was established in 1998, in spite of heavy lobbying against it by corporate-owned cemeteries. There are seven members, two of which are citizen representatives, including a member of FCA.

<www.dpor.virginia.gov/dporweb/cem_main.cfm>

State, county, town, and church cemeteries are exempt from regulation, as are family cemeteries where no graves are sold to the public. The Board must pass regulations that provide consumer protection consistent with the FTC Funeral Rule, price lists being a conspicuous requirement.

Prepaid Cemetery and Funeral Funds

All cemeteries, including pet cemeteries, must have perpetual care funds.

Only 40% of the amount received for preneed *cemetery* "property or services" must be placed in trust. "Constructive delivery" can bypass the trusting requirement. There is no provision for cancellation and refund of preneed cemetery arrangements after the first three days.

Virginia regulations prohibit a funeral licensee from in-person communication to solicit preneed funeral arrangements, including by phone. A consumer must initiate any contact. No such restrictions apply to cemetery sales. As funeral conglomerates buy up both cemeteries and funeral homes, their avid preneed marketers can wear a "cemetery hat" and ignore such a restriction. Consumers receiving unrequested sales calls should tighten a hold on their wallets. Once you're sitting there in person to buy a cemetery lot, the "hats" can change.

A preneed *funeral* contract must have several pages of consumer information disclosures attached. The disclosures are done in an easy-to-read question-and-answer format. The address where complaints may be filed is also included.

Finance charges are prohibited on funeral preneed purchases.

100% of the money paid for *funeral* goods and services that will be supplied at a non-guaranteed price must be placed in **trust**. If prices have been guaranteed, only 90% needs to be placed in trust.

A consumer may cancel a funeral contract within 30 days for a full refund including interest. After 30 days, the seller may keep 10% of what was paid but must return all interest. The contract may be transferred to any provider, presumably minus the 10%.

Funeral directors selling preneed plans must carry a performance bond sufficient to cover the risk of loss and have evidence of such on the premises. A chronological list of all preneed contracts must be kept, but there is no annual reporting requirement to the state and consumer. Although the Funeral Board inspects funeral homes every three years and reviews preneed record-keeping, there is no way for the state to know that all preneed arrangements have been recorded. With the high cost of bonding, there is an inherent motivation to acknowledge or record fewer preneed accounts than have actually been sold. Prepaid funeral money has vanished in other states, including those with 100% trusting requirements.

If selected merchandise is not available at the time of death, substitution of items similar in style and at least equal in quality of material and workmanship is required. The survivor may do the selecting; this is one of the few states with such a provision and should be emulated by all others.

Restrictive Casket Sales

This heading shows up in only three state chapters: Louisiana, Oklahoma, and Virginia.

For years, caskets were the major profit-maker for an undertaker, and markup on caskets was often 300-500% or more. As word leaked out about actual casket costs, some entrepreneurs saw an opportunity to cut the price and still make a "fair" profit, knowing that consumers were growing resentful. In the mid 1990s, the retail casket business was born.

The Federal Trade Commission permits consumers to purchase from a funeral home *only* those goods and services wanted. Since 1994, it has forbidden a funeral home from charging a handling fee if a consumer purchases an item or service elsewhere. The FTC does not address who may sell a casket, but it has very specific language that does oblige a funeral home to accept a casket provided by the consumer.

So what's the problem in Virginia? The following appears in Chapter 28 Title 54.1-2800 Definitions: "Practice of funeral services" means engaging in the care and disposition of the human dead, the preparation of the human dead for the funeral service, burial, or cremation, the making of arrangements for the funeral service or for the financing of the funeral service **and** [emphasis added] the selling or making of financial arrangements for the sale of funeral supplies to the public." With the use of the word "and," not "or"—you would think that one must do all of these to be practicing funeral services. Apparently, however, one small portion of this definition—sale of funeral supplies to the public—is being used to claim that one must be licensed as a funeral director to sell such supplies.

If one is going to enforce this restrictive *funeral supplies* law, it wouldn't be fair to apply it selectively, would it? Wouldn't that also mean the corner stationery store may no longer sell guest books or thank-you cards? What about funeral flowers? Or the flag-case to hold a veteran's flag?

Generally, burdensome laws will be sustained by the courts only if there are reasons of public health, vital statistics, or legal/criminal concerns. Just how does the state of Virginia justify controlling who may sell a box—which is all a casket is? What if we call it a "hope chest" instead? Who may sell it then? There's no law against burying someone in a hope chest.

Clearly, any restriction on who may sell caskets or other funeral supplies in Virginia is a restraint of trade that subverts the FTC's Funeral Rule provision specifically permitting consumers to purchase *only* the goods and services desired from the funeral provider. Until legislators get down to business and change the laws or the Funeral Board changes its interpretation, there is nothing to stop you from ordering your casket from another state via the internet or getting directions for building your own, and the funeral home will be obliged to accept it. Typically, legislators must consider the financial impact of any statute. In this case, that definition may be driving money out of state, not to mention your wallet.

Consumer Concerns

- The death rate in Virginia can support approximately 233 full-time mortuaries; there are, however, 465. Funeral prices tend to be higher in areas where there are "too many" funeral homes.

- There is no annual reporting requirement to the purchaser of pre-paid funeral or cemetery goods and services, paperwork that might be useful to the family of a deceased to indicate prepayment. Such reporting would help to "enforce" the required trusting, as well.

- The 10% penalty for transferring a funeral plan is harmful and should be abolished.

- Until the Virginia laws are changed to require 100% trusting of all money and interest for prepaid *cemetery goods and services* and better oversight for cemetery transactions in general, it is probably a terrible idea to prepay for any cemetery arrangements over and above the purchase of a lot. A trust account in a bank will be safer.

- There is no provision either forbidding a mark-up on cash advance items or requiring the disclosure of how much the mark-up would be. Consumers may want to ask for a copy of the invoice for cash advance items.

- There is no requirement to include low-cost caskets in any display.
- There is no requirement to identify and tag the body at the place of death before removal.
- The medical examiner's permit for cremation in the case of an *anticipated* death from natural causes is unnecessary and creates an additional burden and charge for families.
- The standards for ethical, professional conduct are weak and should be more well-defined. That would make it easier for a consumer to prevail when filing a complaint.

Miscellaneous Information

- The educational requirements for becoming a funeral director in Virginia are mortuary school and 18 months of apprenticeship. All must pass a state exam and the national board exam from ICFSEB. The national exam is deemed out-of-date and irrelevant by many.
- Medical examiners are physicians who are appointed.
- Anybody may designate in writing who will be responsible for making disposition arrangements after death. It should be notarized.
- The FTC Funeral Rule has been adopted by reference.
- Tissue banks must be accredited by the American Association of Tissue Banks. With new standards for non-transplant tissue banks, there should be good regulation of the body parts business.
- A disinterment permit will be issued to a funeral director by the local registrar.
- Complaints may be filed with the following: The Board of Funeral Directors and Embalmers, Department of Health Professions, Perimeter Center, 9960 Mayland Drive, Suite 300, Henrico Virginia 23233-1463. Telephone 804-367-4497 or 800-533-1560

This chapter was sent for review to the Board of Funeral Directors and Embalmers and to the Virginia Department of Health. No responses were received.

Caring for the Dead
In Washington

Please refer also to the general introduction to state chapters: "Caring for the Dead: Necessary Information."

Persons in Washington may care for their own dead. The legal authority to do so is found in:

> *68.50.160 Right to control disposition of remains. . . liability for cost. (1) A person has the right to control the disposition of his or her own remains without the predeath or postdeath consent of another person. A valid written document expressing the decedent's wishes regarding the place or method of disposition of his or her remains, signed by the decedent in the presence of a witness, is sufficient legal authorization for the procedures to be accomplished. (2) Prearrangements that are prepaid, or filed with a licensed funeral establishment or cemetery authority . . . are not subject to cancellation or substantial revision by survivors. . . .(3) If the decedent has not made a prearrangement as set forth in subsection (2) of this section or the costs of executing the decedent's wishes . . . exceeds a reasonable amount or directions have not been given by the decedent, the right to control the disposition of the remains of a deceased person vests in . . . (a) the surviving spouse, (b) the surviving adult children of the decedent, (c) the surviving parents of the decedent, (d) the surviving siblings of the decedent, (e) a person acting as a representative of the decedent under the signed authorization of the decedent. . . . (5) The liability for the reasonable cost of preparation, care, and disposition devolves jointly and severally upon all kin of the decedent in the same degree of kindred, in the order listed in subsection (3) of this section, and upon the estate of the decedent.*

The authors of this statute are obviously concerned about who will pay the funeral bill. There are no other statutes that might require you to use a funeral director.

Death Certificate

Several counties are doing electronic death registration as of this writing, with more going on-line during the coming year. A paper alternative is available for home funeral families. Get a blank death certificate from the county health department. The family doctor, physician's assistant, advanced registered nurse practitioner, or a local medical examiner should be able to sign the death certificate within 48 hours, stating the cause of death. The remaining information must be supplied, typewritten or in black ink. The death certificate must be filed with the local health department within three days and before final disposition. There will be a $1 charge for filing the death certificate in a county other than the county where death occurred.

Fetal Death

A fetal death report is required when death occurs after 20 weeks of gestation. If there is no family physician involved, the local medical examiner must sign the fetal death certificate. The fetal death certificate must be filed within five days. All other procedures apply if disposition is handled by the family.

Transporting and Disposition Permit

The local registrar will issue the burial-transit permit. This authorization must be obtained within 72 hours of death and prior to final disposition of the body. After usual business hours, check with the medical examiner's office.

Burial

Burial must be in an established cemetery. Home burial is not permitted, a strange limitation given the vast regions of unpopulated, rural areas where such might be desirable. That also makes it difficult to set up green burial grounds that were never meant to be platted out as "cemeteries." There are inexpensive county cemeteries where a family might be allowed to handle the burial. The sexton will return the burial-transit permit to the town where death occurred.

Cremation

The burial-transit permit serves as a permit for cremation. Be aware, though, that some counties have added an additional requirement for a local cremation permit; it seems to be a blatant revenue-generation scheme. As of this writing, King County (where Seattle is located) charges $50. Cowlitz County also requires a coroner's permit. Authorization by next-of-kin (or the decedent prior to death) is required, and a pacemaker must be removed. The crematory will file the burial-transit permit.

The crematory must make a note of the casket in which the body is cremated.

There are no laws regarding the disposition of cremated remains. You may do as you wish.

Other Requirements

"Any licensee authorized to dispose of human remains shall refrigerate or embalm the human remains upon receipt of the human remains." However, permission to embalm must be obtained first. No statute makes similar requirements for home funerals. Regulations permit "singing and praying" over an unembalmed body for up to 24 hours, or as otherwise permitted by the local health officer. Some religions require sitting with the body for three days waiting for the spirit to leave, so that would likely be manageable only if the body is kept at home.

If the person died of a contagious or communicable disease, the doctor in attendance should be consulted. The embalming requirement when death is due to plague or cholera has been deleted, thank goodness, "except that embalming is required under certain conditions as determined by rule by the state board of health." This is a strange provision, as embalming serves no public health purpose whatsoever per CDC, which is why they apparently haven't gotten around to any such rule.

Medical Schools for Body Donation

Body donation to a medical school is another option for disposition. Find the information for Washington at <www.finalrights.org>.

State Governance

In 2009 the funeral and cemetery boards were combined. There are seven members. One is a public member, and three are funeral directors/embalmers and three are cemeterians.

<www.dol.wa.gov/business/funeralcemetery/fcboard.html>

Crematories are regulated by this board. One does not need to be a funeral director to run a crematory. Cremated remains disposers must be licensed by this board.

Prepaid Cemetery and Funeral Funds

Only 50% of prepaid *cemetery* goods and services (or wholesale and actual cost, if more) must be placed in trust. "Constructive delivery" is permitted and can bypass the trusting requirement. "Delivery" usually is accomplished by issuing a certificate of ownership and warehousing the vault and/ or marker. Once "delivered," it is almost impossible to get a refund even if the items have never been used.

A consumer may cancel a cemetery agreement, but only 50%—minus what was spent on "delivered" items—will be refunded.

If no claim has been made on a prepaid account for 50 years, the money must be placed in the endowment fund. The cemetery remains obligated, however, for the selected services.

Cemeteries and funeral homes must make an annual report of prepaid accounts to the board.

90% of a prepaid *funeral* contract must be placed into trust. The preneed contract must name the institution where money will be deposited along with contact information. "Reasonable fees," not to exceed 1% of the trust, may be withdrawn for administration, provided that the value of the trust is not diminished.

Substitution of funeral merchandise must be equal or better, according to a state-approved preneed contract, but that may be difficult to enforce because such a provision is not spelled out in the statutes or rules.

A consumer may cancel a preneed agreement within the first 30 days for a full refund of all monies paid. After that, only 90% plus remaining interest will be refunded.

A preneed contract may be made irrevocable only if the beneficiary is to be eligible for public assistance.

Insurance is an alternative to trusting but rarely a good deal for consumers.

Consumer Concerns

- The death rate in Washington can support approximately 165 full-time mortuaries; there are 201. Funeral prices tend to be higher in areas where there are "too many" funeral homes.
- Cemetery trusting requirements are totally inadequate. "Constructive delivery" can avoid even the minimal trusting requirements for merchandise and should not be permitted.
- There is no regulation for an adequate description of funeral goods selected preneed nor for a substitution of equal quality approved

by survivors if the selected item is no longer available at the time of death.

- There is no annual reporting requirement to the purchaser of pre-paid funeral goods and services, paperwork that might be helpful to the family of a deceased to indicate prepayment and would help to enforce trusting requirements.

- There is no state protection for consumers in case of default on pre-paid funeral funds that were never put into trust.

- Until there is an increase in the trusting requirements and better provisions for substitution, it is probably a terrible idea to prepay for a funeral in Washington.

- There is no requirement that low-cost caskets be included in any display.

- The laws requiring embalming or refrigeration after 24 hours is un-necessarily burdensome for home funeral families. The climate in much of Washington makes it realistic to handle a death over several days without embalming.

- Embalming for certain infectious diseases is unwise and should be repealed. This is not only an offense to some religious groups, it puts the funeral professionals at risk.

- A body must be identified and tagged, but this should be required before removal.

- The standards for ethical, professional conduct are weak and should be more well-defined. That would make it easier for a consumer to prevail when filing a valid complaint.

- Complaint procedures are unclear and inadequate.

- The FTC Funeral Rule has not been adopted in this state.

- All cremations must occur in a licensed facility. This will limit the wishes of some Buddhists who would prefer outdoor cremations.

- This state has no laws regulating the body parts business.

Miscellaneous Information

- Educational requirements for becoming a funeral director: two years of college and one year of apprenticeship. For an embalmer: two years of college including mortuary college and two years of apprenticeship. Alas, both must pass the National Board Exam which is deemed irrelevant and out of date by industry practitioners.

- Preference is given to the written (and witnessed) wishes of the deceased. Peoples Memorial Association (a member of Funeral Consumers Alliance) is trying to convince the legislature to pass a law allowing citizens to designate a legal agent for body disposition. Industry forces hostile to the consumer-oriented PMA scuttled the bill in 2009, but it's sure to come up again in early 2011, about the time we are going to press, so it may have passed by the time you read this. Prepaid or prearranged funerals may not be substantially altered by survivors.

- Cash advance items must be billed in the same amount as paid by the funeral home.

- Medical examiners are physicians who are appointed; coroners are elected and do not need to be physicians but may not be an active funeral provider. The county prosecutor assumes the coroner's duties in many counties. The situation varies from one area to another.

- It is illegal to hold a body for debt.

- Counties are responsible for the disposition of indigents.

- A permit for disinterment must be obtained from the local registrar.

This chapter was sent for review to the Funeral and Cemetery Board and the Department of Vital Records Two small corrections were offered by the Department of Health and two more by the Funeral/Cemetery Board.

Caring for the Dead

In West Virginia

Please refer also to the general introduction to state chapters: "Caring for the Dead: Necessary Information."

Families and members of a religious group in West Virginia may care for their own dead. The following statutes are relevant:

> *Title 30-6-22. Disposition of body of deceased person. (a) No public officer, employee, physician or surgeon, or any other person having a professional relationship with the deceased, shall send, or cause to be sent, to any embalmer, funeral director or crematory operator the body of any deceased without first inquiring the desires of the next of kin, or any persons who may be chargeable with the funeral expenses of the deceased. If any next of kin or person can be found, his or her authority and direction shall be used as to the disposal of the body of the deceased.*

> *Title 30-6-31: (re embalmers and funeral directors) . . .The provisions of this article do not apply to or interfere with . . . the customs or rites of any religious sect in the burial of its dead.*

There are no other statutes that might require you to use a funeral director.

Death Certificate

West Virginia has not yet implemented electronic death registration but expects to "soon." If the state doesn't keep some of the old four-part death certificate forms in circulation, it is likely there will be some other paper alternative for home funeral families. You will need to get the medical certification of death (either printed out from the physician's electronic entry or on the substitute form) and then fill in the demographic information about the deceased. This must be sent to the state Department of Vital Statistics within five days and before final disposition.

Fetal Death

A fetal death report is required when death occurs after 20 weeks of gestation and must be filed as above.

Transporting and Disposition Permit

A body may be moved with medical consent. The physician, medical examiner, or coroner will authorize final disposition. After disposition, this permit must be filed with the state registrar.

Burial

Although private graves are mentioned in the statutes, there are none that specifically permit (or prohibit) home burial. It is also unlikely that there are local zoning regulations regarding home burial, but you should review them before planning a family cemetery. If your land is in a rural area, draw a map of the property showing where the burial ground will be and have it filed with the deed. That may be all you have to do to establish your family cemetery. There are no state burial statutes or regulations with regard to burial locations or depth. A sensible guideline is 150 feet from a water supply, 25 feet from a power line, with two or three feet of earth on top. Plan your family cemetery away from boundaries with neighbors, too.

Landowners have an obligation to permit descendants and interested others to visit graves on private property.

When burial is arranged, the family member acting as the funeral director should sign the permit for disposition and retain it as a record. When there is no person in charge of the burial ground, the words "No person in charge" should be written across the face of the permit.

Cremation

Authorization for cremation must be obtained from the state or county medical examiner, or the county coroner. There is a modest fee. Authorization by next-of-kin is usually required, and a pacemaker must be removed. The crematory operator will retain the burial-transit permit.

One must get permission from the person running a cemetery in order to deposit or bury cremated remains there. There are no other laws regarding the disposition of cremated remains. You may do as you wish.

Other Requirements

West Virginia has no embalming requirements. Weather and reasonable planning should be considered.

If the person died of a contagious or communicable disease, the physician in attendance should be consulted.

Medical Schools for Body Donation

Body donation to a medical school is another option for disposition. Find the information for West Virginia at <www.finalrights.org>.

State Governance

The West Virginia Board of Funeral Service Examiners has seven members—five funeral directors, one crematory operator, and one a lay member. Crematories are licensed by this board; one does not need to be a funeral director to operate a crematory.

The Board has an excellent website full of helpful information such as the page on the right to control disposition. It also makes clear what topics would constitute grounds for a complaint and explains the complaint procedure clearly.

<http://www.wvfuneralboard.com/>

The Consumer Protection Division in the Attorney General's office regulates preneed funeral transactions. Cemetery preneed is regulated by the State Tax Department. The Public Service Commission sets the rates that may be charged for setting the government-issued monuments for veterans.

Prepaid Cemetery and Funeral Funds

Only 40% of prepaid *cemetery* goods and services must be placed in trust. "Constructive delivery" can bypass the trusting requirement altogether for vaults and markers. There's no indication that the state has a procedure for verifying that these are waiting for you in the warehouse, so the cemetery probably feels free to pocket all your money right away. (In one state, there were only 200 of the 500 pre-sold vaults in stock when someone finally went to check.) If you've paid for a vault and the opening-and-closing charges for a full body burial, it's probably unlikely that you'll get much money back if you later decide on cremation instead—with only modest interment needs— or move to another state and want to cancel the whole deal and sell the lot. To their credit, legislators require any substitution of cemetery goods and services be approved by the representative of the deceased. Too bad that doesn't apply to funeral goods as well.

One rather garbled statutory paragraph states that interest may be withdrawn for "any appropriate trustee and auditor fees, commissions and costs," but once those are paid, interest is to accrue. Pretty damned generous since the cemetery already gets to pocket 60% of what was paid.

Cemetery vendors may sell unconstructed mausoleum space for up to seven years before construction must start—or until 80% of the space has been sold, whichever comes first. If each sale represents a simple 50% mark-up over cost, then 100% of the construction money will have been raised after selling half or 50% of the crypts. An investor, however, can wait a little longer, selling the next 30% of the crypts, collecting 60% of the total profit to be made without ever having had to build or maintain a thing. State laws seem strangely silent on any trusting requirements for the money from preconstruction mausoleum sales or how to protect consumers in case of default.

How long construction might take doesn't seem to have been considered, either. Funeral directors tell us that most preneed plans are used within six years. Wonder where they'll put the bodies in the meantime? You might want to ask before purchasing anything that hasn't been built. Or ask how to get your money and interest back if you change your mind.

A preneed seller of funeral plans may not make in-person solicitations, including by telephone. Contact must be invited by the purchaser. No such restrictions exist for cemetery sales, so you can be sure that those companies owning combo operations will send their "cemetery" sales reps to your door. Of course, while they are there . . . .

All preneed sellers must be licensed and are not necessarily funeral directors. A preneed seller may retain 10% of the prepaid *funeral* funds as a commission, "to offset administrative and operating costs." The commission can be taken first if you are paying on an installment plan. In other words, on a $5,000 funeral, the funeral director can pocket the first $500. After that, the rest of the funds must be placed in trust with interest to accrue. Constructive delivery of funeral goods is not permitted.

Within ten days of a preneed sale, it must be recorded with the AG's office which will notify the buyer. A preneed seller must make biennial reports to the Attorney General's office. Unless the funds are put in a qualified funeral trust, there should be an annual report of interest earned, but the statutes are silent in this regard.

A purchaser may cancel a preneed contract and receive a refund of the 90% in trust plus interest. There is a provision for transferring a contract, which would be useful for those with an irrevocable agreement, but you can count on only 90% plus interest being transferred.

A provider is obligated to provide the goods and services contracted for in a preneed arrangement even if they are not desired by the next-of-kin. This is a two-edged sword. On the one hand, it's one way for the deceased to make sure that his or her wishes are carried out. Well, sort of. One family did not have the funds to ship a body to Iowa, purchase a vault, and open the grave—services that were not paid for in the initial contract but necessary to complete the original plan. Obviously, an alternative had to be considered. "Otherwise," said the niece, "I'm not sure what you're going to do with an embalmed little old lady at your funeral home. There simply isn't any money left to get her out of there."

Next-of-kin should not be bound by a contract for which there are not sufficient funds to carry out the wishes. Another woman wanted to change her father's plans—he'd outlived all his friends and few relatives were nearby, so who would show up for a viewing? When the funeral home refused to modify arrangements, she got up to leave. "Where are you going?" the funeral director asked. "I'm going to find another funeral home," she replied. "But we've got your father's body," said the undertaker. With more aplomb than most could muster at a time of death she shot back, "And what are you going to do with it?" A second funeral home—far more accommodating—picked up the body a short time later.

When a preneed contract is offered at a guaranteed price, the funeral home must make up the difference in any cost at the time of honoring the contract. Although the statutes provide that excess funds must be returned to the estate, that is unlikely with the current rate of funeral inflation.

There is no provision for an adequate description of merchandise selected preneed nor any provision for a substitute of equal quality and construction that would be pleasing to the family, not just something of equal "value." This clearly leaves the undertaker free to pull mischief, particularly if the undertaker will be stuck footing the bill. A $750 casket chosen 10 years ago is likely to cost $1,750 today, and a casket "valued" at $750 today may be the one the undertaker refers to as "the welfare casket," one he'll suggest as the one that comes with the contract . . . unless, of course, the family would like to pay for "something a little nicer."

A buyer will be assessed a fee of $20 for each preneed contract purchased, of which $8 goes to the Preneed Guarantee Fund. This protection against default is quite limited, unfortunately. If multiple claims are made and the total exceeds the amount in the Fund, claimants will get only a prorata share. West Virginia would be wise to adopt the Vermont plan that is structured to cover all loss to funeral consumers.

Consumer Concerns

- The death rate in West Virginia can support approximately 84 full-time mortuaries; there are, however, 279. Funeral prices tend to be higher in areas where there are "too many" funeral homes.

- There is no state board governing cemeteries. This is a serious omission with the rapid growth of corporate-owned cemeteries. One legislative remedy would be to change the name of the current funeral board to one of "Funeral and Cemetery Services." Then change the make-up of the board to reflect the responsibilities.

- The Preneed Guarantee Fund appears to be underfunded. Provisions should be modified to adequately cover all consumer loss.

- Trusting requirements are inadequate. 100% of prepaid funeral funds should be placed in trust, with interest to accrue and be fully refundable for revocable contracts.

- There is no provision for an adequate description of funeral goods selected preneed or for a substitution of equal quality if the selected item is no longer available at the time of death. Survivors should approve any substitution.

- There is no annual reporting requirement to the purchaser of prepaid funeral goods and services, paperwork that might be useful to the family of a deceased to indicate prepayment. It would help to enforce any trusting requirements, as well.

- Until the West Virginia laws are changed to require 100% trusting of all money and interest for prepaid funeral and cemetery goods and services, it is probably a *terrible* idea to prepay for these arrangements. Your own or a shared trust account in the bank will be safer and may be made irrevocable if you need to shelter assets.

- The coroner or medical examiner's permit for cremation in the case of an *anticipated* death from natural causes is totally unnecessary and creates an additional burden and charge for families.

- There is no provision either forbidding a mark-up on cash advance items or requiring the disclosure of how much the mark-up would be. Consumers may wish to ask for a copy of the invoice for such charges.

- There is no requirement to include low-cost caskets in any display.

- This state has no laws regulating the body parts business.

Miscellaneous Information

- Educational requirements for funeral director: two years of college (60 semester hours) plus mortuary college, national exam, exam of state laws, and one year of apprenticeship. Alas, the national board exam put out by the ICFSEB is deemed irrelevant and out-dated by some industry practitioners.

- The FTC Funeral Rule has been adopted in the regulations.

- Medical examiners are appointed and must be licensed physicians.

- You may express funeral wishes in the advance directive naming a medical power of attorney. This will be helpful for those estranged from legal next-of-kin or when there may not be agreement among them.

- Identification and tagging of the body at the place of death before removal is required.

- Although complaint procedures are unclear, the Attorney General's office does have a Consumer Hotline: 800-368-8808.

- Production blasting is prohibited within 100 feet of a cemetery.

- Disinterment permits will be issued only to a licensed funeral director by a local registrar.

This chapter was sent for review to the Consumer Protection division of the Attorney General's office, the Board of Funeral Service Examiners, the Tax Department, and the Vital Statistics division of the Department of Health. The Tax Department had no idea why they received it and had to be reminded. No other responses were received.

Caring for the Dead
In Wisconsin

Please refer also to the general introduction to state chapters: "Caring for the Dead: Necessary Information."

Families in Wisconsin may care for their own dead. The legal authority to do so is found in:

> *Title 69.18(1)(a) Any one of the following may move a corpse for the purpose of final disposition: . . . 2. A member of the decedent's immediate family who personally prepares for and conducts the final disposition of the decedent.*

There are no other statutes that might require you to use a funeral director.

Death Certificate

Wisconsin is still in the planning stages for electronic death registration. When that is implemented, there will be a paper worksheet for home funeral families. The attending doctor is expected to sign within six days stating the cause of death. In some counties, the coroner must certify the cause when death occurred at home. The remaining information must be supplied, typewritten or in black ink. The death certificate or worksheet must be filed with the local registrar within two days of medical certification.

Fetal Death

A fetal death report is required when death occurs after 20 weeks of gestation or when the weight is 350 grams or more (about 12 ounces). The fetal death report must be filed with the registrar within five days. No forms or documents are required by law for fetal disposition unless transported out of the state, in which case the Report for Final Disposition must accompany the remains.

Transporting and Disposition Permit

The Report for Final Disposition may be obtained from the local registrar or from a funeral director. A body may be moved from a hospital or nursing home by the immediate family only if the family is conducting the burial. In that case, you will also need the Notice of Removal of a Human Corpse from an Institution. If the institution does not have this form, a funeral director or the local registrar may be asked to supply one.

The Report for Final Disposition must be mailed to the local Registrar within 24 hours (or—in Kenosha, Manitowoc, Milwaukee, Neenah, Oshkosh, Racine, Sheboygan, or West Allis—to the City Health Officer). One copy must also be sent to the coroner or medical examiner, located through the office of the county sheriff.

Burial

No state statutes specifically permit or prohibit home burial. It is unlikely that there are local zoning regulations regarding home burial, but you should review them before planning a family cemetery. If your land is in a rural area, draw a map of the property showing where the burial ground will be and have it filed with the deed. That may be all you have to do to establish your family cemetery. There are no state burial statutes or regulations with regard to burial locations or depth. A sensible guideline is 150 feet from a water supply, 25 feet from a power line, with two or three feet of earth on top. Plan your family cemetery away from boundaries with neighbors, too.

When burial is arranged, the family member acting as the funeral director must sign the Report for Final Disposition and retain one copy for two years.

Cremation

A cremation permit from the coroner or medical examiner is required. Although the state fee for a coroner investigating a death is $25, a charge of $50 to families is not uncommon at this writing. In Milwaukee, the charge is $115. There is a 48-hour waiting period prior to cremation. Authorization by next-of-kin is usually required, and a pacemaker must be removed.

One must get permission from the person running a cemetery in order to deposit or bury cremated remains. However, there are no state laws restricting where you may scatter cremains or whatever else you might wish to do.

Other Requirements

Wisconsin has no embalming requirements. Weather and reasonable planning should be considered.

The Health Department may regulate disposition when death was caused by a contagious or infectious disease. The doctor in attendance should be consulted.

Medical Schools for Body Donation

Body donation to a medical school is another option for disposition. Find the information for Wisconsin at <www.finalrights.org>.

State Governance

The Wisconsin Funeral Directors Examining Board has six members. Two are consumer representatives. This board regulates funeral homes and funeral preneed.

<http://drl.wi.gov/board_detail.asp?boardid=15&locid=0>

Crematories, cemeteries, and cemetery preneed transactions are regulated by the Department of Regulation and Licensing.

Prepaid Cemetery and Funeral Funds

Funeral home owners may not also own cemeteries in Wisconsin, but the Wall-Street corporations simply ignored the law and purchased both. In 1997, the state ordered them (SCI and Loewen) to divest one or the other.

If a cemetery lot appears "abandoned" after 50 years and the cemetery cannot locate the owner or heirs, the lot may be resold.

At least 40% (or wholesale cost, whichever is greater) of preneed *cemetery* purchases must be placed in **trust**. When paying by installment, 40% of each payment must be placed in trust. "Constructive delivery" can bypass the trusting requirement with a warehouse receipt. Is the state inspecting warehouses to see if your marker is really there? Money for undeveloped burial space also must be placed in trust in the same proportion. However, a "letter of credit" from a financial institution or bond can eliminate any trusting requirements for the undeveloped cemetery space.

Outer burial containers (vaults) are not included in the cemetery merchandise category (as they are in most other states), and 100% of the vault price must be placed in trust, as applies to funeral preneed merchandise.

Cemetery preneed sellers must report on preneed accounts annually to the Department of Regulation and Licensing.

Religious and certain nonprofit cemeteries are exempt from most of the preneed sales and reporting requirements. How too bad.

Preneed solicitation door-to-door is not permitted. The consumer must request the contact. A prospective purchaser may not be contacted in a health-care facility or similar institution.

100% of prepaid funeral money must be placed in separate trust accounts with the interest accruing. The depositor must be supplied with evidence showing that the funds have been deposited.

Funeral insurance is also permitted as a funding vehicle. If there is a sales commission to be paid, that fact must be disclosed, but not the amount.

Only $3,000 of the funeral funds paid may be considered "irrevocable." An irrevocable agreement may be transferred at any time. This limit is fairly low if a vault is included in the "funeral" merchandise.

A purchaser may cancel a non-irrevocable preneed funeral agreement at any time and request a refund of the amount paid plus interest. This does not apply to cemetery purchases.

Consumer Concerns

- The death rate in Wisconsin can support approximately 185 full-time mortuaries; there are 544 such establishments. Funeral prices tend to be higher in areas where there are "too many" funeral homes.

- Trusting requirements for cemetery merchandise and services are inadequate and should be increased to 100%, with full right of refund for revocable arrangements. Constructive delivery should not be permitted to avoid the trusting requirements.

- There is no provision for an adequate description of funeral goods selected preneed or for a substitution of equal quality if the selected item is no longer available at the time of death. Survivors should have the right to approve any substitution.

- Although the purchaser of a preneed funeral agreement must be supplied with evidence showing that the funds have been deposited, there is no requirement for an annual report to the buyer that would indicate that the funds are still there. Such paperwork would help to enforce the trusting requirement and could be useful to survivors.

- Because of inadequate substitution provisions, limited reporting, and no state protection in case a provider defaults, it is probably *unwise* to prepay for a funeral in Wisconsin. It is probably a *terrible* idea to prepay for any cemetery merchandise and services.

- The 48-hour wait before cremation is unnecessary when survivors are in agreement; it causes extra charges to families for "storage."

- The coroner or medical examiner's permit for cremation in the case of an *anticipated* death from natural causes is unnecessary and creates an additional burden and charge for families.

- There is no requirement to identify and tag the body at the place of death before removal.

- There is no provision either forbidding or requiring disclosure or a mark-up on cash advance items purchased by the funeral director.

- There is no requirement to include low-cost caskets in any display.

- Some coroners may be funeral directors with a conflict of interest. There is only a $50 fine if a funeral director/coroner serves as the funeral director for a body whose death the coroner investigated.

- The law that allows you to name a designated agent to make your final arrangements failed to amend the vital records portion of the law to allow that person, if not a family member, to file the death certificate.

- This state has no laws regulating the body parts business.

Miscellaneous Information

- Educational requirements for a funeral director: two years of college, at least one of which is in mortuary science, one year of apprenticeship, and an exam.

- No funeral director or operator of a funeral home may operate a cemetery or have a financial interest in a cemetery.

- The FTC Funeral Rule has been incorporated in the funeral regulations.

- Preneed sellers must give a Board-generated brochure that explains the difference between trust and insurance funding.

- A permit for disinterment must be obtained from the coroner or medical examiner.

This chapter was sent for review to the Department of Regulation and Licensing and the Department of Health Statistics, but no responses were received.

Caring for the Dead
In Wyoming

Please refer also to the general introduction to state chapters: "Caring for the Dead: Necessary Information."

Persons in Wyoming may care for their own dead. The legal authority to do so is found in:

Title 35-1-418(b): The funeral director or person acting as such who first assumes custody of a dead body shall file the death certificate.

There are no other statutes that might require you to use a funeral director.

Death Certificate

Wyoming is using electronic death registration, although not all doctors and funeral directors are on the system. If you are handling all arrangements without a funeral director, you will need an all-paper system. If your physician does not have a blank death certificate, you will need to get one from a local registrar, coroner, or perhaps a hospital. Some funeral directors may have them, too. It must be signed by the attending physician or coroner within 24 hours, stating the cause of death. The remaining portions of the death certificate must be filled in and filed with the local registrar within three days or before removal from the state.

Fetal Death

A fetal death report is required if death occurs after 20 weeks of gestation. If no family physician is involved, the local coroner must sign the fetal death certificate. All other procedures apply if disposition is handled by the family.

Transporting and Disposition Permit

A body may be moved with the consent of a physician, medical examiner, or county coroner. Take the death certificate to the local registrar or health department to get a the burial-transit permit which must accompany the body to its final disposition.

Burial

There are no state statutes that specifically permit or prohibit home burial. It is also unlikely that there are local zoning regulations regarding home burial, but you should review them before planning a family cemetery. If your land is in a rural area, draw a map of the property showing where the burial ground will be and have it filed with the deed. That may be all you have to do to establish your family cemetery. There are no state burial statutes or regulations with regard to burial locations or depth. A sensible guideline is 150 feet from a water supply, 25 feet from a power line, with two or three feet of earth on top. Plan your family cemetery away from boundaries with neighbors, too.

The burial-transit permit must be filed with the registrar in the district of disposition within ten days.

Land that has been surveyed and platted may be recorded in the county clerk's office as a cemetery. Such land is tax-exempt.

Cremation

The burial-transit permit is sufficient for cremation. There is a 24-hour waiting period before cremation unless a coroner's permit has been obtained. Authorization by next-of-kin is usually required, and a pacemaker must be removed. The crematory will file the burial-transit permit.

Any person in charge of disposition may witness the cremation.

There are no laws regarding the disposition of cremated remains. You may do as you wish.

Other Requirements

Board regulations, not statutes, require that when a body is in the possession of a funeral director, it must be embalmed, refrigerated, cremated, or buried within 36 hours. This would not apply to home funeral families as the Board of Embalming has no authority over non-licensees.

If death has occurred from a communicable, contagious, or infectious disease, the body must be embalmed, the worst possible circumstances under which to embalm a body. Bodies shipped by common carrier must be embalmed. There is no provision for religious objection.

Board regulations require that public funerals for individuals who have died of a "communicable disease" must be held under the supervision of a health officer. This is unnecessary for deaths from AIDS, Hepatitis C, and such. Even the flu is a communicable disease, and we don't restrict families from touching each other when one comes down with it. The only public health concern would be for *infectious* diseases such as meningitis or ebola.

Medical Schools for Body Donation

There are no medical schools in Wyoming. However, Washington, Wyoming, Alaska, Montana, and Idaho participate in the WWAMI Medical Education Program which allows Wyoming students to do their first year of medical school in-state before transferring to the University of Washington. Although body donations are needed for gross anatomy classes, the University of Wyoming does not have embalming facilities and purchases bodies from Colorado. For more information, go to <www.finalrights.org>.

State Governance

The Wyoming State Board of Embalming has five members including one from the State Board of Health. There are no consumer representatives.

<http://plboards.state.wy.us/embalmers/index.asp>

Crematories are licensed, regulated, and inspected by the State Board of Embalming but are not represented on the Board. One does not need to be a mortician to run a crematory.

Prepaid funerals are regulated by the Insurance Department.

<http://insurance.state.wy.us/contacts.html>

There is no state board governing cemeteries.

Prepaid Cemetery and Funeral Funds

Privately-owned cemeteries must establish a perpetual care fund. 20% of each interment space sale must go toward perpetual care. A bond in the amount of 5% of all funds received must be maintained as protection against default. An annual report must be made to the commissioner of Insurance.

100% of prepaid funeral funds must be placed in deposit, "in such types of investments which men of prudence, discretion and intelligence would acquire or retain for their own account." This is the only statutory provision regarding preneed purchases. There are, however, regulations that spell out other conditions for preneed transactions.

Each preneed agreement must be a guaranteed-price contract, with no further money due. That's a raw deal for funeral directors if interest rates don't keep up with inflation.

Regulations permit the funeral seller to withdraw and keep all interest. Furthermore, the seller may retain a penalty of 20% if the buyer needs or wishes to transfer the contract to another funeral home. For those who travel outside their immediate area, this could be a serious problem.

Sellers must make an annual report to the Commissioner. The Insurance Department is regularly auditing preneed record-keeping, according to a local funeral director.

Sellers must maintain a bond in the amount of 5% of preneed trust agreements, hardly sufficient to protect consumers against default.

Consumer Concerns

- The death rate in Wyoming can support approximately 17 full-time mortuaries; there are 32 such establishments. Given the low density of population over a vast geographic area, mortuary careers are not likely to be full-time work. Unfortunately, because of the low volume of business per mortuary, funeral prices will tend to be higher than elsewhere.

- No grave-side services are permitted at the Oregon Trail State Veterans' Cemetery. Services must be conducted in a designated chapel or patio area. This seems an odd and disconcerting restriction.

- If a consumer needs to transfer or cancel a preneed contract, there is a 20% penalty and loss of all interest. Laws should provide that a consumer may cancel a preneed contract and get a refund or transfer arrangements without penalty or loss.

- There is no provision for an adequate description of funeral goods selected preneed or for a substitution of equal quality if the selected item is no longer available at the time of death. Survivors should have the right to approve any substitution.

- There is no requirement that consumers get an annual report of preneed accounts, paperwork that might be useful to next-of-kin and that would help to enforce the trusting requirement.

- There is no guarantee fund to protect consumers against the default of funeral providers.

- Until there is adequate protection, it is probably a terrible idea to prepay for a funeral in Wyoming.

- The law requiring preparation by an embalmer when death occurs from a communicable or contagious disease seems unnecessary. The implication is that the body will be embalmed under the worst possible circumstances for doing so. This is not only an offense to some religious groups, it puts the funeral professionals at risk. The law should distinguish between "communicable" and "contagious." Those who have cared for those ailing from AIDS prior to death should be able to do so after death.

- There is no provision either forbidding a mark-up on cash advance items or requiring the disclosure of how much the mark-up would be. Consumers may wish to ask for an invoice for these purchases.

- There is no requirement to include low-cost caskets in any display.

- Identification and tagging of the body at the place of death before removal should be required.

- Complaint procedures are unclear and inadequate.

- The standards for ethical, professional conduct are weak and should be more well-defined. That would make it easier for a consumer to prevail when filing a valid complaint.

- It would appear that the only choices the Embalming Board has in response to a complaint are a letter of warning, setting conditions on a license, or revocation. The ability to levy fines should be added as a deterrent.

- This state has no laws regulating the body parts business.

Miscellaneous Information

- The educational requirements for becoming an embalmer in Wyoming are one year of college, a year of mortuary school, and one year of apprenticeship. The embalmer must pass the National Board Exam. Alas, the exam is deemed irrelevant and out-of-date by some industry practitioners. One must be licensed as a "funeral director" to maintain a funeral establishment. There are no educational requirements, but the person must pass a Board test on signs of death and state laws.

- The FTC Funeral Rule has been adopted by reference.

- Rental caskets are permitted.

- You may name a designated agent for your final arrangements. In situations where you are estranged or distant from next-of-kin, this could be important.

- Coroners are elected. There is no requirement that the coroner be medically trained, and funeral directors may run for the job.

- It is unprofessional conduct to use "profane, indecent or obscene language in the presence of a dead human body, or within the immediate hearing of the family or relatives of a deceased, whose body has not yet been interred or otherwise disposed of." After that, watch out?

- Embalmers are exempt from jury duty.

- Mausoleum construction must provide for adequate drainage and ventilation.

- Disinterment permits will be issued only to a licensed funeral director by a local registrar.

This chapter was sent for review to the Department of Insurance, the Department of Public Health, and the state Funeral Board. The Department of Public Health was very helpful. The Funeral Board suggested the authors hire their own attorney. No response came from the Insurance Department.

Ethical Standards & Unprofessional Conduct

A

Under Indiana law, a funeral director must "act with compassion." Unfortunately, it's not so easy to legislate what constitutes "compassion." It's easier—based on consumer complaints—to identify what is *unprofessional conduct*, as many states have done. The majority of the following appear scattered in the laws or regulations of one state or another, but no one state has any list so comprehensive:

Unprofessional Conduct

- uses fraud, deceit, misrepresentation, overreaching, intimidation, or other forms of vexatious conduct to influence funeral choices.

- takes undue advantage of a person's ignorance or emotional vulnerability.

- makes false or misleading statements of the legal requirement as to the necessity of any particular burial merchandise or services.

- creates false or unjustified expectations.

- makes statements that are misleading or deceiving because of only a partial disclosure of relevant facts.

- exploits a person's fears in order to sell more expensive items.

- claims or implies that embalming protects the public health.

- claims or implies that embalming preserves the body for more than a brief period.

- claims or implies that certain caskets and vaults will protect or preserve the body.

- claims or implies that there is only one acceptable way to arrange a funeral or that one way is more acceptable than another.

- fails to consider the wishes of the family and/or the family's financial limitations.

- fails to offer the same courtesy and consideration for those receiving public assistance with funeral costs as is offered to others; uses disparaging terms such as "a welfare funeral."
- disparages low-cost options or choices.
- treats any person differently to his/her detriment because of race, creed, color, national origin, religion, sexual orientation, or cause of death.
- fails to determine the cultural and religious preferences of the family.
- shows lack of respect for cultural or religious customs.
- fails to honor requests and make adjustments that are not unreasonable, even if they may seem unusual or different.
- makes assumptions and decisions for the family without first determining exact wishes.
- makes disparaging comments on the condition of any dead human body entrusted to his or her care.
- fails to treat with dignity and respect the body of the deceased, any member of the family or relatives of the deceased, any employee, or any other person encountered while within the scope of practice, employment, or business.
- fails to try to ascertain next-of-kin or a designated agent with legal responsibility for funeral arrangements before providing services.
- fails to determine if all next-of-kin of the same legal order are in agreement before services are provided.
- alters funeral arrangements without the explicit permission of the person who has contracted for those arrangements.
- misrepresents the availability or delay in obtaining merchandise.
- fails to make available at least three low-cost caskets in the same general manner as the other caskets are displayed.
- represents a for-profit business as a "society."
- refuses to surrender the body (or cremated remains) upon the express order of the person lawfully entitled to the custody, whether or not the funeral bill has been paid.
- uses funeral merchandise previously sold without prior written permission of the person selecting or paying for the use of the merchandise.

- fails to return all personal items that were with the body at the time of removal.

- fails to maintain confidentiality.

- solicits future sales during or immediately after at-need arrangements.

- uses uninvited in-person or telephone solicitations.

- sells supposedly at a substantial discount when in fact the actual price has been increased to cover the supposed discount.

- represents that the price is a special price to the purchaser only, if another purchaser would be given the same price.

- obtains a purchaser's signature on a sales contract written in English if the purchaser cannot read or speak English, unless there is a disinterested person present who can explain fully to the purchaser what he or she is buying.

- fails to disclose the charge for services in obtaining cash-advance items if not billed at actual cost.

- fails to follow all provisions of the FTC Funeral Rule.

By having an explicit list of unacceptable behaviors, funeral providers are likely to be more mindful of their actions. When the standards aren't specific enough, consumer complaints are often dismissed.

To meet the needs of consumers, each state should require that a toll-free phone number, website, and address for filing a funeral complaint appear on the General Price List (GPL). Each state should have a pamphlet on-line or to mail out on "How to File a Complaint." It should be a required handout for preneed sales people. The list of unprofessional behaviors should be included, with a request to identify which (if any) are involved with the complaint, along with a narrative report.

Remedies for Consumers

It is important for a state to have the ability to order a refund of money paid, to cancel a debt, or to levy a fine when a mortician is guilty of unprofessional conduct. The fine should be sufficiently large to be a deterrent, not just a nuisance. In some cases, requiring additional education might be appropriate. In far too many states, the only recourse is to suspend a license to practice—something that is rarely done. If the only remedy is too extreme, many who are guilty will go unpunished. The Illinois office handling complaints asks consumers what remedy they are seeking—a nice touch. A complaint form might list the following:

As a remedy I am seeking:

    ___ loss of license___ probation

    ___ refund/cancellation of debt $_____

    ___ fine of $2,000 per violation for ___ violations

    ___ a public, written apology

    ___ other _____

Almost all states provide for a hearing at which the funeral director can explain things and defend his/her actions. But then the Funeral Board makes the ultimate decision on any penalty, if merited, usually without input from the people involved.

We would like to see the settlement process open to the public, with active participation of all parties. All such complaints are heard in open board sessions in Arizona, serving as a good model in that regard for other states. Some consumers may need to be educated about what are reasonable expectations. While it won't be perfect all the time, the consumer should walk away feeling that the state is listening and is concerned about consumer rights and ethical standards in the funeral business. The conscientious practitioners in the funeral industry should welcome an open process, too.

Information Needed for the Death Certificate

1. Full name of deceased

2. Time of death

3. Date of death

4. Place of death

5. Date of birth

6. Place of birth

7. Social Security number

8. Did deceased serve in the US Armed Forces?

9. Marital status

10. Spouse's name/maiden name

11. Occupation

12. Residence address

13. Names of parents: father's name / mother's maiden name

14. Level of education

15. Place of burial or disposition

16. Name, address, and phone number of certifying physician

17. Name, address, and phone number of person with right to control disposition

Index

For additional and updated information, check the following sites.

- The Web complement to this book: *www.finalrights.org*

- The publisher: *www.upperaccess.com*

- The Funeral Consumers Alliance: *www.funerals.org*

- The Funeral Ethics Organization: *www.funeralethics.org*